DOMINATION *without* DOMINANCE

A book in the series

LATIN AMERICA OTHERWISE: LANGUAGES, EMPIRES, NATIONS

Series editors:
Walter D. Mignolo, Duke University
Irene Silverblatt, Duke University
Sonia Saldívar-Hull, University of Texas, San Antonio

DOMINATION

without

DOMINANCE

Inca-Spanish Encounters in Early Colonial Peru

Gonzalo Lamana

Duke University Press

Durham and London 2008

Printed in the United States of America on acid-free paper ∞

Designed by Heather Hensley

Typeset in Monotype Dante by Achorn International

Library of Congress Cataloging-in-Publication Data appear

on the last printed page of this book.

All reaction is limited by, and dependent on, what it is reacting against. Because the counter-stance stems from a problem with authority . . . it's a step towards liberation from cultural domination. But it is not a way of life. . . . The possibilities are numerous once we decide to act and not react.

—Gloria Anzaldúa, *Borderlands/La Frontera*

You too are Peruvian, that is to say, Indian. You are only different from me in your dress and education.

—Miguel Quispe, 1922, quoted in Marisol De la Cadena, *Indigenous Mestizos*

[The old angel smeared the pongo with excrement; the young angel covered the master with honey. Then,]

In the radiance of the heavens, the light of your body stood out, as if made of gold, transparent. . . . And in the mist of the heavenly light, I was ashamed, stinking.

—Just as it should be!—affirmed the master—Keep going! Or, is that the end [of your dream]?

No, my little father, my lord. When once again . . . we were together . . . before our great father Saint Francis, he took another look at us . . . , once at you, once at me, for a long while. With his eyes that saw everything in the heavens, I don't know to what depths he understood us, joining night and day, memory and oblivion. Then he said, "Whatever the angels had to do with you is done. Now, Lick each other! Slowly, for a long time."

—José María Arguedas, *El sueño del pongo*

About the Series

Latin America Otherwise: Languages, Empires, Nations is a critical series. It aims to explore the emergence and consequences of concepts used to define "Latin America" while at the same time exploring the broad interplay of political, economic, and cultural practices that have shaped Latin American worlds. Latin America, at the crossroads of competing imperial designs and local responses, has been construed as a geocultural and geopolitical entity since the nineteenth century. This series provides a starting point to redefine Latin America as a configuration of political, linguistic, cultural, and economic intersections that demands a continuous reappraisal of the role of the Americas in history, and of the ongoing process of globalization and the relocation of people and cultures that have characterized Latin America's experience. *Latin America Otherwise: Languages, Empires, Nations* is a forum that confronts established geocultural constructions, rethinks area studies and disciplinary boundaries, assesses convictions of the academy and of public policy, and correspondingly demands that the practices through which we produce knowledge and understanding about and from Latin America be subject to rigorous and critical scrutiny.

Gonzalo Lamana's *Domination without Dominance: Inca-Spanish Encounters in Early Colonial Peru* is a historical and theoretical tour de force. Theoretically, it questions basic historiographic assumptions. By doing history in this way, he is also able to question the shortcoming of current theoretical debates in the social sciences and the humanities.

A careful, painstaking, and attentive reading of the moving "borders" between Incas and Spaniards in the first two decades of the Spanish invasion of Tawantinsuyu, Lamana's book brings forward the disparity of accounts, then and now, of one of the historical and foundational encounters of the modern/colonial world. Lamana is not just making a claim: he shows how the ideology of writing built on the superiority of Latin alphabet supported an entire theological structure of knowledge that served the Spaniards well (and later on the British and French imperial designs) in devaluing and bringing down Inca's ways of knowing and Indigenous humanity. Epistemology and ontology worked hand in hand to build the foundations of epistemic and ontological racism in which we are still living today.

Walking from the past to the present is one of Lamana's main concerns. Casting a wide eye through the spatial histories of imperial expansion and modern/colonial encounters, he erodes the foundations of the ways of knowing we take for granted in the humanities and the social sciences— ways of knowing that are—willingly or not—complicitous with imperial designs. Lamana realizes, at the end of his journey, that he was doing precisely what Quechuas and Aymaras did in the first two decades of the encounter; and what Waman Puma de Ayala articulated in his decolonial political philosophy, toward the end of the century. Lamana enrolls himself in the genealogy that nowadays we find in the works of the Chicana intellectual and activist Gloria Anzaldúa; the Afro-American radical sociologist W. E. B. Dubois or the Afro-Caribbean critical theorist Frantz Fanon. "As it is clear, the ultimate claim of both sixteenth-century and current, neocolonial projects is that Western subjects know reality as it is while their Others do not," Lamana states in the introduction. And he adds, "if rationality is the way in which a Western subject finds convenient to imagine himself, Christian rationality is the way in which a sixteenth-century Spanish subject found it convenient to imagine himself (gender intended in both cases). Christianity and Science guarantee, in each case, the self-convincing privilege of operating upon the real."

Contents

Acknowledgments

I believe that any intellectual project is by nature collective, in the sense that it owes much to support, conversations, and readings, only some of which one can remember. To all of them, those I recall and those I do not, I thank.

I have traveled with this project for many years. On the way, several institutions have generously supported my work. In Argentina, these include the Universidad de Buenos Aires and the Consejo Nacional de Investigaciones Científicas y Técnicas. In Spain, these include the Escuela de Estudios Hispano-Americanos, Consejo Superior de Investigaciones Científicas, and the Fundación Sánchez-Albornoz. In the United States, these include the following: the Duke University–University of North Carolina, Chapel Hill, Program in Latin American and Caribbean Studies, with successive funding from the Mellon, Tinker, and Ford Foundations; at Duke University, the Department of Cultural Anthropology, the Graduate School, the Center for International Studies, and the John Hope Franklin Institute for the Humanities; and at Indiana University, the Mendel Committee, Lilly Library. This sustained support resulted in several articles, some of which are part of this book. Chapter 1, with some minor changes, has appeared in *Comparative Studies in Society and History* 47, no. 1 (2005). An earlier version of chapter 5 has appeared in *Colonial Latin American Review* 10, no. 1 (2001), under the title: "Definir y dominar: Los lugares grises en el Cuzco hacia 1540." I thank both journals for allowing me to reproduce these articles. I also want to thank Martti Pärssinen for granting me permission to use as the basis for map number 1 the map that appears on page 74 of *Tawantinsuyu* (which is, in turn, based on John Rowe's 1946 map). I am also grateful to the many archives whose personnel have helped me find my way around messy piles of dusty papers. In Peru, these were the Archivo Regional del Cuzco, the Archivo Histórico Nacional, and the Biblioteca Nacional; in Spain, the Archivo General de Indias, the Archivo Histórico Nacional, the Biblioteca Nacional, the Archivo General de Simancas, the Real Academia de la Historia, and the Abadía del Sacro Monte; in Argentina, the Archivo General de la Nación; and in the United States, the Piermont-Morgan library and the Lilly Library, at Indiana University.

I am indebted to many people in Peru, for different reasons. Miguel Glave and Hénrique Urbano helped me take my first steps in Peruvian archives many years ago. Later on, Franklin Pease G. Y. and Teodoro Hampe Martínez also supported my research. During my repeated visits, my friends Verónica Trelles Throne, Silvia Arispe, Miguel Baca and Paloma Visscher introduced me to many respectable venues in Lima, including the Santa Sede and the Kitsch. Donato Amado's erudition guided me through out-of-place archival files and helped me to make sense of sixteenth-century Cuzco places' and people's names. Sonia Velazco Flores was my "alma mater" in Cuzco; she took good care of my human shape when I was exhausted and half frozen after too much archival work in the winter; her *compadre* and *comadre* took good care that I was not too sober.

In Argentina, many on the Ethnohistory Team of the Anthropology Department and in the Program of Latin American History at the Universidad de Buenos Aires helped me persevere until I became a *licenciado*. Roxana Boixadós and Marta Madero were very appreciated sources of energy and intellectual stimulation as I made my years as an *investigador becario*. During those same years, and later as I took my first steps in the United States, I was lucky to have the constant support, intellectual companionship, and friendship of Enrique Tandeter. Unfortunately he could not see the outcome of it all; I send him and his wife, Dora, my deepest gratitude in memoriam. In Spain, Gema Puchal and Braulio Flores opened their house to me; although they meant to make me feel at home, their tortillas—the most fabulous on earth—were too discrepant. Carmen Gómez helped me find my way at the Hispalense, where, as my research led me to interrogate issues of legal history, I discussed ideas and received guidance from Fernando

Muro Romero. In Germany Horst Pietschmann also helped me walk this difficult terrain.

In my years in the United States, many people helped me develop my ideas and turn them into a text. The department of Cultural Anthropology at Duke University was an ideal place to write the dissertation on which this book is based. In particular, I became indebted, scholarly and otherwise, to Charles Piot, Orin Starn, Walter Mignolo, William Reddy, and Irene Silverblatt. Tomas Rogers and Ivonne Wallace-Fuentes, on the other hand, proved to be indefatigable colleagues and friends. Throughout the years, Catherine Julien has repeatedly helped me with erudite answers. The end of this long, serendipitous trajectory took place in the department of Hispanic Languages and Literatures at the University of Pittsburgh. Here, conversations with Elizabeth Monasterios, John Beverly, and Hermann Herlinghaus, and discussions with graduate students in the seminars I taught in the last three years, helped me further put my writing into perspective and elaborate still inchoate ideas. The critiques and suggestions of the anonymous reviewers at Duke University press, finally, pushed me to make the manuscript more coherent. All mistakes, needless to say, are mine.

Of course, without my family and close friends none of this would have ever been written. They know well enough who they are and how much they mean to me. *Gracias a todas/os; köszönöm.*

Situated Interventions   *Colonial Imprints, Decolonial Moves*

This book offers a reinterpretation of the twenty-year transition that bridged the moment of contact between Spanish conquistadors and Andean peoples, and the moment when
a colonial regime with working relations of subordination was
recognizable. The time span is approximately 1531 to 1550; the
main geographical setting is the highlands of South America under Inca control, a 4,000 km (2,486 mi) mountainous landscape
that extends from present-day Ecuador to the north of Argentina and Chile, and in particular the city of Cuzco—navel and
capital of the Inca empire—and its surroundings. The book's
overall contention is that a pervasive colonial imprint still per-
meates accounts of what happened almost 500 years ago, and
its goal is to provide an alternative historical narrative that at
once examines the imprint and shifts away from it. The aim is to
present, then, not an anticolonial narrative, since what is "anti"
is constrained by (and inadvertently echoes) the conceptual
frames of that which it opposes, but a decolonial one.

The conquest of the Inca empire has long captured the interest of scholars and laymen. A rich literature offering detailed,
vivid accounts of the numerous encounters and battles that took
place during those years is as ubiquitous in academic libraries as
in the kiosks that surround Cuzco's main plaza, an ineludible

stop for tourists wanting to make a well-informed tour of the Inca capital. Classic works that intend to convey the dramatic character of this clash of civilizations, such as Prescott's *History of the Conquest of Peru* or Hemming's *The Conquest of the Incas*, continue to be influential and popular today, 256 and 22 editions, respectively, after their first printings.[1] In addition, local readers can access numerous indigenous accounts, most notably those penned by Peruvian nationalist historians, which empty the story of any glamour, qualify the conquistadors' achievements by stressing their alliances with ethnic groups and the role of internecine imperial strife, and highlight heroic instances of Inca resistance.

Regardless of current accounts' various emphases and goals, a common trait characterizes most of them: they restore agency to native peoples, undoing one of the biases of the self-centered Spanish sixteenth-century accounts. But they do it at a high price: they render events intelligible by endowing all actors with Western ways of making sense. Both the objects to be recognized and the kinds of reasoning used to articulate them in a plot are those present in the conquerors' accounts. The result is a master narrative of what happened that makes native accounts of the same events appear at best wrong (imprecise, confusing) and at worst nonsensical (they tell stories that do not match, either because the Spaniards do not mention them or because the elements included look weird). Discrepant stories, such as books that were expected to talk, horses that were said capable of being angry and eating people, or attacks that were launched for an entire year only on the full moon, are largely absent from current histories of the conquest, and, if mentioned, are rendered into curiosities, incidental to the overall plot. I argue, in contrast, that these stories and the discrepant ways of making sense of events they involve were key parts of the overall plot. In fact, once they are taken into account, the history of the conquest reveals itself in a different light: as a full-fledged contest to define the new order of things, and a contest in which no party managed to have the upper hand.

But if reinserting different understandings of the same present debunks the conquerors' favorite narrative strategy—that of presenting a transparent politicomilitary interaction of which they are in full control—it solves only half the problem. Present and past accounts also veil the fact that Spaniards and native peoples were not only different but also similar. In the battlefield as much as in everyday arenas such as conversion, market exchanges, politics or land tenure, the parties blurred into each other in repeated instances of mimicry. Conquerors and Incas copied each other's ways of waging war, dressing, and practicing politics; Spanish clergymen tried to appropriate Inca religious forms and cosmology, while Incas did likewise with Christian ones. The result of these and other repeated acts of copying was doubly troubling: on the one hand, they undermined the colonizers' claim of distinctiveness and superiority; on the other, they empowered creative politics by indigenous social actors who not only reappropriated the colonizers' designs but went beyond them. For instance, challenging the Spaniards' will of mastery, new Inca kings were crowned right when Inca armies were defeated, ruled over ethnic lords and received tribute as much as the conquerors did, and publicly outdid the latter in their Christianity while at the same time leading Inca religious lives. The resulting landscape of plural attempts to define the order of things, attempts often pillaged, flipped, or disempowered, reveals that—unlike Spanish clergymen and conquerors conveyed in their accounts and reports—there was no single or stable configuration of meanings, at any time.

This lack of Spanish mastery undermines in a fundamental way prevalent understandings of the setting that past and present accounts privilege: the battlefield. Like the literature of the conquerors, most current scholarship portrays the transition as a chain of battles at whose end order is supposed to be in place. Although casting order as a by-product of military action seems reasonable, since at the end of the day the Spaniards won, it is not. It rests on a fallacy that makes it look reasonable: the translation of *military superiority* into *cultural superiority* and, in terms of the unfolding historical process, of *domination* into *dominance*. Thus, while widely read, general works that use the Inca conquest as an example—such as Jared Diamond's *Guns, Germs, and Steel* (1997)—give this implicit slippage of specialized studies the rank of open statement, the actual historical process makes plain that military superiority resulted in no ascendancy.[2]

Dominance was elusive also because the complex political process within which battles took place made simplistic readings of their outcomes impossible. First, the Inca empire was a large mosaic of different peoples with several million inhabitants traversed by many tensions (see map); distinct

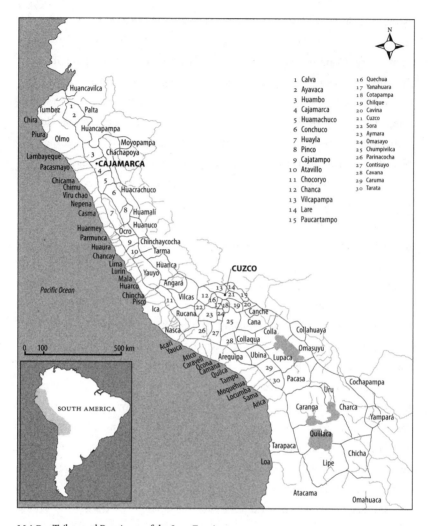

1 Calva	16 Quechua	
2 Ayavaca	17 Yanahuara	
3 Huambo	18 Cotapampa	
4 Cajamarca	19 Chilque	
5 Huamachuco	20 Cavina	
6 Conchuco	21 Cuzco	
7 Huayla	22 Sora	
8 Pinco	23 Aymara	
9 Cajatampo	24 Omasayo	
10 Atavillo	25 Chumpivilca	
11 Chocoryo	26 Parinacocha	
12 Chanca	27 Contisuyo	
13 Vilcapampa	28 Cavana	
14 Lare	29 Caruma	
15 Paucartampo	30 Tarata	

MAP. Tribes and Provinces of the Inca Empire

agendas, at times simply diverging, at others radically conflicting, guided the different ethnic lords and the different Inca factions.

Second, the Spaniards, whose number went from less than 200 when they captured the Inca Atahualpa, the head of the Inca empire, in 1532, to only about 6,000 twenty years later, were also internally divided. This fragmentation and disparity of numbers resulted in shifting conflicts and alliances between different Spanish captains, different clergymen, different Inca factions, and different ethnic lords (see the Basic Political Chronology of the Spanish Conquest at the back of this book before the endnotes). As a result, different parties were able to claim victory, and to different ends, adding further ambiguity to a landscape where plural political and cultural visions coexisted.

Put differently, the alternative history of the conquest uncovered in the pages to follow shows that questions of difference, similarity, and mastery were constitutive to Spanish colonialism. It is through juggling these elements that the Christians (what Peru's conquerors chose to call themselves; throughout this book "Christians," "Spaniards," and "Spanish" are used interchangeably) intended to make their acts and ways of making sense alone look coherent. To unsettle this effect, a double narrative move is necessary: *to reintroduce cultural difference* and, to avoid the risk of orientalization, *to simultaneously de-occidentalize the conquerors*—that is, to question the distinctive image they intended to convey of themselves and their acts. The strategy is twofold because it seeks to respond to the two main Spanish, imperial mechanisms of subalternization, at work both on the ground and in the narratives: exotization and erasure. Allow me to elaborate.

The exotization of the Other makes her or him particular and therefore inferior at the same time that it makes the colonizer universal and superior. The erasure of the Other makes the Spanish rules of recognition the only ones available and everyone's acts intelligible only through Spanish ways of making sense, implicitly cornering other ways of living and thinking the same present into nonsense. Each of these imperial means of subalternization has received a distinct academic response. On the one hand, there is a critique of empire that aims to question Western attempts at making its own logic the only logic possible. *Culture* is here the key word. It allows one to debunk Western renditions of other peoples' acts as nonsensical by showing that the latter in fact made sense, only in their own, different terms. On the other hand, scholars engaged in a critical reading of empire that highlight the power of representations stress that culture, understood as the natives' way, is constitutive of colonial projects. The language of "culture" and "custom," and the practices of intervention it legitimizes, allows imperial agents to exercise control over the clearly different and inferior Other, cajoling her or him into a given set of options enforced through politics of authenticity.

While each of these academic responses can be effective against its in-tended target, the birth of Spanish colonialism in Peru shows that on their own, they fail as decolonial strategies. The power of these two imperial mechanisms, what makes them effective, is that they can work as a catch-22: a response to only one of them runs the risk of reinforcing the other. Thus, stressing similarity in response to exotization may end up supporting the Western claim of universality of its forms and epistemology, and stressing difference in response to erasure may end up supporting the exotization of other forms and epistemologies. And in fact, the dilemma this catch-22 poses to any current narrative was also faced by native actors during the conquest: to enforce their elusive claim of mastery, the Spaniards' repertoire included resorting (self-consciously or not) at times to one means of subal-ternization, at other times to the other, and at times to both at once. Con-sequently, the book will unfold as the account of the conquest progresses, as *situated interventions* on renditions of particular events. That is, they are interventions with no overall coherence; they intend to make visible, in each case, the conquerors' particular strategy of subalternization, both on the ground and in their narrations, and to flesh out native peoples' creative ways of facing, and often trumping them.

For different reasons, I suggest that the import of a new narrative of the conquest of Incas has a significance that goes beyond the case itself. The first reason is its particular location in the history of the world, and because of how that history is often told. The conquests of Peru and Mexico (1519–21) seem to testify to European superiority: Spaniards ranging in the hundreds manage to conquer an empire of several millions. This is the reading the conquistadors intended to convey, and they did so with success. Veiling the fact that a comparison of the achievements of European and Amerindian civilizations would have shown no clear winner, the conquests ignited the Europeans' sense of superiority and manifest destiny. At the same time, the conquests also gave Spain the resources to become the leader of the first modern global configuration, which—as nations of the second, northern European modernity developed it—changed power relations across the globe making the West, in fact, superior to its contenders. In a mystifying circle, current Western taxonomies of human capacity of Westerners and their Others seem to confirm and are confirmed by past ones.

Second, it is significant because it speaks to dynamics of power and subalternization in other temporal and geographic scenarios. Since the transition that made colonial Peru was constitutive of the forging of the material and conceptual matrix of the world we live in, its study sheds light on the building blocks of modernity's Janus other: coloniality. Neither the concrete mechanisms through which the Spaniards' attempted to subalternize indigenous ways of thinking and acting, nor the ways in which native peoples recognized these mechanisms and strived to disarticulate and go past them, are particular to this case alone. Current debates on violence and human rights, assumptions of superiority taken to be self-evident, declarations of civilizing duties and images of authenticity, and subaltern attempts to disable hegemonic frames validating other epistemologies, all have their sixteenth-century doubles. Furthermore, because the story is of a colonial encounter, the contested dynamics through which some peoples seemingly cease to make sense—in experiential, political, or epistemological terms—while others become literally the embodiment of sense, is visible to a much larger degree than in mature colonial scenarios and in neocolonial ones.

Before I address questions of sources and concepts, I stress that there is nothing original in what I have strived to do; it is, in fact, what some of Peru's native peoples set themselves to do some 500 years ago. They recognized the Spaniards' certainty of superiority and its limitations, their imperial gestures and their double binds, and tried to figure effective ways to both disable and move beyond them. This parallel came to me as a surprise when I was trying to make sense of my archival notes, and it made me realize the endurance of Spanish colonialism's imprint. I present this narrative of the events in question, then, with the hope that a different explanation of the past serves alternative understandings of the present and imaginations of the future.

SOURCES AND READING METHODS

As is known, studies of colonial encounters often face the problem that the sources available to study them were written, overwhelmingly, by one party: the Europeans. This is particularly true in the case of the Inca conquest, in which the social process of subalternization that took place during the twenty-year transition was entirely anticipated by a narrative one. As

Table. The Asymmetry of Available Narrative Sources

NATIVELIKE[a] ACCOUNTS	TIMELINE OF INCA KINGS	SPANISH CONQUEROR ACCOUNTS
	End of 1532. Capture of Atahualpa	
	Mid-1533. Execution of Atahualpa	H. Pizarro, 1533
	End of 1533. Coronation of Manco Inca	Mena, *1534*[b] Xérez, *1534* Sancho, 1534
	1536–37. Manco Inca's War	Estete, 1535 [?]
	1537. Coronation of Paullu Inca	Anonymous (RS), 1539
	1544. Manco Inca is killed	Enríquez de Guzmán, 1543
	1549. Paullu Inca dies	Ruiz de Arce, 1543
Betanzos [1551]		Trujillo, 1571
Tito Cussi Yupangui [1570]		P. Pizarro, 1571
Garcilaso de la Vega [*1609* and *1617*]		Plus all chronicles, Oviedo's (1547) being the first
Guaman Poma [c. 1615]		

[a] I call them "native-like" to avoid the image of immaculate native knowledge retrieved; they are all colonial products, some written by mestizos, some by Spaniards married to Inca princesses, some by Incas with the help of friars, some by natives born and submerged in the multicultural colonial world.
[b] Italics indicate that the text was published soon after its finishing date.

can be seen in the above table, Andean peoples' lack of a writing system intelligible to either Spaniards or current scholars resulted in a strong asymmetry in the surviving documentary record: while the conquerors wrote and at times even published accounts from the day they set foot on the empire, the first narrative that presents a native point of view was finished after the transition was over.

In both political-history and social-history studies of the transition, precise instrumental constraints governing the way in which the narratives are built often reproduce the sixteenth-century asymmetry. First, the kind of *sources* privileged: by and large, Spanish conquistadors' accounts and Spanish notarial records. Allegedly because the conquerors' proximity to the events—both as eyewitnesses and writers—makes their narratives the most reliable, the political historiography of the conquest uses them as the main source. Spanish chronicles, in turn, are used to fill in the gaps. Native-like sources are used to add veracity to the story, or, as in the case of Peruvian nationalist historiography, to change the politics of the story, but not its terms, which are set by Spanish accounts. Social historians, in contrast, rely largely on Spanish notarial records to circumvent the military focus of Spanish accounts and their political bias (Spaniards often fought each other). However, notarial records are not neutral either, but respond to a particular way of "coding" reality (Ginzburg 1989:161); the coding in this case reifies Spanish legal categories and makes of Indians, if mentioned at all, only objects.[3] As a result of this twice-embodied asymmetry (sixteenth-century and contemporary), the history being narrated replicates both the Spaniards' field of visibility—the objects to be recognized and the kinds of reasoning used to articulate them in a plot are Spanish—and the stories the conquerors wanted to tell.

Second, in the case of political-history works—by far the most numerous—the imbalance of the available documentary corpus is also reproduced because of a *methodological priority*: the production of a standardized historical narrative—what Seed (1991:9–11) calls "historical realism." Contradiction and incongruity within and between documents are not studied, and in particular, whenever something in the conquerors' accounts does not fit, it is left aside. This reading pattern reinforces the conquerors' accounts' own imprint: they are retrospective simplifications that give events a coherence and conquerors a mastery over acts they did not have. One can then go full circle: as a consequence of these constraints and priorities governing the way in which current narratives are built, the conquerors appear to be in control of all interactions—even when in trouble—and the colonial order seems to be a natural outcome. In other words, history is set before it began.

To tackle these and other problems springing from the historical record and the ways in which it is commonly read, I resort to alternative sources and methods. First, whenever possible I use local documents produced when the events were taking place, such as urgent reports or city council records—what Guha (1988:47–48) calls "primary discourse." Although due to both sixteenth-century and more contemporary events of looting and destruction, most documents of this sort have disappeared, some are available. In them, one can recover the uncertainty and ambiguity of events, and at times pick up traces of silenced plots that reveal the conquerors' accounts' craftiness. Notorious lies—in which scholars will recognize parallels with key scenes in other colonial scenarios, such as the 1519 encounter between Hernán Cortés and the Aztec emperor Moctezuma or the signing of the 1840 British-Maori treaty of Waitangi—involve moments climatic of the conquest and foundational to the Peruvian nation, such as the 1533 conquerors' entry in Cuzco city, capital of the Inca empire, and the reasons triggering the most serious military challenge the Spaniards faced, the 1536 war led by Manco Inca (see chapter 3).

Second, I use *probanzas*. They are legally recorded depositions by witnesses brought forward and questioned by an interested party, who could be a person or an institution, private or public (if carried out by a royal officer commissioned to certify a private person's request, they are called *informaciones*). A probanza certified a certain state of affairs; it could be presented as a proof element in a trial, sent to the king in support of a claim, or kept on file for other uses. What I find important about probanzas is that they catch an array of people, Spanish and indigenous, in partial, momentary attempts to make sense of things, for themselves and their inquirer; while at times the answers are in conformity with the questions, at others they are discrepant. The stories, the objects in them, and understandings included in these momentary attempts allow one to destabilize the master version, carefully edited in order to sustain coherent political claims, provided by narrative sources.[4]

Third, I use often-dismissed or purged nativelike narratives. Given the dates on which they were written, I take them to be situated interventions in the Spanish colonial order of things that try to reinsert different understandings and epistemologies. That is, I do not read nativelike texts as immaculate repositories of native knowledge, but as examples of "border thinking" (Mignolo 2000) that strategically introduce alterity. The value of reading nativelike texts in this way, I suggest, is that it destabilizes the master narrative in a particular way: situated difference is subversive because it makes the "rules of recognition" (Bhabha 1994, 110, 119) visible, thus arbitrary. For instance, I suggest in chapter 1 that books talk because they can be, in fact, *huacas*—deities, powerful beings. Once other epistemologies shape understandings, a "book" ceases to be a self-evidently silent object, and the epistemology making it appear so ceases to be neutral, unmarked. This in turn forces a rereading of the entire contact scene between Incas and conquerors.

Finally, I use lapses in the conquerors' accounts—what de Certeau (1991: 223) calls "faults in the discourse of comprehension." Because, despite their attempts, the conquerors' narratives are not seamless texts; there are moments in which their coherence falters, and a different image of events is visible in a flash. These fragments often are what Ginzburg (1989:164), building on Bakhtin's (1973) notion of polyphony, calls "dialogic indices": narrative cracks in which odd things emerge, and where one can recover "an unresolved clash of conflicting voices." Based on his work in Italian inquisitorial trials, Ginzburg thinks the dialogical element as resulting from the clash between the repressed culture (of the interrogated) and the dominant one (of the inquisitor), a clash that allowed subaltern voices to be heard. In the present case, at times I take dialogic indices in conquerors' accounts in Ginzburg's way; for instance, when they report dialogues in which natives' answers are discrepant. At other times, I think of the dialogic element as resulting from an inner clash between the narrator's will to control his narrative (only men wrote) and the resistance of hard-to-tame elements that clearly escape it—that is, as outcomes of the "chance" (*hasard*) of discourse (Foucault 1971:9, 23).

The existence of these lapses denaturalizes the conquerors' accounts' elements and reasonings and calls into question their intended coherence. For instance, in an official account tightly ordered by images of daring military action against sinful, treacherous Indians, we are told that the valiant Spanish captain Hernando Pizarro, brother of the famous Francisco Pizarro, asks native lords to clear a plaza full of Indians "because the horses are angry and will kill them"[5]—the horses, not the conquerors. This snapshot is neither preceded nor followed by an attempt at making sense of it: the way in which native peoples understood horses or Spaniards, their auras and statuses, and what the conquerors knew about native peoples' understandings and did with them—all are completely absent from the text. The sentence appears then to the reader's eye as a flash in the flow of "Christian realist" plots (I will explain this concept in the next section). One could overlook it, thinking that it is just a mistake, or not even notice it, as so much action of a different nature precedes and follows it. And yet, the odd turns out to be revealing: the "mistake" matches clues in dismissed native accounts, which in turn restore the complexity of the plot and give native actors and ways of making sense a coherence the texts of the master narrative deny (see chapter 2).

CONCEPTS AND DIALOGUES

To foster new visibilities of the birth of the Spanish colonial regime in Peru, I dialogue with critical thinking from different disciplines and traditions. This dialogue works throughout the book as a two-way process: on the one hand, theory helps me undo silences and subvert plots of sixteenth-century narratives; on the other, these unplottings and rethinkings illuminate precise order-producing mechanisms that escape those theories' original formulation, making the case in point speak to larger issues. This dialogue situates, then, the present study in a broader context, both in terms of areas of study and academic traditions.

To apprehend the convoluted dynamics of transformation that sprang from the colonial encounter, my starting point is to consider reality as being constituted through meaning. While "semiotic realism" (Daniel 1987:16) is a longstanding tradition that draws on different theoretical foundations, the basis of my work is Saussure's (1995) theory of langue. Along this path, I find suggestive Sahlins's (e.g., 1981, 1985) attempts to put Saussure's structuralist theory to work to understand historical transformations. However, I part company with Sahlins in that I share neither the strict systemic character of values (or categories) nor the emphasis on the synchronic nature of the oppositions between them. I deviate from these two Saussurean principles as follows. On the one hand, my analysis focuses on the fractured signifying landscape during the transition (cf. Fish's [1980] interpretive communities) and emphasizes the importance of sustained heterogeneity and ambiguity; on the other hand, I suggest that oppositions—and therefore social forms—are defined not only synchronically by the other forms' attributes but also diachronically: something is what at other moments it is not, and in relation to what other similar forms have or have not been. For instance, as I show in chapter 5, the success of an Inca crowned king in defining who was Inca and what it meant to be so—just when the Spaniards proved that they could be defeated and another Inca king was still alive—depended on his capacity to make another future with not-yet-existing forms imaginable, therefore plausible, rallying understandings.

In this and other cases, I try to identify the precise mechanisms through which Spaniards and native peoples attempted to control what was at base an unstable and fragmented reality, making events mean or crystallize in one or another form. In contrast to Dirks (1992:7) and Guha (1997), I find the Gramscian notion of hegemony to be a productive concept to study colonial dynamics, in particular as developed by Williams (1977) and J. and J. Comaroff (1991, 1992). I use it, though, with two caveats. First, I consider it useful to think *Inca* political practices, as it allows one to dispel simplistic (and demeaning) understandings of difference that notions such as "custom" or "worldview" entail. For example, a war waged during an entire year through full-moon-only attacks does not express mental deficiency or conservatism but a deliberate attempt to prove that Inca hegemony was valid "as usual." The Spaniards' acts, in contrast, were clearly disruptive and violent, therefore visible and far from capable of grounding a hegemonic project.

Second, when studying the emerging colonial order of things, I share the Comaroffs' emphasis on the dynamic between the tacit and the explicit, but part company with them when conceiving its actual mechanics; likely because battles failed to effect the ascendancy the Spaniards longed for, in the Inca case the genesis of a colonial quotidian involved an asymmetric dynamic of the tacit and the explicit. In that dynamic, powered by the libidinal energies of the colonial encounter, violence is paradoxically prominent, because, regardless of what native peoples thought of it, they were "interpellated" (Althusser 1971) in everyday situations by a certain way of acting and feeling that embodied the conquerors' sense of what was normal— what, *for them*, went without saying. As an alternative to hegemony, then,

I introduce the concept of the "colonial normal" (see chapter 4). By this, I mean a series of everyday habits, of configurations of what is usually done, without thinking, beyond words, that becomes "habit memory" (Connerton 1989)—configurations that involve implicit relations between people, and between people and objects. It is through them, I suggest, that the cultural and political fragmentation of the contact period and the lack of Spanish dominance turned workable—neither consensus nor homogeneity are assumed.

My use of Althusser's (1971) "interpellation" as a means of understanding how reality came into being in a colonial setting also involves some adjustment. In the case of the deeply embodied understandings of hierarchy and humiliation of the colonial normal, I stress the libidinal energies (rather than "ideologies") at work and the violence behind the hailing act—there were no "subjects" yet. In other cases, I question its directionality. The effect of interpellation is the constitution or confirmation of the subject position of the one being interpellated; the "subject" is not the policeman but the person walking by on the street, whom the former hails with "Hey, you!" In a contact-to-domination process, configurations of meaning and power ("ideologies" in Althusser's terms) are fragile; therefore, interpellations imply as much a top-down valence as the opposite: the authority that interpellates is searching for self-confirmation or constitution. For instance, when an Inca king gave a local lord a gift (the material equivalent to hailing), the gift as much constituted the lord's subject position as vassal as the Inca's as king.

In yet other instances, political practices of a nature other than that considered in most studies of power gained center stage. The essence of these practices can be defined as "magicality." By magicality, I want to evoke ways of acting and interacting that are not fantastic or magic (that is, that do not violate rules of nature), but involve dimensions of social action ordinarily deemed to be so. (I follow here Anderson Imbert's [1976:7–25] distinction between the real, the supernatural, and the preternatural.) As I show in chapter 2, to counter their numerical disadvantage and challenge the awe the Inca as a supernatural being awoke, the Spaniards resorted to supernatural imagery: for instance, horses that could eat people, or be angry and attack on their own. I chose magicality instead of magic for three reasons.

First, magic has too much baggage; it is opposed to science, and therefore evokes an easy-to-dispel falsity or illusion, while I am referring to complex acts with actual effects. Second, I want to evoke the loaded emotions and embodied notions of awe and respect that surrounded acts of magicality. Third, magicality is neither esoteric nor does it relate only to odd situations; rather, it refers to a principle of *political* action of the Western civilizing project its subjects most often deny. While Marx used "commodity fetishism" (1977: 165, 176) to tease political economists' implicitly magical explanation of the production of value, I want to make a point of it: magicality was (is) foundational to Western neo/colonial projects, and it was (is) denied in order to defend the authoritative aura of rationality sustaining them. The denial both erases their nonrational sides and reinforces their self-proclaimed aura, a strategy that allows neo/colonial agents to mark themselves off from, and make themselves superior to, their Others—whom, it is often suggested, incantations and irrationality suit well.

Because magic and rationality are inextricably tied, magicality as analytic concept becomes effective when "Christian realism" is also considered. The latter describes the kind of scenario in which sixteenth-century Europeans preferred to present (and imagine) themselves as different from pagans and idolaters. I say *Christian* realism because a "real" scenario with "rational" actors is the second, enlightened modernity's claim. The imperial actor of the *mission civilisatrice* presented itself as rational, in contrast to the irrational Other that would benefit from it. "Occidentalism" (Coronil 1996) and "Orientalism" (Said 1978) comprise the sets of images underlying both ways of thinking and seeing the West and the Rest. Regarding Spanish colonialism, the situation is similar in formal terms: the conquerors possessed something (Christianity) the Other would benefit from. Faith replaces Civilization; Idolatry or Sin replaces Irrationality. While the notion of orientalism is immediately useful in the study of sixteenth-century colonialism, occidentalism is not. Sixteenth-century Spaniards were not rational from a post-Enlightenment point of view: they inhabited a religious-based world in which irrational, nonscientifically sound things could happen. For "occidentalism" to be useful, an adjustment is necessary: if rationality is the way in which a Western subject finds convenient to imagine himself, Christian rationality is the way in which a sixteenth-century Spanish subject found it convenient to imagine himself (gender intended in both cases). Christianity and Science guarantee, in each case, the self-convincing privilege of operating upon the real.

As it is clear, the ultimate claim of both sixteenth-century and current, neocolonial projects is that Western subjects know reality as it is while their Others do not. This makes visible, as Mignolo (1995, 2000) argues, that past and present processes of subalternization of indigenous peoples are in a last instance epistemological in nature. The word choice intends to question resilient power asymmetries coined in colonial times. One could say *ontology* instead of *epistemology*; however, ontology, like "culture," places the object in a distant, nonagentive position laden with the colonial difference: epistemology is a concept useful to study Western peoples because they *know* reality in a scientific manner; ontology is all one needs to study non-Westerners because they simply *inhabit* it. This current geopolitics of knowledge, with its concurrent asymmetry in terms of agency (who knows and who is being known), was crafted in the sixteenth century: even Spaniards harshly critical of their countrymen's acts, such as Bartolomé de Las Casas, who praised Indians' moral order and devoted his life to defending them, never considered that it could be possible to learn from them.

Because of their privileged relation with the real, the conquerors believed their cultural particulars to be universal and self-evident. Thus, for instance, Christianity and literacy played a key role in Spanish narrations of the encounter scene between the conquerors and the Inca Atahualpa, as Seed (1991) shows. I develop this belief in self-evidence in two directions. First, I disentangle different levels of consciousness behind such beliefs and examine the way in which the acts of believing responded, not only to discursive strategies but also to embodied senses of fair action (see chapter 1). Second, I examine the way in which the Spaniards' claim of a privileged relation with reality "as it is" grounded practices as seemingly trivial as to use Indians as loaders (*cargar indios*) (see chapter 4). Peru's native peoples, in contrast, were well aware of the epistemological claim Christianity entailed, and flipped it to their advantage: they acted publicly as better Christians than the Christians, troubling the latter's desire for ascendancy, and at once inserted a situated difference (see chapters 5 and 6). Through these reappropriations they effectively blurred the "colonial difference" (Mignolo 2000), anticipating in practices solutions Andean intellectuals such as Guamán Poma de Ayala would reach decades later.

My understanding of the challenges that the process of subalternization posed to indigenous subjectivities and epistemologies, and the responses it received, owes much to the work of Chicano thinkers, in particular Gloria Anzaldúa's *Borderlands / La Frontera*. As I show in chapters 5 and 6, the predicament of Incas and of other indigenous peoples when facing Spanish colonialism in many ways parallels Anzaldúa's "being zero" (1987:63)—the inadequacy resulting from hegemonic gazes and imposed identities. In turn, denaturalizing these gazes shifts from a reactive politics to a productive one, creating a liberatory potential that also has sixteenth-century echoes. To my mind, Anzaldúa's work is a logical continuation of Du Bois's (1995:45) "double consciousness," which I read as an initial decentering of the Western subject, who in academic writing had previously been taken to be universal and unmarked by his particularity. Furthermore, I suggest that these assumptions were by no means a fruit of the Enlightenment. Du Bois's visual emphasis is to me particularly revealing in the study of sixteenth-century colonial dynamics; as Spanish colonialism advanced, Peruvian native peoples increasingly found it necessary to see themselves through the eyes of their Others. This "third eye" (Rony 1996) allowed them to find ways to build respectable selves vis-à-vis a system that marked and constructed them as lesser beings—to borrow Rabasa's expression in his study of evangelization in colonial Mexico, as "subjectivit[ies] at fault" (1993:67–68).

While to question colonial inheritances, Anzaldúa or Du Bois face the obstacle of a reality already constituted, during the birth of Spanish colonialism in Peru the arbitrariness of power, and thus of the to-be reality, were clearly visible. In the different instances in which the Spaniards tried initial definitions of the order of things, native peoples were effectively "before the law" (Derrida 1992). Studying this moment made transparent Foucault's (to my eyes) obscure statement that he was not concerned with truth, but with effects of truth within discourses that are neither true nor false (1980:118). "Truth effects," for instance, capture the essence of some land disputes in Cuzco's valley: there, the key was not to determine how things had really been, but to make things look like they were in any particular way that proved effective to particular ends. That is, for "things" to turn into "goods" (objects of law), a prior, arbitrary definition of them as certain kind of things had to take place. The interesting fact is that despite the power asymmetry between parties, the Spaniards could not define reality entirely on their own: they had to appropriate and copy Inca practices (see chapter 6).

The general point I want to argue is not that the field was in a last instance level (it was not), but that it is important not to reinscribe the mystifying tale of impotent Indians facing all-powerful colonizers, which ends up confirming all-too-familiar taxonomies. The case of land disputes is just one example of a larger dynamic: despite the clear-cut distinctions the conquerors so wanted to convey between themselves and native peoples, they *needed* to engage in repeated acts of mimesis (Taussig 1993) and mimicry (Bhabha 1994) in which the parties blurred into each other. Mimesis explains why, in open battle, Incas and Spaniards copied and tried to outdo each other, for instance retaliating full-moon-only attacks with Corpus Christi attacks on Inca shrines (see chapter 4); mimicry explains that the Christians imitated Inca forms of authority (being carried like an Inca, or many Inca political and labor practices), while Incas imitated the Christians (their dressing, manners, and cosmologies). If it is true that when they perceived in it a threat, the conquerors reacted to similitude by orientalizing the Indians, this should not hide the fact that colonial power was inherently fragile.

These observations lead me to divert from theories that conceive of order in terms of the hegemony-coercion axis and suggest that Cuzco's social order resembled one in which power was about having the capacity to be one step ahead in the coin-flipping game. It was a chain of punches and counterpunches, fetishizations and appropriations of the fetishes' energy, acts of copying and assertions of distinctiveness, that accounted for much of early colonial Peru's particular type of order (see chapter 6). It is perhaps this point that makes the present study diverge more clearly from studies of the colonial process in the Andes along cultural lines (e.g., Wachtel 1971; Stern 1982; Spalding 1984; Silverblatt 1987; Ramírez 1996). While these studies largely leap from precontact to the colonial world without engaging the transition, they ground their analysis on clear-cut differences between Spaniards and Andean peoples resulting from functionalist or structuralist studies that veil the constant dynamics of copying and assertion of difference constitutive of the early colonial order. To define who or what had which attributes, and what treatment should follow from it, was by no means given. For instance, the Spaniards strived to present themselves as Christians, therefore distinct and superior, but Andean peoples both destabilized those self-representations and quickly learned to co-opt the epistemological claim of superiority Christianity entailed. As a consequence, an account of religious dynamics along the familiar lines of cultural difference expressed as "Christians versus Andeans" echoes the conquerors' masking of their resort to supernatural, non-Christian elements, and reduces to nonsense native responses that questioned those lines. In turn, by displacing the focus from political domination and material exploitation to the contested dynamics of subalternization in which questions of distinctiveness and superiority played a key role, my study brings to light early instances of the disputed terrain that scholars show characterized late Spanish colonialism in the Andes (e.g., Semiński 1987; Dean 1999; Serulnikov 2003; Silverblatt 2004; Spalding 1984:270–93; Tandeter 1995).

FROM CONTACT TO DOMINATION

The present study consists of six chapters and a coda. They examine, in chronological order, the nitty-gritty of the contested production of order during the transition from the Inca mode of domination to the Spanish colonial regime. The plot tries to capture the incessant attempts by different actors to define what events meant, what was possible or thinkable, which in turn made certain projects more plausible or sensible than others, rallying understandings and support. I take studying these contested attempts to be crucial because the subordination of indigenous epistemologies and ways of making sense neither followed a linear path nor was given at any point. On the one hand, there were numerous "blind alleys" (Thompson 1966:12) and losers, among both natives and Christians, which retrospective readings of social forms and subjectivities often neglect. On the other hand, there was almost no event in which Spanish and native peoples' internal tensions did not tangle and overlap with each other, often in ambiguous ways; there was neither "us" facing "them" nor, even in battle, clear acts. To make waters muddier, to gain control over events Spaniards and native peoples actively copied each other in successive acts of mimicry, further blurring contrasts between (would-be) dominators and (would-be) dominated. If it is true that the end of this period is domination, this should not hide the fact that dominance was elusive, as shown by the palimpsest of stabilization attempts, which changed in nature as previous ones proved inefficient. And native peoples were, in fact, as active in the flipping-of-the-coin game as the Spaniards were. Ignoring these dynamics, making it all an outcome of battles or economic drive, would be to mystify history.

The study begins with a reinterpretation of the most iconic moment of the conquest, the encounter between the conquerors and the Inca Atahualpa, head of the Inca empire, on 16 November 1532 in the plaza of Cajamarca, and his capture. I argue that the scene can be understood only by considering the central but often ignored role alterity and uncertainty played. To build my argument, I examine Cajamarca's coming into being as an ongoing contact process in which Spanish, Inca, and ethnic lords' sense making and politics tangled and clashed. To that end, I shift away from textual analysis and narrative strategies and consider differences between sources as indices of distinct ways of making and producing sense of events that coexisted when the events occurred.

Departing from most sixteenth-century and current histories, the narrative focuses on the exchange of messengers between Atahualpa and the Christians, and uses the latter's advance as its context. The question it addresses, as messengers, rumors, and political intents circulate, is how the extraordinary was being rendered meaningful, both by Spaniards and native peoples. This question is examined in dialogue with debates on cultural encounter and colonialism in other spatial and temporal scenarios, such as the Hawaiian and the Mexican. In particular, by focusing on diversity and politically informed improvisation within and across the cultural divide, I seek to avoid the current double bind plaguing representations of non-Westerners, in which cultural difference is denounced as exotization and likeness as an imposition of Western rationality (an academic echo of the two imperial means of subalternization already outlined).

Chapter 2 examines Cajamarca's complex nine-month aftermath, during which the Spaniards gathered an exhilarating ransom as they kept Atahualpa prisoner, only to finally execute him. I begin here the study of what happens once initial contact is over but domination is not yet in place. The landscape is mosaic-like: there were different kinds and degrees of interaction among Christians, Inca factions, and ethnic groups, as conquerors, rumors, ethnic lords, and loads of gold and silver circulated throughout the empire. In the shrine of Pachacámac and in the cities of Jauja and Cuzco, where small parties of conquerors went, the case is of renewed instances of first contact; in Cajamarca, of sustained cohabitation. In all four scenarios, complex struggles over meaning that paralleled acts are visible, short-circuiting empiricist and culturalist explanations of a contact's aftermath.

Historiography often narrates these nine months as starring Western-like rational actors involved in transparent political or military action. By matching lapses in conquerors' accounts with clues in nativelike sources, I provide a different plot, in which the alleged transparency and normalcy are exposed as selective ways of representing actions and emotions, and murky exchanges of supernatural energy and imagery gain center stage. To advance their respective agendas in the extraordinary and convoluted context, both Incas and Spaniards resorted to acts of magicality that challenged familiar Pagan-versus-Christian scripts. Horses that could eat people, for instance, served both parties, although for different reasons, and in different ways. These entanglements of the different but overlapping kinds of political action bring back to light the unusual means through which the parties competed to gain control of what was going on.

The coexistence between the Christians and the Inca factions opposed to Atahualpa, which extended from November 1533, when the former entered Cuzco city, heart of the empire, until April 1536, when Atahualpa's successor, Manco Inca, began an all-out war against the Spaniards, is the topic of chapter 3. During much of this time, Inca and Spanish attention focused on their prime enemies, Atahualpa's generals and a rival Spanish conquest company respectively. My reading suggests that this coexistence was more uncertain than often assumed. To sustain this reading, I question the field of interactions prevalent in most sixteenth-century accounts of the coexistence: that provided by the civilizing discourse. On the one hand, I expose lies in the conquerors' accounts that mystify key scenes of this period, such as the Spaniards' entry in Cuzco city and their alleged reading to the Inca elite of the Requerimiento, the Crown-mandated legal text requesting submission. Once the mystification is undone, the actual dynamics on the ground tell that at the beginning of the coexistence both parties' main strategy was veiling their final goals from each other and pretending to believe each other's lies.

On the other hand, the conquerors' lies silence the fact that the Crown's civilizing discourse played a key role in the conquerors' internecine conflicts, as different factions used it to fight against each other. Through these recurrent uses, however, the conquerors made increasingly effective a political design not of their own making. Tracking instances of these uses allows an alternative plot of the events from 1533 to 1535 to gain center stage. The plot, silenced in sixteenth-century Spanish accounts and largely absent in current literature, casts the endpoint of this period, the war led by Manco Inca, in a different light: it had a chance to start because, after being used as a handy tool, the Crown's civilizing discourse haunted the conquerors, and the best way out of that predicament was a war—a war that fit also the Inca elite's desire, since their principal adversaries, Atahualpa's generals, had already been defeated.

Chapter 4 studies the main Inca military attempt to regain control: Manco Inca's all-out war, which began in April 1536. The war plays a main role in all histories of the conquest and the Peruvian nation. By and large, conquerors and current scholars privilege an image in which two sides battled each other in endless heroic encounters. Anticipating the outcome of the war—the Inca defeat and the subsequent consolidation of the Spanish colonial regime—a single order of things makes these encounters intelligible. To dispel this implicit illusion of Spanish mastery, I reexamine events on the battlefield and show that it was at base a contest over meaning. For all actors involved in the war, what was at stake was as much achieving victory as *how* to do it. That is why Manco attacked the Spaniards only on full moons throughout an entire year, and why the conquerors, despite the self-confident tone of their narratives, felt it necessary to engage in their own struggle over meaning, attacking, for instance, Inca huacas on Corpus Christi. These acts make evident, in turn, the import of mimesis and mimicry in colonial scenarios and blur the neat difference between the colonizers and the colonized that the former so want to convey.

In the second part of chapter 4, I shift the focus away from the site of military action that Spanish and Inca accounts privilege, and examine everyday instances of cross-cultural interaction. Focusing on logistics, and in particular on the use of Indians as porters (cargar indios), I study the emergence of a quotidian order that was taking place before and during the war, an order to which Manco Inca's offensive also responded. I suggest that through the conquerors' de facto reappropriation and reshaping of precontact forms, a colonial normal was coming into being. It was a way of acting and feeling that embodied the conquerors' sense of normalcy and was being institutionalized beyond institutions, and most often beyond words.

Reassessing the aftermath of the failure of Manco Inca's war is the goal of chapter 5. Both sixteenth-century and contemporary accounts tend to cast the war as a watershed: after it, Spanish authority effectively displaced the Inca's, and the (Spanish) "civil wars of Peru" began. I suggest that this image fundamentally misrepresents the aftermath of the war: Inca power did not end after Manco's failure but reinvented itself. The head of this project was a new Inca, Paullu Inca, crowned in 1537. Unlike his brother, Paullu chose to be an Inca among Christians and to lead native life in Cuzco city. Current scholars, if they mention Paullu at all, portray him as a traitor to his race or nation, a Hispanicized, acculturated man—an image consistent with the dominators/dominated binary the conquerors aimed for. I suggest instead that Paullu was the first example of a mestizo consciousness that emerged when the Spaniards' presence was a given but not yet how it was going to actually materialize.

Paullu's and the involved ethnic lords' project worked through sustained improvisations that put practices ahead of discourses—very much as it happened to Frenchmen and even for the African slaves during the Haitian revolution (Trouillot 1995:88). Initially, Paullu's attempt to be an Inca among the Christians was uncertain because he was caught between the impossibility of what had just failed and the plausibility of what did not yet exist. Discourses caught up with practices toward 1540, when major military action paused and the weight of interaction moved to everyday spaces. In Cuzco, the intersecting paths of this new Inca and of Spanish clergyman critical of the conquerors gave life to an order of things that challenged the latter's fledging colonial normal. While the priests appropriated precontact forms to support their reality-making project, the Inca appropriated the Christians' cosmology, deity, and legal forms to support his own. He thus created a gray space that subverted Spanish domination from within, effectively keeping the Spaniards' claim of mastery at bay.

Chapter 6 examines how this inconclusive status quo evolved between 1543 and 1548. It begins by studying key arenas of quotidian interaction: conversion, economic entrepreneurship, and land tenure. There, the obstacles that a new mestizo consciousness posed to the conquerors' designs only multiplied. In the case of land tenure, for instance, native peoples recognized the Christians' capacity, by then, to redefine what things were, and they mimicked Spanish royal cosmologies to secure land claims—in fact, a mimicry and co-optation that imitated Spanish clergymen's of Inca forms. The conquerors, on the other hand, resorted as well to mimicry: they asked to be carried like Incas and married like the Incas did, exploited the same resources, and used the same currency (coca leaves) the Incas did. In the case of conversion, native peoples engaged in an active politics of de-occidentalization that challenged the conquerors' dominance: they exposed the Spaniards as bad Christians and at once exploited the certainty of superiority that according to the Spaniards, Christianity conveyed, by being better Christians than the Christians. In turn, to reclaim ascendancy, the conquerors resorted to the exotization of native practices and to forcing native peoples into double binds. This uncertain landscape of dominance resulted in open conflict only when its implicit subtext (colonizers and colonized were, although different, equal) was discursively articulated and publicly legitimized—which, ironically, only an absolutist viceroy could do.

The second part of chapter 6 focuses precisely on the conflict that started in 1544, when, as part of the advance of absolutism, the Crown attempted to reorganize the way its colonies were run. This true revolution from above met a decided resistance, led by the last Pizarro brother alive in Peru, Gonzalo. Diverting from the common focus on the politicomilitary conflict among Spaniards, I examine native people's predicament and acts during the conflict. On the one hand, the wars reveal the colonial normal as it was shaping up toward 1545. In his attempt to enforce absolutism, the first Peruvian viceroy threatened what for the conquerors was "the way things are," and native peoples took advantage of it. Their actual exercise of their rights as free vassals entailed the threat of similitude, and was met once again by exotization. On the other hand, ethnic lords and Incas showed themselves to be increasingly savvy about Spanish cosmology and royal mechanisms: many sided with the Crown, which allowed them to claim the credit of fighting "in service of God and the King" when battling conquerors, thus flipping on its head the Spaniards' preferred motto during the early stages of the conquest.

The numerous changes that took place during the governorship of Gonzalo Pizarro's defeater and successor, Pedro de la Gasca (1548–49), mark a watershed that puts an end to this study, in chapter 7. I do not argue that these changes marked an absolute before or after—that would contradict my overall characterization of colonial Peru's power relations—but I suggest that they signal a convenient endpoint because some of the main dynamics that animated the long transition from contact to domination began fading then, while new ones that would animate the political and cultural arenas during the next thirty years began gaining center stage.

CHAPTER I

Beyond Exotization and Likeness
Alterity and the Production of Sense in a Colonial Encounter

The scene that unfolded in the plaza of Cajamarca on Saturday, 16 November 1532, is one of the most baffling in the Spanish conquest of the Inca Empire. That day the Inca Atahualpa, head of an empire of several million extending from present-day Ecuador to Chile, surrounded by his powerful army, was captured by 168 men. The attack took place after the exchange of a book and words in the middle of the plaza, between the Inca and Fray Vicente de Valverde, head clergyman of the conquest party lead by Francisco Pizarro. The scene has been the object of much debate, both in the sixteenth century, when it rapidly became part of Europeans' colonial imagination, and in the present. The goal of this chapter is to offer an alternative interpretation of Cajamarca, which addresses a simple, underexplored question: Why did the meeting occur *in the way* it did? (Why was Atahualpa *there*, exposing himself to some dangerous looters? Why did the Spanish not attack directly if the ambush was ready?) I will argue that Cajamarca happened as it did because it was the necessary final act of a long chain of improvised moves, which responded to culturally specific political dilemmas. Its dynamic reflected a radical uncertainty common to contact processes, but left aside by most scholarship. Recovering it, I suggest, speaks not only to the case in point, but to the mechanics of power and coloniality across space and time.

Cajamarca has been studied with different interests and approaches. Social historians focus on the socioeconomic dynamics of the conquering force (Lockhart 1972; Varón Gabai 1996), while traditional historiography, cleaving to an Enlightenment vision (e.g., Del Busto 2000; Porras Barrenechea 1978), focuses on the Spanish advance. In both cases what happens occurs only because the Spanish act, while native actors are in a secondary plane without agency. This image has been contested by works that reveal the complex native political landscape, relocate agency, and revise the dynamics of the conquest. These studies stress the alliances between ethnic lords and Spaniards from a Marxist perspective (e.g., Espinoza Soriano 1973), or the late moments of Inca resistance from a nationalist one (Guillén Guillén 1974, 1979, 1994). Similar goals drive John Hemming's (1993) detailed account of Cajamarca. In all cases, the scene is narrated by staging rational actors in full control of a clear politicomilitary interaction. This approach has a political agenda: to reject marks of native inferiority. Peruvian native peoples took the Spaniards for what they were: ordinary human beings, nothing else. They did not take them for a native god returning—Viracocha—as all nativelike sources mention. Difference is effaced and native sources purged for good ends. As a result, however, the political goal backfires: Agency is indeed restored to native peoples, correcting one effect of Spanish sources, but at the price of echoing another: *everyone* is endowed with the rationality proper to a Western subject—or rather, proper to how Westerners like to think of themselves.

Recent studies of how native peoples saw the Spaniards that do not engage an actual historical dynamic have introduced a related assertion: the idea that native people mistook the Spaniards for a native god is in fact a late Spanish invention and imposition (Pease 1991, 1995). That is why, it is said, early Spanish accounts do not mention it—the Incas had no writing system, while late native and Spanish authors do. Again, the political intent backfires: Indians appear to be dupes, while the Spanish have the capacity to shape their minds with odd ideas. These options lead to a paradoxical situation: while a large body of scholarship shows that cultural dimensions played a key role in the actual dynamics of colonial Peru (e.g., Wachtel 1971; Spalding 1974, 1984; Stern 1982; Duviols 1986; Silverblatt 1987; Ramírez 1996), they are almost totally absent from the twenty-year conquest period that made colonial Peru possible in the first place. Domination, understood as the *effective pretension* of a single order of things, is in place even before it began.

The coherence of the dominant, neat image of Cajamarca's scene has been questioned by MacCormack (1989) and Seed (1991). They show how the political goal and narrative strategy informing each source condition the way in which the exchange between Valverde and Atahualpa is portrayed. MacCormack argues that what had to be narrated changed across time: from the conquerors' portrayal of a just, transparent interaction, to its interrogation in the 1550s, to a "mythified" view in the 1570s, to the view of end-of-century native authors who accept the mythification but stress Atahualpa's proper behavior, questioning the moral standing of the parties. Seed questions "historical realism"—Hemming being an exponent of this genre—because by privileging eyewitnesses' accounts and standardizing differences it reifies one view of the story, that of the conquerors. She contrasts the 1534 account of Xérez (Pizarro's secretary) with native ones, and argues that the former expressed the Spanish claim of transparency and universality of its values (literacy and Christianity), which the latter challenge in several ways. Both works, which remain within the limits of a textual analysis, open dimensions of analysis that I will develop when I focus on the final scene.

But that scene does not stand on its own as a form of encounter; it is the result of an ongoing contact process that I will examine by engaging debates on cultural encounter and colonialism (Sahlins 1985, 1995; Obeyesekere 1992/1997; Todorov 1978; Clendinnen 1991). In particular, in order to avoid the double bind that plagues representations of non-Westerners, in which cultural difference is denounced as exotization and likeness as an imposition of Western rationality, I will stress uncertainty and diversity, within and across the cultural divide, and the politics of their simplification by both natives and Spaniards. To that end, instead of solving differences between sources to produce a unified historical narrative, I consider them as indices (Ginzburg 1989; De Certeau 1991) of distinct ways of making and producing sense of events that coexisted when the events occurred—narrative strategies and political goals aside. Following these indices, and considering nativelike sources as responses to colonialism from within that imply a positioned difference, a border thinking (Mignolo 2000), one can grasp another, though silenced, sense (alterity) in Cajamarca. Likewise, reading indices in Spanish sources through poststructuralist work on violence (Taussig 1987; Feldman 1991; Das 1998), one can destabilize the dominant image of the Western subject as a purely rational actor in full control of all interactions.

By exposing the mechanisms through which the actors tried and often failed to control their unstable present, Cajamarca regains its character as a contact situation in which different senses of order competed and tangled. As interactions lose their neatness and the Spaniards their mastery, an alternative image begins to make sense on its own. After all, domination is to a large extent precisely about rendering some views unintelligible, and ethnography should serve as an element to counterbalance it, as the Comaroffs point out (1991:xiii–xiv).

IN THE INCA EMPIRE IN 1531–32

The small *compañía* (company) that began the conquest of the Inca empire landed in the empire's very northern tip sometime in early 1531. It took its men almost two years to reach Cajamarca, and some sixteen months to contact Atahualpa. During this time all attention and military resources were concentrated on a war of succession between Inca political fractions, whose visible heads were Huáscar and Atahualpa, sons of the last emperor, Huayna Cápac. Atahualpa's base was in Quito, not too far from the fistful of Spaniards but in the highlands, where Inca political action always gravitated; Huáscar's base was in the heart of the empire, Cuzco, some 1,500 km (932 mi) south. As chroniclers and scholars alike point out, this coincidence gave the conquerors a chance to succeed.

A compañía was a private enterprise contained within the legal frame given by the Crown's authorization. It was organized around several captains with a "prospective governor" (Spalding 1984:116) as its head. Each captain had his own ambitions and several mini-compañías existed, and there was thus potential for political fission. This local tension tangled with another between the Crown and the compañía. The Crown was present through its royal officers, although their task was mainly to secure that due taxes were paid; a real challenge could only come from a competing compañía with good political connections at court. But during its early stages, as Lockhart stresses, a compañía's real danger was that it might fail and dissolve (1972:7).

The 1531 compañía was the third attempt organized by Diego de Almagro and the would-be governor, Francisco Pizarro (throughout the book, called Almagro and Pizarro). The first (1523–24) had been a fiasco that only reached Mesoamerican lands infested with mosquitoes. After a disastrous start, thirteen survivors of the second attempt (1526–28) navigated south, and reached some towns in present-day coastal Peru. They gathered two young natives, who would serve as interpreters, plus enough information and proofs of a viable future to negotiate a conquest permit and a governorship at court. Organizing each expedition meant borrowing and investing large amounts of money, as well as rallying manpower. Pizarro and Almagro had exhausted most of their capital when the third compañía landed in San Mateo Bay, in northern Ecuador, while most of its men had indebted themselves to pay for their equipment and travel. Everyone's most urgent need, then, was riches to pay off debts, while the second was to find large native populations to exploit, which the compañía needed for propaganda.

The mechanism of advance involved a constant definition of the limits of the possible. When the compañía encountered a new group, if the local lord welcomed it, then exchanges and behaviors were contained; he would only have to provide them with all the goods and services they wanted. If, rather, he attempted any resistance, a clear politics of fear was put into place; with violent punishing actions the conquerors would kill as many Indians as they felt necessary and loot with few actual limits. Finally, more stable relations were set by Pizarro's political alliances with native lords, required because his goal was not extermination but domination.

One can see these dynamics in different combinations. The Christians (that is what the conquerors of Peru called themselves at almost all times) landed in a tropical coastal area with few inhabitants and plenty of mosquitoes. Their initial way south was slow because the native groups along their way emptied their small towns and withdrew supplies. When the Christians arrived in Coaque, the first town of significant size, they attacked to prevent this and looted it (Xérez [1534] 1985:64–65). Pizarro then seized most of the bounty to pay off debts to the ships' owners, who provided reinforcements and supplies, and spread in Panama and Nicaragua the news that there was something to gain there, preventing the conquest from fading. The idea worked. After eleven months of enduring tropical illnesses, in November 1531 the compañía greeted two ships that brought it fifty men and twenty-five horses (Lockhart 1972:8). Even so, they still numbered fewer than 100 men.

Their reputation and military might opened the way south. Some lords they encountered welcomed them, and when they did not, as in La Puná Island, the resulting open war set the pattern of encounters to come: the better-equipped Christians crushed the numerically superior natives and suffered only two casualties. In Túmbez, their next stop and Pizarro's original goal, they suffered their last three losses in a skirmish (Xérez 1985:71–76). From there, with a reinforcement of 100 men and twenty-five horses, Pizarro moved south and the conquest entered a new stage: he began realizing his governorship by blending fear and alliance. Aware of the Christians' might, the lord of Poechos welcomed them, and Pizarro received his vassalage, opening the door to a regulated flow of goods and services. Yet nearby lords in the sierra and on the coast refused to serve them, and some men arriving by sea reported fearing an imminent overnight attack. As in any neo/colonial enterprise, the frightening of a colonizer by locals required immediate action. After a military operation, hierarchy was reestablished through exemplary punishment: Pizarro had a main lord, several principals, and some other Indians burned alive; but he also kept one of the accused main lords in office, and even extended his lordship over the executed lord's people (ibid.:78–80).

This blend was an effective political strategy, because it knitted local and foreign orders causally, turning events into structure: the local lord acquired a new authority, with the Christians' presence at its base, while, simultaneously, Christian authority was fortified in being so recognized. Each new social position depended on the other, both arising from a temporally ordered indebtedness—much like a Melanesian Big Man to whom exchanges of gifts are owed. This mechanism secured indirect rule and the sought-after ascendancy: as Pizarro's secretary summarized, from then on "they all served better, with more fear than before" (Xérez 1985: 79). When he reached an exceptional coastal zone of rich valleys, Pizarro began to objectify his governorship in Spanish terms as well: he founded the first town (San Miguel de) Tangarara at the end of July 1532.

During these months Atahualpa's generals were closing in on Cuzco, defeating Huáscar's armies in battle after battle, some 1,500 km (932 mi) away from the compañía. This no doubt organized Inca attention, as many have argued; yet, if the conquerors' production of order seems uncontested, it is because I am condensing here only what their own accounts disclose. Their narratives have a narcotic effect: one has to adjust to only a certain way to actually make sense, of only certain kinds of events, which take place within clear, intelligible boundaries. Actions become reasonable because in the Spanish eyewitnesses' regime of visibility, there is nothing else in sight. To correct this, I will introduce nativelike sources and contrast them with Spanish sources. This will flesh out the steps of Atahualpa's production of order vis-à-vis the newcomers, and will render visible silences and hidden objects on both sides, denaturalizing critical actions and categories. To that end, I will depart from most prior histories by focusing on the exchange of messengers between Atahualpa and the Christians, using the latter's advance as its context. The first exchange originated in Tangarara, to where I now return.

MESSENGERS: FROM NEWNESS TO OBJECTIFICATION

All so-called native chroniclers (Tito Cussi [1570] 1985; Guaman Poma [1615] 1987; Garcilaso [1617] 1960) include extraordinary, often flustering elements when they give people's first images of the Spaniards. Yet, they quickly erase this uncertainty, which corrected the narcotic effect of the conquerors' narratives; they associate the New People with a native deity, Viracocha, and jump immediately to the scene in Cajamarca. This is not the feared revelation but rather an interested simplification that conceals uncertainty and local politics. Behind this simplification, one can identify four stages: newness, inquiry, containment, and objectification. I will study them signaling the locations of strangeness, the means for making sense of them, and the mechanisms through which they are harnessed in pursuit of clear political goals. This shows that, twisting Bhabha's (1994:88) idea slightly, "the representation of difference always *can turn into* a problem of authority."

Newness

According to Guaman Poma—a native intellectual who toward 1615 finished a political letter of more than 1,000 pages to the Spanish king—the first news about the Spaniards was bewildering. When they reached Atahualpa, his captains and other Indians:

were frightened because the Christians did not sleep, it was said because they spent the night awake ready for an attack, and that they ate gold and silver, they and their horses. And they had shoes made of silver, it was said of the bridles and horseshoes and the iron arms, and red hats. And that day and night each talked with their papers, *quillca*. And that all were shrouded, the whole face covered by wool, and that only the eyes were visible . . . And they had their penises hanging backwards, very long, they said of the swords, and they were all dressed in fine silver. And they had no lord, they all looked like brothers in their clothing, way of talking and chatting, eating and dressing. (f. 381[383]; 1987:388)

Within the extraordinary, different locations expressing strangeness can be recognized. First, it had to do with unexpected social behavior: not sleeping at night, no clear order in the group, no hierarchy (i.e., all dress, behave, talk, and eat in the same way and place). These last two contrasted markedly with Andean politics, particularly Andean high politics. Second, uncanniness has to do with the body. They had very long penises tied in the back, and ate gold and silver, as did their "big sheep" (horses); they had silver shoes, dresses, and objects around their bodies, which were shrouded; only a small part of their faces was visible, most being covered by wool (Andeans had no facial hair). Wool suggests an analogy with animals that can be read as a crossing-over of categories between animals and humans, and eating minerals signals mixed matters and unnatural acts. Gold and silver in particular were high-status markers associated with the Inca. This signals not bodies per se but what arises from them, bringing to consciousness how fundamental body imagery is to worldview (Douglas 1966, 1970). Finally, there is an excess of markers with no local parallels (horses described as big sheep, guns described as thunder, and fireballs in other nativelike chroniclers).

These elements point to a concrete problem common to any contact case: someone who is strikingly different cannot be predicted; since the taken-for-granted that makes interaction appropriate is missing, relations to the Other can only proceed by guesswork. The sole source (recently found in its complete version) that allows for chronological study of such Inca guesswork, and its politics, was finished by 1551 by a Spaniard, Juan de Betanzos. Married to Cuxirimay Ocllo, an Inca princess of high rank, his narrative is composed largely of oral history from his wife's kin, who were close to Atahualpa (Julien 2000a). It is not a pure native text, yet it contains much more native material than Betanzos could marshal, and is full of uncertainties and contradictions that are absent in any other nativelike source, which make it a dialogic text (Ginzburg 1989:159) par excellence.

According to Betanzos (II, 17, 1987:253), Atahualpa knew of the strange people just after his generals had achieved the final victory over Huáscar in Cuzco. Tallán messengers from Tangarara reached him near Huamachuco, south of Cajamarca, with odd images similar to Guaman Poma's. Soon after, three other messengers arrived with gifts and a message from Pizarro: the *capito* (*capitán*, captain) had come from Spain to see him because he had heard of Atahualpa's grandeur, and he carried a message from a very great lord which he would give to him once they met (ibid.:254). Atahualpa's reaction allows one to see how unsettling newness is turned into a fact. The first step was inquiry, and included endless questions, which I present summarily.

Inquiry

From the first, bewildering news was followed by a short inquiry in which a godly element was brought in. Atahualpa asked for the New People's name—naming is a means not only for condensing and controlling reality in general (Foucault 1971), but in this case also of locating the other within the map of the known, of containing newness. The messengers said that they did not know it, but they called them *Viracochacuna* (plural of Viracocha)—"that means the gods" (Betanzos II, 17, 1987:253)—because, as their elders had told them, "Con Titi Viracocha" after having made the people went into the sea and did not return until a few years ago, when they saw some of them (there were sparse contacts during Pizarro's second trip). That is, facing eerie people coming from where none were known to come—the sea—to reach a familiarizing conclusion, experience and myths are used. I use the word *myths* in a very practical sense: they are, among other things, ways of making sense of the present through past, archetypal events that can be actualized. Some extraordinary beings had disappeared toward the north by the sea, and some had appeared from there.

I will analyze the godly label in detail later. For the time being, I stress that there was nothing exotic in Andean politics and culture about supernatural beings of some sort at work. I am, indeed, pushing a natural/supernatural distinction on indigenous categories only to make my exposition clear. The Inca, for instance, was a semidivine, supernatural being, and the supernatural was not confined to bodies. When the messengers reached Atahualpa, he was involved in a godly contest. On a hill near Huamachuco was Catequil, a main *huaca* (sacred, powerful being or shrine). Some huacas were Inca, but most were local, related to each ethnic group's ancestors or gods. Depending on the case, the Incas paid recognition to local huacas, built an imperial one beside them, or both, but confrontation was also an option (MacCormack 1991:58–62). Most huacas were oracles; they forecast the future through their *port-parole*. Atahualpa had asked Catequil about his war against Huáscar, and after an adverse answer he had declared the huaca to be an enemy and ordered it to be literally annihilated—the port-parole killed, his body and the huaca's idol burned and ground, the ashes dispersed, the hill burned and flattened (Betanzos:II, 16, 1987:250).

With the second messengers the inquiry was exhaustive. He ordered them to be locked away, and continued his daily affairs. Next morning he and some of his captains met behind closed doors with the messengers. The first questions aimed at determining the strangers' status by searching for ordinary markers that we have already seen: the name of he who sent them, what kind of man he was, how he dressed, how they talked, and what they talked about. The answers, too, follow known lines: the capito was tall, his face covered by a beard; he was wrapped to his throat in cloth, and they all dressed alike—no familiar dress nor signs of hierarchy. The second questions aimed at the excess. Besides the never-before-seen tall sheep, the New People had something long hanging that when one stranger took it out shone like silver and could cut a sheep's (llama's) head. Trying to render the swords ordinary, distinctive from the lighting and thunder that were the Inca's double and arm (Ziólkowski 1996:126–42), Atahualpa said that they must be *macanas* (wooden clubs or swords). But this interpretation could not be conclusive: swords shine while wood does not, and the main Inca captains had silver or gold arms. Thus the messengers responded to it with "that might be the case." The last element investigated was food. Asked if the strangers eat raw meat, and in particular human flesh, the messengers said they ate only animals, roasted. This inquiry had clear goals. In Inca warfare eating the enemy's raw flesh gave an explicit message of total war and requested final submission (Ziólkowski 1996:239–44). Also, eating human flesh was a prehuman behavior proper to pre-Inca ethnic huacas (*Huarochirí* [1608?] 1987:45, 121). Without reading Atahualpa's inquiry too narrowly, it is clear that he was not simply curious in a general fashion, but rather was trying to determine the *kind* of people that he might have to face.

Containment

At this point Atahualpa's captains intervened and told him that he should see which kind of people they were, whether they were gods or people like themselves, whether they meant to harm or good. If they were *runa quiça-cha*, destroyers of people, and they could not be defeated, then they should run away; if they were *"viracochacuna runa allichac*, that means gods who are benefactors of the people," then they should stay (Betanzos:II, 17, 1987 :255). This polarization, besides excluding the possibility that the New People were seen as conquerors, constrained the unknown within familiar forms: either vandals or gods. Atahualpa then solved the uncertainty remaining in his captains' double hypothesis: he declared himself very happy to hear that gods had arrived in his time. This was a far more convenient idea for an aspirant to omnipotent lordship in a convoluted political terrain than was the idea of unknown people that no one could stop wandering around and looting. Although the solution did not end Atahualpa's guesswork, it made the New People *his* affair alone, a point to which I will return.

Objectification

Next Atahualpa began backing his version through actions. This production of sense had at least three targets: the strangers, the men in his camp, and his men in Cuzco. First, he sent back the messengers with orders to tell "to the great Viracocha the capito" (Pizarro) that he was very happy of his arrival, would be happy to meet him in Cajamarca, and "que le tenía por parte," meaning that he considered the two of them to be of a similar kind, which he also expressed through some high-ranking presents. Second, he told his men to rejoice for two days, after which he wanted to leave for Cajamarca and meet the capito (loc. cit.). Finally, he sent an envoy to Cuzco with a message to his generals in control of the city, Calcuchima and Quizquiz.

The news reached them in a clearly packaged way: "The Viracocha and many other viracochas had emerged from the sea, and it is believed that they are the ancient viracochas that made the people. The Inca, pleased by these news, [decided] to meet them" (Betanzos:II, 19, 1987:261).

Atahualpa's production of sense acquires more significance once the broader context is considered. On one hand, at the Inca level, Cuzco was by then an unsettled place. His generals had just defeated Huáscar's last army, captured him and his close kin, and made all Incas ritually recognize Atahualpa through his *bulto*, or body double. Cuxi Yupangue, the envoy, carried also several orders intended to strengthen Atahualpa's position. Among them, to punish Topa Inca Yupanqui's (Huayna Cápac's father) *panaca* because it supported Huáscar;[1] many members were killed and the Inca's body was burned. It was commanded that all traces of Huáscar be erased, and his relatives and all nonvirgin women near him be killed (Sarmiento de Gamboa [1571] 67, 2001:163–64; Murúa [1590–1611] 57, 1987:202). Finally, Atahualpa ordered that messengers be sent to ethnic lords who should order them to go and recognize him in person and that Huáscar be sent to Cajamarca.

On the other hand, beyond the official Spanish-Inca channel which nativelike chroniclers privileged, rumors about the New People were spreading throughout the empire, reaching lords and common people. In 1573 Don Diego Mocha recalled hearing in Atahualpa's camp in Huamachuco of their arrival, and that they had founded a town in Tangarara (*Probanza 1573* . . . 1974:95). As far away as Cuzco, 1,400 km (870 mi) to the south, Sebastián Yacobilca heard news that "certain people had arrived to the coast of Peru that were called capacochas, that meant 'sons of the sea,'" who had peopled a town (ibid.:62–63); it was generally known that they "were coming by all towns by the seashore conquering and fighting with the Indians, . . . and that they defeated them all and took their gold and silver" (ibid.:114–15). Another of Huáscar's soldiers, Francisco Caro Allaulli, adds that "they and their horses eat gold and silver" (ibid.:41). Similar news was reported in Huarochirí, halfway between Cuzco and Atahualpa's camp. Although each rumor highlights different details, there is a mix of unsettling elements, such as the New People's unstoppable violence and hunger for silver and gold, with civilizing gestures such as the peopling of towns. That the New People were coming from the sea only added bewilderment since no one had been known to come from there.[2]

In short, if Betanzos allows one to see that identifying the Spanish as Viracochas was neither natural nor conclusive, the world of rumors exposed in local native testimonies reveals another perspective that is hidden in the nativelike, Inca-biased chronicles: Atahualpa badly needed to keep things under his control. Atahualpa's guesswork did not end, however, with his declaration of the newcomers' identity; it continued in his combination of gracious words and direct action during the next exchanges of messengers.

SPRINKLING GROUND DUCKS AND TUGGING BEARDS

Although the conquerors mention several "spies" sent by Atahualpa,[3] the first messenger—identifiable as the one mentioned in Betanzos—met Captain Hernando de Soto in Caxas, a reasonable place to choose since Tangarara-Caxas was along the easiest route to Atahualpa. The conquerors' accounts subsume the meaning of the meeting within their politics of fear. After Pizarro left Tangarara (24 September 1532) the lord of Pabor, whom Atahualpa's father, Huayna Cápac, had severely punished, welcomed him and told him that there was an Inca captain nearby in Caxas, up the sierra. Enforcing the policy of fear, Pizarro ordered Captain Soto to go there, "so . . . that they would not become arrogant" (Xérez 1985:84).

Captain Mena, who went to Caxas, reports that it was destroyed and many Indians were hanged—Atahualpa's punishment for their having sided with Huáscar. When the local lord showed up he complained about Atahualpa, but said that they were hiding "because of their fear" of the Spaniards. Soto responded by offering him friendship and asking him for vassalage. The lord accepted, and took some women from an Inca house and gave them to Soto. What was a politically loaded gift exchange became then a local fear exchange. When a captain from Atahualpa arrived, the local lord panicked. He had broken all rules by taking the women, and he tried to fix things by standing up (there was a strict protocol governing sitting and standing; the one seating had the highest rank); but Soto had his own politics of fear and ordered him to sit by his side (Mena [1534] 1937:80–81). Diego de Trujillo ([1571] 1953:135), who was also present, adds that since the captain was arrogant and threatened them, Soto sent a messenger to Pizarro asking him what to do and that the answer was that they should put up with the arrogance and pretend that they were afraid of him.

Eight days later, along with a messenger from Atahualpa, Soto arrived in Çarán, where Pizarro was then. The messenger told Pizarro that Atahualpa wanted to be his friend and would await him in Cajamarca. He brought as gifts "two fortresses made out of stone, shaped as a fountain, with which he could drink, and two loads of dry, skinned ducks, with which, after grinding them, he could sprinkle himself" as native lords do.⁴ Pizarro welcomed him and told him that he was happy that he had come, and that after hearing that Atahualpa was waging a war he had decided to meet him and be his friend and brother, and to help him. He ordered that the messenger be treated well, and at his departure (mid-October 1532) sent with him some presents for Atahualpa (Xérez 1985:86–88).

Echoing the conquerors' narratives' plot, recent historiography focuses largely on the events at Caxas and pays little attention to either the meaning of Atahualpa's odd gifts or to his envoy's activities. Making sense of these illuminates further the Inca's goals and strategy. I know of no source that says the Incas used stone drinking vessels, or that Andean lords sprinkled ground, dried ducks on themselves. Years ago Kubler (1945:417, n. 27) suggested a sensible interpretation: the birds ("ducks") were means to void the Spaniards' potency.⁵ According to Juan Polo Ondegardo ([1567] 1990:579), the Incas "sacrificed birds from the Puna [highlands] when they had to go to war in order to diminish the strength of their enemies' huacas."⁶ In this light, Atahualpa's present becomes a sensible improvisation: he knew by then that the strangers had a powerful huaca, which they adored, and that they mocked all native ones, including the Sun (Cieza de León [1553]:40, 1996:124). Uncertain about their nature, he pursued different options and since in the Andes, political struggle was always both natural and supernatural, with huacas at work on all sides, he used appropriate tools to test the strangers' potency.

One can discern more of Atahualpa's guesswork by analyzing his envoy's activities among the Christians and understand the kind of practical knowledge he was trying to gain. Summarizing after-the-fact information, the conquerors render the envoy's actions intelligible as those of a spy: after counting the men, horses, and arms, he informed Atahualpa that they were few in number and that they were thieves, and that although they had big sheep they could be killed and only a rope to tie them up was needed

(P. Pizarro [1571] 1965:179). Only Miguel de Estete adds that the envoy also asked other things: "from what land we came and what we wanted" ([1535?] 1918:21). The "spying" involved in fact an exchange of perceptions characteristic of contact situations that blend bodies and objects (Comaroff and Comaroff 1991:180–97), key means for determining the status of unknown beings (Connolly and Anderson 1987), and that exposed the Christians to situations that would have been unthinkable otherwise. In addition to counting how many Spaniards there were, the envoy tested their strength by pulling and pushing "as if scoffing," asked some to take out their swords, and even pulled a Christian's beard—particularly telling since beards appear as a marker of strangeness in all native accounts. The beard tugging earned the envoy a slap, which led Pizarro to order that no one should touch him in any way (P. Pizarro 1965:176).

THE POLITICS OF BEING AN INCA

The messenger or spy, called Ciquinchara, reported to Atahualpa in Ybocan, on his way from Huamachuco to Cajamarca. Their exchanges present new perspectives on the complex politics informing Atahualpa's actions, and allow one to unpack the divine implications of being an Inca under the exceptional stress of contact dynamics. As we will see, bringing native orderings into the analysis does not generate a picture of rigidly ritualized responses, as one finds in Tzvetan Todorov's (1978) portrayal of the Aztecs in the Mexican case. Quite the contrary.

Secrecy surrounded the matter again. Atahualpa took Ciquinchara aside and asked him about the New People in terms of the by now familiar lines: if they were "gods" he was ready to welcome them, happy that they had come "in his time." Ciquinchara told him that the Tallanes—the messengers with the first news—were wrong; that although when seeing the strangers for the first time, he was as flummoxed as the Tallanes, after observing them he had concluded they were not the "Con Titi Viracocha" and the other "Viracochas." His argument is twofold: (a) they do things that ordinary men do; and (b) they do not do things that gods do. Thus, they (a) eat, drink, dress, mend their costumes, and talk to women; and (b) they do not make miracles, do not make sierras or flatten them, nor make people, nor make rivers or water fountains flow on their way—if there is no water they need to carry it. And if they are not gods, they are men of the worst kind: they take everything they see and desire—young women, gold and silver vessels, rich clothes—and force bound Indians to carry their things. Concretizing his findings in a known category, Ciquinchara says that they must be "*quitas pumaranga*, that means people without a lord, loose and highwaymen." Matching the conquerors' narrations, he added that they should be killed (Betanzos:II, 20, 1987:264).

This report shows a clear advance in the process of turning newness into a manageable object. In contrast to the exhilarating exchange between the Tallanes and the Inca, full of mesmerizing details and questions, this one is a contained exchange concerning the *grounds* for interpretation. Yet Atahualpa's next questions about the New People and Ciquinchara's answers bring the status quo back into uncertainty. There is an excess of markers: They walk on top of very tall sheep; when they run the earth trembles and the din they make sounds like thunder. They carry something hollow, made of something like silver, which they fill with something like ashes and light on fire from below, and as it catches fire a large flame and a thunder come from the opening. Ciquinchara adds that the thunder from the sky kills people while this thunder does not, but there is a clear similarity to the Inca's supernatural arms and his thunder/lightning double. Thus one of the reasons Tito Cussi, Atahualpa's nephew, gives for identifying the Spanish as *Viracochas* was that they had "*yllapas* . . . because we thought that they were thunders from the sky" ([1570]:f. 3, 1985:2). Finally, there is the fact of their odd bodies: they are white, bearded, and dress in a way never before seen.

This presents a clear problem: because of their strange personas, and the strange acts and objects surrounding them, the Spanish belong to a separate category. Difference is established, and it is not removed by arguments that they are not "gods" because they do not strictly qualify. If men often play the trickster with the god (Sahlins 1985:124), in the Andes the god or huaca can be the trickster or antihero who embodies the destructive virtues of the god (Urbano 1981), or it can be, simply, the wrong god or huaca. Atahualpa's decision is consistent with this dilemma: he ordered Ciquinchara to return with two gold vessels for the capito, and to tell him that he loved him and would like to meet him; but he begged Ciquinchara to be careful and to help him find out what *kind* of people they were, "that they could be gods and be angry, and do those things that you say and show themselves as you saw them, . . . because I would not want something to happen to us because we do not understand what they are" (Betanzos:II, 20, 1987:265).

Recall that Betanzos is the closest we have to a royal historical account, however much it is shaped for a Spanish audience. The kinds of reasoning used and the options considered express an Inca's way of ordering reality. Atahualpa's moves are only logical: if receiving a god in the wrong manner was going to impact someone, it was him. As an Inca, he was a semidivine being; mediating between the ordinary and the supernatural was his job.[7] The extent to which this was believed and how exactly it was understood by different people likely varied, but the extraordinary problem the Spanish posed for Atahualpa was clear.[8] As Obeyesekere (1997:219) points out, the fact that there exist experts on native taxonomies and cultural orders does not mean that everyone is so knowledgeable. However, as Clendinnen shows (1991), this does not justify dismissing complex cultural readings of events altogether. If anything, the variety of interpretations only made Atahualpa's position more unstable in the terms of Andean high politics: within the exceptional conjuncture of the Spanish arrival and the succession wars, improvisational decisions subjected his divinity, as a political category, to unknown "empirical risks" (Sahlins 1981:5–6).

To fully understand these risks I will revise the identification of the Spanish as Viracochas, a controversial point that has been rejected as a Spanish invention imposed on the Indians (Pease 1991:148–55; 1995:137–60), a clear case of Western mythmaking in Obeyesekere's (1992) sense. In my opinion, the problem has been misframed; Viracocha is not relevant, per se. First, the exchanges between the Tallanes, Ciquinchara, and Atahualpa, and the subsequent research and guesswork, all fish elements out of a pool of godly attributes, which are used in a bricolage-like fashion to make sense of something out of the ordinary. Second, this sense making was politically informed. Finally, though the Viracocha label is a poor encapsulation of a much more fluid and complex situation, it is not an imposition, but rather the result of a colonial process of transculturation (Pratt 1992) involving Spanish actions as much as native "border thinking" (Mignolo 2000). Let me extrapolate on these three points.

First, the *bricolage*. As we have seen, the Spanish were strange for many reasons, and the gods (or rather huacas) were used to make sense of them. In such a multiethnic (multimyth, multi-huaca) space as the Andes, any identification was necessarily composite. This is hard to illustrate with the available sources, but I can give one example. In the first encounter with Atahualpa, the Tallanes explained that they were calling the New People Viracochas because "Con Titi Viracocha" had disappeared in the sea. "Con" was soon dropped in Betanzos, and no other nativelike writer uses it. This makes sense. Con was a northern, coastal god, and therefore a familiar element of intelligibility for the Tallanes. Pressed to make sense of strange beings for a semidivine king to whom Viracocha was proper, they combined the two names. As Pease G. Y. objects, Viracocha was neither associated with landscape changes, nor a local deity in the north (1991:152), but Con was (Zárate [1555]:I, 10, 1995:50). Further, Con had many qualities that resonated with *the terms* according to which the Spanish were discussed both by the Tallanes and Ciquinchara: both Con and the Spanish had strange bodies; Con could shorten distances, and the Spanish moved so fast on their sheep that they, too, compressed distances; Con could command water, whereas the Spanish needed to carry water.

Second, since in the Andes all high politics was huaca based, defining the identity of powerful beings was no game; actual beliefs aside, it had important consequences. As Rostworowski de Diez anseco points out, Con's and similar accounts can be read as mythical narratives of political events (1983, 1989a:167–74). Con disappeared in the north, superseded by Pachacámac, a coastal huaca coming from the south who, like Con, was son of the Sun and the Moon. Pachacámac turned Con's Indians into animals, and made new people and taught them how to work the land and plant trees, superseding Con's order. Now strange and powerful beings were coming from the north. Besides, Con was only one among many huacas in the northern and central sierra some of whose features resembled some of the Spaniards', and we have seen the rumors about them that were spreading throughout the empire. This complexity must have increased with the simple impact of translation: each time the Spaniards interacted with an ethnic group, to which deity was God equivalent? Furthermore, together with interpretations, actions were taken. At some point Atahualpa asked the powerful huaca of Pachacámac about his encounter with the New People, who responded that he would kill them all (Xérez 1985 :127)—here "he" could refer to either Atahualpa or Pachacámac. After Huáscar's defeat, his supporters made a sacrifice to Viracocha, asking him for help against Atahualpa (Cieza [c.1553]:5, 1988:39–40). Finally, as we will see in the next section, a local lord used the Spaniards' aura against Atahualpa's captains.

Third, the Viracocha label was no European imposition. The equation Viracocha = Maker is a simplification, as many scholars have noted. Viracocha was a deity related to the Sun and to agricultural tasks, whose virtue was to make things achieve fruition; he had the power to transmit the capacity, including different kinds of knowledge, to ensure reproduction, but he was not himself a maker (Itier 1993; Duviols 1993). Or he was merely one manifestation of a multiple deity; another was the antihero of uncontrollable power and disorder, incarnate in Tunupa or Taguapaca (Urbano 1981). Or he had attributes that tangled with several other huacas or ancestors, including diverse creative and destructive forces, and thus had several manifestations, only some of them anthropomorphic (Gisbert 1990). It is likely that local specialists did not agree either on these interpretations and that they had their own agendas. But in any case, Atahualpa's guesswork and actions were far more complex than is suggested by the simple Christianized image of a "goodwill god" returning. Much more was at stake.

How much of this complex panorama the conquerors understood is an open question. I show in chapter 2 that some of them recognized that supernatural elements were in play and took advantage of them accordingly. But it is also clear that Andean peoples were not dupes whose heads were simply filled with Christian conceptions, replacing what was otherwise of a Western secular event. Neither were the Christians so powerful nor the natives so passive. Supernatural beings did not come out of nowhere. The elements that informed the politics of defining the Spaniards' status had little to do with a Judeo-Christian frame, and the reduction of Andean peoples' huacas or ancestors to such a frame is not an imposition upon them, but rather an accomplished erasure of a rich dynamic that I am trying to recover here.

Behind this erasure different agendas can be seen. On the Spanish side, the result conforms to a common colonizing gesture: seizing and flattening native reasonings.[9] For instance, it appears to the chronicler Pedro Cieza de León that the Incas are aware of the Maker and associate him with the Spanish God ([c. 1553]:43, 1984:203–4), which allows Cieza to condemn his fellow men as unworthy carriers of the faith. Friar Martín de Murúa includes recognition of the newness to the native people of the strange, white, and bearded people who reach Atahualpa, but the uncertainty ends there: to native eyes, he asserts, the Spanish were Viracochas carrying the message from the Maker and were felicitously welcomed ([1590–1611]:58, 1987:205).

Nativelike accounts, on the other hand, were colonial creations, but they were not simply colonial inventions, nor were they created through top-down processes or for top-down reasons. They were efforts by native intellectuals to render their views intelligible within the hegemonic frames that defined reality, similar to Du Bois's double consciousness (1995:45). They thought it necessary to edit out guesswork and politics, and to purge pagan elements. The Viracocha = Maker equation made Guaman Poma, Tito Cussi, or Garcilaso accept Spanish categories, but it also enabled them to contest the Spanish order by inserting a *positioned difference*, an example of border thinking (Mignolo 2000). This rich politics took place too long after 1532 to be detailed here, but its importance will become clear when I analyze the final scene of the events in Cajamarca. I return now to the exchange of messengers, and the murkiness of the ongoing contact process.

CRACKS IN THE COHERENCE DURING A "NEGOTATION OF FEAR"

In the Christians' final approach to Cajamarca one can recognize, in action, the effects of the divided opinions in Atahualpa's camp that we saw in Betanzos (i.e., the Spanish are dodgy thieves; the Spanish are some sort of godly beings). One can also see a local use of the Spaniards' aura, and, in a moment in which the coherence of the conquerors' accounts falters, that Spanish and local intentions converged.

After Ciquinchara left, the compañía headed for Cajamarca. On its way there, it faced a shift: there were no more messengers, supplies, or loaders, and it received no information as to what lay ahead; most towns were empty, and in one case the Indians opened irrigation channels to overflow a river the Spanish had to cross (Trujillo [1571] 1953:135). This new strategy of passive deterrence matched Atahualpa's uncertainty, being a halfway measure that fell short of his counselors' more aggressive advice. Some Indians that the Christians captured to obtain information told them that the Inca had ordered war people to confront them along their way to Cajamarca (Mena [1534] 1937:81; Xérez [1534] 1985:92).

As a result, the compañía's journey up the sierra was plagued by a constant fear. As they traversed narrow, vertical paths that over short distances climbed 4,000 to 5,000 m (13,100 to 16,400 ft), the advantage of horses disappeared, and even a simple attack with rocks would have been devastating. In this milieu of uncertainty, Pizarro made a standard move: he attempted to regain control by inverting the balance of fear. He sent a messenger, a Tallán principal named Guachapuro, to tell Atahualpa that he should not be afraid, that they were peaceful people who only fought those that attacked them. But before Guachapuro could return, Atahualpa shifted his strategy again; after four days in which the Spaniards faced no attacks, saw no one, and obtained no supplies, contact resumed.

The first exchange was anything but neat. Atahualpa's envoy brought supplies and told Pizarro at length about the wars between Atahualpa and Huáscar, stressing that the latter had already been defeated and imprisoned. The intent seems to have been to impress upon the New People that ahead they would find a single interlocutor. Pizarro, however, misunderstood it to be an attempt to scare him with Atahualpa's power, and, as usual, he responded by mirroring. He said he was vassal of a very great lord, in fact lord of all the world, who had made other great lords his vassals. He added that this lord had sent him to make all know and obey God, and that if Atahualpa welcomed him he would befriend him, but otherwise he would battle him (Xérez 1985:97–98). The bewildered messengers asked for permission to return and inform Atahualpa. There is no way to know how Pizarro's response and status were understood—Betanzos does not mention them, but the concepts perfectly fit a huaca's port-parole. And this murky exchange of words tangled with and echoed murky acts. For instance, because of their fear, the Christians had been lodging in distinguished, well-built constructions which were Inca-only places. Occupying them must have added to their peculiar aura a meaning legible to any native: who or what is this that lodges where the Inca kings lodge, and yet is not punished? And more generally: who or what are those that can thus break all social rules and taboos?

This failed exchange was mitigated by the next envoy to arrive, Ciquinchara, whose behavior matched Atahualpa's orders (to be careful and welcome the capito). He told Pizarro that Atahualpa, "Pizarro's son" (Betanzos:II, 21, 1987:267), awaited him with many people to befriend him. Ciquinchara also brought golden vessels from which he invited several men to drink chicha, a clear gesture of recognition and friendship. Yet this brief moment of clarity was blurred once again with the return of Guachapuro, Pizarro's messenger and spy. Infuriated by how he had been treated at Atahualpa's camp, he attacked Ciquinchara and accused him of being a spy. He said that he had been refused entry but that an uncle of Atahualpa's emerged to meet him. Guachapuro was then asked, "What people are the Christians and what arms do they bring?" He responded that they were valiant warriors, with horses that ran like the wind and long lances that killed anyone "because with two jumps they reached them, and the horses with their feet and mouths kill many" (Xérez 1985:100). He added that the swords could cut a man into two, and the fireball throwers could kill many. The uncle—and other men of high rank since the account switches to "them"—said that the Christians were few, had two fireball throwers only, and the horses were not carrying arms; they could kill them. Guachapuro answered that they could not penetrate their leather. Cristóbal de Mena, departing further from both ordinary beings involved in ordinary interaction and the trope of the good god returning, adds that Guachapuro was asked at Atahualpa's camp, "from where does the messenger of the devils that had crossed so much land and no one could kill come?" ([1534] 1937:82).

Guachapuro's comments reveal a non-Inca interest in defining the terms of the encounter: he was making the Christians uncannily scary, using their aura for his own ends (horses could eat people; men could throw fireballs) in an indigenous "negotiation of fear" (Adorno 1991) that echoed the Christians' policy of fear. At the same time, one can see for once that the terms in which the New Peoples' status was being discussed were other than the simple military ones that the conquerors privileged, and closer to those in Betanzos's account. Their features, actions, and objects had surrounded them with weird, out-of-the-ordinary signs that lacked clear shape. These "faults in the discourse of comprehension" (De Certeau 1991:223) destabilize the Spanish eyewitnesses' explanations of their journey up the sierra: that the Inca had been simply too confident of his power—an idea that most historiography accepts in an almost 500-year coincidence in the production of coherence.

A FAILED MEETING

There was one last scene before the capture, a meeting in Atahualpa's camp between the Inca and two Spanish captains, Hernando de Soto and Hernando Pizarro. Contrary to what a committed empiricist might expect, Atahualpa's first contact with the Spaniards clarified nothing. The meeting unfolded, as with the previous contacts, as a messy exchange of improvisations and fear blows, making the final act necessary.

The Christians arrived in Cajamarca on a Friday, 15 November 1532. They advanced in military formation but met no opposition—the place was "empty." Disturbing Inca order once again, they lodged not in the native town (which still exists) but in the Inca *tambo* nearby. This state facility consisted of several large buildings surrounding three sides of a large plaza, with a wall on the forth side. Near the middle of the plaza was an *usnu*, a large platformlike ceremonial center from which the Inca solemnly commanded rituals (Hyslop 1990:69–100). The tambo was, in sum, a controllable space, and the Spaniards needed the feeling of control.

"Empty" meant that upon their arrival they faced no enemy army, but when they approached the tambo its inhabitants "lost control [*se desmandaban*] to come see us" (Estete [1535?] 1918:22). This proximity was unsettling, as was the sight of Atahualpa's huge camp, half a league away. Fear at first sight is an element of all the accounts, but it was not simply size that mattered here; it was also order. This threatened a key element in the Christians' ability to control their fear, their certainty of their superiority: "the tents were so many . . . that it certainly frightened us because we did not think that Indians could have such magnificent dwellings nor so many tents, nor so perfect" (ibid.:22). Some conquerors were aware of the importance of the delicate balance of fear in giving bizarre situations an appearance of solidity, providing a frame for orders to be given and obeyed, for actions to refer to some unstable but effective context of sense. After all, they were 168 men, days away from help, having broken all political rules and about to face a feared king with some 40,000 to 60,000 men. As Estete says, the sight of Atahualpa's camp "led all Spaniards to be very confused and scared, although it was not convenient to show it nor, even less, to walk back, because if they felt any frailty in us, our own Indians would kill us" (loc. cit.). He refers to their mostly forced porters; their command over them was, in his view, grounded in the momentum that the constant irresistible advance had given them. Sense was being produced in and by motion; stopping or even hesitating was dangerous.

The Christians wanted to know Atahualpa's intentions and power, and also to establish contact. A first group of twenty horsemen commanded by Captain Soto went to meet him, followed by a similarly sized reinforcement commanded by Hernando Pizarro. Atahualpa had finished a ritual confirmation of his triumph over his brother by stepping on Huáscar's dress and insignias when he learned of Soto's approach. Ciquinchara, the first to reach Atahualpa, told the Inca that one "capito" (Soto) from "capito" (Pizarro) and thirty to forty men were coming, walking on top of their sheep, more heavily armed than ever before. Atahualpa asked the names for horses and of the man approaching, and what he wanted; Ciquinchara told him that Soto wanted to ask him to meet the "capito" (Betanzos:II, 21, 1987:268).

During this encounter a mix of curiosity and protocol guided Atahualpa's actions, which intertwined with the Spaniards' goals. The first entanglement can be read through spatial rules. Soto and his horsemen approached the camp passing through heavily armed squads that stood still. They had to cross several creeks, and since the bridges were not strong enough they passed them swimming on the horses. The last creek was of hot water and deep, so they stopped and asked for Atahualpa to cross over to their side. The Indians on the other side asked who ordered so, "and the interpreter told them that that captain calling him was son of the maker" (269)—not a "capito." Atahualpa sent a main captain, Unan Chullo, to tell Soto to tell *him* what they wanted. Soto responded there was nothing they wanted from him, but from Atahualpa. Unan Chullo insisted, and told Soto to tell him what they wanted because he had been sent for that end. He said to "let them know that if they wanted to talk to the Ynga he did not talk to people like them" (loc. cit.). There is a clear defense of protocol rules—Atahualpa knew Soto was just a messenger and refused to meet him—and there was a safety concern too, as some counselors wanted to treat the Spanish simply as enemies. This first exchange anticipated the way in which things would unravel: once the hope of a contained, defined interaction failed, Atahualpa's curiosity, his desire to see with his own eyes, prevailed. He ordered Unan Chullo to show Soto the ford.

The next scenes are very rich; I focus only on the constant oscillation between protocol and improvisation. The Inca was a semidivine being, and contact with his persona was restricted not only because of his highness but also because of the powers inherent in his body. When the Spanish first entered the patio where Atahualpa was, he sat behind a piece of cloth, beyond the reach of most of his men. Indeed, only women could reach him ordinarily. During the meeting Atahualpa did not lift his eyes nor talk to Soto; the interaction went through his port-parole. Soto told Atahualpa that "the governor" was waiting for him and would not lodge nor eat without him, Juan Ruiz de Arce recalls ([1543] 1953:95). Atahualpa answered, through Unan Chullo, that he was celebrating a feast and was fasting and that he would go the next day (Betanzos:II, 21, 1987:269).

Then Hernando arrived. Seeing Soto lost in Inca protocol, he circumvented it by making his dialogue with Atahualpa an exchange of discursive blows. When Atahualpa responded to his goodwill opening through his port-parole, Hernando asked him to talk to him directly, as he was Pizarro's brother. Atahualpa said then that a lord from Tangarara had told him that they had mistreated his Indians but were not good for war, that he had killed three of them. Hernando responded that the lord was a liar and the people of Tangarara like women; the Christians were good for war, and if he had any enemy they would help him. Atahualpa said one lord refused to obey him, and Hernando said that ten horsemen would be enough, that his Indians would be of no use except to find those hiding. Atahualpa smiled, Hernando Pizarro describes it, "as a man that did not esteem us much" ([1533] 1953:54).

After this bullish exchange Atahualpa tried to regain control through two calculated improvisations, shifting the field of interaction from words to acts. First, he ordered food to be presented and invited the capitos to eat. His intent was to see them eat, and to make them get down from their horses and up again (Betanzos:II, 21, 1987:270) in order to gain personal experience of their bodies. The Christians refused, afraid as usual of a trick, but being aware (for once) that this was an improper response, they justified it by invoking a sense of order outside the immediate context: they said they had no permission to do so, but were only to ask his intentions and return (Ruiz de Arce [1543] 1953:95). Then Atahualpa ordered that gold vessels with chicha be offered to the capitos. A unique honor, it was granted to see if they would keep the vessels after drinking, as he had been told they did (Betanzos, loc. cit.). The Christians feared the drink was poisoned, but, as Estete says, "there was no way to avoid doing it" (1918:23): some drank and some did not, while some pretended to drink and spill theirs. The two nativelike accounts that explain this scene do so differently. For Tito Cussi ([1570] 1985:3), it was a clear sign of discourtesy that would justify Atahualpa's dismissal of the Bible in Cajamarca (Seed 1991:21), while for Betanzos it was a practical exercise. It may well have been both.

Before departing, Soto tried to recover the initiative lost to Hernando. He took a ring from his hand and offered it to Atahualpa, who refused it and, setting limits again, ordered Unan Chullo, his porte-parole, to take it. Soto insisted that it was for Atahualpa, not for Unan Chullo. During the negotiation Soto got so close to the Inca's body that his horse's breath blew the fringe that was the royal insignia, the *borla*, in his head. Atahualpa stood still, showing no sign of fear, and angrily ordered that the ring be returned and the capitos leave.

I stress a few points here. First, reality was suspended. All possible breaches to Inca protocol occurred at once: the rules governing personal contact (visual, oral, and corporal), drinking, and eating were broken. When Ciquinchara first met the conquerors, he was allowed to do what no Indian could, and now the tables were turned. Since there was no signifying context to frame their interactions, the actors exposed themselves to limitless risks. Atahualpa could have been slaughtered or Soto and Hernando poisoned. Second, the meeting solved little. Although the strangers' hierarchy left some of them below Atahualpa's status, he still had to meet the powerful being and capito, and although Ciquinchara's "capito" did not reconcile with Soto's interpreter's "son of the maker," Atahualpa's tests had largely failed. Thus when the capitos left the Inca said *"Mana unan changa runan caicuna,* that means 'these are people whom it is impossible to understand'"* (Betanzos:II, 21, 1987:270). Perceptions, rather than being unveiled, were being redefined through continued, politically informed improvisation.

My third point is that personal differences between participants mattered. Even if the cultural divide was striking, different actors had an uneven ability to cross it. Soto stubbornly tried to reach the Inca but never managed to, nor to challenge the rules. Hernando, as usual, relied on a bullish strategy to undo the hierarchy that ordered action and was more effective. Ciquinchara and some Inca captains had no interest in the strangers and wanted to fence them off, but failed. Atahualpa oscillated between maintaining royal protocol and exposing himself to experimentation, and in the end reached no conclusion. Finally, in this chaotic meeting key elements escaped the realms of neatness that predominate in practice theory. On one hand, it was a cross-cultural contest of fear, as shown by the exchange between Hernando and Atahualpa and the latter's tight control of his emotions. On the other, the risky, close contact that broke all rules occurred because of Atahualpa's curiosity, however politically interested it might have been.

CAJAMARCA

The next day, Saturday, 16 November 1532, the Spaniards would capture Atahualpa in a quick and bloody act. Historians have tried to explain how this was possible in a way that contests demeaning images of the Incas not defending themselves, fooled by taking the Spanish for Viracochas (that is, good gods). Consistent with a politics of anti-inferiority and of objective actors engaged in mutually intelligible acts, their answer has been a military one. While Atahualpa miscalculated the Spaniards' might (they were few) and was too confident of his power, the Spanish attacked by surprise and without provocation. This version of events makes only limited sense, and it does so at the price of ignoring numerous clues. As I have argued, the mythifying version of the encounter is a colonial product that kidnaps native reasonings, but to dismiss alterity altogether is a Pyrrhic victory. Explaining Atahualpa's acts as a simple miscalculation echoes a Eurocentric fable in which capturing him was a neat military deed. Furthermore, the stress of a perfect contact scene triggered uncertainties and emotions on both sides that are poorly conveyed by a portrayal of reified rational Spanish subjects in control of all events. My interpretation aims, consequently, to recover alterity and to destabilize occidentalist (Coronil 1996) images of the Christians.

The first point to address is the idea of a unified native conception of what was ahead and what to do. I argue that there was no consensus. After the capitos left the Inca's camp, the Inca and his captains debated what to do the next day. Although new indices were considered, the arguments followed familiar lines: Ciquinchara said the New People might look like gods but were not; the generals wanted to attack; Atahualpa was undecided. It was agreed finally that they would leave with all the warriors at the ready, and send Ciquinchara to find out and report on the strangers' intentions (Betanzos:II, 22, 1987:272–74). Had Atahualpa been so certain of what was ahead, he could simply have sent his men to capture the Spaniards, but he did not. The compañía's size did not make choices easier: a large number would have been an army, providing a frame for military action, but a small number of powerful, strange beings, if anything, signaled heroes or ancestors and called for improvisation. The Spaniards' might, Atahualpa's attempt to disempower their huaca, and that he had asked the most powerful huaca in the empire, Pachacámac, about the coming encounter (Xérez 1985:127) show that the Spaniards worried him.[10] Besides, as before, the strangers were a pressing issue not only for Atahualpa and his council, but for everyone. For instance, Sebastián Yacobilca, a "soldier" of Huáscar Inca when the first news of the Spanish reached Cuzco, shifted sides and went to Cajamarca, driven by curiosity "to see the said Atabalipa Inga and know what the Sons of the Sea said" (Probanza 1573 . . . 1974:63).

The second point to question is the rational image of the compañía. Things were not easy at the Christian camp, either; indeed they were closer to the hallucinatory (Taussig 1987; Das 1998) than to the ordinary. If the size and order of Atahualpa's camp had troubled many, making their own fragility blatant, the expedition's news of his power unsettled them further. Uncertainty and fear increasingly mingled. Many were afraid because they had not fought with Indians of such a kind and order, and they knew not what to expect (P. Pizarro 1965:12). All knew the numerical odds against them were some 400 to 1, and far from any familiar face, they "expected no help but from God" (Mena 1937:83). While they spent the night sleeping by turns, with the horses saddled and bridled, their view of the fires in the Inca camp resembled a sky in its vastness.

What was their idea for the next day? Most scholars do not ask this question, the ambush and the attack seem to speak for themselves. Hemming contradicts himself. He starts by saying they planned to attack by surprise, and adds paragraphs about their military training. Then he says that they chose to let Pizarro make decisions as events dictated: they might attack if feasible or attacked, or Atahualpa might willingly give some sign of submission, or, if neither occurred, they would pretend to be friends (1993:37–39). However, there is reason to think that things were more complex. The neat version of "leaving things open" comes from Xérez. As usual, he presents Pizarro as in control, the sole organizer of his men (1985:109). Estete complicates matters by relating that there was a long debate, but he does not explain the different opinions (1918:23). Hernando Pizarro opens another window of possibility: the Christians knew from some of their service women that Atahualpa planned to kill them; some of the messengers were the women's kinsmen and had told them so (1953:55)—which reveals, again, that there were cleavages other than between Spanish and Inca at work. Not surprisingly, Pedro Pizarro (1965:177) describes it all as an ambush pure and simple, since he was certain that the Inca wanted to kill them; for him it was all a game of mirrors.

Before the encounter, both sides took good care to assure that the supernatural would be on their side. Sacrifices were carried out in Atahualpa's camp (Cieza:43, 1996:134), while, after a night of vigil, the conquerors heard Mass to uplift their souls and pray for help (Estete 1918:23). The compañía was divided into six groups: Soto, Hernando Pizarro, and Benalcázar would command cavalry units, Pizarro the infantry. They hid in the buildings encircling three sides of the large plaza to surprise Atahualpa with a sudden charge. Finally, in the upper terrace of the usnu/fortress was a Greek captain named Candía with the handful of musketeers and the two small cannons.

Atahualpa, surrounded by thousands of his men, took the entire day to cover half a league. His slow pace and ceremonial display have been interpreted as a sign of majesty, and that the head squad carried only disguised arms a sign that he had underestimated the Spaniards.[11] These interpretations can be reexamined. The ceremonial display and the hidden arms show majesty, but they make little sense if the goal was simply to capture a few vandals. Instead, they were necessary for a flexible, open-ended plan to work—to neither offend nor be unprepared. This open-ended approach was full of tension. Atahualpa sent two messengers during the day. The first said that his men would come armed, since the Spanish had done likewise the day before; the second, that they would be unarmed (Xérez 1985:108). In the plaza all the organizing and praying were not enough for everyone, and fear was in crescendo; some men urinated in their pants without noticing (P. Pizarro 1965:17). At one point the Inca stopped completely. Pizarro understood that he intended to spend the night in the field and, panicking, sent a footman, Aldana, to urge that he join Pizarro for dinner. After many gestures, and a new debate in which each party among the Inca repeated his opinion, Atahualpa resumed his slow march (Betanzos:II, 22, 1987:276). Meanwhile, after Aldana said that Atahualpa's men had disguised weapons and seemingly bad intentions, Pizarro and Hernando reassured their people that God was literally going to fight on their side—not unlike the way Pachacámac had reassured Atahualpa—because God always helped those at his service (Xérez 1985:109).

Some time before dusk Atahualpa finally made his majestic entry. Men dressed in different colors ceremonially swept the floor. Another group followed singing and dancing, and a third entered with golden and silver patens that flashed in the afternoon sun, carrying diverse weapons, many of them ceremonial ones made of gold or silver. Some 4,000 to 5,000 men crowded the plaza, and in the midst of them was Atahualpa in his gold *andas* (litters) covered by feathers, carried by ethnic lords and surrounded by his guard, each group distinctively dressed. Outside the plaza were other squads of up to 40,000 men. After the long day, whether due to terror or military calculation, there was no one to welcome him.

The next scene between Fray Vicente de Valverde and Atahualpa condensed all emotions, intents, and expectations, and is present in all accounts both sixteenth century and current. As MacCormack (1989) and Seed (1991) show in detail, what happened, with a book passed between parties, was of key significance to the Christians, and hence to native thinkers too. There are, still, two tangled aspects of the exchange that have received little attention. The first is the question of why it ever happened as it did. Why was Atahualpa *there*? If capturing a few vandals was the issue, he could have waited elsewhere while the task was done. His presence only makes sense if he had something to gain in person. Likewise, if Pizarro simply wanted to attack, all was in place: the Inca in person, surrounded by walls in a flat space, and the ambush at the ready. He did not need Valverde. The second question is what each party understood about the exchange between

Atahualpa and Valverde: *What* was being exchanged or who was *what*? My answer to both questions is that it was *a matter between* huacas, and therefore required high politics, although for each side in different ways and for different reasons.[12]

As I have suggested, the encounter with the New People was problematic for Atahualpa, among other reasons because he was a mediator between the normal and the supernatural, and many of the capitos' features were extraordinary. This takes on more significance if one considers an Inca's role in war. He rarely engaged in battle in person; his armies and generals battled literally *in his place*, carrying his bulto, or body double. The outcome of the battle showed his *atao*, or warlike luck—not that of his generals', expressing as it did his huacas' or gods' support and power. That is why a consecrated Inca could never lose a war. His personal intervention was a last resource involving the deployment of his supernatural powers (Ziólkowski 1996:215–57), and as such it was a public test of his semidivine condition, of his *cámac*—energy or power (Salomon 1991:16; Taylor 2000:1–34). Thus, up until the final battle, when Huáscar had no option but to try his atao in person, neither he nor Atahualpa took part in the battles between them. On that occasion Huáscar had assured his men that "he would turn into fire and water against his enemies" (Sarmiento [1571]:66, 2001:161).[13] Without invoking narrow cultural readings, within the *extraordinary* context that the New People had produced, these roles, restrictions, and powers make Atahualpa's presence in Cajamarca intelligible: the improvised task (there was no script) of facing an extraordinary being was his alone, as was the risk of doing it wrong. The New People could end up being simply dangerous thieves, but he had decided to wait and find out on the spot.

In this light, the exchange between Atahualpa and Valverde gains new meaning. For Seed (1991:30) and MacCormack (1989:165), it is impossible to know what happened with the book; the answer depends on each narrator's intentions and when he wrote. But, one must ask: What *was* the book for Atahualpa? Valverde approached him when no other Spaniard was in sight to welcome him, making the opening act a murky one, considering the elaborate Andean protocol. And, as on the previous day, during the interaction the words and forms muddied the waters further. Betanzos, like Garcilaso, says that the interpreter could not translate well. According to the former (II, 22, 1987:277), Valverde, holding a book, began addressing Atahualpa, and what the interpreter said was that "that father/friar was son of the Sun, who sent him to tell him [Atahualpa] that he should not fight and should give obedience to the captain [Pizarro], who was a son of the Sun too."

That is, *God* was translated as "the Sun," and Valverde and the capito claimed to be his sons and to carry his message. This must have sounded strange and problematic because it is exactly what an Inca would claim. Further, the interpreter said that all that the father said was "in that book . . . , thus *said it* that painting" (loc. cit.; my emphasis). *Painting* (*quillca*) was the closest word to *book*, but there were no images in the book; the word *written* was out of the question since the Inca system of recording information involved no writing as such; so the book *said* it. As Guaman Poma (385 [387], 1987:392) makes explicit, Atahualpa's immediate reaction was to ask for the book *because* he expected it to *talk*: "Give it to me, the book, so that it will tell me that. And . . . he began leafing through the pages of the said book [and said] 'What, how is it that it does not tell it to me? It does not even speak to me the said book!'"

This makes sense: the only object that could *say* something was a huaca, and as we have seen Atahualpa knew that the New People had one that claimed to be the most powerful, mocking all others. Atahualpa had tried to disempower it; he had his own, and he was one as well. The New People had also shown their atao in several battles. It was clearly a matter of high politics. The moment at which Atahualpa asked Valverde for the book condensed all of Atahualpa's expectations: rather than responding to the odd words, he chose to literally face the huaca—it was the moment of truth. And yet the alleged huaca failed to perform—it did not speak. The much-anticipated moment was a fiasco. Once the loaded object lost its powerful aura, Atahualpa looked at the silent pages and said:

> "This speaks and says that you are son of the Sun? I am son of the Sun too," and all his Indians answered . . . all together "thus is, *Çapa Ynga*." And the Inca turned to say very loud that he also came from where the Sun was, . . . and his people answered him once again: "thus is only lord." (Betanzos:II, 22, 1987:277)

It is, then, not only that *words* such as *Dios* (God), *libro* (book), or *escrito* (written) had no translation—the interpreter seems to have chosen the right words given the pressing context—but also that the *form* (object) through which the encounter was to be rendered intelligible failed: the huaca and book did not talk. This was no simple miscalculation. So far, Atahualpa had magisterially handled the extraordinary stress to which the contact scene had subjected him: to publicly test his semidivine nature vis-à-vis odd beings (the equivalent of asking the pope to perform a public miracle when facing aggressive aliens). Once the situation proved to be ordinary politics, Ata-hualpa threw away the *quillca*, likely shifting to plan B: to face bandits and undo all the damage they had caused to his authority. As all sources report, he asked for everything they had taken to be returned immediately.[14]

I diverge thus from MacCormack's (1989) and Seed's (1991) view of Guaman Poma (and of Garcilaso), based not on selected clues but on their own readings. In my view, both native authors presented the key elements of what had happened—the huaca failed to talk, Atahualpa *needed* to be majestic, and what Valverde said made *no sense*—within an account of the advent of Christianity, the frame acceptable to hegemonic eyes. They did not simply deploy rhetorical strategies to subvert Spanish claims of transparency and universality, pointing out that the book did not talk, questioning the moral standing but accepting the mystification. Rather, they presented, within a "colonial semiosis" (Mignolo 1995:7–9), a native understanding of what things had looked like. Their writing choices were rooted in a different order that they could not present bluntly—they had to accept the rules— but only suggest. The act of making another sense that is silenced (alter-ity) is, per se, challenging, because doing so renders the hegemonic rules of recognition visible and thus arbitrary (Bhabha 1994:110). And yet, in doing so they were caught in the double bind of being both different *and* sensible, what Salomon (1982) calls "chronicles of the impossible." From a Spanish point of view, however majestic Atahualpa was in Guaman Poma he still reconfirmed the Indians' inferiority (ignorant, he expected a book to talk), and as Seed signals (1991:24), Garcilaso had to conclude that the Incas' language lacked adequate abstract terms with which to express the mysteries of the faith.

The scene's dynamics were similar from the Christians' perspective. Why was Valverde there? Even if some so wished, Pizarro could not permit a direct attack because he had to comply with the Requerimiento—the legal text the Crown ordered to be read to any lord a compañía encountered, a must in this perfect encounter scenario.[15] Failure to do so would open the door for anyone to question his authority in the king's name. He needed contact and, like Atahualpa, had to wait and decide his course on the spot. This does not mean, however, that Valverde did not have an agenda. We lack his account and up to this point he had been almost invisible, but based on his later actions it seems clear that the Dominican friar was convinced of his duty: to protect good, powerless Indians from predatory conquerors, showing them the way to salvation.[16] When walking toward Atahualpa in the crowded plaza emptied of Christians, Valverde was, again like Atahualpa, on the spot. It was his turn to show that he carried water.

After the faulty opening, during which no Spaniard was in sight, Valverde approached Atahualpa with a native interpreter. Although the exact sequence of events varies from source to source, all mention the same events that nativelike accounts do: after some words were exchanged the book Valverde carried passed to Atahualpa's hands; it was soon on the floor, and Atahualpa asked for all that had been taken to be returned. Further, most Spanish narrators make explicit the connection between Valverde's words (a request to befriend the Spaniards because God had said so) and the fact that what God had *said* was in the book.[17] Also matching nativelike accounts, Atahualpa asked Valverde for the book, looked at it, and dismissed it. Immediately after, Valverde went back to Pizarro, and sources portray him in radically different ways: ranging from a sorrowful, concerned priest to an outraged crusader.[18]

And yet, regardless of this variation, whatever Valverde said was only an after-the-fact matter; most men were simply too far away to hear at all. For them the exchange was a silent yet clear scene in which gestures mattered. As several men who were present in Cajamarca, but who did not write about it, declared in a trial in 1544–45 (AGI, Ec 1007c, pza. 1, ff. 41–954), they read the interaction from a distance as a turning point. They saw Valverde going to Atahualpa and talking; a sacred book changing hands and ending up on the floor; Valverde running back and Atahualpa standing defiant and calling his men, who responded with a loud shout. For Valverde, it must have been a frustrating blow that put an end to his intention—not unlike Atahualpa's frustration when the famous huaca failed to perform. But unlike Atahualpa,

Valverde had no plan B. In the same act by which Atahualpa proved the New People's huaca to be false, the Christians saw it drop to the floor. This was clear regardless of what they thought afterward about Atahualpa's understanding of Valverde's words. Once the need for a peaceful performance was over, there remained only contained fear and hatred.

The attack was chaotic and frenzied. What has been narrated, following Xérez, as an orderly military deed was to others more of a hallucinatory bloodbath. As the conqueror Pedro Cataño recalled in 1543, "It was agreed that all people grouped with their captains should come out when a shot was fired . . . and since it was not fired all Christians were confused" (AGI, P 90a, n. 1, r. 11, f. 183v). The signal did not come, and there was no epic start. Some began going for the Inca. Not surprisingly, Soto and his men took the lead. Others followed soon, and at some point the shot came and the tension exploded. They were 168 men among 5,000, and they could barely see. Like a camera, Cataño remembers returning after the first cavalry charge "and as they passed through them, when they turned right around upon them they saw that all the others were already mingled with the Indians" (loc. cit.). Meanwhile, Pizarro with his footmen went straight after Atahualpa, but found it hard to pull him down from his andas; they had to literally chop down the carriers, which were quickly replaced by others defending the Inca.

The plaza was a crowded, closed space, and to elude the cavalry charges many of Atahualpa's men tried to open a breach in the wall and eventually managed to push down some of it. In the center of the scene, Pizarro continued his attempt to capture Atahualpa. As Don Diego Inga Mocha recalls (1573), "they suddenly assailed Atahualpa and the people coming with him killing and chopping many of them, and thus [his guards] began to cluster around Atahualpa to defend him, the Spaniards were only wounding and killing" (*Probanza 1573* . . . 1974:96). In the frenzy, before managing to take down and imprison the Inca, Pizarro even had to stop a sword blow with his hand to secure Atahualpa's life.

By then, bodies were also being chopped outside the tambo, where the horsemen continued their (dis)charge. As I have said, Xérez's account of the battle as an orderly deed with Pizarro in command is a biased, after-the-fact simplification. Success came from compressed energies that poured out for hours until they were mastered. Following Pizarro's orders, Valverde and Hernando Pizarro tried to stop the attack after the plaza was cleared. Invoking all available sources of order, they asked the men "in the name of the king and the governor to retreat because the night had fallen and God had given them the victory"; they would continue the next day (AGI, P 90a, n. 1, r. 11, f. 184). Some did so, yet—as "it would not be right to leave the enemies so close and go to sleep" (loc. cit.)—most decided to continue the massacre, which went on until midnight, when Pizarro fired a cannon, "and then the horsemen retreated . . . thinking that the Indians were attacking the camp and the same did the footmen" (Mena 1937:87). Once order was reestablished, the panorama was Dantesque: "there remained . . . dead, . . . six or seven thousand Indians, and many others had their arms chopped and other wounds" (loc. cit.).

Unlike the portrayal in most scholarship, in Cajamarca there was nothing coldly ordered by the mastermind Pizarro, an embodiment of Western reason. As Feldman points out in his study of Northern Ireland, the idea of power as being contained in the center and flowing toward its peripheries, external to violent action, is a "myth of rationalization" (1991:3). Violent action is not simply instrumental, it has to be thought of as having a semantic and material autonomy. Power's effects, as in Cajamarca's outcome and aftermath, rest largely on local practices, on concrete material forces; legitimation is related not necessarily to arguments laid out from the center but to performance and contingency.

This has direct consequences. Seed argues that Xérez's account of Cajamarca celebrates the Western belief—culturally particular but assumed to be transparent—in the superiority of literate people. Atahualpa was punished for the arrogance that prevented him both from marveling at the form (an object containing speech) and from accepting its content (Christianity), thus justifying Pizarro's reaction. I want to interrogate the assumption of transparency. No doubt Xérez, like any European, would have been endlessly happy to see Atahualpa marvel at the book, "the sixteenth-century equivalent of green vibrating crystals carried by Martians as evidence of the obvious superiority of their culture" (Seed 1991:28). Yet, it must have been clear to a thoughtful sixteenth-century reader that it was impossible for Atahualpa to understand what a book was, much less to marvel once exposed to (alphabetic) writing: Crystals vibrate on their own; books do not. Rather than frustrated cultural expectations universally taken to be transparent, Xérez's *pretension* of transparency was necessary to expurgate any question as to the performance of the Requerimiento, and was a result of the surging emotions that effaced the opacity of the moment.

Spanish colonialism was a complex mix of royal and private mechanisms, ideas, and components. There is a constant tension, during the production of the colonial order in Peru, between the conquerors' actions and the Crown's dispositions. As the Crown demonstrated in practice, it was ready to open tenacious legal proceedings against anyone whose actions were not pleasing and who had lost political backing at court. As a result, few governors could afford to be in office without someone writing a "true" account of their task.[19] Honor and career were at risk. To Pizarro, complying with the Requerimiento or something similar was crucial. In order for his compliance to be safe from a trial, the act *had* to be transparent, no matter what actually happened. Mentioning that Atahualpa might have misunderstood the interaction, that something had not been transparent, would have undermined the deal.[20]

That said, I do not mean to argue that the pretension of—and even the belief in—the universality and transparency of cultural particularities is not a powerful, effective, and even key tool of any colonial or neocolonial project. To the contrary, it is precisely in spaces of murkiness when acts are assumed to be transparent that strategies of dominance are empowered, both because it is difficult to recognize the slippage as such, and because assumptions and slippages are enacted and embodied by imperial subjects. I argue, then, that in Cajamarca's case the slippage was less rhetorical than *bodily powerful*. What was crucial were the heightened emotions that for those in the front line, suspended murkiness. Actors, events, and narratives were "achronic" (Feldman 1991:13, after Lyotard 1973)—each constituted the other. That is why conquerors all agreed, whether they wrote in 1533 or 1571; it was not a generational difference (MacCormack 1989). And that is why many of those far from the action (Cieza 45, 1996:140; Zárate [1555]:5, 1995:75) could not share in the agreement. By the same token, this local dynamic re-empowers the center's discourse (the Requerimiento), legitimizing and replicating its *own* slippage into universality. It is to these consequences that native intellectuals responded, and tried to destabilize by inserting alterity, unsettling embodied senses of fair action. Theirs was a constant struggle to define reality, a struggle which indeed marked the entire path to the establishment of the Spanish colonial regime.

CHAPTER 2

Christian Realism and Magicality during
Atahualpa's Imprisonment

Between the Spaniards' capture of the Inca Atahualpa in November 1532 and their execution of him in July 1533, the empire's political status quo was uncertain and full of paradox. Huáscar, the defeated Inca, was prisoner of the generals of the victorious one, who was prisoner of strange new people. Soon an agreement was reached in the shape of a ransom, and messengers, rumors, loads of gold, Christians, political intents, and native lords began moving across the empire. How exactly was the situation being rendered intelligible by each of the parties, what were the resulting actions, and how effective were they?

This chapter engages these questions by examining several attempts to cast the unstable context. So far I have highlighted improvisations, the politics of alterity, and the attempts to contain newness, mainly between Atahualpa and the Christians. Now things become increasingly complex; interactions multiply and turn particular as Christians, Incas, and ethnic groups engage in different scenarios. This diversity results in different contact dynamics, and in different degrees of contact, multiplying places, acts, and politics. Consequently, the in-between that bridges contact and domination can begin to be studied. What happens once contact has occurred but domination is not in place? How do different ways of signifying reality relate? How is certainty achieved, if at all?

Scholars often write this nine-month period as starring Western-like rational actors involved in transparent political or military action. This corrects Spanish accounts' order, turning native peoples into agents, but echoes it at another level: in both kinds of texts, when a passage revealing an alternative understanding appears, it is controlled by using it as a *curiosity*. This obscures the fact that at work were experiential ways of living the same present and epistemic orders other than those dictated by *Christian rationality*. By this, I mean the terms in which sixteenth-century Western subjects liked to imagine themselves, since rationality is a claim of the second modernity—French, British, and so on. By matching faults in the conquerors' accounts with clues in dismissed nativelike sources, I provide a plot in which alternative understandings abandon the space of curiosities and become key parts of the story. This plot exposes the alleged transparency as a selective way of representing actions and emotions, and illuminates the murky exchanges of supernatural energy and imagery that were taking place.

Because, as will be seen, to advance their respective agendas Incas and Spaniards needed to resort to acts of "magicality." By magicality, I want to evoke ways of acting and interacting that are not fantastic or magic (that is, that do not violate the rules of nature), but involve dimensions of social action ordinarily deemed to be so.[1] These acts of magicality responded, though, to different epistemological understandings of political action: while the Inca *was* a supernatural being, the Spaniards could only *try to evoke* the perception of being supernatural. My argument is that the dynamics resulting from the difference and overlapping of both kinds of political action bring to light the epistemic dimension of the transition from the Inca mode of domination to the Spanish one, as well as the import of murky acts in the working of power. In turn, this makes visible the complexity of the struggle for meaning that paralleled that of acts, circumventing culturalist and rationalist shortcuts to explain the ongoing transition from contact to domination.

CRAFTING A RANSOM

The uncertainty on the way to Cajamarca did not vanish with the encounter. Atahualpa's capture meant an eerie credit for the Christians and a problem for him, since another authority and sense of order could be seen at work. His strategy for damage control was twofold: sense making and overlapping. He immediately asked Pizarro for some of his men to be brought to him, and once they were there he ordered them to tell his people that he was not dead and that they should come to serve him *and* the Christians (Mena [1534] 1937:88). He thus stopped rumors of his death that were already spreading according to Pizarro's page, Pedro Pizarro ([1571] 1965:179), and also wrapped the Christians' authority in his own. For instance, the conquerors' next morning task was looting Atahualpa's camp, taking numerous gold and silver pieces, men and women, and supplies; they brought so many *piezas* (war captives) that Pizarro ordered them to be freed once each of his men took the captives he needed. To reclaim control over the shared scenario, Atahualpa then ordered his men to return to their lands too (Hernando Pizarro 1953:58).

The story of the "ransom" can be read as the next ring in the struggle to shape reality. Although Pizarro promised Atahualpa no harm, all eyewitnesses report the Inca's fear of being killed right away. After the bewildering events, I suggest, the question was how to control interactions, what to offer; the answer came from seeing the Christians looting his camp: "the *cacique* showed himself to be happy, and told the governor that he knew what they wanted. The governor told him that the war people wanted nothing but gold for themselves and their lord, the emperor" (Mena [1534] 1937:88). Atahualpa promised then to fill up the room he was in with gold and another with silver. The current historiographic version—that this treasure was a ransom offered in exchange for his freedom—is, I suggest, an after-the-facts closure of complex and crossed politics and intelligibilities, Inca, ethnic, and Spanish. As Raúl Porras Barrenechea signaled years ago (1937:89, n. 44), in most conquerors' accounts the offer has a clear shape only at the execution—not at the capture. As will be seen, there are good reasons for it.

The 168 men waited for months for the treasure—and much needed reinforcements—to arrive. Leaving aside logistic reasons (the loaders had to cover huge distances on foot—Cuzco was some 1,400 km [870 mi] south of Cajamarca), Atahualpa faced several problems in collecting a "ransom." First, while a ransom was a form of interaction familiar to Spaniards, who used it to free captives in the Muslim-Christian frontier (Rojas Gabriel 1995:153–269), it was something that *made no local sense*. Ethnic lords might surrender to or ally with the Incas, their resources might be used to pay tribute, eventually something could be looted, but hostages and payments had no precedents. Among nonmonetary polities, in which the capacity to mobilize human energy expressed wealth, the request must have been a puzzle. Second, the Inca was not the beloved ruler of all peoples, but a ruler of rulers. There were several levels of mediation between him and the native groups from which the empire received tribute, and reciprocity and redistribution ruled all exchanges (Murra 1978); nothing could be simply ordered or extracted. Third, Atahualpa's position was fragile. His authority was still being settled when the news of his imprisonment shook it. Local lords and Inca elites could refuse to help him, either hoping for a comeback of Huáscar's faction or simply waiting to see how the strange conjuncture ended, since the Viracochas were an odd but amazing chance.

In this complex, fluid context a clear politics of sense was crucial. Atahualpa had to render rumors into facts to secure his position and ensure the collection of the treasure. For that end he used both, the aura of the New People and the New People themselves; they, in turn, engaged in their own acts of meaning making, often involving magicality; finally, both attempts tangled with local ways of making sense of the conjuncture. This dynamics unfolded in four scenarios with two different textures, that of first contact—Pachacámac, Jauja, and Cuzco—and that of everyday cohabitation—Cajamarca.

SUPERNATURAL CONTESTS IN PACHACÁMAC AND JAUJA

Atahualpa suggested that Pizarro send a party of men secured by two main Incas to gather the treasure of Pachacámac, a main coastal huaca, arguably the most important non-Inca one. This allowed Atahualpa to advance his authority where it was facing limits. In Cajamarca, he put into place the authority of the "bishop" of Pachacámac: using a Spanish chain, he asked the "bishop" to free himself if his huaca was as powerful as he said, and told him he would not remove it until Pachacámac's treasure was brought to Cajamarca to meet his offer.[2] In Pachacámac, continuing his fight with local deities that began in Huamachuco (see chapter 1), Atahualpa used the

Christians to punish the huaca and collect the treasure. For the Spaniards it was an occasion to obtain gold and gain knowledge of the land. Or so, at least, their accounts declare.

Pachacámac's shrine, still standing, crowns the top of an imposing hill on the seashore south of Lima. The compound has several buildings and walls one has to go through to reach the chamber of the huaca. Ordinary people had to fast an entire year to set foot in the compound, and only the highest ministers would enter its chamber. Christian accounts (recall that by and large Peru's conquerors called themselves Christians) present the expedition as an opportunity to do . . . Christian things. It took the expedition of twenty-five men twenty-five days to arrive in Pachacámac. In a fearless task, after breaking all taboos, the Christians entered the temple, publicly scoffed and destroyed Pachacámac's idol (the Devil), and planted a cross in the huaca's chamber, securing the Faith against the idolaters of the "mosque." All natives present reacted in awe.[3]

Current scholars often echo the conquerors' image and praise their bravery—so far away from any help and yet so daring. Others, like Mac-Cormack (1991:50–65), offer a reading of the acts at the huaca in terms of cultural divides: the Spanish could only understand non-Christian religious practices in the terms provided by Christian doctrine, making the Devil or deception the sole possible explanations. Perception was conditioned. That is why the Captain Hernando Pizarro, head of the expedition, in an example of religious zeal tortured one of Pachacámac's ministers to get him to confess that it was all priestly fabrication. In all cases, actions seem to take place within the field of Christian realism the conquerors chose.

There is, however, a strange dissonance. In his official 1533 report, Hernando Pizarro chooses to narrate only one scene of the torture session designed to have the huaca's minister confess that he did not talk to the Devil and that it was all a fakery: he tells that in spite of the torture, the minister stubbornly stuck to his words, and continued to maintain that it was indeed "the Devil" (Pachacámac) who had spoken to him, "and told him not to fear horses, that they were scary but did no harm" ([1533] 1953:64).

That is, it was about horses that the Devil talked to his ministers. This makes little sense. Why was the Devil concerned about such a trivial matter? One would expect more esoteric topics, perhaps Who were Christ's soldiers? Equally intriguing to us, Why was Hernando fixated on horses? The Devil's appearance or the tongue in which he spoke would seem more relevant matters. Besides, horses play no role in any Spanish account of the events at Pachacámac. The passage is a paradigmatic Ginzburgean dialogical clue: a strange fragment, in which coherence fails and a clash of two voices can be heard (Ginzburg 1989:149–50). And what is odd turns revealing if one reexamines the conquerors' privileged image of the events at Pachacámac: it exposes Christian realism as a selective way of representing actions, emotions, and understandings.

Let me begin the reexamination by questioning the expedition's aura of a neat, Christian-like deed. If in general I would argue that the weight of medieval treatises has to be counterbalanced by common people's unorthodox beliefs, as studied by Ginzburg (1980, 1983), in the case in question there was more to it than that; crucial too was the way in which the conquerors chose to portray themselves as in control of all emotions and devotional energies. When the expedition was approaching Pachacámac, the earth shook—one of the huaca's main attributes—which made all the accompanying natives flee; they took it for a warning, Estete tells ([1535?] 1918:27). Seemingly, the event had no effect on the Spaniards; in reality, approaching the huaca was not easy for them either. Despite the confident tone of their narratives, they had taken good supernatural equipment: crossing sources reveals that the small expedition had at least two Christian priests as members, a record considering that altogether there were only four in the entire compañía.[4]

What were the effects of the expedition? Hernando, coherent with his idea that the huaca's ministers had ignorant people subdued by fear, reports nearby lords telling him that "until then they had served the mosque because they were afraid of it, but that now they were afraid of nothing but of us, that they wanted to serve us" (1953:65). Apparently the status of those who could break taboos even the Inca would not dare to, and still remain unaffected, was unclear. But the fact that the New People were immune to their acts did not erase local orders of things: in his official report, Estete tells that local lords marveled at Hernando's daring, but were scared of what would happen *after* the Spaniards' departure (in Xérez [1534] 1985:138).[5] I suggest that there was no cultural abyss separating Christians and Indians, but rather a slippery blend in a hallucinatory milieu. The *value*—in Saussurean terms—of the supernatural was being shaken and reconfigured, in no simple direction.

Second way of questioning the Christian-realist image of the expedition is to by ask why the Devil, his minister, and Hernando were interested in horses. The answer lies in silenced acts involving magicality, performed by both Spanish and Incas. To make this visible, I will revise the larger context of the expedition using dismissed native accounts. They make plain that the events at Pachacámac were determined by factors that remove us further from the cross and the Devil; it was not only about shocking acts but also about shocking beings—which, in turn, makes the odd passages in Spanish accounts intelligible.

Nearby *curacas* (ethnic/lords) brought to Pachacámac most of the gold and silver the Spaniards gathered at the huaca. Why were the lords there? What is known about it comes mostly from the testimonies of eighteen native witnesses (seventeen from the ethnic group of Yauyos and one Inca) and one Spaniard interrogated in 1573 by request of the royal prosecutor in the Yauyo province, some 90 km (56 mi) up the sierra from Pachacámac. It was a tax trial.[6] As far as the dialectic between questions and answers is concerned, the prosecutor made some mistakes about the order of the events, to which the witnesses bent,[7] but there is nothing in his questions suggesting either the kind of elements or the motivations for action the answers articulate—which are my target.

Don Gonzalo Zapayco distinguished three waves of rumors arriving in Yauyos. The initial one said that that unknown bearded people no one could stop had come by sea in houses asking for gold and silver; they called them "sons of the sea." The second wave said that those men had reached Cajamarca, where "they had thrown into confusion and imprisoned Atahualpa, and from this all natives marveled . . . how being so few those men the sea had thrown out, they had done so much" (*Probanza 1573 . . . 1974:77–78*). The shocking news relates in all testimonies to events *beyond the limits of the possible*; Sebastián Yacobilca, a man of Cajamarca, declared that "it was their understanding that in the whole world there were no people that could dominate or defeat or were more valiant than them" (ibid.:64). The third wave Don Gonzalo recalls came with messengers from Atahualpa who made the news even more strange. They told

> how those men that had imprisoned . . . Atahualpa had some sheep into which they entered and that with a puff [*soplo*] they threw fire and killed many Indians even if they were far where they were, and that with the tail it would cut a man in halves, and that those sheep eat gold and silver. (ibid.:78)

They asked the curacas to collect gold and silver to free Atahualpa and feed the horses. In this milieu of eerie images the Yauyos went to Pachacámac.

All was bewildering. That the New People entered sheep made no sense; in the Andes there was no animal that could transport people (although deities could transform themselves into animals), which signals, again, the importance of bodies when locating uncanny difference. A horse has a piece of metal in his mouth, chewing it constantly, and his feet have nails, making him an organic and metal hybrid. In the effort to denaturalize our familiarity with horses, a good parallel is the awkward sensation that body piercing and artificial members provoke, as violations of body boundaries; and it is not about bodies per se but about what is normal in them, bringing to consciousness how fundamental body imagery is to worldview (Douglas 1966, 1970). The same is visible in death: to a Western person some *kinds* of death seem acceptable, while some are horrifying. Radical alterity is about that: when something is so much out of the Normal it challenges and turns uncertain the order of things. Other indexes of estrangement in the testimony point to the same direction: *soplo* is how guns' action is described—like that of animated beings—and swords are horses' tails.

These images echoing throughout the empire served overlapping interests and intelligibilities that are important to discern. The stranger and more dangerous the Spaniards were imagined, the better for Atahualpa: the Inca had not been captured by ordinary beings. His messengers' images saved his aura and solidified his role: he was still mediating between ordinary and extraordinary realms. By the same coin, Atahualpa chose the format within which to ask ethnic lords for gold and silver; the ransom was not a form that made local sense, but that the eerie "big sheep" were hungry seemed to work. This example shows that his capacity to shape rumors does not have to be overstated; the images were *plausible*. They made *local sense* of how something as flummoxing as the Inca's capture had happened, and they were of the same eerie order of things as the images preceding contact. Atahualpa was not then pulling out of his little finger a version that best fitted his interests, but was *riding on circulating images*. And the Spaniards' amazing acts only added to the bizarre context.

If I am right, this signals a crucial dimension of the way in which the transition from contact to domination worked: it was about maneuvering uncertainty, about producing valid, exchangeable units of sense, *not* about unveiling truth. There was no moment of enlightenment, rather a plurality of perceptions that continued to evolve and overlap. Consider asking for gold because the horses are hungry: native peoples will soon realize who eats the gold, but there is no return to zero. Next interactions will work upon this first interpretation, and its consequent relationship—the link established in Pachacámac—will not simply fade. This is important because the rationalist argument assumes not only that finding out is a primary drive—an implicit attribution of a prevalent scientific pulsation to humans—but also that as a result of it reality will appear naked, beyond the draperies of misperception, and mystification will cease. This line of thought results in another mystification: of history. It makes time an unnecessary variable, it endows all agents with the most valued treasure of occidentalism (Coronil 1996)— scientific drive—and it assumes that reality is "there" and that power operates through the visible. I am trying to challenge ethnographically all these assumptions that spring from the opposition of truth and mystification.

The Yauyo testimonies clarify why the curacas were at Pachacámac in the first place, and why they declared to fear the Christians from then on. When Atahualpa's messengers said that Inca captains were going to show Pachacámac to the Spaniards, "the Indians were frightened by how the said captains had dared reveal the Sun house and shrine of the Maker of the Earth, and were very scared of it," Martín Atrico recalls (*Probanza 1573 . . . 1974*:59). This echoes, forty years later, Estete's register of the Indians' terror when the Spaniards desecrated the huaca. The events in Pachacámac were neither simply about the cross and the Devil nor plain, and there was as much local sense making as imperial politics involved in them. It is an effect of the conquerors' accounts, often replicated by current scholarship, to accept Christian realist images, cornering native ways of making sense into the space of curiosities.

And reintroducing them was not easy. That by 1573 the process through which cultural difference turns into "colonial difference" (Mignolo 1999) was a fait accompli explains why not all Yauyo witnesses included alterity in their responses. Studying the political and epistemic effects of those testimonies that did so illuminates the economy of their game within the colonial semiosis. The witnesses carefully picked the way in which to present radical alterity to a Spanish audience (the magistrate) who *did not need it and was in power*, and still be intelligible and respectable subjects. For example, Yacobilca narrates all precontact news using terms such as "sons of the sea," or *capacochas*, while after contact he rapidly switches to "Spanish" (*Probanza 1573 . . . 1974:63–64*). This narrative choice reinserts an-other subjectivity into the context of interrogation and protects his persona. It says: "OK, now I do not say anymore capacochas because it is after contact, and now you listeners and your order have entered the picture and it (I) would look silly if I keep on saying anything of that sort."[8] The effort of alterization when describing events for which the interlocutor uses another key was not simply tiring; it also meant a conscious epistemic challenge: it introduced a way of making sense that ran against accepted conventions, decentering them and putting at risk the intelligibility and respectability of the subaltern subject. It is not simple difference; it is *a situated one*—in essence like the Italian miller Menoccio's choice in end-of-sixteenth-century Friuli to explain the Creation to his inquisitor through the cheese and the worms (Ginzburg 1980).

Accepting radical alterity as a key factor not only lends an ear to the consistency of native accounts, but also makes sensible the strange passages in Spanish ones. One can now understand Hernando Pizarro's torture session in Pachacámac, and why he chose to narrate only that scene: what had angered and unsettled him was that the huaca's minister *knew* that horses did no harm while everyone else was terrified. This fascinating line, a true lapsus (De Certeau 1991), makes sense only if the horses' status was at stake. The key in the torture act lay, then, not in Spanish religious zeal but in silenced acts involving magicality. The Christians' acts in the next scenario make this even plainer.

From Pachacámac the tiny expedition went back north along the coast, turned east to climb the sierra, and then south toward Jauja, main city of the Huancas. Hernando knew that Calcuchima, a general of Atahualpa's, had gold and silver and a large army there. Hernando and the general had exchanged messengers and agreed to meet on the way to Cajamarca, but he never showed up and repeatedly tried to mislead Hernando. For the twenty-five men the situation must have been trippy and uncanny. They were being welcomed as beings of the highest class, and they were seeing treasures they had only heard of in fables: on the way to Jauja they met an Inca captain with 150 loads of gold sent by Calcuchima, soberly 1,725 kg (3,804 lb);[9] the nobleman they ran into in Huamachuco carried 300 loads of gold, some 3,450 kg (7,607 lb); and in Pachacámac they had collected 85,000 pesos and 3,000 marcos, roughly 387 kg (853 lb) of gold and 682.5 kilograms (1,505 lb) of silver.[10] And yet they were constantly afraid of a sudden attack, since they were only a fistful of men in the middle of nowhere and surrounded by millions of aliens, all potential enemies.

In this exhilarating atmosphere they arrived in Jauja, on 16 February 1533. When approaching the town they saw a "black spot" in its middle, but could not tell what it was. Ready for battle, they met a celebratory ambiance that included large welcoming festivities—the black spot was Jauja's crowded plaza. As usual, neither Estete nor Hernando Pizarro—the only members of the expedition who narrated it—make any attempt to explain it; their plots focus on the absence of Calcuchima and his army. One of the Inca captains who accompanied the expedition left to find out the general's intention. When night fell the Christians decided to spend it ready for an attack, the horses saddled and bridled. Flat, open spaces being the best for horsemen to charge, they wanted to camp in the plaza, but the disturbing celebrating people crowded it. To clear it, Hernando "ordered the lords of the town that no Indian should appear in the plaza *because the horses were angry and would kill them*" (Estete, cited in Xérez 1985:143; my emphasis). The horses, not the Spaniards.

The quote comes from Estete's official report, included in Francisco Pizarro's secretary account, published in Seville in 1534. As in Pachacámac, things make an-other sense: horses, out-of-place beings, can be angry, attack and kill, on their own. What the Yauyo witnesses recalled in 1573 was at work in 1533. No surprise that in a battle during the compañía's second attempt to reach Peru (1526–28), the natives run away upon seeing a Spaniard fall from his horse, saying that it had turned into two (Estete 1918:15);

or that according to Garcilaso, son of an Inca princess and a conqueror, Indians gave the Christians gold and silver to feed their horses in Cajamarca and Pachacámac ([1617]:XVII, 17, 29, 1960:40, 58); or that in Pachacámac Hernando asked native smiths to make silver and gold shoes and nails for the horses (Mena 1937:94).

The scene in Jauja is telling on yet another account: Hernando Pizarro could have made the same request by saying that they would punish anyone remaining in the plaza, but he did not; he used supernatural imagery to empower it. This exposes both Christian realism as a faked field of interactions and the hallucinatory milieu the conquerors actually lived in. The Christians were terrified by the idea of an attack; few among thousands, their life depended on their aura. And still, for the move to be effective it had to ride on local ways of making sense, valid exchangeable units, which reminds one of the spatial and temporal complexity of the ongoing contact process. Through his request, Hernando mirrored back his own fear of the alien places and bodies around him, exorcising it. I recognize the practical side of making oneself feared, but I argue that this is not enough; it was not a unidimensional act in a single signifying field. The "epistemic murk" of rubber seekers in the 1900s Amazon basin Taussig (1987:xiii) identifies was inherent to the conquest. But what happens with Christian rationality and the conversion deed then? Were all Christians aware of, and using, magicality? To address these questions I will examine first how Spanish sources present alterity, and then try to answer why they do so.

CONTAINED ALTERITY AND PARTIAL RECOGNITION

The reader may by now have the impression that radical alterity and magicality are extensively present in Spanish eyewitnesses narratives. After all, this could fit a part-medieval imagination. Nothing could be further from truth. The quotes I have presented are drops in a glass of water. To understand how Spanish eyewitnesses deal with alterity is crucial because it opens the door to recognizing that Christian realism is the way in which the conquerors *chose to represent* themselves. Confusing this with the way the Spanish *acted* has obscured the epistemological ground of the transition from the Inca mode of domination to the Spanish one.

The historiography of the conquest often narrates action as taking place between Western rational actors engaged on a clear political terrain. There is no alterity, magicality, or radical uncertainty. We have examined the political aims of this decision: to move native peoples away from marks of inferiority. There is another argument to examine: as Hemming in his widely read *The Conquest of the Incas* argues, the idea of the Spanish being taken for anything but ordinary beings has to be dismissed *because* Spanish eyewitnesses do not mention it (1993:97–98). Yet as we saw at times radical strangeness emerges, unsettling Christian rational frames. Where does the difference between nativelike and Christian accounts lie then? My argument is that it is not the simple absence of alterity that differentiates one from the other; it is rather *the way in which it appears*, a difference that reveals the epistemological violence behind interactions.

The conquerors' accounts are closed narratives that make it sound as if there were little to explain and a lot to describe. They are organized as a counterpoint of sections full of Spanish military action followed by long descriptions of the land and natives (their dressing, religious beliefs, sacrifices, hair styles, houses, bridges, sexual customs, etc.). It is true that by portraying the Indians as infidels, traitors, idolaters, and so forth, these descriptions serve the purpose of celebrating the conquerors' deeds, but that is not the point I want to make. The point is that these descriptions are *fully disengaged* from the actions taking place. They never challenge the actors' Christian rationality and the interactions' transparency; the conquerors simply go from one place to another; there are no lines of intelligibility to cross, no unclear realities to face. The Indians are mere military counterparts, and the long descriptions reconfirm the conquerors' mastery, since they are not only able to defeat the enemy but to describe their mores, filling the space of curiosities, of objects that are being collected. This trivializes difference, relegating alternative ways of making sense to museums and disempowering them, as Anzaldúa (1987:86) points out.

In this feature, Spanish eyewitnesses' narratives echo other colonial sources. In the case of India, for example, Guha (1988) analyzes primary, secondary, and tertiary discourses ("the prose of counter-insurgency") and shows that what peasant upheavals were about is progressively replaced by an increasingly doctored and sanitized version. Alterity in particular is displaced, and ways of reasoning other than the ones the colonizers use vanish. If one accepts the image the latter want to give, then the option of realist historians is reasonable. (In fact, studies of colonial Peru often replicate the conquerors' accounts' structure—action and description—making cyborg-horses and silent books, if mentioned at all, notes of color to military action.)

There is, however, a second way in which difference appears in conquerors' accounts: in the form of *snapshots*, flashes of alterity *tangled with the Spaniards' actions*. These are the passages I focus on. They differ from long descriptive sections because they are short sentences, followed by no elaboration, and because *they do not pause the plot but are part of it*. Restoring for a second the alternative orders that the narrators want to erase, these snapshots signal moments in which become visible what De Certeau, when analyzing French travelers' narratives, calls "faults in the discourse of comprehension" (1991:223). In these fragments Spanish and native parallel realities intersect, Christian realism falters, and alterity bursts beyond any attempt to render it intelligible, unsettling the pretension of transparent action—like a lapsus in psychoanalytic theory.

Combining Guha's and De Certeau's observations, my argument is that in conquerors' narratives alterity—and the resulting murkiness—is *not* absent; they are mostly *controlled*. Difference is shown and contained; it does not alter the plot; it is a curiosity, accidental to what *really* happens. This control fails only in the snapshots, and the clues that surface in them match the epistemological ground, elements, and reasonings of native accounts, showing that their ways of making sense were not nonsense. And vice versa: by giving an alternative, complex image, in which alterity and murkiness have a concrete impact upon the unfolding events, nativelike accounts challenge Christian realism and turn Spanish lapses intelligible.

I will next risk some answers to *why* Spanish eyewitnesses handle alterity in this way. A first answer is that it happens because alterity was too overwhelming. Narratives are people's tools for making sense, and one has to believe in one's own reasons to pursue a particular line of action. Accepting alterity implies acknowledging that there is more than one plot, and that the other one is not simply driven by evil, arrogance, sin, and so forth. This puts at risk the necessary blindness-derived drive of a conquering task. If the Other is a sensible being, then the door to uncertainty is open.

Second, as I mentioned, there are two ways in which the Other appears in eyewitnesses' accounts, via *snapshots* and via *descriptive sections*. The latter are not only disengaged from action but use proper portrayals of Otherness: human sacrifices, *pecado nefando* and other sins, mosques and idolatry—all Christian technology (vocabulary and sites) for dealing with usual Christian others: the Devil and the Muslims. It is arguable that the conquerors' slot for Otherness was loaded with known forms that rendered it manageable to themselves and their metropolitan audience. Including alterity would have implied seeing themselves as exotic creatures, therefore particular—for actors of an imperial project carried in the name of a universal (Christianity).

I argue that it is precisely in response to these reasons that native sources include out-of-the-ordinary beings and actions. Their versions of what happened were ignored and their ways of making sense were nonsense. Presenting alterity *in action* was for them a means to remedy their dismissal. Peruvian native subjects include other reasonings in their accounts for the same reasons that in the inquisitional processes studied by Ginzburg (1980, 1983), peasant mobilizations studied by Amin (1989), Chicana border crossings narrated by Anzaldúa (1987), or politics of the indigenous mestizas studied by De la Cadena (2000), subaltern subjects defend their own frames for reality from given ones: to produce *respectable selves*. Escaping from given subject-positions always needs alterity because colonial domination operates upon a (denied) epistemic violence that makes of colonial subjects at best opaque, nonsensical characters to be ignored, and at worst evil, idolatrous ones to be punished. Reinserting difference and questioning the Spaniards' treasured self-representations result in no glorification of the conquistadors nor in any sign of native inferiority as in Obeyesekere's (1992/1997) understanding of Western mythmaking. To the contrary, it opens up a space in which the non-Western subject is coherent by being different *and* equal.

A third and last answer for how the conquerors handle alterity is that it was emotionally and politically complex for most of them. At a personal level it would diminish the glory of their enterprise. What is there to be proud of if the enemy does not surrender or fear as a result of glorious action but by mistake? At a public level, the conquerors were agents of a Christian monarch; their duty was to bring the light, fulfilling the virtues of Christian knights, not to use foolish local beliefs—not by chance they choose "Christians" as their primary self-characterization. If one considers the conquerors' aims (Xérez, Mena, Hernando Pizarro, and Sancho wanted to be published in Europe and/or were official accounts, Ruiz de Arce's is a tale of glory destined to his successors, and Trujillo and Pedro Pizarro wrote to back hard anti-Inca politics), it is clear that by erasing murky acts they chose how to be remembered.

Whichever the answer(s) there remains a crucial issue: Were these literary reasons—by which I mean reasons that responded to the constraints of a certain discursive regime—or the result of a way of making sense? The point is doubly key. It determines the consciousness one will endow the conquerors with—they can be expressions of their cultural frame or of smart writers; and it determines how the work of power is conceived— through murky struggles for meaning or through neat, transparent acts. I argue that there is, in fact, no need to choose. If one accepts that reality is plural, it follows that different persons had different ways of making sense of what was going on, including the place they were able to give to Indians and to themselves. A pure literary or culturalist argument misses human diversity and reduces the relationship between practices and representations to one of schism or collapse, respectively. Avoiding the either/or choice detrivializes domination because it recognizes the import that the "realm of partial recognition" (Comaroff and Comaroff 1991:22–30) has for settling the relationships between would-be dominators and would-be dominated, away from simplistic politics. Without this realm, in Pachacámac there was only faith, and in Jauja only daring.[11]

This plurality of partial understandings is visible in the differences among Spanish accounts. Many snapshots appear in Estete, and he alone is able to register that Atahualpa, beyond saying that he planned to kill or to come in peace to the Christians, wanted to know *who* they were, and *where* they were coming from ([1535?] 1918:22). Not by chance, Hernando Pizarro operated through fear in Pachacámac and Jauja, since fear and bulling were his modus operandi even toward fellow conquerors (AGI, P 90a, n.1, r.11, ff. 236–38v). My claim about diversity is linked to its logic consequence: it is not only that reality is made sense of in different ways by different actors, but that different actors have more or less monolithic ways of perceiving how reality is. To some reality is only in one way, the evident one, while others have a more flexible definition of what may or not take place, what may or may not be.

Returning to the situation in Jauja, it is impossible to say what all Christians understood of native rumors and images, but at least some of them saw in them a good tool. Hernando Pizarro's resort to the status of the horses shows that he recognized that something was going on, and explains why torturing Pachacámac's priest was important. We have no sources to tell how the Huancas understood Hernando's request, but the plaza was emptied. The Inca general Calcuchima showed up the next morning, and after some hesitation decided to go with Hernando to Cajamarca, leaving another captain in his place.[12] The group left for Cajamarca on 20 March 1533 with thirty loads of gold and between thirty and forty loads of silver (345–402.5 kg [761 lb–888 lb]). They entered Cajamarca on 25 May, more than five months after their departure.

POLITICS OF GODLINESS AND GOLD IN CUZCO CITY

I move the focus now to Cuzco city, the second scene of treasure collection. On 15 February 1533, forty-five days after Hernando's expedition left for Pachacámac, three Christians left for Cuzco. One returned on 13 May with amazing news, the others a month later with the treasure. There are differences between cases: in Cuzco's we lack firsthand narratives—there are no snapshots—but we can examine the dynamics of the intra-Inca conflict. However, at a structural level the cases resemble each other on a number of accounts. First, the reason for going: It was Atahualpa's idea. He complained that gold was not arriving as quickly as he wanted, "that since he was prisoner the Indians did not do what he ordered" (Mena 1937:91). Atahualpa not only had a godly contest with Pachacámac and had to shape rumors to obtain gold and silver from ethnic groups; he also faced resistance from the Inca elite in Cuzco city. His answer lay, again, in using the New People to overcome local limits. For Pizarro, it was another chance to secure the treasure, know the land, and stake his governorship's legal claim to Cuzco (Xérez 1985:129).

Second, the signifying landscape shows blurred statuses. The three Spaniards (and at least one black slave) were carried the 1,400 km (870 mi) to Cuzco in litters (andas), a privilege the Incas strictly controlled, and were provided with all they needed. This readable display of status plus the circulating rumors shaped first contacts along the way. According to Betanzos, the Spanish chronicler married to an Inca princess, "as they were not known they were taken for gods, and the old men and women of the towns as they saw them . . . they offered them their eyelashes and eyebrows blowing them in the air in their direction, calling them *Tici Viracocha Pachayachi runa yachachic*, which means gods from the ends of the earth makers of the world and the people" ([1551]:II, 25, 1987:281). The act, called *mocha*, expressed recognition of political and religious authority across the Andes.

Third, there was Inca politics invested in taking control of the meaning surrounding the New People, but this time it was shared. Cuzco was by then under control of Quizquiz, another of Atahualpa's generals. After Huáscar's defeat, while Calcuchima moved to Jauja to control the Huancas, Quizquiz punished Huáscar's supporters in Cuzco and began taking control of the administrative imperial machine. Although he was forced to treat the Christians well, for him they were enemies. For the Inca elite that had fought Atahualpa they were, literally, miraculous appearances that had defeated their most hated and powerful enemy. Like Atahualpa, Huáscar's partisans had reasons to make the Christians supernatural. The chroniclers Cieza de León ([c. 1553]:5, 1988:39–40) and Polo Ondegardo ([1561] 1940:154) tell that after Huáscar's final defeat, his supporters made a large sacrifice to Viracocha, asking him for help. When the extraordinary news of Atahualpa's capture arrived in Cuzco, they thought that Viracocha had responded and the Christians were his sons, and named them after him.

Beyond the father-son Christian overtones, it is worth noting that Cieza and Polo do not simply add new data; they give authoritative opinions: both acknowledge that there were many other versions of why the Spaniards received the name Viracochas. Cieza in particular tells that some *orejones* (Inca noblemen) corrected his mistake—that they were called so because Viracocha meant sea foam ("espuma de la mar"). This adds more ways of making sense of the Spaniards, by different people in different parts of the empire, and also shows the active imperial politics behind it. The Incas of Cuzco welcomed the Viracochas according to their take: they performed the mocha and prostrated themselves on the floor; the women of the Sun temple served them; and they were lodged as honorably as possible (Cieza:49, 1996:155). If Huáscar's supporters could now claim the huacas back on their side, fixing their Inca's *atao* failure, on the other end of this culturally informed spectrum Quizquiz ordered Atahualpa's *bulto* and brothers to be hidden, away from the city (Betanzos [1551]:II, 25, 1987:280). Hiding the bulto was a way of preserving Atahualpa's—and his own—authority, since it was in command of the city as much as the general; by hiding the brothers, he likely wanted to prevent a new Inca from allying with the New People.

Fourth, politics of godliness and gold went hand in hand. Quizquiz welcomed the three men and showed them the way to the Sun's house, where they could obtain the gold they were looking for (Mena 1937:93). In the huaca they marveled at two rooms whose walls were covered by gold panels, its quality decreasing as the Sun's shadow increased during the day. Not only had the Sun temple not been touched to collect Atahualpa's ransom, but as in Pachacámac the Christians were again used to do the unthinkable: the three men had to strip down the walls by themselves "because [the Indians] did not want to help them because it was the Sun's house, saying they would all die" (loc. cit.). Quizquiz's pragmatism was also informed by Inca godly politics: the Sun's priests played a key role in Huáscar's crowning and supported him thereafter; as on the coast, allowing the desecration was a way of punishing them and their divine support.[13] In this intricate Inca chess game, whose unaware pieces were the Spanish, Atahualpa showed concern for his father's body. When the Christians entered Huayna Cápac's palace, they saw by the Inca's body a woman with a gold mask blowing away flies and dust, who asked them to leave their shoes out before she would let them in; after entering and observing the body, they took only some gold pieces "because the cacique Atabalipa had begged them not to take them saying that that one was his father" (loc. cit.).

Fifth and last, for the Christians the situation was, again, surreal. They were only three, 1,400 km (870 mi) away from anything familiar, welcomed as awing beings in a city full of treasures. They operated upon the surreal accordingly: they took as much gold as they could carry, but left behind all the silver in a house whose doors they sealed in His Majesty's name; and they also took possession of the city through a notarial act (Xérez 1985:147). These do not have to be seen as empty, formal acts, but as attempts at navigating the surreal, making it real, at turning the absurd and fragile into tangible forms. The seal and the record were means of realizing Pizarro's jurisdiction by having a proof of his marking of the city, and also of making the totally alien place theirs by playing on the limits of the possible. If Hernando resorted to animal magicality in Jauja to gain control, the three Spaniards resorted in Cuzco to legal magicality. We do not know of its reading by Incas, but if we trust the 1543 testimony of Martín Bueno—one of the three—the silver was still there ten months later when the compañía entered Cuzco (AGI, P 90a, n. I, r. II, f. 239v).

It is then clear that different politics, acts, and meanings molded the situation as the Christians moved throughout the north and center of the empire. Local signifying acts tangled with Inca and Spanish forms and goals, creating a mosaiclike, reverberating terrain of contacts and rumors. Meanwhile, after several months of cohabitation, what was the situation back in Cajamarca?

COHABITATION IN CAJAMARCA

Unlike these three first contact cases, Cajamarca was a space in which reality—who was what, and what was possible for him—was acquiring form out of sustained cohabitation. A spatial analysis provides a venue to understand it. Pierre Bourdieu (1978) argues that "habitus," the system of dispositions that provides the frame for everyday action, is embodied, and a result of it social action takes place in structured spaces that reflect class differences (1985, 1998:1–34). It is because behaviors and statuses are spatially readable that certain actions are "out of place" or unthinkable, while others are acceptable. Regarding Cajamarca, the important point is that there was no habitus structuring the cohabitation, because each group embodied its own while they coexisted, and in an unclear milieu. Whom to obey and why? What were the limits for action? What was proper or reasonable and what shocking? Did the different forms of being and of feeling operate across groups? I now turn to these questions, beginning with native high politics.

As the other side of his attempts to produce order *from* Cajamarca to achieve his goals (ransom and imperial politics), Atahualpa was producing order *inside* it. The scenario had a set of permanent actors, plus temporary ones entering and exiting: local lords bringing their shares of the treasure and paying obedience. One can see that even in everyday spaces, super-natural energies—indigenous ones—animated and shaped interactions. Ac-cording to Xérez, curacas were both coming in peace to Pizarro and paying ritual recognition to the Inca. In these acts of double reading, the native side worked as usual: before the Inca the lords "showed him awe, kissing his feet and hands, [and showing hauteur] he welcomed them without looking at them; strange thing is to say Atahualpa's gravity and the great obedience all showed to him" (1985:125). That is, neither the Spaniards' success nor their sheer presence had collapsed the native system of privileges; Atahualpa's divine aura stood in place, which shocked Xérez—and in light of the Chris-tians' repeated resort to the aura of the horses, likely annoyed him as well. The Inca regulated as well some curacas' movements. The lord of Huayllas asked him for permission to visit his land and returned to Cajamarca after the term given him for the visit; he approached the Inca with a present "and arriving in his presence he began to tremble in such a way that he could not stay on his feet" (P. Pizarro [1571] 1968:168).

The currency of his sacred status was spatially reinforced. Regarding Ata-hualpa as a son of the Sun, a semidivine being mediating between humans and deities, anyone entering his space had to carry a load to signal humilia-tion and recognition and also had to be barefoot. This Durkheimian divide between sacred and profane places, a rule at work in Huayna Cápac's palace too, required distancing to work. And yet, these testimonies come from Spaniards, and there is no evidence that they paid attention to Inca prohi-bitions. They were, rather, in close contact; Atahualpa and Pizarro even lodged in the same large building. This surely mixed their auras and marked them off from others. In this context at stake were Atahualpa's sacredness and the Spaniards' ambivalent relations to it, which oscillated between an-noyance and mimesis.

When Atahualpa complained to Pizarro because a Spaniard had stolen a dress, Pizarro ordered Pedro Pizarro to find out and punish the thief. The problem was clear. No man was ever close to the Inca unless by permission; only his sisters surrounded and served him at all times—served in turn by daughters of curacas. This rule expressed hierarchy of a divine kind: an Inca did not wear twice the same cloth, did not spit but on their hands, his hairs were collected, and so on. When Pedro inquired into the robbery, he was shown a house full of different wrapped items where the stolen cloth had been. The number and kind of things stored puzzled him: used cloths, eating utensils, leftovers—in short all that Atahualpa had been in contact with. He was told that it was collected "because what was touched by the lords that were sons of the Sun ought to be burned and turned into ashes and dispersed in the wind" (P. Pizarro [1571] 1968:187).

Atahualpa's politics also involved the Viracochas in more ordinary ways. Huáscar was being taken as a prisoner to Cajamarca, but once the Christians changed the political status quo his life threatened Atahualpa. And yet as Pizarro wanted to meet Huáscar—a potential source of riches—Atahualpa had to test the waters. All accounts tell that he pretended to be sad because his brother had been killed without his orders, testing Pizarro's reaction. Once Atahualpa found out there was no danger, he had Huáscar killed, together with many relatives and captains. Atahualpa also tried to knit Pizarro into his web of kinship ties, a key Inca way of regulating social and political relations (Silverblatt 1988). Some two months after his imprisonment, he ordered one of his sisters, Quispe Sisa, to be brought to Cajamarca and gave her to Pizarro (Hilaquita and Hilaquita [1555] 1976a: 22; AGI, Ec. 1007c, pza. 1, ff. 218, 392v).[14]

But all this was high politics. How were ordinary relations being defined? How were hierarchy and normalcy being settled in everyday arenas? I suggest that the same mechanisms were at work: murky acts and blurring statuses. The chronicles do not talk about it; although the conquistadors spent nine months in Cajamarca, in which they had sex, ate, and consumed native goods, they, like classic movie heroes, are portrayed as doing only heroic things. This portrayal corsets the reader's sight, making history a mystified by-product of military action (they fought, they won, they ruled). To recover what is possible of the evolving perceptions, changing subjectivities and varied motivations for action, I will use a *probanza* resulting from the long-lasting struggle between the Crown and the Pizarros. Unlike chronicles, which edit events to make coherent moral or political claims, this probanza includes an array of persons in partial, momentary attempts to make sense—for themselves and their inquirer—of themselves and of things that were hard to explain once they were out of the context in which they were sensible. In other words, they had to made sense of *local normalcy*.

How did the Christians manage to eat while in Cajamarca? One could think that they were supplied from Inca state deposits—after all, they were in control; but this was not the case. In question 6 of the probanza the royal prosecutor asked if during that time, the land being in peace, Hernando Pizarro allowed Spaniards to commit many cruelties, taking the Indians' food, sheep, gold, and silver without payment (AGI, P 90a, n. 1, r. 11, f. 75). The question interpellated action thousands of kilometers and of Weberian social spheres away from where it happened (at royal court one pays for what one gets), and consequently uses the term Spanish instead of Christians. That nothing was paid for during conquests was a public secret (Taussig 1993:86–89, 1999), but such secrets are more secret closer to the center, so the witnesses had to come up with reasons.

Antonio de Vergara solved it by saying that after sorting the piezas (captives) "the Indians served so willingly . . . that they went by the whole region bringing sheep and all other food to their lords" (AGI, P 90a, n. 1, r. 11, f. 178v). That is, the Indians serving the Spaniards "brought" the food. This makes some sense. They were *yanaconas*, Hispanized Quechua for persons that are no longer members of an ethnic group, have lost any rights to collective resources, and whose position is contingent on their lords' position (Julien 1982; Rowe 1982), now on the Spaniards' position. Yet, how did they "find" the food they "brought"? Alonso Pérez de Vivero saw how footmen and horsemen "went by the land searching for food, and most times sent Indians they had, and they with the Christians' support went and stole the land and brought food" (AGI, P 90a, n. 1, r. 11, f. 203v). That is, the raids were joint ventures in which the emerging border subjects, the New People's yanaconas, were breaking local rules empowered by their relation with the Viracochas—not unlike Atahualpa.

But these responses are, still, descriptions. How was looting *accounted for*? Hernán Beltrán tried to make sense of it: it is true that "Indians," "Christians," and "war people" went by searching for food, taking it wherever they found it—the governor knew it, everyone did—"and if they did not do so they would die of hunger, and that wherever they found gold they took it because that is what they were looking for in the Indies" (AGI, P 90a, n. 1, r. 11, f. 207). The looting parties become clearer now: *everyone knew it*, it was *normal*, and it was a need, otherwise they would die. Ransacking turns into everyone's usual thing, the colonial normal (I will develop this concept in chapter 4), a normal that became so by blending through violence the need for food with the appetite for gold, and the conquerors' and their yanaconas' interests and statuses. After all, plunder as a form works for all these ends.

Yet one does not need to fall into predatory images. Public secrets work upon partial truths; the terrain was not only of plunder. If according to Martín Bueno nearby native peoples soon learned to run away and hide (AGI, P 90a, n. 1, r. 11, f. 237), some curacas wanted to support the New People. Guaman, a Chachapoya lord, told that he provided food and other supplies to the Christians—despite the fact that he was some 135 km (84 mi) away (AGI, P 28, r. 56, f. 1). These supplies, signs of clear political plans, were likely used by high-rank conquerors, but were not by common men and their yanaconas, as we saw.

These were male-only tasks; what happened in cross-gender relations? The prosecutor asked in question 4 if Hernando Pizarro had let the men take Atahualpa's and other main lords' wives, sisters, or daughters as lovers, and in question 5 if such thing was the worst possible affront (AGI, P 90a, n. 1, r. 11, f. 75). In 1543, at the peak of the influence of Bartolomé de Las Casas, the conquerors' sexual behavior was a good object of condemnation; also, rape was one of the few crimes in which royal jurisdiction could act in the first instance regardless of place (Barros 1990:208), and it fit images of conquerors as having an endless sexual appetite. Rape no doubt occurred, but things were more complex. As we saw, some women were given to some Christians as means for political alliance. But since that did not fit Catholic forms, only one witness dared saying that at times curacas gave sisters or daughters to their Spanish lords (AGI, P 90a, n. 1, r. 11, f. 203); all other witnesses closed ranks, saying that taking their women was something native lords could not tolerate and acknowledged that yet it happened. This, paradoxically, turned native political forms unspeakable, but there are still windows into the situation.

To question 4 Hernán Beltrán responded that after dividing the *piezas* "each did as he pleased with his Indians [*yndios*] as people that were in war" (AGI, P 90a, n. 1, r. 11, f. 204v), locating agency in the conquerors alone. Yet after acknowledging that "it is true that those wanting to have sex [*acceso carnal*] with Indian women, that no one would stop them," Pérez de Vivero adds that "this witness saw that the Indians [*yndias e yndios*], even if the Christians regretted it, were coming to their lodges and they could not push them out" (ibid., f. 203).[15] This image of yanaconas flooding the Christians allows one to glimpse the complex subjectivities and motivations at work, questions agencies, and resonates with ordinary people's reaction in other colonial settings—like Hawaiian commoners' behavior toward the British (Sahlins 1981) or Highland Papua New Guineans' behavior toward Australian gold seekers (Connolly and Anderson 1987). After all, the Viracochas were powerful beings and did amazing things, and their yanaconas were part of their sphere; if a close relation with an Inca could be empowering, so it could with one of the New People.

One has then to recognize the complexity of this early scenario—to stop short from giving the Indians solely the emotion of victims, and to avoid taking Christian positivities for truths. It would be easy to simply denounce the conquerors' actions, but that also erases diversity. Not all conquerors were the same. If warlike talk worked for men of low social standing such as Beltrán, educated ones such as the notary Juan Pantiel de Salinas justified that they had Indian women by saying that "in this witness' opinion they had them . . . to sustain themselves because the women made the meals, because for that [service] a *pieza* is worth a lot in that land because otherwise the Spaniards could not sustain themselves nor recover" (AGI, P 90a, n. 1, r. 11, ff. 358–358v), and adds that those women in close contact were probably being converted.[16] This can be read as simple hypocrisy, but that would miss its power: it was a satisfactory explanation for an unacceptable behavior to a notary residing at court. One should not dismiss denial and delusion, or attempts to make a certain reality bearable; after all, some of these men had chosen to leave the conquest of Peru.

LOCAL VIEWS AT THE DELIVERY SITE

At the same time that high politics and ordinary acts were defining the forms of normalcy, the ransom was being collected. While large shipments handled by Inca captains or Spaniards were spectacular, much of the treasure was gathered and taken to Cajamarca by ethnic groups. The collection, perhaps assumed as a simple delivery, has not been an object of analysis. Examining it offers the chance to study local points of view. If we consider the blurred social statuses, the politics surrounding them, and the frightening acts and rumors, approaching Cajamarca could not be simple. Also, if the New People and horses were strange creatures, so was a ransom; what the gold and silver were for and what was going to happen at the delivery point had to be uncertain. Finally, to make things even fuzzier, delivering the loads overlapped with the curacas' acts of recognition in which they paid obedience to the just-victorious and imprisoned Atahualpa.

These issues speak to a current debate. It is presently accepted that many curacas sided with the Spanish, playing a major role in the Incas' defeat. Since Spanish accounts silence it (conquerors completely, later chroniclers mostly), the sources to study are probanzas made by curacas. Correcting mystified images of native inferiority, Espinoza Soriano (e.g., 1967, 1971) has used many of them to present the ethnic groups as active political players. Pease has warned, though, that one has to avoid easy readings of these documents because they are interested versions; ethnic support may have been exaggerated or not occurred at all (1991:135–38). What I want to question is not the actual event of ethnic lords' siding with the Christians but the ordinariness and transparency of the act. I am not concerned with invention or exaggeration—both conscious acts on a clear terrain—but with the retrospective rationalization of uncertain and complex situations and intents.

We have seen acts of double recognition in attempts by curacas and Atahualpa to keep things under control. The lords' point of view is harder to grasp because sources are rare and actions tend to be normalized; it was simpler and there was more to gain in erasing uncertainty and ambiguity than in keeping them. Thus when Don Pedro Marcalloclla made a probanza in 1612 in a trial for the title of curaca of the *guaranga* (1,000 households) of Ychoguánuco (Huamalíes, halfway between Cajamarca and Jauja), he said, simply, that when his uncle Ynpalloclla knew of the presence of the "Spaniards," he went to Cajamarca to give obedience and offer himself to "His Majesty's service" (LL, Puric Huanca, f. 121). The witnesses are less polished. Juan Yupari, more than 100 years old, recalled carrying Ynpalloclla's *tiana* (the seat of a lord) and going with other minor lords (ibid., f. 125). Martín Llaxa, more than ninety years old, adds that Ynpalloclla took "gold, silver and single women to distribute" among the Spaniards (ibid., f. 130v). Gold and silver fit the ransom, and taking women, carrying the tiana, and going with the entire political establishment signal the will to establish a political relation, but with whom? The questions mention no further help to the Spaniards, suggesting Marcalloclla and his relatives were on the Inca side; but *even* if it was with the Inca and the Christians, we know little of how each party imagined the act and how it was understood.

One can tell more of the Huancas. According to Don Jerónimo Guacra Páucar, curaca of Hurin Huanca,[17] gold, silver, yanaconas, and other goods were given in Cajamarca to Pizarro, sealing an alliance. He claimed so in his *memorial* (1558) and probanza (1560) published by Espinoza Soriano (Espinoza Soriano 1971). But accepting the meeting in Cajamarca as crystal clear forces Espinosa Soriano to undermine his political goal: he has to call the Huancas "inexpertos políticos," who thought to free themselves, while Pizarro, lucid mastermind, knew what was happening all along and used the Huancas (Espinoza Soriano 1973:61, 64, 69, 93). This not only does not fit the Huancas; it also ignores the meanings surrounding the act that made it possible when it happened. To move out of the comforting idea that it was a rational deal— in the sense of operating upon the way in which Westerners like to imagine their political action—one has to circumvent interested simplifications.

There are alternative local accounts, from some of the Yauyo witnesses in the 1573 probanza who had been in Jauja in 1533. Since they had no claim to stake, they did not trim their versions. Causation and context change radically. Don García Tocari declared that Atahualpa's messengers told them to collect gold and silver, carry it to Cajamarca, and give it to Spaniards "because they greatly needed that, that their horses did not eat anything else, that they would free him [Atahualpa]" (*Probanza 1573 . . . 1974*:100). Don Hernando Curi Huaranga added that Guacra Páucar gathered a large amount of gold and silver to free Atahualpa following the messengers' orders, transported it with 300 Indians, and gave it to Pizarro the same day that Atahualpa was killed, "and this witness saw it, and scared by Atahualpa's death and afraid that they would kill him Guacra Pacora, that was carrying the said treasure, gave [it] . . . to the marquis [Pizarro]" (ibid.:108). García Tocari was in Bombón when the news of Atahualpa's death reached him and other loaders. The different lords who were there (it was a main crossroad) deliberated and decided that one of them should continue and deliver the load, so that the horses could eat it (loc. cit.); yet others in other points reacted differently and after hearing the news returned afraid of what could happen to them (loc. cit.). (Recall that these flashes of alterity were neither in the royal prosecutor's questions nor in his allegation.)

As I mentioned, chronology is difficult to establish in these testimonies, but it is very unlikely that Guacra Páucar, with a large Inca army settled in his territory, could manage to collect and carry gold other than in response to Atahualpa's messengers.[18] Also, the quotes suggest a far more complexly motivated and emotionally loaded scene than a transparent alliance. Even if one accepts that Atahualpa was alive there was no single order at work, and both recipients inspired awe. Inés Huayllas declared in Guacra Páucar's probanza that she saw him give the "presents" to Francisco Pizarro, who asked him to return to Jauja and have things ready for their trip southward; Guacra Páucar refused, and it was only because Atahualpa ordered him that he finally did it (in Espinoza Soriano 1971:255).

Finally, if the rational aura of the deliveries is questionable, what can be said about their reception? I know of only one testimony, Don Gonzalo Zapayco's. He arrived after the Inca's execution and gave his load in person to Pizarro, who told Don Gonzalo that he had killed Atahualpa because he had killed Huáscar. According to Don Gonzalo, Pizarro also asked him to go back and collect more gold and silver, "because I greatly need them so that these horses I am coming in will eat, because they eat a lot, and that all that Atahualpa and his captains gave me and I took because of his death these horses have eaten" (*Probanza 1573* . . . 1974:79). Seemingly, Pizarro as well resorted to horses to make sense of things. That this was a (erased) discourse addressing native peoples is reinforced by the fact that Pizarro explained his decision to kill Atahualpa in terms of Inca politics—punishing Huáscar's death, which appears as a justification in no early Spanish source.

KILLING AN INCA

Atahualpa was executed on 27 July 1533. Examining the factors accounting for it, one can see how crucial shaping reality was and how deeply entangled the different plots. Plots that, as usual, involved an exchange of energies. The frame was fluid because freeing Atahualpa was militarily absurd and killing him politically risky; and he was paying the "ransom." In the awkward landscape of power in which Christian and Inca values, authorities, and techniques overlapped, any option meant crafting a clearly and convincing visible form. The first factor at work were rumors of "treason." Already when Hernando Pizarro left for Pachacámac, there were rumors in Cajamarca of war people coming to kill the Christians and free Atahualpa. The rumors continued for the entire period—Atahualpa never managed to control them—and eventually peaked. They were powered by different native actors; Estete reports a rumor among Indians (1918:29) which was produced by Huanca yanaconas (Trujillo 1953:141); Xérez tells of an actual denunciation by a curaca of Cajamarca, confirmed by an *orejón*, an uncle of Atahualpa's, some lords, and Indian women (1985:153). Although the conquerors never found an army—they searched for it repeatedly—the constant uncertainty and fear made his death equally sensible.

Second, these political plots mingled with a mundane one. All native-oriented sources tell that Felipillo, one of the interpreters, had or tried to have sex with one of Atahualpa's women. Either way, he was alive only because of the Christians' presence, and needed Atahualpa to be dead. Using his key position, he mistranslated when the Inca and other witnesses were interrogated about the presumed attack, and even forged evidence of Inca armies nearby (Betanzos:II, 26; Murúa 1987: 63; Hilaquita and Hilaquita [1556] 1976b:51).[19] If these examples tell that the production of reality is at least a 500-year-old technique, so is the awareness of it: Felipillo was "objectifying things" (*orgectivándolo*), the chronicler Cieza summarizes ([c. 1553]:54, 1996:175).

Third and last, this reality-crafting of a treacherous prisoner and an imminent attack was entangled with a previous, decisive one: the ransom. Felipillo's interest coincided not only with that of many Indians, but also with that of some Spaniards. Although Diego de Almagro, Pizarro's partner, had arrived with some 150 men in mid-April, because the events in Cajamarca had been shaped as a ransom, only those present at the capture had a right to a share. As long as Atahualpa was alive, Almagro's men would get nothing of the huge loads arriving, while the Inca's death would solve the problem.

These tensions tangled with the one between the compañía and the king. Pedro Riquelme, the royal treasurer, argued that an attack would endanger his majesty's share. However, as always the king needed not his officers; a footman, Pedro Cataño, invited him to the scene. Cataño made a *requerimiento* to Pizarro in the name of the king, asking him to keep Atahualpa alive because much more treasure could be obtained from him. This move was not trivial: Almagro *had* to take the time to ask Cataño, explicitly, to desist from continuing with the requerimiento (AGI, P 90a, n. 1, r. 11, ff. 187–88v), besides likely helping Felipillo produce evidence. Finally, there was Pizarro's attempt to guide actions through a convincing form. I say "execution" and not "murder" because it was the active frame at work. Pizarro *had* to make an inquiry about the attack—no matter how faulty. The label "execution" allowed him to objectify the situation, solving uncertainty at the exact time that some horsemen were still searching for traces of the Inca army.

The so-called execution gives one clues of a last exchange of imaginings and energies. While many yanaconas and Inca enemies of Atahualpa rejoiced because of his death, many of his sisters killed themselves or tried to in order to serve him, as customary (Estete [1535] 1918:29; Mena [1534] 1937:100); others searched for him in his room, since he promised to return if his body was not burned, and only once convinced of his death began the crying recitation of his deeds (Estete [1535?] 1918:29; P. Pizarro [1571] 1965:187); and when he was taken to be executed, all Indians present threw themselves to the floor, trembling like drunk people (P. Pizarro [1571] 1965:186). Pizarro, like his brother Hernando in Jauja, engaged the supernatural energies surrounding him. He had Atahualpa's body burned "a bit" after the strangling (Sancho [1534] 1986:66–68). It seems trivial, but it is not; as Atahualpa had converted at the last moment, the way of executing him was changed from burning to strangling; burning some parts of the body was therefore religiously improper but, I suggest, secured that there would be no return. Also, Pizarro ordered a solemn Mass the next day and had Atahualpa's body buried in the improvised chapel's holy ground. After all, the horses' hunger had not stopped after Huáscar's death.

The fabulous ransom was also uncanny. The foundry was open from 10 May to 6 August 1533. The total amount the compañía gathered was 1,326,539 pesos of gold and 51,610 marcos of silver (Xérez 1985:150), some 6,035 kg (13,307 lb) and 11,740 kg (25,887 lb) respectively. Footmen received on average some 20 kg (44 lb) of gold and 412 kg (908 lb) of silver (5,345 pesos), horsemen the double, captains more. (Horses were also revered by the Spaniards: horsemen received two parts because one was for the horse, and many men gained half parts because they owned half-horses.) By comparison, the annual income of a Spanish marquis was 8,000–40,000 pesos (Domínguez Ortiz 1974:113), and all gold and silver pieces exhibited in the 1497 royal marriage of Juan, son of the Catholic Kings, was worth some 65,000 gold pesos (Oviedo [1547] ILIX, 1, 1959:231).

I will not analyze the details surrounding the foundry; they can be found in Loredo (1958:5–99) and Lockhart (1972). I will just highlight two points related to the project of reality making it anchored. The main point is that the foundry was a magical moment of transformation, key to the early status of the enterprise. By the simple act of taking a piece of gold, giving it to the royal treasurer, paying the tax, and getting it marked, property was irrevocably established and the piece transformed into an exchange commodity.[20] It was a self-referential act working upon others' things and orders, a trick with the king being everyone's magician. This is, I would like to suggest, just another expression of the magical powers kings (Bloch 1993) and states embody (Coronil 1997; Taussig 1997), and it gives a precise, historicized beginning for magical realism (Anderson Imbert 1976:7–25; Carpentier 1974:85–99) as social practice. The other point is that this magic trick was only one among many. As we have seen, shaping Atahualpa's imprisonment as a ransom was a master move that excluded all men coming with Almagro from a share in the treasure—they received a symbolic amount only. This was arbitrary, as Lockhart points out (1972:78); undoing what was a fact, in the next foundry those absent received a share too—otherwise they would have refused to be left behind.

In the crucible of unthinkable acts and images, of silenced reasons and actual behaviors, of earth shakings and failed intents, of looting and founding, reality was turning real. Through a bricolage of these elements, systems of privileges and expected behaviors were being tested, and subjectivities shifting. This ongoing process had no linear path, no moment of truth; the way from contact to domination did not work through replacement or annihilation. The initial political turbulence, however, would only worsen from then on. In this sense, contact was the most stable moment of the transition, because it involved only basic strokes.

CHAPTER 3

Why Betting a Barrel of Preserves Can
Be a Bad Thing to Do   *Civilizing Deeds and Snags*

Those in power often push forward their political agendas by inscribing them into stories that sustain, and are sustained by, particular fields of visibility. Thus, to give a current example, labeling someone a "terrorist" sustains a plot of irrational hate versus love of freedom that legitimizes political initiatives radically different from those arising from labeling the same person as a member of a "resistance." This effect that narratives and fields of visibility have, at once restrictive and productive, played its role as well during the Inca conquest. As we just saw, Christian realism defined a field of intelligibility that dictated the possible plots by which the aftermath of Cajamarca could be narrated such that the conquerors appeared as coherent actors while native peoples resembled irrational, nonsensical beings.

To study the period between November 1533, when the Spaniards and the Incas of Cuzco first encountered one another, and April 1536, when open war between them began, I will stress the importance of another field of visibility sustaining sixteenth-century Spanish accounts: the civilizing discourse. By this I mean not the ideas of manifest destiny, immanent ascendancy, or delivery of the light (understood either as political order, moral customs, or religious knowledge), elements others scholars have pointed out, but the Spanish Crown's capacity to provide "positivities" (Foucault 1969:164–73): objects that appear natural, appear reasonable, and are difficult to question because, to the Western eye, they make sense. Because "discovery," "foundation," "to see the land," or "to pacify," provide logics for action that both objectify elusive dynamics and make the Other dispensable even if present, historical narratives that build on their field of visibility give events a coherence appealing to the Western reader, whose interpretive skills they reconfirm.

Although the civilizing discourse is not absent from accounts of events prior to 1533 (in fact, the main narrative of the events up to Cajamarca, Xérez's *Verdadera relación* [True Account], often uses it), I suggest that it is only in the years 1533 to 1535 that it is recognizable as the key field of visibility at work. It guides the cornerstone account of this period, the 1534 "Relación" of Pero Sancho, Pizarro's secretary after Xérez. All events in its matter-of-fact–looking plot, battles included, are subservient to it, while Christian realism plays a secondary role. Moreover, at the level of the actual practices on the ground, the civilizing discourse proved to be the conquerors' most effective tool for handling the very elusive situations they found themselves in.

The critical exercise I propose is double: to pierce the civilizing discourse's bubbles, and at the same time see the period using them as lenses. The piercing reveals Spanish lies carefully crafted to both please metropolitan audiences and sustain political agendas on the local scene. Scholars will recognize in these lies' structure and elements similarities with key scenes in other colonial scenarios where civilizing narratives abound, such as the 1519 encounter between Hernán Cortés and Moctezuma during the Mexican conquest, or the signing of the 1840 British-Maori treaty of Waitangi. On the other hand, if one sees the period using the civilizing discourse's bubbles as lenses, an alternative plot of the 1533–35 events gains center stage. The plot, silenced in sixteenth-century Spanish accounts and largely absent in current literature, threads a number of instances of snowballing import in which the conquerors resorted to the Crown's civilizing discourse to solve internecine conflicts. Its dénouement changes past and present understandings of the endpoint of the period, the all-out war that began in May 1536 when Inca armies attacked Spanish Cuzco, capital of the Inca empire and heart of the fledging Spanish colony. It tells that the war was as much an achievement of part of the Inca elite, the view of many sixteenth-century and current narratives, as the only way some conquerors found to free themselves from the civilizing snags.

This silenced underplot also suggests alternative ways of thinking how power works at large: as being effective by making itself available. To solve the obstacles they faced in the local scene, the conquerors found it necessary to resort to the reality-making effect of the civilizing discourse. And yet, in the same acts in which they invoked it, they made effective a design that was not of their own making. As a consequence, they ended up tangled in it, giving actual power to an actor that had few means of its own in a locale thousands of kilometers away from court: the Crown. The advance of central power (the Western state-building process) in this colonial setting appears then not necessarily as a forceful imposition, as studies of metropolitan cases suggest (Foucault 1991; Bourdieu 1996, 1998:35–63), but as fragile and effective only when locally invited, dependent largely on making itself available. That is, the efficacy of power lay in its weakness.

The narrative spans from November 1533, when the Christians and the Incas opposed to Atahualpa first encountered one another in Cuzco, and May 1536, when open war began. During much of this time, both parties' main challengers were the remains of Atahualpa's armies and rival Spanish expeditions, which postponed their facing each other. Since the plots are multiple and simultaneous, I will privilege the coherence of certain stories over synchronicity, at times rerunning the same event from different angles—a narrative strategy, but one that reflects also the fleeting, fragmented sense most actors had of what was going on. I begin by presenting a rereading of the period up to the threshold of Manco Inca's war that at once questions the objects provided by the civilizing discourse and testifies to their power; I then move on to present the silenced plot, parallel to all events considered that far, and that explains differently what is most often seen as a heroic Inca war of resistance.

PIERCING THE BUBBLES

After Atahualpa's execution in July 1533, the compañía allied with a fraction of the Inca elite backed in Cuzco. While the city—like most of the empire—was under control of Atahualpa's armies, in Cajamarca Túpac Huallpa, a son of Huayna Cápac (as was Atahualpa), was recognized as new Inca. Soon after, the joint party marched southward along the sierra toward the Inca capital, repeatedly battling on the way Atahualpa's generals Mayta Yupanqui and Quizquiz. On 13 November, at the door of the city the compañía met another son of the last emperor, Manco Inca, who was soon crowned new Inca (Túpac Huallpa had died on the way). Until the end of March 1534, when Pizarro and Manco left toward the city of Jauja (halfway between Cuzco and the coast), the two leaders remained in the Inca capital taking care of several items of urgent business.

The main account of these events is the 1534 "Relación" of Pero Sancho, Pizarro's second secretary. Its influence cannot be overestimated. As Lockhart (1972:276) points out, together with the work of his predecessor, Francisco de Xérez, the account forms the backbone of modern histories of the conquest of Peru. However, despite its thorough, matter-of-fact air, the "Relación" is a carefully crafted text that silences as much as it tells in order to stage Pizarro as a conquering-civilizing master in command of all acts and actors. Thus, for instance, in a plot timed by the urgency of constant military action, the morning after entering Cuzco, Pizarro "made [Manco Inca] lord of the land," "ordered" Inca nobles and *curacas* to obey him, and then "ordered" Manco to gather men and go after Quizquiz; everyone bowed to Pizarro's command ([1534]:11, 12, 1986:112–14).

Sancho's staging, however, encounters one obstacle. Since the expedition against Quizquiz (composed of Captain Hernando de Soto with 50 horsemen, and Manco with 5,000 men) chased the general away from the Cuzco area but did not defeat him, Pizarro hurried Manco Inca to gather more men and go after him right away. Manco did not. Instead, he spent three days fasting, after which he was recognized as new Inca, and then gathered some 10,000–20,000 men, allegedly to go after Quizquiz. But his departure was then postponed for a long while despite Pizarro's renewed urgency because, Sancho explains (13, 1986:115–18), it was raining heavily, rivers were carrying much water, and hanging bridges had been destroyed.

The reference to the weather explains the delay by causes Pizarro could not master, but it does not account for Manco Inca's initial disobedience: to carry out (again) his coronation. To reinstate his boss's control, Sancho narrates a daring scene: Pizarro walked among the several thousand men gathered by Manco in Cuzco's main plaza, gave a speech "as used in these occasions," and then had Sancho read to the main lords present the Requerimiento, the legal text that requested the submission of Indian lords to the Spanish king, and that included the threat of war and enslavement. Dissipating any doubts a reader might eventually have had about the bizarre situation (a handful of men among thousands asking for submission in rather harsh terms), Sancho stresses that an interpreter translated the content of the text and the main lords declared "to have understood it well." "It was then asked them that they considered and called themselves vassals of His Majesty, after which the Governor welcomed them in peace and with the same solemnity used in other occasions; that is, by lifting twice the royal standard" (12, 1986:116).

This civilizing epiphany, although brief, plays a key role in Sancho's account, as it reinstates Pizarro's mastery and casts it in a positive light: by understanding the terms of, and willingly accepting their submission to, the Spanish king, the native lords realized colonial imaginings of manifest superiority ("if explained, they will accept"). Also, this particular kind of epiphany has echoes across time. Scholars of the Mexican conquest will recognize parallels with the Aztec emperor Moctezuma's 1519 speech, as reported by Hernán Cortés, in which the former spontaneously ceded to Charles V the sovereignty. Students of British colonialism will notice the similarities with the signing of the 1840 treaty of Waitangi, through which, according to neo/colonial narratives Maori chiefs voluntarily ceded their sovereignty to Queen Victoria. While the Mexican and New Zealand scenes have created wide controversy,[1] Cuzco's has not. Specialized accounts of the Inca conquest either adopt the scene as is or flatly skip it; the solution depends on the author's political agenda. If, instead, one chooses to interrogate it, the scene reveals that Sancho's tale is at best a lie, and at worst an attempt to veil a fuzzier situation—that acts and their meaning escaped any clear plot. Let me present a counterreading of the events up to that point to foreground this idea.

The reasons Manco Inca did not go a second time after Quizquiz make plain that against Sancho's staging, not all things were in Pizarro's hand. When both parties first met, Manco bore no signs of power; he was alone, escaping Quizquiz's men. Soon after, he entered Cuzco, carried in *andas* and wearing the *mascapaicha*, the Inca royal insignia, as several elder native witnesses declared in a tax trial in the 1580s (ARC, Bet. 5, 1589, ff. 971, 992, 1030v). While Sancho attributes this status shift to Pizarro's prowess, it is clear that only Inca forms, times, and sanctions made it real. After three days of fasting in total isolation outside Cuzco, which marked the time during which a new Inca was only seen by the Sun, Manco emerged to be conse- crated according to royal protocol. He was first installed by the Sun priests, Villac-Umu and Tiçoc, and sworn in by several of his brothers and high- ranking Incas in the Sun house (ibid., ff. 759, 837, 856–856v, 955). Then ethnic lords recognized him in a massive gathering in Cuzco's main plaza, where a large and elaborate political ceremony unfolded for thirty days. After ritu- ally going to the Sun House Manco visited the mummified bodies of former Incas, which were then brought to the plaza with all their paraphernalia and servants. There, from sunrise to sunset, among a lavish consumption of prestige food and drinks, the new Inca ceremonially exchanged gifts and rec- ognition with the imperial elite's political bodies, the *panacas*, while his pre- decessors' deeds were sung—a scene that vividly impressed the conqueror Miguel de Estete ([1535?] 1918:53), and also tangled ordinary people into a web of customary generosity, serving to strengthen his authority (ARC, Bet. 5, 1589, f. 936). In fact, traditional Inca protocol explains also why Manco did command the first expedition against Quizquiz: while he would have had the time to carry out the crowning before it (gathering the 5,000 men took him four days, while he fasted for three), he needed a battle to test his *atao* (war luck) and show his *cámac* (personal potency), proving the adequacy of his condition (Ziólkowski 1996:245). Only once his success made the ad- equacy evident, his coronation took place.

Once an Inca-organized plot is in place, the scene of the Requerimiento can be revisited. The daring act allegedly took place while thousands of men celebrating Manco's coronation crowded Cuzco's main plaza. Did Pizarro ever give a speech and have the text read in such a context? He apparently was there, but the meaning of his acts was different from the one Sancho reported. Don Francisco Guaman Rimache declares in the tax trial that when Manco was sworn in as the new Inca, Pizarro indeed gave a speech, which said, in short, "that Mango Ynga was their lord as Guáscar Inga and his father Guaynacaua had been" (ARC, Bet. 5, 1589, f. 948). What about the alleged reading of the Requerimiento and the main lords' vassalage? Al- though, tellingly, no other account mentions it, clues in the four-item ordinances (*ordenanzas*) Pizarro gave to his governor-lieutenant at the end of March 1534 expose Sancho's as a crafty tale. The ordinances were registered in the Cuzco council log on 26 March and cried after Mass three days later, right after Pizarro gave the first *encomienda* titles (which gave conquerors the right to collect tribute from groups of Indians).[2] The goal of the ordinances was veiling. Item 3 ordered that no one

> dare make the caciques and Indians understand or tell them . . . that they shall not obey the . . . cacique [Manco] Tupa Inga and do what he . . . who is the main lord of all the land and who all serve and obey, shall order, but to their [Spanish] lords because if this . . . they were made understand and told, there would be much outrage among the . . . naturals and the caçique [Manco] Tupa Inga . . . and much damage and de-service to His Majesty could follow. (PML, MA 155, f. 180v; my emphasis)

Item 4 added that if Manco Inca wanted to take out of Cuzco, for any purpose, Indians that had been given in encomienda, no one dared prevent him from doing so.

In other words, not only was there no Spanish command and Pizarro's alleged clarification of the order of things had not occurred, but the prospective governor asked his men not to expose the lie.[3] But *lie* may be a misleading word, as it reinstates what it seems to question: someone's mastery over events, and their certainty; for a lie to be effective reality has to be clear, so that the agentive party can neatly operate upon it, duping the other. If acts, perceptions, and meanings are elusive, a lie loses its potency, and agencies become blurred. Several indices point in that direction.

While the Spaniards had no political command over the Incas, their acts were not ordinary either. The Christians' way to the Inca capital had been no simple affair. Although native logistics and information facilitated it enormously, in their three-month, 1,500 km (932 mi) advance against Atahualpa's generals Mayta Yupangui and Quizquiz, the bulk of the fighting had been largely done by the Spanish vanguard, of some forty horsemen.[4] They not only won the four major battles, but suffered casualties in only one of them, in Vilcaconga, some 40 (25 mi) before Cuzco. One could explain the relentless advance against the most powerful armies known in the Andes that far in plain military terms: the Spanish weaponry was clearly superior. They had steel swords and armor, while the Incas had wooden shields and clubs, did not use long-range weapons such as arrows, and could not stop a cavalry charge, as they did not know horses.[5] This explanation would fit the conquerors' narratives' choice, which let military events carry their alleged self-evident logic, but would hide the ongoing ping-pong of imaginings and potencies, which they silence.

First, there was the issue of the horses' awesome aura. At times believing them to be immortal (Cieza:58 and 61, 1996:194–95, 205), on the way to Cuzco Quizquiz's men repeatedly celebrated in a fetishized manner every horse they killed, turning their tales and manes into battle emblems (Trujillo [1571] 1952:142). And the conquerors played the game too: although erased from their accounts, which stage action in the field of Christian realism, in Vilcaconga, with five of forty men dead and several wounded, the vanguard made the effort of burying overnight the dead horses, as two of its survivors declared in a 1563 *probanza* (AGI, P 107, r. 2, ff. 5, 26). The contest also involved the Christians themselves. The morning after Vilcaconga, the encounter between Manco Inca and Pizarro took place. Unintentionally exposing as a crafty tale Sancho's version of a plain political meeting (11, 1986:110–11), the conqueror Juan de Pancorbo declared in a 1567 probanza that during the meeting Manco told Pizarro that Calcuchima, a general of Atahualpa's carried by the Spaniards as prisoner, had been sending constant advice to Quizquiz on how to best attack them, "and before this witness [Manco brought as proof some messengers and] he heard them say how Calcuchima had sent them to tell Quizquiz *that they were mortal* and dismounted from horses at rough passes," where they should be ambushed (*Información 1567* . . . 1970:163; my emphasis). Once again, the conquerors played the game: overnight the vanguard also buried its human casualties (AGI, P 107, r. 2, ff. 5, 26).

The way in which the Cuzco elite dealt with the Spaniards was not ordinary either. Narratives that present an Inca point of view tell that the Spaniards were welcomed into Cuzco and held in some special status, somehow related to the Inca deity Viracocha. Although they neither elaborate nor explain how the situation evolved,[6] the choice made political sense. It secured Manco's fledging command—it extended his task as mediator with out-of-the-ordinary beings and protected his semidivine status from being debased by quotidian contact with them—and it fit previous sense-making strategies: Atahualpa's labeling of Christians as Viracochas, and prayers by

Huascar's partisans to the deity for help against Atahualpa. The Incas also let the 230 men loot Cuzco with little if any restriction despite its religious and political significance.[7] In turn, the Spaniards showed themselves to be extraordinarily mild mannered: although the city and its valley were home to several hundred huacas that received regular offerings (the so-called *ceque* system),[8] and although mummified bodies were publicly acting in non-Christian ways, the only act of Christian zeal was to designate a building as a church. This act was not only a far cry from Hernando Pizarro's epic deeds in Pachacámac, but it was also of unclear meaning, since the building in question was located inside the compound of a former Inca called Viracocha (Garcilaso [1617] 1960:123a).[9]

I suggest that the indefinite meanings and agencies behind these trades also characterize the larger picture and that attempting to discern how things *really* were is the wrong task. If both parties pretended to believe each other's script and performed accordingly, agencies and lies were illusory and reality hard to pinpoint. Incas and Spaniards were involved in exchanges that as in the case of the Putumayo River studied by Taussig, bound "Indian understandings of white understandings of Indians to white understandings of Indian understandings of whites" (1987:109). Manco knew the conquerors were convinced that the Indians regarded them as some sort of special beings, and acted accordingly; to secure their military help, he satisfied their self-esteem and their (literally speaking) known hunger for gold, labeling them Viracochas and letting them loot. In turn, to protect what they thought Indians thought about them, the conquerors hurriedly buried men and horses and practiced religious tolerance, while Pizarro took pains to veil his colonial project, forbidding anyone from saying what should not be said.

SEEING THROUGH THE BUBBLES

But, if veiling and pretending were both parties' strategy, why did Pizarro give encomienda awards before rushing to Jauja in April 1534? Not only did he risk exposing his plan, but the awards were so small and restricted that the conquerors complained to him right after he gave them (PML, MA 155, f. 179). The answer takes us further away from the certainties of Sancho's narrative into a chain of reality-making attempts set between Cuzco and Jauja. The attempts show that if it is important to pierce the bubbles, diverting from their neat, rewarding objects, it is equally important to recognize that they can be effective tools to define the meaning of things—acts and actors included. As it happened, to install a certain semiotics of power that would make their political projects tangible, both the prospective Inca and the prospective governor mobilized civilizing imaginaries.

At the end of March 1534, Pizarro had been in the city four months. However, at that point, within the course of only one week, he founded Cuzco, registered its *vecinos* (neighbors), appointed its *cabildo* (municipal council), gave encomienda titles, and left for Jauja with 190 of his 230 men. Sancho's "Relación" glosses over the timing of these acts and mentions as a reason for leaving the danger Quizquiz's forces posed to Jauja (15, 1986:123). But this mystifies more than explains; not only had the general been by then defeated by a joint force of Huancas and Spaniards (eighty conquerors had stayed in Jauja instead of advancing to Cuzco), but an expedition of fifty horsemen led by Diego de Almagro and 4,000 men led by a brother of Manco, Paullu Inca, had left after him earlier (Hemming 1993:137–38). Pizarro rushed to make his governorship tangible because his project was endangered by a rival and more powerful conquest company: news had reached Cuzco telling that Pedro de Alvarado, the governor of Guatemala, was headed toward the northern capital of the Inca empire, Quito, and also threatened to send a ship south beyond the legal border of Pizarro's governorship, whose 200 leagues ended well before Cuzco (Cieza:77, 1996:261).[10]

Alvarado's menace and the murky status quo in the city give special meaning to the foundation of Spanish Cuzco. While foundations are often presented as cornerstone moments in which the groundwork of a social building is completed, in this case a foundation signals the moment of highest instability. Its import lay in its capacity to make things looks real, objectifying several "interpretive communities" (Fish 1980). Key to its effectiveness were elements provided by the Crown's civilizing discourse, which Pizarro deployed in at least three ways. The first was by physically occupying the space, setting a material claim to it that incorporated it into the Spanish order of things: once it had a sign of possession, literally carved in stone in its main plaza (RB, II/1960), Cuzco ceased to be a virgin, unmarked space. Second, the mechanics of the act made a net of interdependent interpreters come into being at once: in accordance with the authority that his king's titles conferred him, Pizarro founded the city, registered its vecinos, and appointed its cabildo; next, the cabildo he just created received and recognized him as governor in the name of his majesty (PML, MA 155, ff. 169v–74v). Third, driven by their need to make the uncertainties of the colonial encounter crystallize in recognizable and handy shapes, all parties involved in the act recognized the king as the ordering source of it all and enforced in the local scene the forms he provided.[11]

Cuzco's foundation was but the first move in a number of frenzied, sense-making interventions. Pizarro founded Cuzco once he knew of Alvarado's plan from a messenger sent by his allies in Nicaragua. On his way south the messenger told Benalcázar, Pizarro's governor-lieutenant in San Miguel, about it. Benalcázar saw in it a chance to carve a space for himself in Quito, but he did not go directly after Alvarado; first he convinced the cabildo to request him to go to Quito to "defend and pacify the land." This allowed him to both escape Pizarro's authority and have a case before his king (Cieza, 1996, chap. 57). By the same token, when Alvarado landed north of San Miguel he carefully avoided any contact with the city, a way of denying recognition to Pizarro's authority—a move that Almagro, who flew from Jauja in pursuit of Alvarado and Benalcázar, took care to tell Charles V of in a letter ([1535] 1884:111). Finally, Almagro, aware of Alvarado's superior power, as soon as he managed to locate the latter and before facing him quickly founded Riobamba by Pizarro's proxy, right where he was, and appointed a cabildo. The next day he sent a member of the cabildo and its notary to make Alvarado a *requerimiento*, asking him "not to give room to scandals or oppress the royal justice or to enter the city" (Cieza:75, 1996:256). The effort paid off: on 26 August 1534, Almagro bought Alvarado out for 100,000 pesos.

Meanwhile, Pizarro and Manco Inca arrived in Jauja at the end of April 1534. The scenario there had different plots and readers. On the Inca-Christian front, on 13 May a joint party composed of a brother of Manco Inca with 4,000 warriors, some 600 Huancas, and Hernando de Soto with 50 horsemen and 30 footmen, left northward in pursuit of Quizquiz and returned some twenty days later after having forced the general to retreat toward Quito (Sancho:16, 1986:130, Espinoza Soriano 1971:204, 283).

On the Spanish front, uncertain of what was going on in the north, Pizarro tried to consolidate further his fragile position. In the local scene, he founded Jauja immediately after he arrived there on April 1534.[12] Next, he sent the royal treasurer, Pedro Riquelme, to the coast as proxy to found a city and prevent Alvarado's pilot from claiming possession of the unmarked land. Riquelme founded the city (San Gallán) and named its cabildo as instructed (Cieza:77, 1996:262), only to undo it all when the news of the agreement between Alvarado and Almagro reached Jauja. Pizarro also took care of remote interlocutors. On 25 May, he and the three royal officers of his governorship (who also needed it to exist) sent a letter to the cabildo of Panama. The civilizing frame orders the text. It narrated all they had done in "his majesty's service" and for the "good of the land," mentioned that the news of Alvarado had unsettled it, and invoked the cabildo of San Miguel and the conquerors in general, who were very concerned and had asked the four to solve the problem (F. Pizarro et al. [1534]:1868:134–44).[13] A month and a half later, on 7 July, and still with no news of Alvarado or Almagro, the cabildo of Jauja sent a longer letter to Charles V. Using the same frame as the previous letter, it plainly added that Alvarado had to be sent somewhere else and Pizarro's governorship extended to include Cuzco (1884:114–34).[14] Finally, on 15 July Sancho closed his "Relación" addressed to the king by describing, after much effort and solid civilizing achievements, the uncertainty Alvarado had caused. Although neither text could determine the outcome of facing Alvarado, they carefully prepared the context in which that outcome was going to be rendered meaningful: in a land in which a governor guided by civilizing principles was praised by its vecinos, the former could only be an unsettling intruder.

On the Inca front, Manco tried to consolidate his authority by restating an indigenous semiotics of power. One can only glimpse at it because the Spanish civilizing discourse, besides mystifying the conquerors' action by reducing it to only certain objects, makes native practice and its logic unnecessary. As a self-referential frame, indigenous peoples can only be subjects, never agents; otherwise its pretension of totality would be debunked. In the case in question, the only piece of information Spanish accounts give of Manco Inca in Jauja casts him as a friendly Indian. After the joint force drove Quizquiz away toward Quito, the Inca organized a spectacular *chaco*, a so-called royal hunt. As one of the conquerors present tells, several thousand men encircled the area and began gathering animals by shouting and closing up; when nearing Jauja, Manco invited the Christians "to go hunting," which they accepted (Estete [1535?] 1918:36). This well-known episode is often seen as a moment of celebration and friendship after defeating Atahualpa's general; I suggest that it can be read differently: as Manco's attempt to consolidate his command by using the Inca civilizing discourse.

A chaco was a large public display of men and concerns that staged the Incas as ordering leaders. As explained by the chronicler Garcilaso, son of an Inca princess and a Spanish conqueror, Inca chacos were carried out every four years and involved a complex task of selection and sharing of animals in a given territory aimed at controlling their multiplication. They showed the Inca's sapience as regulator and guarantor of nature's reproduction and also expressed his generosity—commoners received in a ritual manner part of its fruits ([1609]:VI, 6, 1995:339–42). However, the mestizo chronicler's civilizing portrayal veils the fact that a chaco delivered a clear political message: it regularly reminded both ethnic lords, who monopolized the control of *their* nature, and commoners of their place by giving them only their kind of wool and meat—those of the lowest quality.

The chaco was no isolated attempt to stress the validity of traditional Inca political practices. At the end of the century there was a complex suit for a title of curaca (*segunda persona*) of Hurin Huanca, one of the Huanca groups of Jauja. Among the claimants was Don Francisco Páucar Guacra, son of Don Gerónimo Guacra Páucar, whose main asset was that although he was his father's last son, his mother was an Inca woman of royal lineage, Vispa Ocllo. She was given to his father in 1534 by Manco Inca. Saying more than the question asked, Don Hernando Apaiche, at ninety years old, declared in don Francisco's probanza that

> coming Mango Ynga to this province of Xauxa in Yucai, where the main tambo of Hatunxauxa is, being in its plaza, and being there jointly all the caciques from these nearby provinces, the said Mango Ynga, successor in these kingdoms, called . . . don Gerónimo Guacra Páucar, main cacique . . . of this repartimiento, and told him that he was giving him Vispa Ocllo as his wife . . . , and together with her to honor him he gave him a skirt with silver embroidery and a very rich *cumbe* [finest wool] blanket, and . . . don Gerónimo Guacra Páucar took and received and had her as his wife. (LL, Guacra Paucar, f. 79v)

That is, Manco also tried to objectify his fledging authority through a solemn deployment of indigenous political practices. Twisting Louis Althusser's (1971) interpellation schema a bit, in the particular given the context of the 1534 Jauja the weight of the gift-giving act lay as much in defining Guacra Páucar (or any other lord) as an imperial subject as Manco as the locus of power. Giving a woman, a royal shirt, and a cumbe blanket—prestige goods of the highest politics (Murra 1975:145–70)—had a univocal reading; by accepting them, Guacra Páucar was confirming the status of each of the parties and the political relationship between them.

Although no source gives a direct response to how the Spaniards' presence was being assessed, some indices suggest that they were seen as transient. In a 1560 probanza Don Gerónimo Guacra Páucar listed among the services he wanted to be rewarded for, men and goods given to the Spaniards when Jauja city was moved to Lima, at the end of 1534 (in Espinoza Soriano 1971:220). While most witnesses simply agreed, the conqueror Alonso de Mesa clarified that the men were Huanca but the supplies were not; they came from Inca *collcas* (storehouses), filled up by the Huancas (ibid.:244). That is, almost four years after contact, two years after capturing Atahualpa, and with several Spanish cities in place, Inca state deposits received tribute from the so-labeled staunchest Spanish ally.[15] It is likely, though, that Manco Inca framed, again, the Spaniards as service providers: according to the registry of the royal accounts, before the joint force left after Quizquiz on May 1534, he gave Pizarro a "gift" weighing 24,386 pesos (Cook 1968:80–81).

A DÉNOUEMENT

Despite the sense of fait accompli the conquerors' narratives convey, it is clear that in mid-1534 uncertainty still tainted all actions. It may be that the coexistence of parallel plots fueled by each of the parties' internal politics, the sparse scenarios in which actions were taking place, and their fast pace suspended the need for a clarification. These conditions changed in early 1535, when two main political plots ended. On 5 January 1535, in the about-to-be-founded Lima, Pedro de Alvarado was effectively bought out; four days after fulfilling the 100,000-peso payment, Almagro took possession of Guatemala's governor's fleet (AHNP, PA 717). In another arena, as a result of the concurrent actions of Almagro, Alvarado, and Benalcázar in the Quito area, the armies of Atahualpa's generals' Zope-Zopahua, Rumiñahui, and Quizquiz were all but gone.[16] Political action gravitated then toward Cuzco, where the status quo was soon clarified. I will briefly present the dénouement following the narrative plots and fields of visibility prevalent in both sixteenth-century Spanish accounts and current scholarship, to, in turn, question them later on.

On the Spanish front, Almagro, with whom were most of Alvarado's men, received news that he had been awarded a governorship that began where Pizarro's ended, an uncertain place. The key question was to whom Cuzco belonged. In late May 1535, on the verge of open confrontation, both governors sat down in the city to negotiate. On the Inca front, tensions were also running high. Manco had managed to destroy Atahualpa's armies (a wild idea a year before), but the Spaniards' presence undermined his authority, which was questioned by some main Incas. Both sets of conflicts mingled in practice.

Following traditional Inca political ways, Manco Inca eliminated adversaries within the Inca elite. With Almagro's assistance, he had three of his classificatory brothers killed, and openly confronted Pazca, a high-rank Inca who had Pizarro's favor.[17] The Inca also asserted once again his role as guarantor of divine and earthly order by carrying out a majestic Sun festival (Inti-Raymi), a celebration of the past harvest that lasted eight days in a row and in which the Sun was thanked for the past harvest and begged for a rich one to come; it closed with a plowing of the land that opened the plowing season across the empire. Cuzco's main huacas were taken to an esplanade in Cuzco's outskirt and richly displayed according to their hierarchy, showing the divine order; in the same manner the Inca elite displayed itself, with Manco Inca as its head (Molina [c. 1553] 1968:81–83; MacCormack 1991:74–78). Significant unto itself by claiming and reenacting an explicit continuity with the past, in the particular conjuncture the Inti-Raymi worked as a reminder of Inca imperial rule: it publicly stated Manco's role as mediator with the divine realm, his position before the elite, and the elite's before its imperial subjects.

The coexistence of Inca and Spanish authorities, and the mutual veiling and pretending, ended in the following days. On 12 June both governors reached an agreement: Cuzco would remain under Pizarro's authority, and

Almagro would leave southward to the discovery of Chile (Cieza 1996, chap. 84). After the expedition (which included some 500 conquerors and about 10,000 Indians led by Paullu Inca and Villac-Umu, supreme priest of the Sun) left the city at the end of July, Pizarro sent captains to conquer other areas (Hemming 1993:172), at once decompressing internal tensions and encroaching on Inca authority. Finally, he asked Manco Inca for detailed records of the empire's tributary population (Betanzos [1551]:II, 28, 1987:289), and on 1 August 1535 made a general distribution of encomienda awards (Julien 1998a)—this time with no restrictions. The Inca response was quick: in a meeting of high-ranking noblemen it was agreed to begin a general war taking advantage of the Spaniards' dispersal (Betanzos, 1987:289).[18]

ANOTHER REASON FOR STARTING A WAR:
A CIVILIZING SNAG

In past and present narratives of the conquest of the Inca empire, the events reviewed so far set the stage for the war led by Manco Inca, which began in May 1536 when he finally managed to escape Spanish-controlled Cuzco. The war appears thus to be the natural outcome of the Incas' eroded position, an ineludible part of a conquest-resistance struggle. I argue, though, that the events examined and the overall plot of a finally unlashed resistance respond only to the way in which the conquerors wanted the story to be framed—there is nothing natural about them. The success of this restricted field of intelligibility lies, I suggest, in its capacity to provide a straightforward plot that makes sense, convincing regardless of whether Manco is cast as the hero or the villain.

In order to be effective, the conquerors silenced—to the point of making it unrecognizable—another chain of events that ran side by side with everything considered thus far. Once organized in an alternative narrative, these events explain Manco Inca's war differently: it had a chance to start because, after being used as a handy tool, the civilizing discourse haunted the conquerors, and the best way out of that predicament was a war. Key to understanding this underplot is the fact that the order of things was fragile not simply because of the numerous battles and conflicts but because, to paraphrase Marx and Engels's famous dictum (1998:54), "all that [was] solid melt[ed] into air," while air itself proved to be solid. To solve internecine conflicts, the conquerors engaged in the game of making things mean one thing or another. In this game, the forms provided by the Spanish Crown's civilizing discourse proved to be good tools, but by using them the conquerors also gave the weakest player unprecedented efficacy—things ended up meaning what the Crown wanted them to. As a consequence, royal order became tangible in a colonial setting where it had few means of its own to, and ended up catching the conquerors in the dilemma of having to respond to its designs—a civilizing snag.

The entry point into the story is the foundry that ran in Cuzco from 20 May to 1 August 1535. The dominant conquest-and-resistance plot makes it look irrelevant; it plays, in fact, no role in any account of the conquest, past or present. There is, however, something odd about it: only three persons registered metal from 20 May to 30 May; then no one during the entire month of June, and from 3 July to 22 July, 173 men did (*Fundición* . . . [1535] 1868:503–82). Why did the foundry stop for thirty days if so many had metal to register? To answer the question, my narrative has to go back to Cuzco after Manco and Pizarro left for Jauja, toward June 1534, a time when the city was the backstage of the political drama and all energies focused on the space between Jauja and Quito. A conflict began then whose import escalated during 1535 and whose dénouement triggered Manco Inca's war, questioning past and present understandings of it. It is a story no one was fully aware of until it grew out of control—everyone involved was too busy, and later all tried to silence. To make it intelligible, I divide it into four parts.

Part 1: Inviting in the King

When Pizarro departed for Jauja in March 1534 to fence off Alvarado, he took with him 190 of his 230 men. The forty men left were a tiny island in the Inca heartland, days away from Jauja or the coast. For several months no reinforcement came. Although a key piece in Pizarro's claim to the land, for the men in Cuzco they were those *left behind*, being where no one wanted to be, in the murky status quo Pizarro had crafted. Pedro del Barco evokes the atmosphere in his probanza by saying that "some people said 'what were we staying there for?,' that we were staying for the carnage (*carniçería*)" (AGI, L 204, n.12, f. 3). They spent eight months on guard in the main plaza, the horses saddled and the arms ready, Lope Sánchez tells (AGI, L 118, n/f).

Clearly, they saw themselves not as the vanguard of an unstoppable colonial enterprise, but at best as its cul-de-sac.

However during that time, each man tells, "we had" (*ovymos y llegamos*) 35,000–45,000 marcos and 37,000 gold pesos, with which to graciously serve His Majesty (*servicio gracioso*). How did they manage to "have" so much money being in such a frail position, and why did they behave as loving vassals? The answer has two parts. First, both conquerors silence that they obtained the money from a ransom. Probably in June 1534, the forty Christians panicked and, as another of them, Mancio Sierra, tells in his probanza,

> [while] we were guarding and defending there was news of the Incas wanting to kill everyone and to take control of the city, bringing Billaoma as their captain; and so that it would not occur . . . Mansio Sierra and another eleven soldiers dressed like Indians and with their arms, went where . . . Villaoma was, and they found him with many war people . . . and brought him prisoner to . . . Cuzco and handed him in to . . . captain Beltrán de Castro [governor-lieutenant]. (AGI, P 107, r. 2, f. 6)

Then "the Incas tried to rescue him [*lo rescatar*], and gave for his ransom a large amount of gold that was worth more than two hundred thousand pesos" (ibid., f. 7). The picture is familiar: superior as they felt, the Christians were terrified by the prospect of an attack. There is no way to tell if Villac-Umu, appointed "supreme priest of the Sun" after Atahualpa had his predecessor killed, actually intended to attack, but they felt threatened; capturing him was a means to regain control. Once the main Inca was imprisoned the situation was shaped as a ransom, a known figure to all parties.

Yet why in fact did they so generously give such a large amount to their king? What the three conquerors avoid saying is that they did it to resist their governor's authority; being weak, they invited in their king. On 5 July 1534 Joan de Quincoçes, one of Pizarro's men and a councilman in Jauja, appeared before the Cuzco cabildo with a provision from Pizarro, authorizing him to "search for and take away the gold that seemed to be in this city of Cuzco" (PML, MA 155, f. 175v). To reject the attempt, the councilmen reworked the signifying frame. They said that they obeyed the provision because it was their governor's, and yet Quincoçes should do nothing of what he intended, because having the governor in the name of His Majesty populated this . . . city and installed in it cabildo [*justicia e regimiento*] in which His royal service can be trusted, there is no need and it is not convenient that any vecino or councilman from any other town be dealt with in matters related to justice in this city, . . . because their Honors had sworn for the good and common pro

of Cuzco, and not those of Xauxa; should their answer be rejected, they would appeal Pizarro's order before the Council of the Indies (Consejo de Indias) (ibid., f. 176).

The exchange illuminates the fragility of what was supposed to be solid, and the solidity of what was supposed to be fragile. Pizarro's provision interpellated Cuzco's cabildo as his dependant; they were nothing on their own—nor was the city; that is why Quincoçes presented a proxy. Pizarro needed only to *authorize* someone. The cabildo's response acknowledges Pizarro's authority as governor, but rejects the interpellation by shifting the signifying frame: *they* were in charge of the city's well-being, and there was no reason why a councilman from another city should meddle with it. After turning forty conquerors into an abstract body, the council completed the shift in the source for making sense, ordering acts and relations by mentioning that if it was true that Pizarro had installed them as councilmen, he had done it "in the name of His Majesty." And to turn the move operative, they threatened to resort to the ultimate Spanish authority in colonial matters, the Royal and Supreme Council of the Indies.

Pizarro responded to the move by doubling the bid. Quincoçes appeared again before Cuzco council a month later, on 4 August, with a letter from Pizarro ordering its members to comply; otherwise they were condemned to death and loss of all property (PML, MA 155, ff.—176–176v).[19] Now, in addition to having to give or tell Quincoçes of any known gold or silver, they should surrender any Indian they had imprisoned related to obtaining the gold. The cabildo stood its ground. It said it obeyed and was ready to give Quincoçes "the said Villaoma whom, so that he would be well treated, it had had some days in [its] power"; but regarding the metal, they said they were giving it to Quincoçes so that he and two city representatives could give it to His Majesty, for he might need it (ibid., f. 177). The servicio of

30,000 gold pesos and 35,000 silver marcos was formally attested to before a notary on the same day, and 38 of the 40 conquerors signed it (ibid., f. 185).

I pause the story before introducing its second part to point out some implications. One is that in the same way that official accounts (such as Sancho's "Relación") use the civilizing discourse to erase the actual dynamics, replacing them with fantastic objects ("discovery") and motives ("to see the land"), the conquerors "had" gold and wanted to "serve" the king—both unobjectionable acts. In other words, the objects, the techniques invoked to erase actual dynamics, and the effects of closure of the civilizing discourse could be of use to local agents. It was not a Machiavellian expression imposed from above; it was a handy tool. And it was so because, since it was a form produced by the Crown, its use implied putting into play a set of values and codes whose interpellation no Spaniard could dodge; as a closed self-referential discourse, its rules constrained, in theory, anyone.

This colonial example also suggests ways of conceiving the advance of central power different from those coming from metropolitan settings. In some influential works, the process of state building is seen as a top-down imposition of a certain kind of rationality powered by particular institutions (Foucault 1991), or as related to a self-legitimizing concentration of resources that advances encroaching local forms (Bourdieu 1996, 1998:35–63). Such was not the case in this colonial scenario. Thousands of kilometers and Weberian spheres of interaction away from court, the microphysics of power bore none of those characteristics, and yet central power was strengthened. Cornered by Pizarro, the men of Cuzco decided to invite in their king. They had nothing to lose and likely something to win, since a servicio was a gift asking for return. Their actions thus point to the sixteenth century as a crucial moment in the European state-building process, as Foucault and Bourdieu do, but suggest a more complex course, one that stresses the role of the colonial experience in the constitution of the Western self—in this case, in the spread of its enlightenment, civilizing fetish.[20]

Finally, the story exemplifies the risks and paradoxes of the colonial project of reality making. The move on the part of Cuzco's cabildo shows that a governor's creation could turn against him. By the same acts with which Pizarro installed cabildos in order to solidify his governorship, it became more real but less controllable. On the one hand, he ceased to be the only representative of royal order in place; on the other, in the magic act of transformation through which Pizarro named a cabildo and was recognized and legitimized by it, both the cabildo and the governor recognized the king. Once the act was over, a cabildo, although subordinated to his governor, could resort to the ultimate source of its coming into being—the magician.

Part 2: Naming a Ransom "Ransom"

The second part of the story bridges Villac-Umu's treasure that served as ransom and service with the apparent anomaly in the 1535 foundry registry. It consists of a number of small events, all springing from the dispute between Pizarro and the Cuzco council. If the twists in the story make it hard to follow, I beg the reader to bear in mind that it was at least as obscure for those involved in it, a quality that contributed to putting it, eventually, beyond anyone's control.

The ransom episode would become significant because it took place at a liminal moment in the inchoate Spanish colonial order: when Pizarro was ceasing to be the boss of a compañía in order to become a governor. In turn, this transition happened when he was waiting to hear from Almagro, who had the order to fight or buy out Pedro de Alvarado, and since Alvarado was more powerful, either task would require new funds. And yet at that point, there was no longer a compañía and therefore no common bounty (*montón*) Pizarro could use to pay the unexpected expenses. For that reason, at the same time that he sent Quincoçes to Cuzco, Pizarro went to Pachacamac in search of the huaca's treasure,[21] and even tried to renew the compañía, making all metal found during the next year part of a new common bounty (AGI, Ec 496b, f. 755v), although with little luck.

Villac-Umu's ransom thus came timely: out of it 20,000 marcos were coined and given to Alvarado pursuant to the agreement reached with Almagro. The only problem left was to fix the *status* of the metal. Quincoçes arrived in Jauja in mid-August and gave the ransom and servicio to Jerónimo de Aliaga, acting royal accountant. Aliaga weighed it and gave it to the royal overseer (*veedor*), García de Salçedo, for deposit until the royal treasurer, Riquelme, returned from the coast (where he was founding the mock city of San Gallán by Pizarro's proxy). But when Pizarro had the silver coined, it was not registered nor was the royal fifth paid to the king (Berlanga [1535] 1868:244, 247, 281).

The governor and the royal officers worked as a team to hide the fraud. Pizarro tried to make the servicio vanish. He sent Captain Hernando de Soto to Cuzco with verbal instructions to ask the cabildo to void it and turn it into a donation to himself, later to Almagro (Berlanga [1535] 1868:256, 272).[22] In case this plan failed, he ordered Soto—this time in writing—to enforce the ordinances of 26 March, proceeding against those who had violated them (AGI, P 90a, n. 1, r. 5). Item 2 forbade any conqueror from taking from Cuzco's Indians gold, silver, or cloth, or anything else they would not give voluntarily, and set a penalty of 500 gold pesos and confiscation, to be applied "to whom and as I see that is convenient" (PML, MA 155, ff.—180–180v).

While either plan would have solved the problem, the status and destiny of the money remained ambiguous because at that point Pizarro could not alone define the order of things, what was *what*. In Jauja, on 23 May 1534, he had received a *real cédula* (royal decree) dated 8 March 1533 with general directions on how to proceed on the distribution of encomiendas. In it, Charles V ordered Indian *cabeceras* (main towns) to be reserved for him (AGI, L 565,1. 1, f. 118v), which clearly included Cuzco. Pizarro did not enforce the troubling instruction until, as in Cuzco, his creation invoked the civilizing discourse to rebel against him: on 27 June, Jauja's cabildo made Pizarro a requerimiento, asking him—among other things—to lift the restrictions on obtaining gold and silver in Cuzco, because from it many bad consequences to the land followed, and "His Majesty is de-served" (Berlanga [1535] 1868:294). Pizarro's answer was twofold. He invoked the risk of an Indian uprising as a reason to uphold the prohibition; however, reappropriating the civilizing discourse, he said that His Majesty had ordered "the caciques and province heads [*cabeçeras*] to be signaled and given [to him] . . . , and because that city of Cuzco was the head and its lord the principal it has been signaled and given to him"; therefore, all in Cuzco or belonging to Manco or his antecessors was the king's (ibid.:301).

This drastic change in the order of things allowed Pizarro to contain his men's dissatisfaction and to appear as a loving vassal before his king when he most needed to (recall Alvarado's threat), but undermined the frame he intended to apply to Villac-Umu's ransom: either by way of servicio or encomienda, it belonged to Charles V. The fraud had no immediate consequence only because by then the "structural rivalry" (Lockhart 1972:75) between the king's agents and the prospective governor had turned into a partnership. The royal treasurer, Riquelme, helped Pizarro against Alvarado by founding a town on the coast, while Pizarro in exchange stole and destroyed a probanza he had made against Riquelme in 1532 (AGI, P 28, r. 55; Berlanga 1868:246), awarded him a large encomienda (in Lee 1926:7–8), and granted him the right to plunder (*tratar*) gold and silver while on the coast—from which he obtained 1,956 gold pesos (Cook 1968:84). As a result, when Aliaga, the acting accountant who had received the ransom/servicio in Jauja, later urged Riquelme to request it of Pizarro, he refused (Berlanga 1868:252). But the problem was not solved, and in fact it only worsened.

Part 3: "All that [was] solid melt[ed] into air"

The second part of the story suggests that if as Lockhart (1972:65–89) argues, their internecine fights guided the conquerors' acts, the fights involved not only the distribution of political power and monetary rewards, but the capacity to define order at a more fundamental level—what was *what*. In this game of naming things and giving them meaning, a very effective player turned out to be the weakest one on the ground: the Crown. In the same acts that the Cuzco conquerors fenced off Pizarro, and Pizarro fenced off the Jauja cabildo, a door was opened for a radical challenge to the order of things as conquerors and governor understood it. The challenge both explains Cuzco's 1535 foundry's odd pace and forces a change in past and present understanding of the reasons triggering Manco Inca's war.

As mentioned earlier on, the foundry registered only three entries on 20–30 May, then stopped completely for the entire month of June, and on 3–22 July registered 173 entries (*Fundición* . . . [1535] 1868:503–82). What explains the strange pace is that at the end of May, Jerónimo de Aliaga, by then acting accountant general, put the problem on the table: he publicly said that he was planning to make a requerimiento to Pizarro, asking for all gold and silver (ransom/servicio *and* foundry) to be given to the king, as it had been declared it should be (Berlanga 1868:250–52). While it is not clear if Aliaga actually did as he declared, the threat his announcement posed was real enough to prevent all conquerors from taking metal to the foundry.

In other words, the radical shift in the order of things that meant actually making the city, the Incas, and all their treasures the king's was possible.

The fact that everyone's gold and silver were up in the air gave way to two opposing responses. The first one was to take advantage of it. The treasurer, the veedor, and the accountant-lieutenant visited conquerors, offering them to exchange their uncertain possessions for clean metal—of course with a discount. This was a skillful use of their position: because they were the keepers of the royal mark, they could deploy the magical power of transformation held by the king, turning things fragile in their "thingness" into solid (and secure) ones. In other words, the idea that objects are unstable in their "objectness" (Thomas 1991) was mastered—at least—four centuries ago. Several men accepted the deal (Berlanga 1868:260, 262, 266, 273, 277, 290) and later complained about their loss, but never so loudly as to put the entire "public secret" (Taussig 1999)—the fact that they had no right to it—at risk.

The second response was to undo the twist in sobriety that "Cuzco belongs to the king" meant, a threefold job. First, Pizarro tried to protect the frail positivities in place by disqualifying Aliaga: he accused him of "searching for new things" and of "sowing discord" (Berlanga 1868:250–52)—very much like someone refusing to join a war can be accused of creating dissent and labeled antipatriotic. Second, he commissioned the issue to a licentiate named Calderón, and after he cunningly declared the foundry's metal to be the conquerors' (Berlanga [1536] 1921:44),[23] Diego de Mercado replaced Aliaga as the foundry's accountant on 30 May (Fundición . . . [1535] 1868). Finally, on 20 June Pizarro sent a cryptic letter to Juan Vázquez de Molina, nephew of the all-powerful secretary of state of Charles V, Francisco de los Cobos, and later secretary himself (Lynch 1998), mentioning more than once a servicio that is never clearly stated, hoping that Molina would take care of his business in Spain as he took care of Molina's in Peru (AGI, P 192, n. 1, r. 10).

The story could have ended there; however, right when Pizarro seemed to have recovered the capacity to define what things meant, new events challenged it: on 20 August 1535, Fray Tomás de Berlanga, bishop of Panama, commissioned by Charles V to inquire on several matters, began his work in Lima. Although Pizarro did not allow him to go inland, alleging the danger of an Indian uprising, the bishop managed to question fifteen witnesses in Lima and two more in Panama. He also obtained copies of Jauja cabildo's requerimiento to Pizarro of 27 June 1534 and of Pizarro's response. The result of his inquiry and his report are the documents I have referred to as "Berlanga [1535] 1868" and "Berlanga [1536] 1921." Without him, part 2 of the story would have been well buried, part 3 unintelligible (a simple anomaly in the foundry's record), and part 4 unthinkable.

Part 4: Why Betting a Barrel of Preserves Is a Wrong Thing to Do

In August 1535 the conquerors were dispersed throughout the empire, and Manco Inca's faction getting ready to wage a war. The war began eight months later, in May 1536, when the Inca finally managed to leave Cuzco and escape the Spaniards' control by tricking them—or so conquerors' accounts tell and sixteenth-century chroniclers repeat. Guided by the overall narrative of a war of resistance with a movielike start, current narratives of the Inca conquest cast the war as Manco's goal and achievement. I suggest, however, that if the war was a result of the dissatisfaction of the Inca's followers with the way things had turned, it was also some conquerors' attempt to solve what was, by then, a snowballing problem. In a last instance, the problem was that they had fallen prey to the civilizing discourse they had strategically used more than once—a civilizing snag. The prospect of a war fit, then, although for different reasons, both parties' goals. There was no trick.

From August 1535 to the actual beginning of the war, there was a steady encroachment of Inca authority by the Spanish. After Pizarro left Cuzco for the coast, his brothers Juan and Gonzalo subordinated Manco to their control. Twice he tried to leave the city; twice they captured and brought him back.[24] From the attempts, and the fact that some Spaniards were killed when visiting their encomiendas, followed spiraling degradations of Manco's status. The sequence included throwing the Inca into jail, taking some of his women by force, even raping some, humiliating him with such actions as burning his eyebrows or urinating on him, and making requests for gold. Iteration and uncertainty reigned during the entire period.[25]

The Inca remained in this humiliating condition until Hernando Pizarro arrived in Cuzco in February 1536. The oldest Pizarro brother had left for

Spain before Atahualpa's death to deliver an advance on the royal fifth and take care of several items of family business at court (among them obtaining seventy additional leagues for Pizarro's governorship). Upon his return Pizarro sent him to replace Juan as governor-lieutenant of Cuzco. Hernando freed Manco and played good cop, while repeatedly asking him for gold and silver in exchange for protection against other Christians. This went on until mid-April, when Villac-Umu, the Sun's supreme priest, returned to the city after having deserted Diego de Almagro's expedition to Chile. Together both Incas played their often-cited trick on Hernando: after having gained his trust, Manco obtained Hernando's permission to leave the city and carry out some celebrations in the nearby Yucay valley, promising to bring at his return the solid-gold statue of Manco's father, Huayna Cápac. They left the city on 18 April and returned in early May, only to wage the fiercest war.

Why did Hernando make such a big "mistake"? The implicit or explicit answer that conquerors' accounts and sixteenth-century chroniclers give is that it was a perfect trick: Manco hid well his intentions, and Hernando's greed took care of the rest. However, Hernando was not tricked. As many Peru veterans—friends and enemies of Hernando alike—declared in a trial in 1543, it was "public and notorious" in Cuzco that Manco and Villac-Umu were leaving to rise up. Several conquerors told Hernando about it at length, some of them urged to do so by high-ranking Inca women afraid of Manco's ire if he managed to escape.[26] Moreover, the Cuzco cabildo made Hernando a requerimiento, before a notary, asking him to imprison both Incas at once (AGI, P 90a, n. 1, r. 11, e.g., ff. 139v, 166v, 192).

Why, then, did Hernando let Manco go? I argue that it was a deliberate move driven by risky political calculation. The war had a chance to begin because, as a consequence of the spiraling underplot, Francisco Pizarro was as much in trouble as Manco was. Hernando arrived in Lima from Spain when Berlanga, Charles V's envoy, had done most of his inquiry and begun questioning Pizarro and the royal officers at length about all he had found contrary to the king's interests. Among others, Berlanga touched on two sensitive points: he asked for the 1534 servicio to be given to the king, and for Cuzco and Manco Inca to be the king's encomienda ([1535] 1868:311–13). The first request meant that Pizarro had to pay back 100,000 to 200,000 pesos.[27] This was no small amount: 8,000 to 40,000 was the annual income of a marquis or duke (Domínguez Ortiz 1974:113), and 68,758 was Pizarro's share of Atahualpa's ransom (Arocena:1986:238). Moreover, the request implicitly accused Pizarro and some other main conquerors of fraud. To *encomendar* Cuzco and Manco Inca in the king's encomienda had a large monetary impact: as Berlanga told Charles V when reporting the findings of his inquiry, all past Incas' treasures were the king's because they had not been obtained through conquest, Pizarro had declared them to be so in his response to the Jauja cabildo's requerimiento, and he had also given an ordenanza saying that all gold and silver found in Cuzco was going to be seized; therefore, all metal registered in the 1535 foundry had to be returned to the king ([1536] 1921:43–44).

When questioned, Pizarro rejected Berlanga's accusations with evasive responses and lies, claiming to be the king's advocate. Regarding Cuzco and Manco Inca, he told Berlanga he had informed the king about it, and there was nothing to do by then. He made no reference to the servicio, but five days later sent a letter to Charles V saying that it had never been made—it was all a misunderstanding, but he would give it to him as his own—which he never did (AGI, L 566, ff. 324–25). At the same time, Hernando sent the king his own letter, which cast doubt on Berlanga's report not by denying the accusations, but by replacing the legal frame at court with local needs; he said it was "too early" to send someone requesting the kind of things Berlanga did (H. Pizarro [1535] 1959).

This points to the political problem underlying the monetary one: the civilizing discourse, after having legitimated Pizarro's acts of magical transformation and served the conquerors' moments of resistance, was coming back to haunt them. Berlanga clearly tried to impose the king's order of things over local, colonial dynamics. The ultimate claim was that what was property of past lords or public property belonged now to the king, since he was the inheritor of the native lords' sovereignty (Pietschmann 1989).[28] Although such was the legal frame of all Spanish conquests, enforcing it meant advancing over the ambiguous character of the conquest compañías, overturning in practice the status quo that had ruled Atahualpa's ransom.[29] The shift meant not simply an economic loss to the conquerors; it also countered their ambition of being absolute lords of vassals in the medieval way, rooted in their self-image as men in service of God and His

Majesty who deserved rewards—rather than viewing themselves as soldiers (Lockhart 1972:17–22).

The bishop's report sprung concrete action in Spain. Soon after it reached the court, the royal prosecutor accused its main protagonists of having committed a major fraud against the royal treasury (AGI, P 90a, n. 1, r. 13), and in July 1536 the Crown commissioned Bishop Valverde (then in Spain) to act on the issue, punishing whomever he had to, and to recover the servicio and the total of Cuzco's 1535 foundry (Comisión [1536] 1943; Instrucción 1536 [1943b]). In this light, letting Manco Inca rebel was the reasonable thing to do: it would sever the link between the king and Cuzco's riches, redraw the signifying landscape, and bury, literally, the move under a pile of ashes. Hernando wanted to take Manco out of the equation—a move Berlanga foresaw and tried to thwart[30]—because the Inca embodied the native lord that the king needed to both make cabecera mean something (there had to be an Inca for Cuzco to be an encomienda) and make the property of all past lords be his. The war also changed the signifying landscape: once the conflict was over, the Crown's claims over Cuzco and Manco, and therefore over the total production of the 1535 foundry, would seem far-fetched and unimaginable.[31] Finally, the war hid the reasons behind Hernando's move from sight; the "war matter" rhetoric and the narrative of a handful of men's survival against masses of rebel Indians mystified all events. That is why, when in April 1536, right after Manco left Cuzco for good, Juan Bautista Ordóñez jokingly told Hernando that he "bet him a barrel of preserves that the . . . Inca would not return but to wage war," Hernando responded sharply (AGI, P 90a, n. 1, r. 11, f. 167v); he found nothing funny in someone inadvertently making his move visible.

CHAPTER 4

Illusions of Mastery   *Manco Inca's War and the Colonial Normal*

This chapter analyzes the war led by Manco Inca between May 1536, when he attacked Cuzco, and April 1537, when the return of the expedition led by Diego de Almagro and Paullu Inca from Chile stopped it. During this time, Cuzco was besieged by an enormous army, Lima attacked, and all Spaniards in between were killed. The war, the most serious challenge the Spaniards faced, plays a prominent role in all narratives of the Inca conquest and the foundation of the Peruvian nation. By and large, current scholars privilege an image in which the two sides battle each other in endless heroic encounters. The (quite repetitive) acts are transparent to the reader, and so are the dynamics energizing them: they reflect the self-evident logic of military action. In what follows I suggest that this is an illusion which was well crafted in the sixteenth century, a result of the way in which the conquerors *chose* to portray the war in their public narratives: a heroic struggle in which, God's grace aside, their military savvy and courage allowed them to overcome their overwhelming numerical inferiority. They are, in other words, celebrations of Spanish mastery, "against all odds."[1] This framing matters doubly. In terms of sixteenth-century dynamics, it sets the stage for an understanding of the ensuing colonial rule as a matter of exercising this (alleged) superiority. In terms of current accounts, regardless of whether they celebrate Manco Inca's attempt or not, the forms used to narrate the war end up reinscribing still-current myths of Western superiority. In both contexts, the Other appears as either stubbornly resisting or constantly trying to catch up with the modern man (gender intended), unable to compete as different but equal.

The goal of the present chapter is to revisit Manco Inca's war in an attempt to foster new visibilities. To that end, I will draw on different concepts. If conquest, a transition from contact to domination, is a period of active production of reality, this production is asymmetrical. If a power formation is conceived as a continuum encompassing domination and hegemony, the former related to the direct exercise of control enforced by a visible apparatus in recognizable acts, and the latter expressing the capacity to define the everyday order of things beyond the actual exercise of violence (Gramsci 1992; Williams 1977; J. and J. Comaroff 1991), then Incas and Spaniards were at opposing ends. The latter's actions were, even in an unsettled milieu, an open disruption of the order of things, while the opposite is true of Manco's. For him, the war was as much about annihilating his adversaries as about confirming that Inca hegemony, the unspoken constellation upon which order had run until four years before, was valid "as usual." The production of order, and the distinction between revalidating it and creating it, played a central role during the war.

As all parties were involved in a struggle over meaning, in order to be effective their successive attempts at gaining mastery resulted in a process of observation and copying. Far from a clear-cut military scenario, the siege resembled a mosaic-like signifying terrain in which mimesis (Taussig 1993) became a primary form of interaction. The chain of mimetic acts reveals, in turn, that Incas and Spaniards had more in common than sixteenth-century narratives (and most current ones) are willing to concede. The threat this similarity posed to the conquerors' pretension of dominance was double: distinctiveness became elusive, as did asserting mastery, since acts of copying could always unfold. Yet native peoples' acts during the war did not necessarily revolve around the Spaniards as the latter suggest in their accounts; rather, the former often followed their own agendas, which dispersed the political center of gravity. It is these challenges to the Spaniards' will toward dominance that, I suggest, required order to be defined not in the battle-field but in everyday interactions—and in a particularly violent manner at that. In seemingly irrelevant quotidian arenas, such as travel and lodging, the conquerors' hegemonic *pulsations* worked as "structures of feeling" (Williams 1977), actively lived ways of being and thinking that challenged Manco's hegemonic project because they prefigured an alternative order, a colonial normal.

HEGEMONY AND MENTAL DEFICIENCY

To narrate Cuzco's siege, past and present accounts must attend to its most striking feature, the asymmetries between parties. In Cuzco there were initially some 180 Spaniards and 100 horses, and some 1,000 Indi-ans fighting Manco, while the besiegers numbered between 100,000 and 400,000. By the end of the siege some twenty Spaniards and thirty horses had died, while on Manco's side losses were in the tens of thousands.[2] Specialized military studies of the siege converge in stressing the supe-riority of Spanish weaponry and tactics. The Incas had neither effec-tive defensive weapons against swords and lances (firearms apparently played a minor role), nor offensive ones against steel armors and helmets (Guilmartin 1991). In addition, they were unable to stop cavalry charges (Himmerich y Valencia 1998), which proved lethal.[3] Manco's men tried to counter this imbalance in numerous ways, but never managed to funda-mentally challenge it.

Sixteenth-century Spanish accounts address this disproportion of re-sources by organizing the narrative as a (long) succession of massive attacks and heroic resistance lead by cavalry charges, a plot some epic encoun-ters and daring Spanish counterattacks punctuate. Current scholars (e.g., Hemming 1993:184–217; Guillén Guillén 1979:51–80, 1994:81–106; Del Busto Duthurburu 1994:223–60, 2000:2:269–91) largely adopt this narrative schema. The result is a clear image built with military shapes: the Incas fought bravely; the Spaniards, thanks to their advantage, managed to survive. As a consequence of all actors attaching the same meaning to events, cultural differences vanish from sight or are mentioned only as a footnote. The logic guiding all acts is a self-evident (Western) military one. Equally important, the conquerors, despite their desperate situation, appear to have mastery over all events; their superiority (manifest in their survival against all odds) in turn assures their distinctiveness.

This image fits both current political agendas and the goals and silences of Spanish sixteenth-century accounts, although for different reasons. While current scholars often try to place native peoples and Spaniards on the same footing, dismissing any sign of inferiority, the men of Cuzco, concerned with the way in which they were seen back home, privileged stories that cast themselves in the light of heroic, self-confident struggle, and silenced the uncertainty and murkiness of the war. Yet, neither were the Christians self-confident nor was their superiority—and therefore distinctiveness— manifest, not even to themselves.

A good access point to begin undoing these silences, promoting other visibilities, is to revise common understandings of how the war was waged. In particular, one can question superficial readings of the fact that Manco's attacks were tightly coordinated with the lunar calendar. While conquerors who fought the siege often refer to the lunar cycle in their *probanzas*, in their accounts they silence it. Of all their narrations for public consumption it is only mentioned in one, the anonymous *Relación del sitio* (RS [c. 1539] 1879), and in a rather casual manner; the plot focuses on the massive attacks and the valiant cavalry charges. Current scholars usually do not mention it either; if they do, they cast it either as a curiosity or as a lamentable handicap, as the men of Cuzco were ready to defend themselves every full moon, and to launch counterattacks and expeditions to obtain food during every new moon. Even rich studies of the ideological underpinnings of Inca warfare consider it a "surprising conservatism" with "negative" effects (Ziólkowski 1985:161, 1996:230).

There is clearly a political concern: the lunar rhythm is seen as something demeaning to mention. I argue, however, that the strict observance of the lunar cycle was only logical. Manco Inca's war was not simply an attempt to annihilate the Spaniards and recover his command; it also was an attempt to revalidate the principles upon which that command rested. His tactics expressed not conservatism but politics. Among Andean polities warfare was a contest with supernatural dimensions. Each of the contenders' *huacas*, their power, and their leaders' power were active elements in the battlefield. As far as the Moon is concerned, it was a central deity of the Inca (Silverblatt

1987), likely considered a container and expression of the energy available to him (Ziólkowski 1996:72–80), and somehow related to the Sun, the Inca's father. It follows that because of his role as mediator and semidivine character, for an Inca the full moon was the moment when his *camac* was paramount and thus the right time for an attack. Moreover, Manco's refusal to alter the lunar rhythm of attacks throughout signals not the incapacity to innovate but a clear political decision: changing it would have meant acknowledging that the Inca mode of power manifested in the synchronization of military deeds and celestial phenomena proved noneffective.

The war was not over self-evident facts—if there are ever such things— but clearly about their meaning. The siege can be read then as an effective cultural dispute over the definition of reality, and more precisely, over the definition of the valid cultural parameters that sustained each of the contending reality projects. It was not only about *what*, but equally about *how*. This struggle over meaning can be studied in a number of instances. The initial attack took place on 3–6 May. The night of 5 May had a full moon, and was the most propitious time for military action.[4] On 6 May Manco's men commanded by Villac-Umu, supreme priest of the Sun, won Sacsahuaman, the military-religious complex dominating the city, and launched a massive attack. Soon the Christians gathered in a few buildings around the main plaza, the only flat, open space they could defend, while the rest of the city was on fire. The offensive was overwhelming. As one of the besieged evoked, "It was so much the stone from the slings entering the doorways that it did not seem but very thick hail when the sky hails much, and so much the screaming of the Indians that there was no man that felt no great fear" (*Sucesos ocurridos* [so] [1543?] 1884:381). To counter the horses, Manco's men walked on top of the walls, built barricades that blocked the streets, and inundated fields. Fighting took place relentlessly, day after day, house by house.

The next major event was the fall of Sacsahuaman back into Spanish hands. The fall, which has been fairly labeled as a turning point in the war, can also be read as a key point of the overall struggle to prove which the right order was. All Spanish eyewitness accounts, including the *Relación*, the cornerstone of any current narrative of the siege, attribute the idea to Hernando Pizarro—and so do many scholars. Fighting with no sign of progress, many Christians began arguing that the best option was to abandon Cuzco and escape toward the coast. In a crucial meeting, Hernando proudly refused to leave the city his brother had won, and, in an example of Western military genius, argued that without winning Sacsahuaman they could not resist much longer—or so the story goes. The story does not explain, however, why the attack was launched *when it was*, neither before nor after. It began around 15 May and the fortress fell on either 18 or 19 May. Tellingly, the moon had been fading and 19 May was the new moon, the most unpropitious time for Manco Inca.

One can guess that local knowledge and agency had a key role in making the Christians do the right thing at the right time. As it happens, Pazca, a high-ranking Inca and general of the native forces inside the city, took part in the meeting (Murúa [1590–1611]:66, 1987:234), which the conquerors' accounts silence. The faction of the Inca elite and the other native groups in Cuzco not only provided intelligence; they made some crucial interventions too. When Captain Juan Pizarro was seriously injured during the attack on Sacsahuaman (he died soon after), his men retreated, loosing most of what they had won thus far. Hernando Pizarro returned the next day with reinforcements and led a new attack (that would finally prove successful), but that night the crucial siege over the fortress—stopping Inca reinforcements, food, and military supplies—was sustained to a large degree by Pazca's men (ibid.: 67, 1987:236).[5]

What were the consequences of Sacsahuaman's fall? From a conventional military point of view, it led to increased Spanish control over the city and deeper counterattacks that forced Manco's men to retreat somewhat. Manco himself moved back to the stronghold of Ollantaytambo, some 30 km (19 mi) from Cuzco. Also, the final balance of casualties was appalling: 2 Christians versus 1,500–2,000 Indians in the main tower alone (RS 1879:33; SO [1543] 1884:386). And yet, the fall meant neither an immediate decrease in the intensity of Manco's attacks, nor a change in their overall pattern: every full moon there were renewed attempts to take Cuzco, followed by new moon pauses and ritual offerings (RS [c. 1539] 1879:36, 92).[6] This sustained correspondence is no conservatism but rather a move in the struggle to revalidate the basis of Inca hegemony; it meant doubling the bid vis-à-vis the fall's possible readings.

First, all native actors could read the failure as evidence of the limited value of observing Inca restrictions related to the *hanan pacha*, or upper world; Manco's men were defeated even if led by the Sun's supreme priest—that is, failure would be an ideological and religious setback. Second, they could read it as an index of Manco's inferiority, because while he *had to* observe the restrictions, others did not—that is, a personal limitation. Third, many could claim credit from it. The Incas in the city could challenge Manco's command or the particular foundation of his political project or both, and all the other ethnic groups could claim their own huacas' victory over those of the Incas. The Christians, finally, not only reasserted their military might, but they also made evident that they were immune to the rules and restrictions guiding Inca warfare, and validated once again their huaca's power.

There are other indices of Manco's struggle over meanings beyond the lunar calendar, which also call into question modern interpretations of the war. When pondering the causes for the initial failure, Hemming, among others, mentions Manco's delay in launching the initial attack, and his lack of personal engagement in combat (1993:196–97). Although both explanations (losing the surprise factor and lack of command) make Western sense, they run counter to Inca warfare rules. The initial "delay" matches the overall political claim: to stress the Inca's connection with the hanan pacha by attacking when it was propitious. The fact that Manco did not command the attack in person expresses rank of a divine kind. An Inca's personal engagement in battle was reserved as an exceptional, final measure (see chapter 1). It implied an open, definitive test of his *atao*, or warlike luck, the expression of his huacas' support and of his supernatural powers. As the war had just begun, it would simply not have been proper, particularly for someone reclaiming Inca protocol. One can also guess that Manco knew the risk posed by the Spaniards' cavalry, and knew their strategy of going for the chief when in an inferior position.

Finally, the fact that *how* the war was fought was crucial to the Inca elite can be seen in the account written by an Inca, Manco Inca's son, Tito Cussi Yupangui. He narrates a dialogue between Manco and his generals after their retreat to Ollantaytambo. When criticizing the generals for failing despite their overwhelming numerical superiority, Manco mentions as partial palliatives that he had not been there in person, and that the Spaniards received help from their huaca, Viracocha. No mention is made of weaponry. The generals' response follows the same lines and, among other reasons, criticizes his absence, saying that he would have been a *definitive means* to "finish them" ([1570] 1985:23–24). That the war was to a large extent a struggle to prove the validity of Inca order is explicit in Manco's commands to his people before abandoning the Cuzco area, at the end of the siege. Among other instructions was that they should pretend to adore the Christians' huaca—"some painted pieces of cloth [paper sheets], which they say is Viracochan" (ibid.:26)—and remain loyal to what they know, "because as you see the *vilcas* talk to us, and the Sun and the Moon we see with our eyes, while what they say we do not see well" (*vilcas* = *willkakuna* = "sacred things or beings").[7]

In summary, reintroducing alternative epistemologies turns the implicit mental deficiency underlying the "lamentable conservatism" into a deliberate political bid, undoing long-drafted taxonomies of human capacity; however, it also reifies the neat difference and distance between Indians and conquerors the latter so wanted to convey. Such was not the case. Despite the privileged role that the conquerors give in their narrations to their allegedly effective cavalry charges, they not only took notice of the lunar cycle to better fight Manco Inca, but also found *necessary* to engage in their own struggle over meaning. Their attempt was, in turn, returned by Manco Inca. This exchange opens the door for mimesis as a principle ordering acts, which in turn blurs stark differences between colonizers and colonized. Both elements—blurring and need—question the main illusions the Spanish narratives of the siege tried to convey: distinctiveness and mastery.

DOMINANCE, MEANING AND MIMESIS

In Cuzco, by mid-June 1536 the war had turned into a siege with a regular rhythm. Manco's armies, even after their partial retreat, controlled the area beyond the city proper and attacked regularly. As all accounts report, the Christians stayed inside the urban perimeter, with the exception of two prompt counterattacks and one foray out to gather badly needed food in the nearby Jaquijahuana valley. But not quite; although no conqueror account or chronicle narrates it, on 22 June 1536 they carried out a daring attack on a compound, on a hilltop 11 km (7 mi) south-southwest of Cuzco, Huanacaure. The mission was carefully executed. The party rode late at night avoiding major roads, and once at the bottom of the hill approached the enemy with caution, crawling silently across harsh terrain. They attacked the compound by surprise at sunrise; they met little resistance, killed all men on the site, and rapidly withdrew to the city, as two of the attackers tell in their probanzas (AGI, L 118, Salas; AGI, P 93, n. 9, r. 6). Why this risky and senseless attack? The answer points directly to the struggle for meaning, and opens a new dimension of it: the Spaniards' awareness of, and ways of fighting it.

Although hilltops may have military value, Huanacaure's remoteness made it indefensible. It was way beyond the limits of the city proper, in vertical terrain (Bauer 1998:106–9) inaccessible to cavalry. No Spanish garrison could be stationed there. What makes the attack sensible is that Huanacaure was a central shrine in the Inca religious and political landscape. It was the place where one of the original Inca ancestors turned into stone before the Incas descended on the Cuzco valley, working as an embodiment of Inca memory and power, as much a milieu as a "lieux de mémoire" (Nora 1989). Considered to have a beneficiary influence over the Inca realm, it received offerings throughout the year and played a main role in two important annual ceremonies: the ritual initiation of new Inca noblemen, and the imperial ritual of purification, the Ciqua (MacCormack 1991:101–16, 171, 191–95). More to the point, Huanacaure was an important oracle consulted by the Inca in person; it was an intermediary with the Sun, the Inca's father, and was carried during Inca military campaigns to secure victory (Ziólkowski 1996:65–71, 156–64).

Attacking Huanacaure thus makes sense if one abandons the logic through which the conquerors narrated their actions: of self-confident cavalry charges heroically battling with massive attacks (over and over). Although sensible only against the grain of the conquerors' narratives, the attack fits well within a large, well-known Christian civilizing-conquering tactic: to control local beliefs, however expressed, by overwhelming them with Christian ones (Alberro 1994)—for instance, building churches upon pagan temples in Italy, in the same way that they would be built upon local shrines in Cuzco, or overlapping indigenous religious celebrations with Christian ones. The attack on Huanacaure is a clear example of the same logic of orienting action: it is an attack on a main Inca huaca, with warfare-related potency, done during the main celebration of Christian triumph, Corpus Christi.

The Spanish expedition left Cuzco on Corpus eve—the night of Saint Basilio Magno, perhaps by chance an active evangelist in a heathen land, Cappadocia, present-day Turkey. It was a Wednesday, 21 June 1536.[8] They attacked at the crack of dawn on Thursday and returned to the city in time to observe Corpus—which, incidentally, is also calculated according to the lunar calendar. Twisting meanings saturated the event. Although celebrating the transubstantiation of Christ's body in the holy host, Spanish performances of Corpus always incorporated non-Christian Others, who were ritually defeated as the host was paraded through a city. It was a triumph over difference. While in Europe the Other was mainly Muslim, Turk, or Jew; in the Americas Indians took the stage (Dean 1999). One wonders who played the part in 1536 Cuzco. The attack becomes even more revealing if one considers that the date is significant from an Inca point of view: 22 June was the winter solstice, the time when Manco Inca would begin the important celebration of Inti-Raymi. The celebration established the Inca's control over natural cycles; the Inca in person opened the plowing season throughout the empire, and confirmed his personal relation with his father, the Sun, who began its annual rebirth. Last, Huanacaure was a mediator with the Sun, a star Christian iconography also claimed as central figure—the monstrance holding the host was often shaped after it (ibid.:83, 127).

In short, the attack aimed at debasing Manco Inca's privileged relation with supernatural forces. It was a challenge to his attempt at proving that the hanan pacha (upper world) was backing him "as usual" and an attempt at claiming, instead, the Spaniards' mastery over the latter. In other words, the Christians were fighting Manco Inca *through imitating him*.[9] This departs from a usual way of understanding colonial relations. Scholars have often suggested that once the evangelization began actually taking place, Peruvian native peoples chose to cloak their religious practices under Roman Catholic ones—for instance, by choosing as patron saints those whose days calendrically best fit indigenous celebrations (Ziółkowski 1996:389–98), or, more to the point, by celebrating Inti-Raymi during Corpus Christi. The multilayered example of Huanacaure suggests that overlapping forms can be read as part of a different interpretive paradigm of cross-cultural dynamics, that of mimesis.

I would like to draw attention to a difference between mimicry and mimesis. Using the notion of mimicry points out the central role imitation and the reinscription of difference have in colonial relations (Bhabha 1994: 85–120). In the case of mimesis, the emphasis is on the fact that when parties blur into each other, like when a shaman wears a leopard skin, there is an actual trade of potencies and imageries (Taussig 1993). The latter concept illuminates best, I suggest, the events under consideration. The Spaniards were fighting Manco Inca through imitating him in his overall claim, trying to turn the sacred potencies he embodied and commanded to their advantage by obliterating them and possessing them at once. In this simultaneous desacralization of the Other and resacralization of the Self, Huanacaure reveals then a case that is as much of sympathetic magic, in which mimesis aims at controlling and co-opting the Other's energy (Taussig 1993:44–51, after Frazer 1911), as of the release of the sacred, in which the Other's potency is celebrated through its destruction and unmasking (Taussig 1993:85, after Bataille 1955, 1986).

Allow me to stress the consequences of thinking the attack on Huanacaure through mimesis. First, it reveals that available narratives of the siege, colonial and current, often misrepresent it: it was the fact that there was no self-evident superiority manifested in neat military deeds that made the attack *necessary*. I suggest that it is precisely these dimensions of the attack (it being necessary and the blurring of the parties into the other) that determined its subsequent silencing. This is because mimesis exposes the distinctness to tell the colonizer apart from the colonized as *a mere voluntary act*, revealing the arbitrariness of the former's claim of superiority. Second, when mimesis orders interactions, the ability to assert dominance becomes elusive. On the one hand, as a chain of mimetic transformations unfolds, the chances of identifying an original, true act vanish. The uncertainty resulting from the imitation of the imitation makes establishing a mastery over the meaning of events fragile. On the other hand, the acts of copying can always be unfolded, adding new twists to the reading. In 1536 Cuzco, the Christians began the game by using their sacred calendar to overwhelm local beliefs; Manco arguably returned the mime three months later.

On 8 September 1536, five days after the new moon attack was over, Manco had delivered to the besieged the heads of several Christians, together with a large number of torn letters. Spanish narratives explain it as an attempt to undermine their morale by letting them know that all reinforcements had been annihilated (RS 1879:52–53; Enríquez de Guzmán [c. 1543] 1960:154; P. Pizarro 1968:206).[10] They also say that while the heads had the desired effect, the letters undermined it in part; from them, the men of Cuzco learned that Pizarro was still alive in the coast. Why the apparent mistake?

One could guess that the precise nature of alphabetic writing was not fully understood by the Incas. This would be consistent with the fact that a *quipu*, the system of cords and knots the Incas used to record information, according to many specialists was readable only by its creator or someone trained in his particular encoding.[11] If writing was thought to work in the same way, the letters were useless without their carriers. And yet, this answer in itself would not explain why to tear up the letters and deliver them together with the heads. I suggest that it is because through them Manco made a new move in the mimetic contest, a move that involved a chain of associations of a fetishistic nature.

During colonial times, documents in their materiality progressively became objects endowed with power for Indians, regardless of exactly how writing was understood and what documents actually said (MacCormack 1989; Rappaport 1994b). Although one could think of it as a result of the asymmetric character of colonial power relations, and of the fact that often authority was exercised through papers Indians could seldom read, this would reify a technical reading of papers. I argue that their potency has also to be thought of as part of a fetishistic trade. Manco's move resulted, like the Spanish attack on Huanacaure, from observing and imitating. Papers were objects endowed with power for conquerors too, most of whom were, like the Indians, unable to read them. In particular, the act of receiving a *real cédula*—there were some among the letters—involved an elaborate gestural ritual in which it was kissed and placed by the recipient on top of his head at the same time that some ritual words in recognition of the king were uttered. (Note that severed heads accompanied the letters.) The ritual embodied the entire Spanish political hierarchy, independently of the cédula's content. The act, paradoxically a Spanish mimicry of Moorish political practices (Cummins and Rappaport 1998:12), had been publicly visible, for instance, during a key signifying act in Cuzco's plaza: Pizarro's foundation of the city and his subsequent recognition by the *cabildo* in his three different capacities (RH, II/1960; PML, MA 155, ff. 171v–74), each requiring the ritual handling of royal documents.

The torn papers then delivered a clear message through mimesis: the submission and destruction of an object fetishized by all parties that stood for the Spaniards' power. By delivering it Manco also disrupted the established route that connected conquerors to their king, legitimating the new order they embodied, and gave himself ascendancy. And if—anticipating the struggle over a British mast (fertilizer of the land or flag carrier) during the 1844–45 Maori revolt in New Zealand (Sahlins 1985:60)—in Cuzco there were different precise understandings of the object in question, ultimately that was irrelevant. Manco enacted a return of the "writing lesson" (Lévi-Strauss 1956:312–22), a challenge to the certainty of superiority that Westerners considered literacy to embody—a theme already displayed in the contact scene in Cajamarca (Seed 1991). Perhaps it was this instance of ruffling barbarism that drove Spanish accounts to describe the heads as being from "Christians," not from "Spaniards."

Against any definitive reading, the attempts and counterattempts during the siege remind one that mimetic claims are by nature open-ended, and signifiers can always escape anyone's clear control. According to Tito Cussi, Manco's son, his father in his faraway speech said the Viracochas' huaca were "some painted pieces of cloth" ([1570] 1985:24). This suggests a reworking of the first news of the Spaniards, which included that they talked to pieces of cloth (*quillcas*) as if talking to a person, in the same way Indians talked to huacas (see chapter 1). By coincidence or not, during the siege most Spaniards had taken refuge in the church, one of the very few buildings that stood after Manco ordered the city to be set on fire. There, as all Spanish narratives tell, in the face of the overwhelming attack the conquerors commended themselves to God and prayed for help. In this, they were joined by the Indians in the city (loc. cit.), who likely considered *mochar* (to pray, adore, offer) the Christians' powerful huaca a sensible act, since their destinies were then entwined. It is to this aspect of papers as embodiments of huacas, which the conquerors likely consciously utilized to play Viracochas,[12] and of places as huacas, that Manco's act responded too: he was returning the attack on Huanacaure in *kind*, trying to level the field of supernatural energy and imagery vis-à-vis both the Christians and the other native players inside the city. Furthermore, according to the mestizo chronicler Garcilaso de la Vega ([1617] 1960:123a), the church had been Inca Viracocha's palace, which begs the question of who was being *mochado* and why. Even the reading of the torn letters and severed heads could be flipped. The men of Cuzco took heart from a royal letter saying that Charles V had defeated Barbarossa and the Turks in Tunis, which restored both their faith in their dominance over barbarians and their self-image as part of a global mission with clearly distinct Selves and Others; also, as the fervent believer Don Alonso Enríquez de Guzmán ([1543] 1960:154) pointed out, the Virgin Mary herself surely had intervened to make Manco send the letters with the news, since they had arrived on 8 September, her day.

THE REBELLION OF THE SECONDARY CAST

Another way of revising the prevalent image of self-evident military encounters, and the resulting illusion of Spanish mastery, is to recuperate the plural politics in place during the war. Unlike what is suggested in most sixteenth-century Spanish accounts, native peoples' agendas and ways of interpreting events were not on the same page with the Spaniards'. At times they were simply opposed, and at others different. This plurality troubles the conquerors' project of dominance, as it decenters the image and in some cases voids it of heroism. In what follows, I examine different scenarios in which actions drifted away from a Spanish-centric view of the war guided by diverging ways of making sense of it.

The first scenario is Cuzco city. Who were the native actors in the city? How did they relate to the Christians and the war? Spanish and Inca narratives seldom talk about the sociopolitical dynamics inside Cuzco. Sustaining the tale of a sharply defined scenario with only two coordinates, Christians and Manco, the other actors go almost unmentioned, and labeled—eventually—as the Spaniards' "allies" or "friends." Current accounts tend to follow the same outline and use the same labels, adding at times the "antipatriotic." The problem I want to stress is twofold. First, either label robs native actors in the city of agency and political projects. As in the case of the Santals rebelling in British India studied by Guha (1988), there is a prose of counterinsurgency at work; the native actors in 1536 Cuzco city are and do in function of someone or something else—the Spaniards or the Nation, not of themselves. Second, the labels obscure that not all acts revolved around the conflict between Manco and the conquerors; nor was there a uniform way of giving meaning to the war. As a result, there appears to be only one plot (and heroic), with the Christians as its protagonists; the "friend Indians" play the part of a surrounding cast, if at all.

This image fits the conquerors' quest well, hiding from sight the fact that at stake was, precisely, establishing dominance and giving actions a unique meaning. The starting point to revise what was going on inside Cuzco is to recognize that the siege was, from its very beginning, an affair as much for the Spanish as for the Indians in the city. As we saw in chapter 3, several high-ranking Inca women denounced Manco's plan to their Spanish partners. This expressed as much alternative political cleavages as shear panic. "The Indians [*yndios e yndias*] of the . . . city," Juan Sánchez recalled in 1543, "were frightened by the sight of the . . . Inga leaving and crying telling each to their Spanish lords 'now we will all be killed'" (AGI, P 90a, n.I, r.II, f. 452). Once the war began, Manco immediately had killed not only all Spaniards in Cuzco's surroundings but also Indians on good terms with them (ibid., f. 453) and black slaves working in mines (ibid., f. 454v), and ordered all *yanaconas* to suffer the same end (Molina [c. 1553] 1968:92b). Manco's attack was thus directed not only against the Spaniards or any actor in particular, but against anything that embodied an alternative order to his; the conquerors may have been blind to it, but the different native groups in the city were not.

Those fighting Manco were a heterogeneous group, and they related to the Christians in different ways. Incas, yanaconas, black and Central American Indian slaves (generally labeled "from Nicaragua"), Cañares, and Chachapoyas can be identified.[13] Their total number fluctuated from less than 1,000 initially to some 4,000–7,000 at the end of the siege.[14] The increase reflects the number of those changing sides, and eventually of captives. The sociopolitical dynamics in the city are difficult to study because, as mentioned, available narratives say little of what was going on in Cuzco and even less about what native groups were up to. A way to partially pierce this silence is to use testimonies given by veterans of the Inca conquest during the long trial between the Crown and Hernando Pizarro. The date is 1543, the place, the Spanish court.

In question 10, the indefatigable royal prosecutor Juan de Villalobos asked witnesses at court if Hernando, to obtain gold, consented that Indians be tortured by fire, strangled, cut (*acuchillados*), or dogged (thrown to dogs, *aperreados*) (AGI, P 90a, n. 1, r. 11, f. 76v). The goal was clear: to portray a Hernando consumed by greed and in control of all acts. The witnesses tell that Indian prisoners were in fact mutilated, burned with bundles of lighted weeds, hung by their feet, or dogged. However, the justification for this brutality was obtaining not gold but information about Manco's men and plans (e.g., ibid., ff. 275, 370v, 472). By invoking the fact that torture was a standard means to obtain information in the Spanish—and for that matter European—legal system (Tomás y Valiente 1973, 1979), the shift protected the conquerors' acts. As far as my argument is concerned, the answers replaced one instrumental reason with another and confirmed the conquerors' self-image. However, in some testimonies the legalistic, means-to-an-end reason recedes and a hallucinatory milieu emerges as a driving force. For instance, Diego de Bazán declared that the men of Cuzco resorted to torture "because the Christians that were in Cuzco besieged were not more than 200 men and there were attacking them 200,000 Indians, and to defend themselves they did in them all cruelties they could . . . to *put fear in them*" (AGI, P 90a, n. 1, r. 11, f. 275, my emphasis).[15] That is, terror was an end in itself. The Christians found that the best way to survive in a frightening space was by inspiring terror, and resorted to inscribing in the body of the Indians the dominance they wanted and lacked.[16]

This is, in a way, nothing new; since they set foot on Peru, the Spaniards mirrored the fear they had of the Indians, making sure energies and imageries flew in the right direction; but that the sense of urgency was crushing is new, as it exposes the image of heroic, self-confident warfare as a crafty illusion. Facing Manco's sustained attacks despite Sacsahuaman's fall, the men of Cuzco progressively changed their targets and goal, shifting to a war waged through terror. For instance, aware that in Inca armies women joined their husbands as auxiliaries, they began killing them as means to discourage the men (RS [c. 1539] 1879:44); they also began taking large numbers of prisoners, mutilating and releasing them (ibid.:45)—a practice they resorted to whenever the intensity of the attacks increased (ibid.:91–92).

Nor is it that gold was out of the picture; however, in the same way that the Nuer talked about cows to converse with (the anthropologist) E. E. Evans-Pritchard (1969) about many other things, one can argue that gold is the language through which Spaniards talked to Indians about things other than greed. Question 20 asked if Hernando asked for "gold" from Indians wanting to change sides and come in peace as "vassals of His Majesty," for which end he had placed a scale in Cuzco's main plaza (AGI, P 90a, n. 1, r. 11, f. 79v), and if as a result many decided to continue the war; and question 30, if Hernando asked "friend Indians" for "tribute" during the siege (ibid., f. 82v).[17] Once again, the royal prosecutor casts Hernando as a master of a city in which acts are clear and mutually intelligible; the answers, on the other hand, are snapshots of different stories in which mastery is not as evident as is the attempt to state it.

In some cases, there was a murky mix of gold and violence. Don Alonso Enríquez de Guzmán declared that Hernando tortured a main Inca, the housekeeper of Huayna Cápac's estate, and one of his women, asking them for gold and information under the pretense that they wanted to flee and join Manco. He later held the woman's daughter (Marca Chimbo) for a "ransom" (AGI, P 90a, n. 1, r. 11, ff. 19, 344, 352v). In other cases, gold was the language of political statements. Yanaconas who changed sides "at one point" were regularly giving a certain amount of gold that was measured with a weight, Juan de Hojeda heard (ibid., f. 194). Juan de Aguirre's testimony adds other angles. He in fact recalled seeing the scale in the plaza and that Hernando's yanaconas were standing by it; and "there he saw that other Indians that they call *orejones yngas* [Inca noblemen] were coming there [*sic*], and there he heard it said that those orejones yngas were bringing gold." After contradicting himself—he tried to defend Hernando—he added that

> he was seeing that other Indians were telling [Hernando] 'señor, this one is from this part, and this other from that part;' and thus he [Hernando] was telling them and pointing, 'those are from where?,' and [he was seeing] how today they asked them about the . . . Inca, and where he was, and what people he had. (ibid., f. 475)

The exchanges with the orejones appear to have been framed by the Spaniards also as parts of a radical twist in meaning. Gerónimo de Çurbano was not in Cuzco, but heard as public that

> after the Indians were tired of having the siege . . . and of . . . waging war, having left their houses and arable lands they had by the . . . city, many sent word . . . to Fernando Piçarro that they wanted to come in peace to him and that he gave them their houses and lands to sow.

Hernando responded that because they had "upraised and rebelled they had lost their right" to them; if they wanted them they should buy them back and he would welcome them (ibid., ff. 404–404v). Some refused and continued the war; others accepted and traded gold and silver objects in Cuzco's main plaza to make up the payment (ibid., f. 26). Toward the end of the siege, gold regularly changed hands. The licenciado Francisco de Prado declared that not long before Almagro's return (April 1537), "yan[acon]as," "friend Indians," and "orejones" were regularly giving "tribute" (ibid., f. 54). According to Diego de Baçán, the gold of "friend Indians and caciques" was being gathered by a main Indian (prinçipal) of Cuzco (ibid., f. 37v), suggesting that local hierarchies mingled with those the Spaniards wanted to enforce.

These exchanges can be read as greed, as the royal prosecutor intended. The underlying premise would be that all actors were on the same page. I suggest, though, that they should also be seen as *attempts* by the men of Cuzco to objectify a fragile and unclear social hierarchy through material exchanges, as if objects changing hands signified recognition. If it is true that exchanges are always part of larger social networks that give them meaning (Mauss 1990), in unstable contexts their readings need not coincide, but rather expose tensions (Thomas 1991). The fact that currently there is no way to know how the native actors in the city made sense of these exchanges does not make the Spaniards' interpretation any more likely. I suggest that in some cases it could even have been the other way round: a payment securing that the Viracochas stayed at work, and in place. This would not be exceptional within the local context; although little is known about it, before contact the Incas paid some ethnic groups beyond their political control to secure their military support against third parties (AGI, EC 1007c, pza. 1, f. 59). The hypothesis would, indeed, make some events more intelligible;

for instance, the choice of launching the daring attack on Sacsahuaman (at the right time) instead of abandoning Cuzco. The Spanish self-centered image hides the fact that during the siege the ones in the worst position were the native groups opposed to Manco, not the very well-equipped and much more mobile Spaniards. Such differences between groups would, in turn, explain in a different light the enthusiasm native groups put into regaining the fortress the night when the Spaniards faltered.

I am not arguing for a need to choose between readings—Spanish and native ways of giving meaning to events likely differed and overlapped at once, echoing Lockhart's (1985) framing of Spanish-Nahua interaction as "double mistaken identity"; but I suggest that the Spaniards' calling it "tribute" is an easy objectification that masks a heterogeneous landscape. Consider, for instance, that in some instances circulations of gold reflected, rather, the fact that not everything in the city revolved around the Spaniards' presence; as it happened, native actors during the siege—Incas included—used Spaniards to solve their disputes, as they had done all along. For example, an Inca told on two caciques (AGI, P 90a, n.1, r.11, f. 257) and had Hernando hang one and mutilate the other (ibid., f. 30), and an Indian woman complained about Pazca (Manco's uncle and general of the Indians in the city) and gave Hernando gold, which resulted in the general being imprisoned for a week (ibid., ff. 22–22v).

It seems clear that among the "friend Indians," there were different actors engaging in different relations with the Viracochas, for different reasons and in different circumstances. (The gold changing hands signified accordingly: at times it was tribute; at others, a payment for help; at others, a ransom; at others, a blend of torture and information; at others, buying back rights; and at others, a compensation for punishing enemies.) Few if any of these relations sustains a clear mastery on the conquerors' part, as their narratives suggest. Besides, the conquerors' own everyday acts often failed the heroic trope.

In the midst of so much action the definition of Cuzco's status, and therefore of its riches, was still up in the air; they could be Pizarro's, they could be Cuzco cabildo's, they could be Almagro's, or more decisively, they could be the king's. The Pizarros clashed with their creation over the right to define order once again; Hernando repeatedly confronted the City and abused some its members (AGI, P 90a, n.I, r.II, ff. 8v–9, questions 12–14, ff. 80–81v, questions 22–27, and numerous testimonies). Also, he publicly declared that he had to be obeyed by virtue of the worth of his persona, not of the office he held (ibid., ff. 6–6v, question 6 and witnesses, ff. 81v–82, question 28 and witnesses), disrespecting the king. The men of Cuzco took note of this uncertainty during the siege. Despite (or because of) the fact that they knew of a royal decree (*real cédula*) stating that all belonging to past lords and main caciques was the king's (ibid., ff. 83–83v), at the end of the siege, Pantiel de Salinas recalled, the city was full of holes dug in search of buried treasures (ibid., f. 544)—ironic clones of the holes Manco's men dug in their attempt to stop the horses. And there is no fantasy here, or in any other reference to gold. Toward the end of the siege, from 12 February to 26 April 1537, with Manco's men at a distance of two to three leagues, the besieged carried through a new foundry. The registry of this mundane feat tells that if Hernando Pizarro melted a sizeable amount (55 kg [121 lb] of gold and 98.6 kg [217 lb] of silver), his was just one name in a list that included almost all of Cuzco's men's names.[18]

This image, which bears little resemblance to a clear-cut military scenario, was not unique to Cuzco. In the other settings where Manco Inca's war unfolded, native peoples' agencies and agendas were equally heterogeneous and as elusive as the Spaniards' claim of being the protagonists. On the one hand, some ethnic groups did not support Manco Inca, as scholars have pointed out. On the other, political decisions often had little to do with the war itself. At times the war was a family matter, at others a matter of local rivalries, and at others a chance to finally settle something else. This plurality undermines the Spaniards' way of narrating the conflict (and of understanding its aftermath) in a less dramatic but equally important manner.

After Cuzco, the main scenario of the war was the central sierra, and in particular the failed attempt to take Lima. Pizarro sent five expeditions of forty to sixty men from Lima to help the besieged, the last one in June 1536. Taking advantage of the steep terrain, Manco's men buried the members of the first four expeditions under rocks in deep mountain paths, while the last expedition returned hurriedly.[19] From May until November 1536, when, after receiving reinforcements from other Spanish colonies, a heavily equipped army began, slowly, opening its way up the sierra, there was no

Spaniard between Lima and Cuzco. In between, in mid-August, Manco's generals unsuccessfully tried to take Lima. Behind the failure, diverse local allegiances can be traced.[20] In some cases it was about family ties. Thus, for example, the Hurin Huayllas—whence came Inés, the princess Atahualpa gave Pizarro and mother of the conqueror's children—sided with their father (Rostworowski 1988). In other cases, decisions were guided by endogenous local dynamics and the war was rather a chance for local business, as in the case of the Canta and the Yauyos of Chaclla. The Incas favored the Yauyos and gave them the right to exploit a coca production enclave named Chaclla in Canta territory. Tension over it was constant. Although according to all accounts, during the attack on Lima both groups sided with Manco, the Yauyos of Chaclla claimed in a long land suit that they had sided with the Spaniards, and that in retaliation the Canta killed two of their curacas and 150 porters, and occupied the coca lands (AGI, J 413, ff. 14, 136, published ibid.). Most of their own witnesses give an even less certain image: the Canta killed the Chaclla men on their own, and to justify it and avoid Inca reprisals spread the rumor that the Yauyos of Chaclla had sent information to the Spanish (ibid., ff. 144v–145, 150v, 154v, 164v).

An internally fragmented landscape can be seen in the case of one of the main political units of the central sierra, the Huancas of Jauja. Although work based on documents produced by some Huanca lords portrays them as staunch allies of the Spanish (Espinoza Soriano 1971, 1973), the local map was more complex. Non-Huanca sources tell that a Spanish expedition was annihilated in Jauja (Murúa [1590–1611]:68, 1987:240–42) that the Huancas took an active part in the job (Betanzos [1551]:II, 31, 1987:296), even sacrificing Spanish captives on a regular basis (Discurso . . . [1543?] 1892:45). The discrepancy may signal different cleavages. At the macroethnic level, the curacas of Hurin Huanca and Hatun Jauja only included in their probanzas what fit their quest for rewards, and we know little of the Hanan Jaujas. At the microethnic level, there are several indexes of internal rivalries both among Hurin Huancas (LL, Guacra Páucar, 1600–2) and among Hatún Jaujas (AGI, L 136) tangled with intra-Inca rivalries, which makes a fragmented response to Manco Inca's war likely. In fact, a main curaca of Hurin Huayllas sided with Manco and later joined his general in Huánuco's area, Illa Topa, in his continued fight (AHNP, DI, I. 31, c. 622, f. 18v).

Finally, in the northern and southern parts of the empire Manco's war had little impact, although for different reasons. In the Quito area support for Manco ended by mid-1536, after an Inca princess close to Atahualpa, Doña Isabel Yaruc Palla, told her Spanish partner of the plans of local lords, led by the curaca of the Chachapoya *mitimaes* who had been moved to the Otavalo area by the Incas—the Incas of pure blood did not side with Manco (Oberem 1995). The Chachapoyas' story during the war resembles the Huancas'. Although, after Espinoza Soriano's (1967) seminal essay, this northern group often is mentioned as a firm Spanish ally, that is a simplification. A long history of shifting alliances between particular Incas and heads of local factions resulted in shifting local leaderships (loc. cit.), a dynamic that continued after contact. Guamán, a recently installed curaca in a fragile position at the time of the Spanish arrival, built his power through alliances with main conquerors in the area (AGI, P 28, r. 56). When Manco Inca launched his war, the local lords were split, and only after Guamán defeated on his own Manco's envoy to the Chachapoya province, Cayotopa, did the rebellion end (loc. cit.).[21]

In the south of the empire, the last scenario to be considered, the way in which the war unfolded had less to do with the Spaniards than with Inca internal politics. Although the Collasuyo was still beyond the Spaniards' control, the large Spanish contingent that went toward Chile under Almagro's command managed to cross the Bolivian plateau without suffering major attacks and had its logistic needs well provided for. The reasons behind the Spaniards' survival point toward another case of intra-Inca rivalry. On the one hand, Paullu Inca, classificatory brother of Manco and soon his rival, secured much of the local lords; on the other, the Inca governor, Challco Yupangui, did not follow Manco's orders and helped the contingent continue southward—after which Manco had him killed by one of his generals, who with a large contingent took control of the province (AGNA, Sala 9, 31–5-8, ff. 19–35).

In summary, the plural ways of making sense and acting during Manco's war make evident the difficulties that faced both the traditional Inca way of doing politics and the Spaniards' will of mastery. In what concerns my main argument, the Christians' need to imitate Manco Inca, the uncertainties brought about by mimesis, and the alternative political cleavages during the war, all expose the fragility of the Spaniards' claims of superiority and self-confidence. Neither the war nor its aftermath had as much to do with the conquerors and their heroic cavalry charges as their narratives would suggest. I will examine the aftermath in the next chapter; in what follows, I argue that this fragility made it necessary for the conquerors to state their project of dominance away from the battlefield, in quotidian arenas, and in a particularly violent manner.

THE COLONIAL NORMAL

I suggested in the introduction that the Gramscian concept of hegemony as developed by Williams (1977) and the Comaroffs (1991) helps one to understand the war from Manco Inca's perspective; it was not simply about winning, but about revalidating the order of things upon which the Inca mode of power operated, proving that reality conformed to its forms. However, hegemony seems a less productive concept when one is trying to understand the Spaniards' point of view. Their actions were openly violent, therefore recognizable as arbitrary; that is, there was no given order of things between them and native peoples to validate. Nevertheless, the concept can be of use for studying Peru's early colonial dynamics from the Spaniards' perspective if devoid of its implicit reciprocal character.[22] I argue that the Christians interacted with "Indians" in ways that expressed their hegemonic *impulses* (after Lyotard's [1973] 1994 "dispositifs pulsionnels"). Like the Comaroffs (1991:22–30), I stress the importance of the tacit and the everyday for understanding colonialism's success, but part company with them when conceiving its actual mechanics; in my view, the genesis of a colonial quotidian involves an *asymmetric* dynamic of the tacit and the explicit powered by the libidinal energies of the colonial encounter and in which—paradoxically—violence is prominent. Because, *regardless of what native actors thought of it*, they were interpellated (Althusser 1971), in everyday situations, by a way of acting and feeling that embodied the conquerors' sense of normalcy; what, *for the latter*, went without saying. In quotidian arenas, through capillary mechanisms that contrary to the case of late eighteenth-century France (Foucault 1975) involved no systematic production of knowledge, the new order Manco fought against was becoming functional.

The main obstacle to grasping the tacit understandings upon which domination works is, precisely, that they are tacit. People talk about what is problematic, not about the given; much less do they write down their thoughts about it. It is only when confronted by a way of thinking which escapes that unspoken agreement that people articulate it in words. The sources I will use to study it contain this ingredient of estrangement in two different ways, social and temporal; they relate an arena of early quotidian Christian-Indian interaction that although important has been bypassed by chroniclers and largely by scholars: logistics.[23]

Since in the Inca empire there were neither efficient beasts of burden nor roads good for carts, loads were often carried by hand. During their first six years in Peru the Spaniards moved repeatedly throughout the north and center of the empire, at times in groups, at times individually, often with servants, native women, equipment, and even merchandise. How did such carrying work? (Who were the carriers, how were they obtained, and how did the travelers obtain supplies?) A possible guess would be that pure force secured supplies and carriers; however, while violence certainly played a role, the answer would veil the complex ways in which new social realities were emerging. For instance, early on in Cajamarca the Spaniards' ways of obtaining food and other supplies varied and were informed by their am-biguous status. While Atahualpa ordered the Spaniards to be treated well and provided all they needed, including during their expeditions to Pachaca-mac and Cuzco, some ethnic lords delivered food on their own, and some Spanish ransacked in joint ventures with their newly turned yanaconas (see chapter 2). This motley mix of statuses and situations continued as the conquerors defeated and allied with Incas, who tried to control the mean-ings of the Viracochas' presence and acts and often failed; if in 1533, on their way from Cajamarca to Cuzco, the conquerors had not only their stuff and gold but also their native women carried in hammocks (AGI, P 90a, n. 1, r. 11, f. 203), a privilege strictly regulated by the Inca, in 1535–37, some in Almagro's party to Chile even had their newborn colts carried (Molina "el Almagrista" [c.1553] 1968:84).

The direct relations between conquerors and ethnic lords were not any simpler. Consider, for example, the Huancas of Jauja, a large, rich group residing at a main crossroads. Groups of Spaniards passed by or stayed there on different occasions before Manco's war began. How did these trips and stays work? When curacas of some Huanca parts made probanzas around

1560, to back their claim for rewards they gave detailed accounts of all goods, services, and Indians they had given to Spaniards (which they framed as continued support to His Majesty). The sheer numbers are striking: from 1533 to 1536, the Hurin Huancas alone gave 6,116 men and 485 women as porters, of which they lost 2,589 and 328 because they never returned (in Espinoza Soriano 1971:202–4). The Hatun Xauxas were even more precise, and distinguished among those *given* as yanaconas (60), those *given* as porters *and lost* to the Spaniards (217 men and 437 women), and those directly *taken* by force (110 men) (ibid., 278–85). The latter belonged, in fact, to a separate category: *rancheo*, the supplies-oriented looting of men, women, and large numbers of goods that the Huanca curacas detailed alongside those willingly given. It is clear, then, that vis-à-vis the Christians ethnic lords, even those often labeled "allies" controlled interactions only to a certain extent—like Atahualpa or Manco Inca. Theirs was rather a claim of mastery, expressed through the forms of gift and alliance, than its full achievement.

How did the Spaniards see the same events? Writing some twenty years later to undermine his countrymen's tale of glory, the priest Cristóbal de Molina denounced the way in which the conquerors moved during their first years in Peru. Like a good Lascasean, Molina "el Almagrista" cast Indians as lambs and conquerors as wolves: "There was no Spaniard, no matter how poor, who would go by a town or road and not be given [to eat well] and if the cacique or lord did not give it, he would give him a beating . . . , and there was no Spaniard or justice to protect them" ([c. 1553] 1968:62–63). Although things were not as simple, the point I want to examine is that in each of these repeated, quotidian exchanges, certain subject positions and forms of interaction were being constituted, integrated by a narrative that had, *from the Spaniards' point of view*, them as organizers.[24]

This semiotic rewriting of bodies and objects, done through confusion and sustained in quick rhythm, was being institutionalized beyond institutions and words. This institutionalization becomes clear in instances in which its implicit taxonomies were violated, as the following skirmishes show. When requesting that Pizarro give *encomienda* grants in June 1534, the Jauja council invoked the civilizing discourse. One of its main arguments was that abuses often done by Spaniards to Indians, including rancheo, could be avoided if the latter had an *encomendero* to protect them. Pizarro responded by flipping the (civilizing) coin. He said he was surprised to hear of the abuses, since it was indeed the council's duty to exercise justice within its jurisdiction; therefore its members had been negligent (in Berlanga 1868:294, 299). There is much irony in the response, which plays with a cornerstone of the Crown's political imaginary: the Indians were free vassals and could therefore obtain justice from a cabildo, like anyone else.[25] But while at times conquerors could strategically reuse the Crown's design (recall in chapter 3 the Cuzco cabildo's refusal to give Pizarro Villac-Umu's ransom), an exercise of justice that implied equality was insufferable; it clashed with the conquerors' embodied sense of superiority.

Shortly before Manco's war began, some high-ranking Inca women, among them Marca Chimbo, Manco's sister and his political operator, complained to Hernando about Spaniards stealing fine pieces of cloth from them. Hernando commissioned the *alguacil mayor* (chief marshal), Cristóbal Pérez, to arrest those responsible and return the stolen items (AGI, Ec 1007c, ff. 22–22v, 625). The thieves were, in fact, men of Juan Pizarro. When Pérez tried to carry out his order in Juan's house, the arrest was resisted. As Juan Despinosa recalled in 1544, Juan gave the alguacil the pieces of cloth but did not let him enter his house to arrest the thieves, scorned him, and told him that "that" was not going to happen "in his house" (ibid., f. 626). That is, it was not the accusation that was questioned, but the meaningful implications of acting upon it. The idea of arresting a Spaniard because of an Indian was clearly unthinkable, which made the alguacil's attempt offensive to Juan, a threat to his honor. It undermined inequality as a way of being, as part of a "structure of feelings" ingrained in everyday practices.

As in Williams's original formulation, these "meanings and values actively lived and felt" (1977:132) capture beyond words the sense of a certain generation. Echoing the disciplining of the body as precondition for the emergence of the Enlightenment free man (Foucault 1975:258–59), this disciplining of selves at the genesis of the colonial order was perceived as strange once the latter was a given—a temporal estrangement that makes the tacit explicit. In their 1561 probanza the Hatun Jauja lords asked if it was true that for all things that throughout the years they had given serving His Majesty, they had received no payment or reward (in Espinoza Soriano 1971:277). Most Spanish witnesses said simply "yes," but some felt the need to explain the repetitive enumeration of situations, refreshed in more than sixty questions. Alonso de Santana, for instance, declared that all was either taken or *rancheado* "because *in that time* it was the soldiers' and war people's custom, and he knows that *in that time* nothing was paid to the Indians in this kingdom" (ibid.:338; my emphasis). The testimony clearly invokes as a reason a *different time* in which things were different, but falls short of explaining how these actions were sensible for the conquerors then. One could do it by taking the analytic and political shortcut of saying that they were, simply, evil, abusive beings—as Molina did.[26] However, this would miss the crux of the matter: the reality-making potency of three intertwined rationales driving the Spaniards in their imperial project, *custom*, *need*, and *practical reason*.

In 1544, eight years after Manco's war began, Hernando Pizarro had a probanza executed in Lima to defend his case in Spain. Question 20 asked if during Atahualpa's imprisonment, including the trip to Pachacamac and Jauja, "since until then they had seen no Spaniards," Hernando and his people were served in all towns "in the custom they had with lords," having all supplies ready in their lodgings, "and without asking them for Indians to carry their loads" they provided them, "because thus was the custom among them"; the carriers were never forced nor tied, "it was not even necessary"; the question closed, "had they abused [*hecho mal*] Indians, the witnesses would know it" (AGI, Ec 1007c, ff. 13v–14).

What the question referred to was neither a lie nor the truth, but a specific combination of both. Under the Inca there was a complex transport and communication system that included lodging sites, food supplies, and carriers at regular distances—the *tambos*. Local peoples serviced and stocked them, and provided carriers who worked in shifts (*mita*) within their tambo's limits. The system functioned under the logic of reciprocity: ethnic groups owed tribute in work time to the empire, who in turn provided all supplies, including the shift workers (*mitayos*) (Murra 1978; Wachtel 1971). But the privilege of using imperial resources was given neither to all Spaniards nor at all instances, and given the constant wars the system worked only at times. Hernando's question entailed, then, a mechanics crucial to understanding the emergence of the colonial order: the appropriation and redefinition of precontact forms and its belying, a double move that both invokes and creates a new normal.

If reality is conceived as an arbitrary configuration of social forms whose contents are constantly defined in a negative way, like signs in Saussure's (1995) language system, then the coexistence of different signifying communities (Fish 1980)—Incas, conquerors, ethnic groups, each run through with internal tensions—produced a constant and fractured dispute over forms and contents. During the convoluted time that contact opened, I suggest, the slow emergence of a new order of things has to be conceived as a shifting evolution and overlapping of these communities, resulting in a patchwork-like signifying field—what Žižek (1989:87) calls the "quilt." There is no need to assume conformity. Within the fragmented landscape, the conquerors pushed for their configuration to be, if not accepted as natural, as it could not be, at least functional regardless of context—that is, *working* as if natural.

The appropriation and resignification of social forms such as rancheo and *cargar indios* (to load Indians) are particular examples of these dynamics. Hernando's question achieves a reality-making explanatory force by combining a *historical grounding* of reality (the customary way things work) with the most powerful illusion behind the colonizers' practices: the *need* guided by *practical reason*—an early use of the kind of instrumental logic Sahlins (1976) recognizes in twentieth-century bourgeois thought. They are potent arguments because they are beyond intention and agency (that is the way things are) and are powered by the self-evident (it is necessary), which makes the thinking and practice they legitimize solid as "social facts" in Durkheim's elaboration (1982:2–4, 35–38, 69–71). All witnesses agreed to this basic tenet with few additions. One may think that this agreement speaks only of the obvious (witnesses doing their job), but this shortcut would miss the key point: the consensual character of these rationales. This becomes clear if one considers that Hernando's 1544 probanza was a counterpoint to the royal procurator's 1543 probanza, and despite their utterly opposed goals both shared the same ultimate ground, what went without saying. Moreover, both probanzas build on the same mechanics: resignification and belying.

Questions 7 and 8 by the royal procurator Villalobos ask whether, while Hernando was captain general he consented that merchants and war people load Indians with excessive weights and force them to walk excessive distances "like beasts," tied by their heads and beaten to make them walk when too tired; and whether if they refused to or could not walk, their heads were chopped off (AGI, P 90a, n. 1, r. 11, ff. 75v–76)—all forbidden practices. By setting the court as the natural locus of enunciation from where actions were judged reasonable or unreasonable, the royal procurator at once overran unclear local practices with solid royal forms and hid the move from sight. Thus, he both reified Hernando's command over the *compañía* and the conquest's political frame at large. Note that in his belied generalization and rewriting of actual forms, Villalobos echoed that of the conquerors over the Indians as stated in Hernando's question. In the same way that native peoples found it hard to escape the conquerors' interpellations in Peru without exposing themselves to reprisal, the witnesses could not openly confront at court the royal procurator's move without risking refusal of their interpellation as loyal subjects. And yet, the question's implicit normal was contrary to their experiences as conquerors, regardless of what they thought of Hernando. To restore the local, colonial reality as the axis of sense, they were forced to explain it, opening a window into what hardly received attention in its own time and place.

First, as in Hernando's question, all witnesses resorted to the logic of *necessity*: war people, merchants, everyone used Indians as porters; there was no other way to walk or win the land (AGI, P 90a, n. 1, r. 11, e.g., ff. 98, 106, 165, 186). The second part of Hernando's argument is often given too: using Indians as porters was "the land's custom" (ibid., e.g., ff. 119v, 128, 371). This tenet was qualified in different ways. Cristóbal Martín, who arrived in Peru in 1535, saw that Indians were loaded "like beasts in Castile" and that at times, "because they were going through uninhabited areas, they were made to walk longer, so as to reach places where there was food and shelter . . . and water if there was any" (ibid., ff. 128–128v). This exemplifies the resort to practical reason: it was *to the Indians convenience* to be forced to walk; otherwise they would have died of starvation or thirst. Interwoven is the implicit dehumanization and subordination of the Indians: they have to be taken care of to be good beasts of burden, like cattle in Castile. The fact of the Indians being there in those conditions in the first place is replaced by its consequence, hiding the arbitrariness behind its enunciation. The effect is that it made sense.

Important to recognize as part of this sense making is that it also worked through forcing Indians into double binds. The argument that Indians were loaded because such was the custom of the land could have an orientalist base: "the Indians had it [to carry loads] as a vice (*vicio*) and even since they are little they are shown and given loads," the royal overseer Juan de Turué-gano declared (AGI, P 90a, n. 1, r. 11, f. 490v). Consider that *vicio* in Spanish means not only a bad, regrettable habit, but also a luxurious indulgence, something one cannot help enjoying. The argument of *natural inclination*, even vice, went side by side with an acknowledgment of the fact that Indians were often tied or chained while loaded (ibid., ff. 98, 179, 203v, 212,). This violence was explained, again, by invoking practical reason: to take something from A to B securely one had to tie the Indians, so that they would not run away (loc. cit.). The example shows how well the discourses of custom and need tangled to create normalcy. The fact that the combined arguments were not seen as contradictory (if it is customary, even vice, why tie?) placed the Indians in a catch-22 situation, which made the conquerors' acts' interpellation harder to dodge.

Finally, the rationales behind cargar indios, hegemonic pulsations turned into words, mingled with an explicit argument examined in previous chapters, the fear policy. Some witnesses qualified the porters' situation by saying that while some Indians were tied others were not. Those *willingly* given by curacas (recall the Huanca case) were not tied; those that were not and were "unfriendly" were tied and beaten up to make them walk (AGI, P 90a, n. 1, r. 11, ff. 186–186v, 207v, 370). As in the previous cases, the mechanics behind the conquerors' actions at once asserts dominance and displaces agency: the (to them self-evident) hierarchy had to be recognized; if the Indians failed to be naturally friendly, they had to be punished, presumably to make them so ("if they do not want to be civilized, we will civilize them"). When the self-evident assumptions tangled with practical reason, the result was extreme violence. Gonzalo Gutiérrez tells that when transporting some of the king's gold from Cajamarca to the coast, in 1533, he saw the Spaniard in charge killing two tied Indians who refused to walk; when he asked why the cruelty, he was told "that is was *necessary* to be thus done"; otherwise the others would do likewise, and they would be "forced" to abandon the gold (ibid., f. 258v; my emphasis).

I want to suggest that these examples bring to the surface an important dimension of Western claims of dominance, often overlooked by both studies of Spanish colonialism and studies of the second wave of colonial expansion (French, British, and so on). In the former case, the coalescence of rationales just examined provided much of the reality-making power that drove the Christians in their colonial affairs. It laid the common ground that made possible well-known, more articulated notions that scholars have pointed out, such as social ascent, search for wealth, or religious conversion (e.g., Stern 1992). The displaced agency and taken-for-granted assumptions of superiority at once denied the violence involved in resignifying people's statuses and practices, and provided a powerful rationale that seemed to spring from material conditions, hiding both the fact that they did not, and the act of turning them into being so. This double denial, together with the mechanics of reappropriation and redefinition of preexisting forms, were essential, I argue, to the formation of the *colonial normal*. By it, I try to evoke a series of everyday habits, of configurations of what is usually done, without thinking, beyond words, that becomes "habit memory" (Connerton 1989:22–29)—configurations that implicitly define relations between people, and between people and objects. It is through them, rather than through battles with unclear readings, that the cultural and political fragmentation of the contact period was turned *workable*—without any claim of consensus or homogeneity.

One can recognize ingrained in the colonial normal the Manichean polarity that portrayed Indians as either nice, little brown people to be converted, or as evil creatures (sinful, irrational, traitors) to be policed. As such, the colonial quotidian anticipated and transcended the theologico-philosophical arguments in the Spanish court on the nature of the Indians, which crystallized in the famous 1550–51 Las Casas–Sepúlveda debate (Hanke 1988, 1985; Pagden 1982;, Brading 1991). This polarity, in its contradiction, was functional to Spanish claims of dominance; because, whether the Indians are evil to be punished or pure to be taught, they are beings at fault, never an alternative rationality that can destabilize that of the colonizers. Native peoples were thus caught in the double bind of being so different (and evil) that any action against them was justified, or so similar although inferior that what they felt or thought did not count—a parallel in terms of pulsations and everyday practices to Walter Mignolo's (1999) epistemological "colonial difference."

These dimensions of the Spanish claim of dominance also speak to a body of scholarship specialized in later Western colonial missions. In chapter 2, I argued that the conquerors' erasure of difference had several causes, among them the necessity of retaining the feeling of control; control that as contact was gradually and unevenly turning into settlement, translated into the capacity to produce positivities (Foucault 1969:164–73): only what the colonizers do constitutes the reality upon which everyone legitimately operates. The examples just examined expose a continuity, embodied in the conquerors' everyday actions, which was key to the formation of the colonial order of things. If colonialism is understood as a cultural project of domination, as many argue (e.g., the Comaroffs 1991 and 1997 Dirks 1992; Stoler 1995; Thomas 1994; Pemberton 1994; Cooper and Stoler 1997), the examples I have pointed out suggest that during its period of genesis it functions not so much through intended, studied transformation but through murky appropriations and redefinitions guided by practical reason, everyday moments in which "what the natives do" matches and slips into "what the colonizer needs." In my view, this sphere of coalescence planted the seeds of a working colonial normal, while open violence functioned as its necessary counterpart, not so much by simply defeating armies and leaderships, but by disarticulating the local positivities that provided the institutional frame in which the preexisting forms made local sense. It is precisely Manco Inca's awareness of what was at stake that explains *the way* in which he fought his war.

The newborn yanaconas of the Christians in Cajamarca and their "food" raids, cargar indios, and rancheo, are all examples of everyday forms through which the Spanish colonial regime began to be functional and to acquire concrete material shapes. In all cases, it should be noted that I am making visible what I think was hardly so, at least not for everyone, and more important not in an articulated manner. It was a way of carrying out business in moments during which more important matters were at stake—battles. From this point of view, history enters the picture not as the decisive turning events, but as providing the urgency and murkiness that make possible everyday acts in which a colonial hierarchy becomes functional.

Although the failure of Manco's war can make it appear reasonable to think that "that was it" (an illusion sixteenth-century Spanish narratives sustain), the argument of this chapter has been that dominance could only have been elusive to the conquerors after the war. The challenge to mastery that mimetic chains pose and the diverging political agencies during the siege challenged the conquerors' hegemonic pulsations and resulting subject positions. In other words, the war made evident that the Viracochas could not be defeated, nothing less, nothing else. That is why, rather than opening a period of stability, the end of the siege opened up a time of heightened uncertainty and radical improvisation. As a consequence the conquest took a spectacular turn: instead of moving toward accomplished Spanish mastery, what followed was the emergence of a new mestizo consciousness that, as it snarled up with the open conflicts among Christians and their radically diverging projects, effectively competed for the capacity to define the order-to-be.

CHAPTER 5

The Emergence of a New Mestizo Consciousness
An Unthinkable Inca

The war Manco Inca led was the most serious open challenge the conquerors of Peru faced. Its failure, sixteenth-
century and contemporary narratives say, signaled a watershed.
Upon his return from Chile in April 1537, Diego de Almagro
not only put an end to Manco's siege but also imprisoned the
main Pizarristas and took control of Cuzco as its new governor.
From then on, open conflict among conquerors took center
stage, while Manco presently withdrew to an isolated area north
of Cuzco and founded a so-called neo-Inca state, Vilcabamba.
According to the esteemed Spanish chronicler Pedro Cieza de
León's narrative outline (c. 1553), the "Conquest of the Incas"
was almost over while the Spanish "Civil Wars of Peru" had just
begun. Contemporary historical accounts most often replicate
Cieza's outline; they either focus on the Spaniards' conflicts or
on Manco's and his successors' heroic survival in Vilcabamba. In
either case, the landscape after the siege is clear: Spanish domination spills and overruns Inca authority like ink on blotting paper and a black-and-white colonial order emerges. The objects
to be recognized and the rules of recognition appear given.

I suggest that this image echoes the conquerors' wishes and
imagination rather than the actual cultural and political land-

scape. Inca order did not cease or simply get exiled after Manco's retreat, but reinvented itself. The extraordinary uncertainty that reigned after the end of Cuzco's siege gave an order of things alternative to that of the conquerors the chance to emerge. The key figure to trace this disparate process is Paullu Inca, Manco's half brother, crowned as new Inca in 1537. Current accounts—if they mention him at all—tend to portray Paullu as a Spanish pawn. I argue, instead, that Paullu posed an actual challenge to the conquerors. Through constant improvisations that navigated the fault lines of Spanish colonialism, this new Inca produced rules of recognition that were neither traditional nor Spanish but sui generis. It was a new *mestizo* politics, which enabled native actors to contest the conquerors' sense of superiority precisely when it seemed the most uncontestable: after Manco's defeat.

This challenge has been ignored in most past and present narratives because it was initially unthinkable, and once it ceased to be so and was discursively articulate it turned too troublesome, as it escaped the either/or lenses through which the conquest of the Incas was imagined.[1] This sixteenth-century unthinkability has had a material impact on the historical record: only the conquerors' projects are readily available, which silences the contested visions and plural projects after Manco's withdrawal and in turn renders Paullu's politics unintelligible. Once the different ways of "silencing the past" (Trouillot 1995)—at the documentary production, archival, and narrative levels—are undone, there becomes recognizable a new kind of political thinking based on neither tradition nor confrontation but on appropriation and co-optation. The key to its success was its capacity to challenge Spanish colonialism from within, subverting the spaces of domination and resistance as they are most commonly understood. The result was a "gray space" (Lamana 2001).

I begin my argument by questioning the assumptions behind the past and present field of visibility. To that end, I revisit the 1537 coronation of Paullu Inca, contrasting the well-known Spanish accounts with native ones rescued from archives, pointing out the distinct objects each recognized and the distinct narratives organizing them. This opens the door to a rereading of Manco Inca's war finale, suggesting that it was far from a Spanish-alone affair. There was no watershed, rather a plural landscape of meanings and authorities. The resulting murkiness makes me question the illusion of an easy narrative certain labels tend to convey. In a milieu in which improvisation was paramount and heterodox alliances were common, necessarily fluid social forms (being Inca, being governor, being bishop, or being curaca) could crystallize in different ways, with definite attributes, and the outcome depended on the actors' success in casting reality. The latter proved difficult, though, because at the time of Manco's withdrawal, practices often ran ahead of discourses. Only toward 1540, in Cuzco city, the latter caught up with the former, making it intelligible why a pagan Inca tithed to the Catholic Church while conquerors refused to, why Incas and conquerors claimed credit for the same battle's outcome, or why clergymen sided with native lords against their fellow countrymen. As these images cease to look weird, they reveal an Inca strategy of learning and appropriating the Spaniards—their potencies, cosmology, and forms—to then outdo them.

This strategy expresses a way of thinking whose import extends beyond the case in point; it is part, I suggest, of an "alter genealogy" of still-current global designs, one that decenters the West's pretension of universality. Paullu's project can be seen as an early response to the latter, resembling, for example, those of the seventeenth-century native intellectual Felipe Guaman Poma de Ayala, of W. E. B. Du Bois, and of the Chicana writer Gloria Anzaldúa. They all share an understanding of the West's mechanics of subalternization as being in the last instance epistemological, and react consequently. Because it is a particular project but it presents itself as universal, Western colonialism implicitly defines reality, to then declare itself self-evidently superior to its Others; the effect is to turn alternative ways of making sense into nonsense (superstition, irrationality, childishness, etc.) and alternative ways of being into defective subjectivities (the Primitive, the Indian, the Negro, the Homosexual, etc.). All the aforementioned responses are responses *from within*; they try to contest the modern or colonial order of things by shifting from a politics of confrontation—which in a last instance confirms hegemonic categories—to one of production, going beyond either/or thinking. It is this option that made Paullu Inca's project unthinkable in the first place. I begin my argument by revisiting his obscure coronation.

In April 1537, closing an expedition to Chile of almost two years that had yielded no rewards, Diego de Almagro, Pizarro's partner-turned-competitor, returned to Cuzco with some 500 men. Manco's war gave him the chance to improve his fortune: he proceeded to "liberate" the city and claim it as part of his would-be governorship, Nueva Toledo. What up to that point existed mainly on paper began to look real.[2] Three months later he reasserted his project in the Abancay battle by defeating Alonso de Alvarado, a mariscal Pizarro had sent from Lima in November 1536 to help those besieged in Cuzco. After the battle, convinced that Manco would not come in peace, Almagro crowned the loyal Paullu Inca as new Inca, rewarding his help in Chile and Abancay—or so the story goes. According to most scholarship, from then on the new Inca would remain loyal to Spaniards, betraying his brother and his race. Searching for easy "accommodation," he would never be more than a "puppet Inca" in Spanish hands.

In fact, Paullu's coronation looks like a nonevent: it occupies half of one of Hemming's *The Conquest of the Incas'* 698 pages (1993:226), it is caricaturized as a docile act by nationalist historians who examine it in detail (Dunbar Temple 1937, 1939), and it is skipped by those who focus on Manco's "heroic" struggle (e.g., Guillén Guillén 1994). These narratives narrowly imagine the spaces of resistance and domination (only Manco counts), make agency one-sided (the Spaniards do, Paullu follows), and adopt Spanish forms ("coronation"). Although these choices fit their authors' agendas, I suggest that they cannot be reduced to them. The way in which Paullu's coronation is reduced to a nonevent has a larger history; it replicates sixteenth-century Spanish accounts' order: a "monotopic" (Mignolo 2000:18)—that is, European, but apparently universal—regime of visibility. To revise it I will examine the Spaniards' ways of rendering the coronation meaningful, which make Paullu a subject spoken about, then turn to nativelike narratives, which correct the image, and finally interrogate how both ways of making sense meshed.

Only three Spanish accounts describe Paullu's coronation. According to the 1539 anonymous *Relación del sitio* (RS 1879:125), Almagro, considering Manco's refusal to come in peace and Paullu's goodwill and services, decided to give the latter the *borla* (royal insignia). To that end, he summoned many ethnic lords, who recognized Paullu as new Inca, and then asked them to prepare to fight Alvarado, the Pizarrist mariscal, in Abancay. The chronicler Gonzalo Fernández de Oviedo y Valdés paints a similar picture. Convinced that Manco would not come in peace, Almagro crowned Paullu—"an appreciated and brave person"—as an Inca in a public act, a reward after the battle ([1547] XLVII, 9, 1959:5:160). Each text's agenda explains the only puzzle—the timing of the event. The *Relación*, a Pizarrist piece, uses it to build the case against Almagro: Indians are moved to fight against Christians; Oviedo, an Almagrista, uses it to cast Almagro as taking an act of good government: rewarding an Indian who has served his Majesty. The third account is from a Lascasean priest, Cristóbal de Molina ("el Almagrista"; [c. 1553] 1968:93). His moral agenda is to praise good native order and condemn the brutal conquerors. Manco, a fair ruler embittered by the Spaniards' abuses, turns into a cruel tyrant, which justifies Almagro's decision. In Cuzco, back from Chile, the latter rewarded the loyalty of Paullu, "a good and sensible Indian," with the borla.[3]

The mechanism of subalternization is the same in all three cases. If one translates labor relations into narrative regimes, in each case the coronation is formally subsumed (Marx 1977:1019–60) by an order that turns it into a Spanish affair; the object remains in sight, but it is subordinated. The agency is Spanish and so are both the authority investing Paullu and the logic behind the act. If anything, native actors are puppets on the stage on which the Spaniards play—they are punished, crowned, and told to fight. So far there is a total coincidence between Spanish chroniclers and contemporary literature; not only does one decide and others follow, but a single order of things seems to be in place—what "crowning" meant and the authority validating it seem transparent. The only puzzles—when and where it happened—appear negligible. Such puzzles become revealing indices (Ginzburg 1989), though, if one turns to nativelike sources. In them, as part of a radical shift in the regime of visibility, Inca forms and politics order the plot—Spanish follow.

In 1599 an *información* was made in Cuzco in response to a petition by Paullu Inca's grandson, Melchor. Among the events elderly native witnesses addressed was Paullu's coronation. The shift is total. They declared that Paullu wore the borla before entering Cuzco, that his authority as new Inca was decisive in ending Manco's siege, and that Paullu's authority was established through Inca forms. Two witnesses out of nine went to Chile during Manco's war, three stayed in besieged Cuzco, and four were with Manco.

Those coming from Chile saw that after Paullu wore the borla, all natives in the contingent began to "obey and respect him as king, and as such he commanded them" (BNE, Ms. 20193, f. 152v). Once near Cuzco, the new Inca began weaving his net: he "sent many messengers to all rebel naturals [so that they would recognize him], and thus after it was known . . . that . . . Paullu had the king's borla many naturals that were in the heights and passes [around Cuzco] and those following . . . Mango Ynga . . . that besieged the city" came to him in peace (loc. cit.). Those witnesses who were in the city—Manco's enemies—saw Paullu arriving with the borla and recognized and obeyed him as Inca (ibid., e.g., ff. 158, 163v); soon those in Ollantaytambo with Manco did likewise (ibid., f. 124).

In the new field of visibility, the *mise en scène* ordering relations is Inca. First, Manco's war's end ceases to be a Spanish affair. Until April 1537, those wanting to leave Manco had as their only option accepting the Spaniards' rules and hegemonic pulsations. Paullu's return recast the scenario, opening a new option: to change Inca sides. This shift effectively displaced the Spaniards from the center of the stage, *yet* retained them as players: in his message to nearby lords, Paullu assured those willing to change sides that they would not be punished by the Viracochas (BNE, Ms. 20193, f. 146v). Second, in the new visibility field, producing Inca authority is not in Spanish hands. In Cuzco city, in the mist of the ongoing wars, Paullu organized a solemn coronation in which Inca captains, Inca governors, and ethnic lords took part (ibid., ff. 156–156v). After the act several days of customary Inca celebrations followed, in which the lords' recognition of Paullu had more to do with Andean notions of asymmetric relationships created through gift exchange than with wearing the borla per se. In addition to institutionalized generosity, Paullu obliged lords by giving privileges such as the use of *andas,* named new governors and captains, and carried out the important rite of passage into adulthood of young Incas. In short, Paullu was producing Inca normalcy and authority precisely where there were supposed to be none.

Unlike under the Spanish chroniclers' monotopic regime of visibility, the plot has now at least two sets of social forms, two projects, and two readings. Almagro and Paullu were making allies against their respective enemies; each authority knitted itself with the other. If one goes beyond the game-of-mirrors solution to this coexistence, then the question becomes how the resulting fabric was imagined. The answer of most current scholarship—and that of the three Spanish chroniclers examined—would be clear: Almagro acted, Paullu followed (a docile native); an answer that, in turn, suggests that the native witnesses declaring in 1599 either were delusional or lied to favor Paullu's grandson's case. The established image of an almost-complete Spanish conquest, and concerns about documentary reliability (the Spanish texts were written much earlier than the información) would make this verdict sensible. However, as the 1533 events at Pachacamac involving torture sessions and eerie horses proved (chapter 2), sensibility in colonial settings is often a result of power asymmetries. In the retrospective act of making history intelligible, Spanish chroniclers (and often current scholars) gave conquerors a mastery they lacked.

Although the Cuzco council's logbooks from 1535 through 1545 are lost, a letter from the council to Charles V dated 27 July 1537 has survived. The text justifies at length Almagro's entry into Cuzco and the battle of Abancay, defending his work as governor. In closing, the letter tries to solidify the image of Almagro as a good vassal whose acts aimed at pacifying the land and serving the king; it says that Almagro had sent an army to fight Manco because, seeing the "differences" between Spaniards, the former "returned to wage much war and waged it against the Indian towns that had come in peace to the said governor and had reduced themselves to Your Majesty's service." (HL, PL218–1, f. 852v). That is, Almagro was repairing the damage done by the "differences," helping Indians recognize the king. Forms are neat, and the plot is familiar: the logic ordering events and the stage are Spanish; Indians are the necessary enemy. But the letter continues:

> and these [towns] are many, because . . . it seemed [to the governor] convenient to Your Majesty's service to raise (alçar), and he raised, to Inga and lord of the naturals . . . a brother of the . . . Inga . . . to whom [the naturals] *had come and continue to come from all the land in peace.* (my emphasis)

The image shifts: it was Paullu's authority that was being recognized by the curacas, and Almagro's depended on it. The conquerors' testimony written when the events were taking place replicates the unexpected landscape of potencies they want to deny; to account for Almagro's authority, they cannot escape Paullu's. It was, in fact, an unclear order of things for everyone.

Testifying in a 1540 *probanza*, the licentiate Antonio de Castro declared that he saw how in 1537 "Pavlo Ynga brought many caciques and principals in peace . . . from many places and more than three thousand Indians . . . that he saw together, who were from diverse provinces, according to their dresses, and far away lands, who he saw *mocharon* the said governor don Diego de Almagro" (AGI, L 204, n. 11, f. 17). The *mocha* is the Andean gesture of recognition of authority. Curacas who had responded to Manco were coming in peace to both the new Inca and the new head of the Viracochas, likely uncertain of the effectiveness of either act. This double recognition further troubles the certainty of current and past accounts, allowing one to recover the fledging senses of order in place; senses of order that, in turn, suggest that there is no single answer as to which pattern the authorities formed when they intertwined, because it was not clear to the actors themselves. This political uncertainty was radicalized, I argue, by a more substantial one: there were no effective social forms guiding actions.

ACTS APPROPRIATE TO NONEXISTING FORMS

The untidy status quo of 1537 Cuzco not only subverts the image of a neat, linearly expanding Spanish domination and consequent Inca subalternization; it also makes it necessary to question the categories used to narrate it. The problem I want to stress is that of social forms and their attributes. What is it to be a governor if an Inca is crowned? What is it to be an Inca if a governor is installed? Also, what is an Inca if there is already one, and what is a governor if there is already one? In each case, who should be obeyed, how and why? The issue is not just *who* is what—which characterizes history at large—but also who is *what*. If there were not clear battles involving given actors but instead constant cultural and political improvisations with uncertain fates, then one can wonder if the elements orienting Spanish and native action—categories, social relations, interpretations—were not fuzzy, and their definition part of the game.

To address this crucial question I find useful Sahlins's distinction (1985:x–xii) between "performative" and "prescriptive" action. Prescriptive acts are those that tend to confirm the social form containing them, while performative ones tend to produce it. "Friends give gifts" and "gifts make friends" exemplify each. My analysis applies this distinction along two dimensions, synchronic and diachronic. In the first case, I suggest that in a signifying context fundamentally altered by the presence of an Other, prescriptive actions *necessarily* turned performative (i.e., prescriptive acts were impossible). They no longer responded to social forms but actively created them. And, furthermore, while being a "friend" is clear regardless of context, being an Inca in 1537 was not. Therefore, if one asks, "Was Paullu *really* an Inca?" one has to accept that there was no answer, because its import was being defined as it was being done—by the sui generis way in which others responded to it and by the social relations established vis-à-vis it, rather than by—although in interplay with—its traditional attributes. Likewise, what was the one with a paper saying that he was a governor? What was the precise authority he could exercise? Over whom? It is also this dilemma, I suggest, that made ethnic lords recognize both Paullu and Almagro.

It could be argued that this fluidity characterized the entire transition to the Spanish colonial regime; Almagro-Paullu's relations much resemble Pizarro-Manco's in 1534. I argue, though, that the fluidity peaked in 1537, because at that point in time actions were prescriptive or performative also in relation to past events, which made different futures more or less plausible or imaginable. Let me elaborate. Sahlins's distinction builds on Saussure's emphasis on the relational character of value: the value of a sign is determined in relation to those of other signs (Saussure 1995). This principle of structuralist analysis emphasizes the predominance of synchrony over diachrony; it is always necessary to know what the configuration of a system is in a certain moment to know what a sign means. If one adapts Saussure's idea, maintaining its relational character but emphasizing diachrony, the result is that something is what at other moments it is not. There is no static, synchronic being. The same can be said of the attributes of a social form. Paullu—and Almagro to a lesser degree—had to define the attributes of the social forms they aspired to (Inca, governor) in relation not only to each other and the other actors (curacas, Inca governors, conquerors, priests, common Indians, etc.), but also to the previous forms and their established referents (Manco and Pizarro). The key to their projects lay, therefore, in their ability to make certain futures more plausible than others, rallying imaginations and actions.

This dynamic can be seen in repeated attempts by Almagro and Paullu to reduce the proliferation of ambiguous signifying and political action, turning performative acts into prescriptive ones. In each instance, though, both leaders faced the same problems. First, during the aftermath of Manco's war, acts were "at the limits of the thinkable," blurring futures; often "discourse . . . lagged behind practice" (Trouillot 1995:88, 89), and the latter was inconclusive—just as it was during the long Haitian revolution for Frenchmen and even for the African slaves. Second, in addition to it—or perhaps because of it—each leader's attempts undermined the other's. These problems explain why one project failed—Almagro's—while the other succeeded but only years later, toward 1540. Only then was Paullu able to craft a place for himself *within* the Spanish cosmology of order, which shielded his project from open Spanish violence. Let me begin examining these dynamics by studying first scenarios in which Almagro's and Paullu's attempts coexisted, and then switching to the those of Paullu up to the end of major military action, toward 1540.

At his return to Cuzco Almagro was at a disadvantage in trying to make his authority a practice of the then-given form, as he was acting against what seemed to be settled senses of authority. Pizarro had a large advantage in fixing the meaning of *governor* and making it his: he had performed the original magical transformation that turned native bodies and spaces into objects of the Spanish legal regime, had founded several cities, given encomienda and land titles, acted vis-à-vis the Crown as governor, and—more to the point—gotten rid of "his" Inca (Manco).

To unsettle the disadvantage Almagro, imitating Pizarro, took care of signifying and military action. He first secured Cuzco council's recognition and support, and carried out numerous public acts, at once legal and propagandistic. Once a certain tentative reading of reality was in place, he reasserted his claim in the 12 July 1537 battle by the Abancay River against the Pizarrist mariscal Alonso de Alvarado.[4] Although "battle" evokes clear sides, Abancay's actual dynamics reveals the fluidity of the moment: only a core group of men fought, briefly; most simply changed sides. Some changed sides because Pizarro, after promising Pedro de Lerma the leadership, gave it at the last moment to Alvarado, and Lerma, affronted, agreed with Almagro to change sides and rallied others to do the same.[5] Equally important, many changed sides because at that particular moment in time few could tell who the (real) governor was, whose commands were valid. In fact, the short battle was preceded by lengthy and contested ritualized attempts at defining the true order of things. They included, for instance, Almagro's envoy screaming across the river the reading of Almagro's title, together with a *requerimiento*, to which the Pizarristas on the other bank responded by shouting and plugging their ears—to avoid disregarding their king's words (Molina "el Almagrista" [c. 1553] 1968:93).[6]

Spanish accounts of Abancay make it a Spanish affair, and as such Almagro's success; Paullu, if mentioned, is a figure subservient to Almagro, whom he eagerly helps (e.g., PP [1571] 1965:212–14; RS [1539] 1879:126–30). One can begin questioning the taxonomy by using nonnarrative sources. Forty-five days after the battle, the Lima council made a probanza against Almagro. The city's prosecutor asked if Almagro used 10,000 "Indians" (Paullu's men) to attack "Christians" (Alvarado's men) (AGI, P 185, r. 16, n/f). Most witnesses simply said yes, but Tomás Vázquez added details. He declared that he saw some 4,000 Indians fighting Alvarado, and Almagro

> telling . . . the Inga [Paullu] that why was not he attacking the Christians by their backs with the ten thousand Indians he had promised, and the . . . Ynga said that that day they would arrive [and they never did]; because in this witness's opinion the said Ynga had little will to attack the . . . Christians. (ibid.)

Goals were fuzzy, and so were borders. Asked if Almagro "ordered" Paullu to stop any "Christians" fleeing to Lima after the battle, Pedro Çermeño declared that Paullu's men brought to Cuzco's main plaza the heads of some conquerors, and proof of another they had killed, saying "you see here the arms and cloth of that Viracocha, that means 'Christian' in Indian tongue" (ibid.). The confusing terrain, with a crossing over of Christian and Indian borders and authorities, was in fact a natural result of Abancay's double-sideness. In their 1561 probanza, the curacas of Hatún Jauja declared that Alvarado took to the battle 532 Huancas with him, who fought—and were defeated by—*Paullu's* men (in Espinoza Soriano 1971:267).

That is, Abancay, like Cuzco before it, was a plural scenario in which Paullu tried to strengthen his authority, making his being Inca real. At his return to Cuzco, he was disadvantaged vis-à-vis his brother. Manco had enjoyed a long period of command that settled understandings of his authority, making it a practice of the traditional social form. Traditional action was, as we saw, Manco's program all along. In stark contrast stood Paullu. In 1537 it was clear that the Viracochas could not be defeated, which ruled out tradition and confrontation. Paullu's career as Inca could only be based on the co-optation of the Spaniards' potency and the appropriation of their categories. This can be seen in the untidy scenarios in which Paullu intervened, in constant acts of improvisation, to answer the questions "who is Inca" and what it meant to be so.

His coronation fit the logic of Inca agnate conflict in which brothers competed for the place of Inca, but the ceremony included Spanish priests, the intermediaries with the Viracochas' powerful huaca. He likely received the borla from Almagro, whose potency peaked at that time, but although wearing it did identify an Inca, being so resulted from each native lord's personal recognition and from the confirmation of his special conditions. This explains why Paullu on the one hand multiplied the ritual instances in which personal liaisons were established (the odd iteration of coronations the sources mention), and on the other hand needed battles to settle his authority, proving his *camac* and his *atao*, indispensable sanctions.

The new Inca's next step was to eliminate direct competitors. In Cuzco, he had Almagro kill the high-rank Inca Pazca, commander of the anti-Manco native contingents during the siege (AGI, Ec 1007c, f. 265); then he went after Manco himself. The Inca had by then retreated to Vitcos, a rough mountainous site not far from Cuzco. Spanish accounts report that since he posed a threat, after Abancay Almagro sent his general Rodrigo Orgóñez to Vitcos with a strong force that defeated and disbanded Manco's men. While Manco escaped, on foot and alone, the Christians looted his camp (RS 1879:132–34; Cieza 21, 1991:98–101). Paullu is not mentioned, other than to say that, puzzlingly, Orgóñez kept for him the golden Sun idol. In contrast, in the 1599 información all native witnesses declared that Paullu and many men took an active part in the attack. Moreover, they invert the plot and change its elements. Paullu with some Spaniards attacked Manco, whose men abandoned him to recognize Paullu—they were not disbanded. Besides, Paullu rescued his mother, Añas Collque, and his main wife, Tocto Ussica, whom Manco had taken prisoner (BNE, Ms. 20193, e.g., ff. 124, 132). Finally, making Orgóñez's gesture intelligible, Manco's son, Tito Cussi, tells that Paullu also gained control of several key elements of the Inca imperial apparatus: the

Sun's and Huanacaure's idols, the bodies of several Incas and Collas (Inca queens), and Manco's andas ([1570] 1985:27).[7]

As these examples suggest, neither leader managed to solve the puzzle of murky authorities and imaginations. At the same time, this same murkiness makes clear that Manco's defeat did not signal the end of Inca power. There was no fait accompli nor did Paullu as a content "puppet Inca" (Hemming 1993:226, 249; Varón Gabai 1996:241) simply accommodate the Spaniards' plan (Dunbar Temple 1937, 1939); he was, instead, producing order in a moment that was no longer Tawantinsuyu but not yet a Spanish colony. The conquerors only contradictorily acknowledged his project because recognizing it would have countered their hegemonic pulsations, sharing the definition of order with whom they saw as their subaltern. Once Manco's uprising simplified the scenario, they had stopped making such concessions.

The unclear landscape of authorities lasted several years. From mid-1537 to mid-1539 Pizarristas, Almagristas, Manco, Paullu, and ethnic lords fought each other in numerous battles, forging shifting alliances. To question the common understanding of these events as plainly signaling an advancing Spanish control, which makes of the Spaniards the only agents and of Paullu—if mentioned—a traitor to his *patria*, I will sketch the battles and point out their contested readings. Presenting this alternative view is indispensable to understanding the next point of inflection in our story: Cuzco city toward 1540, once main military action stopped. At that time discourses caught up with practices, enabling Paullu to articulate a political project in open defiance to the conquerors' designs—an Inca with a governor became, then, plausible.

Almagro's career was short lived. After the victories of Abancay and Vitcos he tried to make his governorship look real: he descended toward the coast, founded the villa de Almagro, installed its *cabildo*, and received the royal officers of his governorship. His next, indispensable step was to reach Charles V—so far, only Pizarro's version of an Almagro controlled by "the Enemy" ([1537] 1865:64) (the Devil) was available at court. This proved impossible, though, because Pizarro controlled the sea; he zealously prevented any information from exiting Peru and rallied all newcomers' allegiance. The ensuing negotiations only strengthened Pizarro and weakened an isolated Almagro. On 26 April 1538, Hernando Pizarro defeated him in the battle of Las Salinas, finally to execute him on 8 July.[8]

Paullu's attempt to be Inca continued after Almagro's death. Between August 1538 and February 1539, Paullu with up to 15,000 men and Hernando and Gonzalo Pizarro with some few dozens battled native armies in the southeast of the empire. Testifying to the plurality of plans in place, the campaign was triggered by a request for help by Hatun Colla lords. They were under the attack of joint Lupaca-Pacajes armies, who had decided to recognize neither Incas nor Spaniards (Hemming 1993:233–39; Guillén Guillén 1994:115–17). After defeating the Lupaca-Pacajes, the allies moved farther south to fight multiethnic armies under the command of Manco's general, Tizo Yupanqui. In April–July 1539, once back from the Collasuyo, Paullu with several thousand men and Gonzalo Pizarro with a 400-strong force successfully attacked Manco's stronghold, Vilcabamba.[9] Finally, in October 1539 Villac-Umu, the religious leader of those Inca elites supporting Manco, was captured (Hemming 1993:241–45; Guillén Guillén 117–20).

As studying these battles in detail would repeat the moves in my analysis of 1537 Cuzco, I will only point out elements that illustrate the sustained heterogeneity of the status quo. I suggest that if a 15,000-strong native force and some 60 Christians defeat a several-thousand-strong native force one cannot tell to whose credit the victory redounds; even less, whose personage gained legitimacy because of it. The sources allow one to glimpse this point. For instance, Manco's general and the lords supporting him in the south of the empire surrendered only in response to Paullu's calls; when they did it, echoing 1537 acts of double recognition, they "made reverence with great humbleness, first to Hernando Pizarro and then to Paullu" (Murúa [1590–1611]:71, 1987:254). And the latter was no gracious gesture. During the campaign, Paullu ordered an ethnic lord (that of Pomata) to bring supplies but he refused, saying that "the land is for the Spaniards and thus the Inca has nothing to order me" (Ramos Gavilán [1621] 1988:189). The Inca responded by sending some men who met and beheaded the lord, bringing his head back to Paullu.

There is no doubt that in a way these battles advanced Spanish rule; yet their effects were not those of a black-and-white scenario, with liberated and conquered areas. Such image would only reify the conquerors' discourse, according to which the order they produced ruled all interactions and Paullu was a "good Indian" who quixotically emulated his lords. Power is not as effective, nor, as Derek Sayer stresses (1994:369–71), hegemonic projects as complete as they pretend to be. What they are, though, is effective at writing fiction-history—what François Furet (1984:20) identifies as the second illusion of truth of the historical practice: what happened (Spanish colonialism) is what must have happened.

In the case in point, the illusion filters down, affecting even the way in which sixteenth-century Spanish handwriting has been read. In 20 April 1539, Pizarro gave Paullu a large encomienda. It encompassed coca-production groups in the Andes, corn-production groups near Cuzco in Mohina, and cattle-rich groups near the Titicaca lake, in Hatun Cana (BNE, Ms. 20193, f. 11).[10] Although often framed as a reward to Paullu's servility, I suggest that the title makes clear that mastery was not clear; it was exceptional both because it was not given as part of a general *repartimiento*, and because Paullu designed it. To satisfy the Inca's request Pizarro had to dispossess his brother Hernando (Julien 1998a) and the conqueror Mancio Sierra of several groups. As Sierra explained in his will (AGI, P 107, r. 2, f. 10), Pizarro had to please Paullu because he was "successor of the Ingas and lord of this kingdom" (loc. cit.); yet two modern transcriptions of the document read, "successor of the Ingas and *lords* of this kingdom" (my emphasis).[11] This smoothening (and smothering) of the past echoes wishes that are almost 500 years old. But toward 1540, the order of things was far from settled and still elusive to the conquerors' designs.

PRIESTS, SPANIARDS, AND CHRISTIANS

After the 1539 attack on Vilcabamba, major military action in the Tawantin-suyu paused for two years, which moved the bulk of Spanish-Indian interaction back to everyday urban spaces. What did Cuzco's 1540s religious and political landscape look like? In particular, how did Paullu's project of being an Inca coexist with the conquerors' hegemonic pulsations? According to historians who include Paullu in their accounts of the conquest, his position showed the not-praiseworthy benefits of being on the winners' side. His future was to enjoy his "rewards": his large encomienda, his magnificent palace at Colcanpata, and later his coat of arms.[12] The only clouds on the horizon were rumors that Paullu planned to join Manco against the Christians, and the fact that his wealth tempted some Spaniards of little fortune.

Nevertheless, the rumors soon proved baseless, and the Inca, thanks to his pro-Hispanism, gathered help to conjure away the temptations (Dunbar Temple 1940; Hemming 1993:247–49). The image fits the portrayal of Paullu as a weak, acquiescent puppet Inca; the true challenge was elsewhere, in Vilcabamba.

However, the chronicler Martín de Murúa ([1590–1611]:70, 1986:249) describes these years somewhat differently:

> I'll just say that . . . the Indians in Cuzco and its surroundings that did not go where Manco Ynga was, went to recognize Paulo Topa as son of Huaina Cápac . . . The Spaniards, vecinos and encomenderos . . . , wanting to avoid problems that . . . could arise, and so that Paulo Topa would not become full of himself, ordered none to go to his house if not his servants . . . , and thus they understood . . . that in this way he would not rebel like his brother.

The passage is strange on two accounts. First, it describes native peoples' recognition of Paullu's authority, something chroniclers rarely mention. Second, this recognition seemingly bothered conquerors. If Paullu had proven on many occasions how useful he was to them, it is strange that they doubted his loyalty and compared him with Manco, who posed a real threat Paullu helped contain. Why the contradiction?

In order to address it, I need to bring in a social actor well known to studies of colonialism: the clergyman. They have seldom appeared in my account because they are mainly absent in the record. It is only toward 1540 that they surface in two critical texts. One is a long letter sent to the king from Cuzco in 1539 by Vicente de Valverde, the friar who faced Atahualpa in Cajamarca. He left for Spain in 1534 and returned as Cuzco's first bishop in 1538. The other is a thorough *Relación* sent to Charles V by Luis de Morales, Cuzco *provisor* (ecclesiastic judge), just arrived in Seville in early 1541.

Seeing everyday Cuzco through their eyes reveals the ways in which a different reality could still crystallize, an antidote to the neat, bucolic image conquerors and royal officers conveyed. To ground their alternative project, making it sensible to others' ears, Morales and Valverde resorted to taking the Crown's legal discourse to its logical ends and to recasting precontact forms so as to suggest continuities. In the former case, the clergymen used two legal concepts at the heart of the Crown's colonial political imaginary: *libertad de los indios* (Indians' liberty) and *señor natural* (natural lord). I will begin by examining their use of the Indians' liberty to flesh out 1540s everyday Cuzco, and then situate Paullu in it. My argument is that through his appropriation of the notion of señor natural, Paullu built a subject position legitimate within the Christian imaginary but outside conquerors' designs. This challenge to the embryonic colonial normal signals the point at which discourses caught up with the constant improvisations that began in 1537. As such, I will suggest, it marks the beginning of a mestizo consciousness whose logic was that of appropriation and subversion, instead of tradition and opposition.

After the catastrophic experience in the Caribbean, where the conquest decimated the native populations, the Crown stressed the Indians' liberty as a means of preserving its tribute-paying population—slaves did not pay head tax (Pietschmann 1989). Sanctioned in the 1512 Laws of Burgos, regularly stressed in *reales cédulas*, and bolstered by pope Paul III's 1537 *Sublimus Deus* bull,[13] the Indians' liberty entailed that Indian vassals of the Crown had to be treated on the same footing with Peninsular ones—Christian guidance aside. Most often this legally stated equality did not work in practice; however, when enforced, as in 1540 Cuzco, it clashed with the emerging colonial normal. The dynamics of hierarchy and humiliation in the city at that time resembled that in roads or the countryside we have seen. Morales complained, for instance, that Indians could be taken by force by a Spaniard when walking by and turned into servants (AGI, P 185, r. 24, ff. 14v–15), could be marked and turned into slaves for alleged acts of war (ibid., ff. 3, 8v), or commodified and rented to pay debts (ibid., f. 3)—outcomes local Spanish authorities even legalized.

This quotidian alienation of the Indians' humanity was reinforced through precise practices, which signaled continuities from war to peace and reconfigurations from Europe to the Indies. We saw the use of dogs during Manco's siege to terrorize imprisoned Indians. While in European wars Spaniards used varied means to inflict pain on each other, including dogs, in Peru the latter was reserved for Indians (the J. Varner and J. Varner 1983:122). This reconfiguration of the borders of alterity encompassed regular judicial techniques (torture of Spanish prisoners included fire and dislocation of limbs but not dogging) and the policing of public spaces. There, technical reason blended with embodied pulsations. "It seems more cruelty [and] inhumanity than punishment," Morales complained, that *vecinos* have dogs "fleshed" (*çebados*) in Indians that at times ran loose and attacked them; "and I wish I needn't say that as a pastime, some aimlessly and some to make their dogs bloodthirsty and ferocious, they threaten to set them . . . on the . . . natural Indians, a bit kidding a bit for real," and "by saying 'I did not meant to do it' or 'I did not see it,' " they feign ignorance (ibid., f. 2). The dehumanization was consistent. For instance, roving Spaniards with no fortune would at times loot (*ranchear*) Indian towns, and if while defending themselves the Indians killed any a punishment party from the nearest town would follow (ibid., 16v).

The Indians' liberty was also violated in ways that directly concerned the provisor's authority. Cuzco's Spanish neighbors, he complained repeatedly, lived "as in Mahoma's law," with many native women as sexual partners, at times held in a regime of semi-imprisonment (e.g., ibid., f. 14). This unchristian behavior overlapped with others. Many Spaniards did not let their Indians—sexual partners and others—attend mass and hear doctrine on Sundays, as a result of which "if they were crude (*torpes*) and dirty in their law and sect, they are much more now because of our good conversation and example" (ibid., f. 2v). Morales's irony aimed at a key element of the Spanish civilizing cosmology (still current in that of many other nations): that sheer contact with its bearers is beneficial. As with *ranchear* or *cargar indios*, conquerors took their urban practices to be normal: "it is public," Morales says; no one wonders about it, and—more disturbing—"[those involved] think that it is no sin" (ibid., f. 4v).

One might think that like eighteenth-century British sailors (Sahlins 1981:40), conquerors lost their Christian mores beyond Cape Horn and went wild. However, this would misrepresent Spanish colonialism for two reasons—first, because in the same way that the Crown tried to establish in the Indies a system of government more direct than the one in Spain, some clergymen wanted to put into place a society with tighter moral standards. Morales asked Cuzco Spaniards to behave in ways rare in Spain before the Council of Trent, where extramarital sexual relations were common men's behavior, and concubines often part of even clergymen's lives (Rawlings

2002:78–99; Haliczer 1996). In the intimacy of quotidian Cuzco, Morales viewed Christianization as needed as much by Spaniards as by Indians, because he could not, as other clerics critical of Spanish colonialism did in Mesoamerica (Clendinnen 1987; Florescano 1997:80–90), create spaces insulated from Old World corruption and conquerors' depredation where Indians would turn into ideal Christian subjects.

Second, various dynamics coexisted, from attempts at absolute power to attempts to produce order through mimicry. Consider, for instance, the Spaniards' liaisons with native women. There are two surviving rulings given in 1539 by Fray Vicente de Valverde, bishop of Cuzco, acting as *protector de indios* (Indians' protector) ([1539] 1943:11–15). The first case shows a conqueror's hegemonic pulsation and also shows that if given the means, Indians could threaten it. Mencia, an Indian woman, denounced her lord for his abuses. Being questioned by Valverde he plainly admitted having had Mencia in chains "so that she would not leave" and having whipped her "at times." The bishop condemned him and freed Mencia. The second case suggests a personal relationship. Francisco Hernández charged that Francisco González had taken and held the Indian Pospocolla by force and abused her. After a quick inquiry in which she declared such to be the case, Valverde condemned González and solemnly informed Pospocolla of her liberty. She declared, then, that her will was to be with Hernández. Finally, it is likely that like the Inca they sought to replace, the conquerors did politics through women. Alonso de Mesa, for example, had at home and actively cared for four children by four women in 1542 (Mesa 1927) and eight by eight women in 1544 (BNP, A-397, ff. 363, 365v), one of which was from his encomienda's main town, Caycay (*Tasa* . . . [c.1570–90] 1975:165), suggesting an alliance with the local lord along the lines of Inca political practice. If I am right, this polygamy was part of a larger Spanish mime: encomenderos, for instance, asked to be carried in andas like the Inca (P. Pizarro [1571] 1968:153).

There is, however, a way in which eighteenth-century British sailors and sixteenth-century Spanish conquistadors—who likely would have been horrified by the comparison—resembled each other: both failed to live up to occidentalist (Coronil 1996) myths—in this case, that of mastery. Although the conquerors' behavior tells of their will to absolute power, it also reveals a reality that threatened to escape it. The use of dogs, for instance, was common in the Indies but no Peruvian conqueror ever claimed it as an indication of his merit. Rather, it resembles the resort to terror in neo / colonial settings when being overwhelmingly outnumbered frightens the alleged masters—consider that the total Spanish population in 1540 Peru was only about 4,000 (Lockhart 1968:12) against a native population of several millions. In this case, using dogs to set urban order was the institutionalized version of Hernando Pizarro's 1533 resort to the horses' eerie aura to get Jauja plaza cleared: it was about mirroring fear and about enforcing an ascendancy that was elusive.

The examples examined so far tell that the state of society and culture in 1540s Cuzco differed from both that of Christian knights fighting sinful Indians during the conquest and that of confident extirpators of indigenous idolatries in the 1560s. In the years in question, menace came not from a difference exterior to or eluding in-place Christian designs (Dean 1999), a difference that the Spaniards could straightforwardly attempt to conquer or extirpate, but from an alternative order of things that challenged the fledgling colonial normal from within the frames of the Spanish colonial discourse. The second legal form pushed by the Crown, the *señor natural* (natural lord), gave such order the chance to be articulated. As the next examples will make plain, its strength lay in its potential to effectively link the imaginations of bishops and Incas against that of conquistadors.

Putting together the first Western global design included defining for the first time the status and place in the schema of things—creation included—of people who until then had been unknown and unaccounted for. Testifying to the complexity of the task was the heated debate in all spheres of sixteenth-century Spanish society about the right and procedures of the Spanish conquest (Hanke 1985, 1988). In this debate, the figure of natural lord played a key role. Rejecting the idea that native peoples of the Indies had an innate inferiority that made them unfit to govern themselves, which would have justified a conquest with no caveats, the Dominicans Francisco de Vitoria and Bartolomé de Las Casas argued that the Spaniards' presence was legitimate only if it respected the rights and authority of the natural lords, which did not cease because of their ignorance of Christian order and governance (*policia*) (Hanke 1985, 1988; Brading 1991; Pagden 1982).

The debate had actual consequences. The figure of natural lord constrained the compañías from 1513, when, in response to the 1511 critical sermon of Fray Antonio de Montesinos, the Crown coined the Requerimiento. In short, the text stated that God had created the world and its inhabitants, that the pope was his representative, and that as such he had conceded the Spanish king *dominio* over the new lands and peoples. When the Spanish encountered a new people, the Requerimiento had to be read to its lord; depending on his response—on whether he recognized the Christian king or not—the door to pacific submission or just war was juridically opened. Far from closing the debate, the text stoked it; the Requerimiento's content, its enactment, its right to rule over others' property were questioned. However, as Pietschmann (1989) stresses, the Requerimiento's addressees were not Indians but conquerors. Its performance reaffirmed *before them* the Crown's authority over acts, lands, and peoples that were, in practice, well beyond its control. In particular, the text was the cornerstone of the Crown's claim of mastery, as it made the Spanish king successor to local lords' sovereignty.[14]

The Crown's discourse regulating intervention had conflicting effects on the ground. If a lord acquiesced to the Requerimiento, he opened the door to a pacific relation with the Christians, recognizing the king's authority above his *and* retaining his own. In practice, the highest representative of the king on the local scene was the head of the compañía, whose most urgent goals were to recover capital invested and to solidify his power. Yet since the natural lord had recognized the king, the captain could not simply dispossess him of his lands and vassals; he had to engage in a delicate balance, keeping in mind his own interests, his men's pressure, other compañías' competition, and the threat of direct royal intervention. We examined this game of chess in the Inca case; Manco Inca posed a quandary to Pizarro that ended only once he "rebelled." From that moment on, Manco ceased to be a legal problem and turned into a military one, something manageable to conquerors. That is why, I argue, Manco's war meant to the conquerors not the beginning of the problems, as often maintained, but a change in its nature, provoked to eliminate a troubling status quo.

Even with Manco's quandary solved, natural lords mattered because, as is known, the Christians had to resort to them to exploit native populations. This dependency's institutional form was the encomienda. In theory, an encomienda did not violate the Indians' liberty; it only delegated to a conqueror the royal right of collecting the tribute paid by a given group of

Indians. In practice, Morales denounced, "the natural Indians and lords and caciques of the province of Peru are so constrained to their master's service and to what they [sic] want to order . . . that . . . they are very afflicted and not like freemen or vassals of Your Majesty but like slaves" (AGI, P 185, r. 24, f. 23v). Stressing that this was a deviation from the legal form, the provisor asked the king to order

> that given the tribute the . . . Indians, lords, and caçiques . . . are obliged to and usually give their masters [amos], that they be free of their masters . . . to do what they'd like and work where they'd like and get hired by whomever they'd want and go rejoice wherever they'd want, as with the natural lord and with other lords. (loc. cit.)

Morales's fight against the subjection under which Cuzco's encomenderos held native lords is explained by their key role in the doctrine of the pacific conversion of Indians: if lords converted, their vassals would follow (Assadourian 1994:173). Given that the behavior of Spaniards in Cuzco was more obstacle than help in moving native lords to convert, the way to make Christian vassals of them was to win their will by freeing them from their masters' oppression. Since in 1540 Manco Inca was beyond reach in Vilcabamba, the main figure in native Cuzco was Paullu Inca, who caught Morales's attention. The ecclesiastic judge complained that

> because . . . Paulo Ynga, natural lord, lacks lands in which to sow corn according to his house and lordship, and some lords and caciques of the province *want to sow for him on their lands some plots of corn, to please him*, . . . the masters [amos] of the said caciques do not want to consent nor [do they] consent to it, *not because of the damage that comes to them from it*, but so that they [the curacas] do no good . . . to the said Paulo. (AGI, P 185, r. 24, f. 24v; my emphasis)

The quote is revealing on a couple of accounts. It tells that Paullu Inca received, eight years after Cajamarca and in Peru's main city, tribute in labor time from curacas that belonged to conquerors' encomiendas; they gave it to him in recognition of his authority as an Inca, corn being produce of the highest social value in the Andes (Murra 1975, chap. 2). Also, by doing so the curacas and Paullu openly challenged the colonial normal; they set limits to the conquerors' hegemonic pulsations. The Indians' actual exercise of their liberty targeted the core contradiction between the Crown's legal frame and local practices. The subversive effect of a curaca giving tribute to his encomendero and yet recognizing another—and native—lord was the most striking in 1539–40, as the years of constant war had resulted in an acute famine and sky-high produce prices in the Cuzco area (Assadourian 1994:19–62).

The conquerors reacted accordingly to the tribute payment not because of the economic loss, but because they perceived it—rightly—as a challenge to the order of things they upheld; to have, *again*, a natural lord between them and their vassals was unacceptable. Their retaliation, which targeted both the clergyman and Paullu, make visible the complexity of competing visions and projects in 1540s Cuzco. In addition to their openly unchristian behavior already examined, many conquerors withdrew support for their church. They refused to tithe, disguised their harvests among those of their Indians, or did not bring the produce to the city, telling the clergymen to go collect it, Valverde told the king in his 1539 letter (1865:97). More worrisome indeed, Morales complained, conquerors told Indians that they were not obliged to tithe (AGI, P 185, r. 24, f. 11v).

These actions proved aggravating not simply because of their economic impact, but because they debased the very foundation of the clergymen's program: the divinity of the Church—its men, places, and theories. Valverde and Morales were deeply invested in conveying all this to Indians because their religious project was also one of reality making; to make it plausible, both men were casting still unclear social forms to their advantage by forging continuities with precontact practices. For instance, when Valverde asked the king for Indians to serve churches, he argued that "the [naturales] of this land had Indians and towns reserved for the sun houses; and [to convince them to serve] there is no need to give more reasons than that they are houses of God" ([1539] 1865:105). Likewise, Indians would tithe because they are accustomed "to pay tribute always and to offer from all things they take to the sun, who they had as God" (ibid.:96). The homology could be extended to encompass real estate ownership: since God had replaced the Sun and other local deities, all lands the displaced deities had should be given to churches and monasteries (*Instrucción* . . . [1543] 1978:1:34).

In trying to cast preconquest forms to their advantage, the clergymen were not alone; as we saw (chapter 4) the conquerors justified the practice of cargar indios because it was "the custom of the land," and they clearly claimed absolute control over their Indians as a mime of Inca potency. However, Morales and Valverde were able to assert more fundamental continuities. They flipped the Crown's discourse (at base a Christian cosmology, as the Requerimiento shows) and took it to its logical end: Valverde argued ([1539] 1865:98–99) that if God had given Peru's rich lands to the king, who graciously gave conquerors rights to exploit them, it was only fair for conquerors to give some of those riches back to God. The reasoning made perfect sense and was noted at court.

The radical clergymen's acts (defending Indians) and words (placing a protective king and God at the center of colonial relations) triggered native lords' perception of an order and characters alternative to those embodied and produced by conquerors. The first to take advantage of the fault lines in Spanish colonialism was Paullu Inca. Morales asked the king to order Indians to tithe—they would take it for something "good and holy"; he knew because he had talked about it with native lords, who had told him they wanted to. As a first result, "Paulo Ynga . . . began to tithe and brought to the church his tithe of corn and coca and sheep; and all the other subjects (súditos), as they saw it, they exerted themselves to do the same" (AGI, P 185, r. 24, f. 11v). If the act of tithing when Indians' obligation to do so was contested was already striking, it was even more so in light of the conquerors' refusal or craftiness in refusing to do likewise. By publicly paying the tithe and bringing it to Cuzco's church, located in Cuzco's main plaza, Paullu turned questionable—this time not in military but in moral terms—the total submission of Indians to conquerors that the latter yearned for. The key to the act lay not in the (implicit) material loss, but in its twofold subversive effect. First, it called into question the rules of recognition (Bhabha 1994:110, 119): Indians could act as full subjects, beyond their self-appointed masters. Second, it opened a breach in the emerging colonial normal that undermined the foundation of its hierarchy: it allowed native lords to build respectable selves, proving that they could be better Christians than the Christians—more civilized than the civilized.

To outdo the Christians was, in fact, one part of Paullu's larger project of de-occidentalizing the Spaniards—which anticipated my academic project by almost 500 years; the other was to expose the conquerors as bad Christians. An example of the latter move comes in a dialogue between Paullu and the ecclesiastic judge Luis de Morales, who was instructing him. When discussing marriage and baptism, Morales told Paullu that he should take (only) one woman to be baptized with him, at which point the Inca asked "why the other Christians had so many women . . . if [he] asked him to have one?" To this civilizing dilemma, the clergyman could only respond that those were "villains, bad Christians, who did not do what God ordered" (AGI, P 231, n. 1, r. 4, f. 5).[15]

I will return to this two-sided strategy in the next chapter. For the time being, I stress that the contradiction in the quote by Murúa that opened this section was only apparent: Paullu Inca challenged the conquerors regardless of his relation with Manco Inca. The image of a single order ruling interactions in Cuzco expressed the former's hegemonic drive, not its actual fruition. If, as Bhabha argues (1994:98), the identity of a colonizer is constituted in part by the responses from the colonized, the gaze being returned in 1540 Cuzco did not conform to the conquerors' expectations. It challenged their order, and their selves too—this not by military means but, more unnerving, from within the civilizing frame, blurring the spaces of domination and resistance. To Cuzco's conquerors the crux of the challenge was, consequently, to clarify them.

TO DEFINE AND TO DOMINATE

Although related to that of clergymen critical of Spanish colonialism, the project of Paullu and of the involved ethnic lords went beyond it. The latter embodied an alternative order and authority in Cuzco that at once embraced and escaped Christian forms. The Spaniard Sebastián Hernández de Espinossa declared in Paullu's grandson's *información* that he saw that Paullu was "held in much veneration" by *orejones* (Inca nobles), main curacas, and common Indians in Cuzco. He observed that because Paullu was "in His Majesty's service" while Manco Inca was rebellious in Vilcabamba,

the said Indians had as, and named lord, the said Paullo, who made knights and gave . . . *dúhos* in which the Indians he thus made knights and caciques sat, as this witness saw he did with Anaranca, cacique of the Yanaguaras, who his father Gonçalo Hernández had in encomienda, with certain ceremonies of their own that were reserved only to the lords of this kingdom. (BNE, Ms. 20193, f. 58v)

The image is striking. The dúho was a curaca's seat, whose use and meaning were univocal in the Andes: of the elements that signaled the exercise of authority, such as feathers, trumpets, and andas, the dúho was the indispensable one. It evoked order in a fundamental way—in Andean mythical cycles, the deity or the hero, at the time of civilizing that followed action, sat down (Martínez Cereceda 1995)—and also expressed authority in domestic and public contexts. In Turner's (1967:20) terms, the dúho was the "dominant symbol" that condensed the ritual value during the exercise of power. The Incas tapped this value and strictly regulated and codified the use of dúhos, implicating ethnic lords in the production of imperial order in the act of giving them.[16] In other words, Paullu Inca carried out, in the heart of Spanish Cuzco, years after Cajamarca and Manco's defeat, and despite the encomienda awards, the Inca ceremony through which the power of a curaca was legitimized. Only those to whom Paullu had given a dúho sat on them, Hernández declared; the others were sitting on the floor awaiting the political gift. And, as in the case of the lords giving him tribute, the curacas that recognized Paullu as Inca in the act of receiving the dúho from him belonged to encomiendas of other "masters."[17]

The persistence of this important political ceremony shows that in such hierarchical societies as Andean polities, the role the Inca fulfilled had not been erased by the Spaniards' presence. Those lords who were firmly integrated with the imperial structure, either by necessity or to express their political project, backed the Inca's role in generating order in colonial times. The fact that the conquerors knew of this politics of social privilege (and early on demanded to be carried in andas) makes Paullu's acts in Cuzco's main plaza the most challenging. And yet, as the Inca recognized the Spanish king's authority, he could not be attacked for exercising his own—it fit legal forms.

To solve the presence of a natural lord between them and their Indians, those most affected resorted to the strategy used against Manco and Atahualpa: accusations that he planned to rebel, and abuses to push him to do so. In his 1541 "Relación" Morales denounced the game. He told Charles V that Paullu had to be rewarded for being a "loyal vassal," and protected from the "bad treatment and offences" he received from "Spaniards," because as he is natural lord of the land and the caciques of the Spaniards rejoice with him and have him a palace [*le tienen palaçio*] and drink and eat, because of envy that their cacique had no friendship but with their master and gave to no other but him, . . . they go after . . . Paulo and . . . raise hideous things [*fealdades*] against him. (AGI, P 185, r. 24, f. 18v)

The "hideous things" were raised through rumors, as in Atahualpa's case. Yet in 1540 Paullu had effective means to counter them. In April through May of that year he made a probanza of his merits and sent it to the Spanish king. The document is extraordinary in its materiality; it speaks of a native lord's understanding of Castilian means to contest public meanings at a very early time. In its content, Paullu's probanza—like any of its kind—aimed at proving the services to the king done by its main character; what is notable in it is that, again and again, after describing an action it adds that Paullu could have killed all Christians but instead helped them. This signals not Paullu's proud servility, as some scholars have argued, but politics. Two questions in the probanza directly address the tense context, and illuminate other aspects of Paullu's predicament:

[9] . . . whether you know that many times Mango Inga has raised many wicked insinuations [*vellaquerías*], saying that I was in deals with him against the Christians, and that it has never been found that I have said a lie . . . or talked of any wicked thing. [10] . . . whether you know and it is public that Christians and other persons have said that I had no good heart and was wicked [*vellaco*], and no wickedness has ever been found in me. (AGI, L 204, n. 11, f. 1v)

Two points to stress: First, Paullu's unique project was attacked not only by Spaniards; his adversary for the place of Inca produced rumors as a means of simplifying the political equation, a goal shared with conquerors.[18] Second, and equally revealing, question 10's mention of Paullu's heart suggests that such seemingly disparate experiences of subalternity as that in early colonial Peru and that in twentieth-century United States are in essence the same. It speaks, I suggest, of a 500-year-old "double consciousness," the capacity to "[look] at one's self through the eyes of others" (Du Bois 1995:45). Du Bois's visual accent is particularly pertinent to an understanding of Paullu's case; regardless of his well-known services to the king, of what was visible, he could have a wicked heart—a rationale used in old and modern purifying crusades. The heart was the inner place where a person's true nature resided—recall Christ's—and the trick of the wicked was to pretend. The question showed Paullu's clear awareness of the colonizers' mind, and was in fact effective. All who testified declared that he had always been a good friend of Christians and that they had never known of any wickedness in him; Martyn de Salas added, appropriately, that Paullu "has a good heart, as Christians have" (ibid., f. 8v).

Abuses and violence, reminders of the power asymmetry in place, followed the rumors.[19] In late 1540 the servant of a conqueror "slapped [Paullu] and pulled his hair and did other bad treatments to him," both by act and by word, and went unpunished (AGI, L 566,1. 4, f. 288v). Some disguised Spaniards even tried to murder the Inca (AGI, L 204, n. 11, f. 18v). In another example of the heterodox alliances the figure of señor natural enabled, Morales denounced the local justices (all cabildo members and encomenderos) and asked his king for an independent judge to rule on Paullu's affairs (AGI, P 185, r. 24, f. 24v). The request was granted, along with many others from the clergyman—as also were some Paullu made directly. The Crown's positive response and Paullu's continued exercise of his authority tells that his sui generis strategy of challenging colonial dominance from within proved successful.[20]

This success, in turn, calls into question not only the traditional political history of the conquest but also social historians' picture of an accomplished everyday colonial order (Lockhart 1968; Trelles 1991; Varón Gabai 1996). In light of the examples examined, the entrepreneurial nets linking the encomenderos' resources—which become traceable in the documentary corpus in the 1540s—reflect not so much the actual status quo but the primary sources being used, notarial records. The latter reify Spanish legal categories and make Indians their objects, as also do encomienda titles. Taking products of the Spanish legal regime at face value replicates the conquerors' will and ignores the way in which native actors rendered interactions meaningful. Let me elaborate.

If, as has been argued, in the Andes the movement of goods was always explained by the social relation subsuming it—blurring the Western distinction between the political and the economic—when studying this early time one must stress the distinction, for two reasons. First, the Spanish presence was not readily understood as permanent. Responding in 1561 to his king's inquiry, the jurist Juan Polo Ondegardo stressed that to understand the early colonial order, different areas and times had to be set apart. Until 1534 the dominant dynamic had been rancheo, with ethnic groups by the main roads the most affected. A second era began once encomienda titles were given, and lasted until Lima's High Court was established (1544). Yet often it was not clear where the ethnic groups listed in a title were, nor was there effective control over them. When they were not in nearby cities,

> few came to serve and there was no fixed tribute, but each [encomendero] asked his cacique for what he needed of food and services and he brought it; and those that were farther away went there in person with the soldiers they deemed necessary for their safety and . . . asked for what they could take, and returned. ([1561] 1940:157)

Within this second era, Polo stressed the import of Manco Inca's war; after it, the Spaniards "came to know the encomiendas . . . and the Indians their masters and to understand that they could exempt themselves from the Inca's jurisdiction and dominion and to expel [Inca] governors, and came to serve their encomenderos" (loc. cit.). That is, only toward 1540 did curacas begin considering the Spanish presence as lasting, and even then only in certain areas. As we saw, Paullu's position had worsened by then. This explains from yet another angle why his authority was so problematic: it ran against the general trend, subverting it. The 1537 context of wars made the birth of Paullu's sui generis project—an Inca among Christians—possible. While wars lasted, he apparently was not seen as a threat but as a "friend Indian" helping "pacify the land," a figure common in Spanish accounts. Meanings changed once a time of peace arrived, and as all social forms were revalued, so was Paullu as Inca. It is at this point, I suggest, that clergymen became indispensable, because they gave Paullu the tools to make his political project thinkable, thus possible to believe. And in fact not only Paullu's. The second reason the distinction between the political and the economic has to be stressed is that the fact that curacas gave their encomenderos tribute did not necessarily mean that the giving legitimized the hierarchy. The support that lords with a Spanish encomendero gave Paullu shows that many of them saw legitimacy resting in Inca hands and did not deem the Spaniards' presence significant.[21]

The landscape of authorities and political imaginations in the early 1540s challenges the image of a colonial order already in place and ruled by conquerors. Equally significant, the threat did not come from Vilcabamba. In Cuzco city, alternative orders supported by heterodox alliances between critical clergymen, Andean lords, and a sui generis Inca competed with the conquerors' designs. These factors force a rethinking of colonial political dynamics and subject positions: behind the rumors and abuses targeting Paullu Inca was not the greed of some Spaniards of little fortune, but calculated political goals; they were attempts to resolve into black and white a gray space that escaped the lines of domination and resistance as often conceived.

AN ALTER GENEALOGY OF GRAY SPACES

Manco Inca and Paullu Inca solved their conflicts with Viracochas in different ways. Manco put an end to them by leaving the city and starting an armed resistance he would not abandon. His decision defined the fields of interaction, simplifying them. Paullu Inca, in contrast, avoided resorting to military means to solve his conflicts with Spaniards. Taking advantage of Spanish colonialism's fault lines, he chose to produce order in Cuzco city as a natural lord among Christians. His decision kept the scenario undefined, generating a "gray space" (Lamana 2001).

These are spaces that are disturbing in the act of classifying alternatives, spaces whose challenge arises not from their potential to reverse relations of power but from their capacity to *dislocate* them, because these spaces' simple existence calls into question the implicit classifications upon which those power relations are instituted—power understood in a late Foucauldian fashion, not as located in institutions having the capacity to coerce, but instead as operating at a capillary level and inherently productive, a power whose real risk is facing situations that call into question the naturalness of its order. In other words, if domination is established above and beyond physical force, by defining reality so that it conforms to the available forms, then an Inca in a time of peace was beyond them—in both senses, outside the reach of their power and outside their comprehension. It constituted a source of legitimacy that escaped the conquerors' control, and therefore questioned the status quo because it exposed it as particular, thus arbitrary. It did not threaten the conquest, which Vilcabamba could hypothetically do, but subverted its order, while Vilcabamba confirmed it.

To elaborate on the concept of gray space, allow me to introduce De Certeau's analysis of the relation between production and consumption of cultural goods. He distinguishes *tactiques* from *stratégies* to differentiate the weak and the strong: the strong has a place of power that belongs to him (the *lieu propre*), defined through a particular order of the space, a place from which he advances toward its exterior. That is why a fundamental consequence of a lieu propre is "a victory of space over time" (1990:60). By contrast, the weak has no lieu propre; he operates inside a space whose control is foreign to him, as a poacher (*braconnier*). Because he has to move within the enemy's visual field, it is the sense of opportunity that allows him to appropriate the forms proposed by the powerful. It is this capacity to consume in a differential way that makes the tactique—the "arts of doing *with*"—possible for the weak, avoiding simple submission.

In De Certeau's analysis, order and lieus are given—that is why for him it is *braconnage*, in the Other's territory. But in the case in question, it was unclear who were the producers and who the consumers. If from a distance and in the long run the colonial process suggests a simple inversion of roles, such was not the case while the new order was acquiring its forms. It was not a situation of complete asymmetry, but of competing regimes of visibility and feasibility. To be Inca with a governor was as uncertain as to be governor with an Inca. Ethnic lords faced the dilemma and recognized both; and likely wondered which governor and which Inca was the "real" one. And all—Incas, conquerors, and ethnic lords—wondered if they should or should not tithe, and why. Was it God, the king, or the Inca that owned and defined things? In each case, the solution was not just a matter of determining political allegiance, but of defining how things were going to be.

This indeterminacy troubled the possibility of assigning clear places, and of determining to whom they belonged. From the conquerors' point of view, actions aimed at making their hegemonic pulsations materialize in a colonial normal, defining Cuzco's public spaces as lieus propres. From the Incas' point of view, actions aimed either at maintaining the places of power in an isolated setting, as Manco Inca did in Vilcabamba, or at producing order and normalcy in disputed spaces, as Paullu did in Cuzco's main plaza. There the question was, precisely, to define which logic would mark spaces: his or that of the conquerors. This was particularly relevant at that moment in time, because as the social forms themselves were fuzzy, their embodiments carried especial weight—think of bringing the tithe to the main church and what it said of being Inca or of being Christian.

As is known, History as a material process and History as writing do not necessarily match. Incongruent events, in particular, often disappear in the "long baking process of history" (Foucault 1984:79). The baking responds to clear agencies and programs. It is "the capacity of transforming history's uncertainties in readable spaces" (1990:60), De Certeau argues, that characterizes the power of knowledge. He presents it as the constitution of an instrumental kind of knowledge, as in the case of nineteenth-century British historiography on colonial India (Guha 1997:1–3); however, it can also be thought as the attempt to give historical processes a cohesiveness they lacked. In our case, while Spanish chroniclers—and most scholarship—convey the sense that conquerors are the only agents in a black-and-white scenario, the latter's variety of colonial rule faced obstacles that escaped either/or lenses. The constant improvisations through which Paullu built his being "an Inca among Christians" repeatedly challenged the available frames. His authority was neither a continuation of traditional forms nor a farce. It was (and is) a hard-to-cast practice precisely because the dominator/dominated binary constrains alternative forms and subjectivities, cornering them into nonsense.

Paullu's case—both as a practice and as the narration of it—can be thought, I suggest, as points on the long trajectory of the attempt to deal with Western designs. The unthinkability surrounding him resonates, for example, with that surrounding Chicanas as a result of Anglo and Mexican either/or hegemonic gazes (Anzaldúa 1987). Discourses of allegiance and, purity, of inadequacy and authenticity, corset actions and subjectivities in both cases, however distant from each other. Furthermore, in both cases the response to these constraints is the same: an attempt to move from the limited options of a reactive politics (limited because it echoes the hegemonic categories) to the open possibilities of a productive one, a shift that signals "a new *mestiz[o]* consciousness" (ibid.:77; emphasis in original). Likewise, Paullu's awareness of the Spanish mechanisms of subalterniza-tion resonates, again centuries away, with W. E. B. Du Bois's "double con-sciousness" (1995:45). I by no means ignore the many differences between the three cases, but I want to argue that they belong to the same genealogy of attempts to deal with the West and its modern and colonial pretensions of universality—genealogy here in the Foucauldian sense of a study that rescues incongruent events that signal reappropriations and resignifications and that lays no claim to discovery of an original condition (Foucault 1984). In fact, locating an early instance of this genealogy in the conquest of Peru makes particular sense, as it was a crucial instance in the configuration of still-current global designs.

Within this genealogy, one can locate the first intellectual response to modern/colonial designs in seventeenth-century Peru. Behind Paullu's project—and that of many others as we will see in the next chapter—was a way of thinking that understood the nascent field of power and chose to use the forms and potencies of the colonizer to effectively subvert them. As such, the Inca anticipated in practices solutions Andean intellectuals such as Guaman Poma de Ayala would conceive some seventy years later in *Nueva crónica y buen gobierno*. His work mixes languages and epistemologies (see Adorno 2000) escaping either/or thinking—very much like Anzaldúa's, and challenges the conquerors' dominance by simultaneously exposing them as bad Christians and outdoing them—as Paullu had done. The fact that his unique writing has traditionally been seen as a confusing compilation of cu-riosities echoes the caricaturization of Paullu as a puppet Inca. In both cases, their politics indeed subverted Spanish claims of dominance.

CHAPTER 6

Power as Moves   *A Mid-1540s Repertoire of Flipping the Coin*

The 1540s were also a violent decade in the Andes, although distinguishable because the open conflicts were mainly among Spaniards. In July 1541 some die-hard Almagristas led by Diego de Almagro "the Lad," the son of Diego de Almagro, killed Francisco Pizarro. The ensuing conflict lasted until September 1542, when Cristóbal Vaca de Castro, the Crown's new representative, defeated and executed the conqueror's son. However, peace would be short lived. As a result of contested but sustained political changes taking place in Spain, in 1542 Charles V decided to revamp entirely the way in which the colonies were run. The arrival of absolutism in the Indies, a true revolution from above, was met with determined resistance led by the last Pizarro brother in Peru, Gonzalo.[1] The constant negotiations and battles that marked the conflict ended only with Gonzalo's final defeat and execution, in April 1548.

Sixteenth-century accounts of these years argue passionately about the struggle between the Spaniards, discussing in detail the battles and political intrigues of *The Civil Wars of Peru*. Current works often share this Spanish-centered framework. They examine the military and juridicopolitical aspects of the conflicts, study the settler society—a *Spanish Peru*—developing amidst the violence, or, if focused on the fate of the Incas, largely skip the period altogether. In either case, as if the terms on which Spaniards and native peoples behaved toward each other had already been settled and other more urgent things were at stake, Spanish-Indian relations are not interrogated. I would like to question this perception and argue that not only were they not settled, but that the quotidian contests between colonizers and colonized played a major role in *The Civil Wars of Peru*—civil now in a more encompassing sense. Or, more precisely, early colonial relations were settled only in their intrinsic instability.

If one shifts the focus to examine Indian-Spanish relations during the 1540s, the question becomes What happened to the plural views and projects previously examined? I suggest that although the window of opportunity for Paullu's emergence as a natural lord among Christians was related to the uncertainties of the transition, the kind of thinking it represented was not. The obstacles that the new mestizo consciousness posed to the conquerors' designs only multiplied. In quotidian arenas as diverse as religious conversion, economic entrepreneurship, or land tenure, skirmishes of a similar nature recurred: the Spaniards' dominance was continuously undermined by both the cracks and limitations of their own projects (which they tried to mask), and native peoples' creative ways of relating to them. An examination of conversion opens the door to the study of these skilled acts of signification and reappropriation. Far from popular images of an intolerant Catholicism, mid-1540s Cuzco shows an untidy landscape of beliefs, potencies, and authorities in which native peoples challenged the Spaniards' either/or designs, blurring handy taxonomies. Nor were the dynamics that animated market activities any different. Diverging from the impression of a neat business mentality specialized studies often give, the conquerors engaged in repeated mimicry of native forms, while also trying to reinstate their ascendancy by exoticizing indigenous practices. Disputes over land tenure also involved mimicry, although by native peoples. They co-opted the potency Spaniards attributed to their king and his cosmologies and took them to their logical conclusions, thereby successfully supporting unclear land claims. These and other challenges to the Spaniards' dominance resulted in open conflict only if their implicit undertext (that is, colonizers and colonized were, although different, equal) was discursively articulated and publicly legitimized—which, ironically, only an absolutist viceroy could do.

This mid-1540s everyday landscape speaks, I suggest, to questions about order and how it should be conceived. The coexistence of plural political, religious, and cultural projects and the resulting heterogeneity of practices, potencies, and meanings did *not* make the early colonial society any less functional. This signals sources of stability fundamentally different from those imagined by theories that conceive of order in terms of the hegemony-coercion axis. Rather than on consent or confrontation, Cuzco's social order resembled one based on displacement, which is how Rafael (1993:7) casts Spanish colonial rule in the Philippines. However, the Peruvian landscape differed on two accounts. First, while in colonial Philippines the native peoples (the Tagalog) produced the displacement by not listening or listening only selectively to what the colonizers were saying, Peru's native peoples carefully scrutinized what the colonizers said, as well as what they did. Second, Spaniards in Peru were as involved in displacement as their alleged subjects were. Thus, although order was not about hegemony or coercion, neither was it about the cynicism of "living a lie," in which performance is all that matters (Sayer 1994; after Havel 1987). Meanings and potencies were fundamental, to all parties, and they were *constantly* co-opted and guarded. The result is a repertoire of punches and counterpunches, fetishizations and appropriations of their energy, acts of copying and assertions of distinctiveness, which accounts for much of colonial Peru's particular type of order. It is stability through tension, in which power is defined as the capacity to be one step ahead in the coin-flipping game. I begin the project of tracing these successive moves by examining the religious landscape of Peru during the 1540s.

THE PREDICAMENT OF BEING CHRISTIAN

The role clergymen played in the transformation of indigenous ways of life and subjectivities has made conversion an important feature of the study of Western colonial projects. As is well known, in the case of Spanish colonialism the expansion was carried out under the banner of Christianization and with the presence of clergymen supported by the Crown. While there is a large body of specialized literature on Christian doctrinal texts and moments of open strife, much less is known of the everyday religious dynamics, particularly in the early years of the colonial encounter. In the case of the Inca empire, rich studies on the resolutions of the first ecclesiastic councils (1551–52, 1567, 1583) and the 1560s native movement of religious resistance (the Taki Onqoy), contrast with the few, mainly institutional works on the two decades after Cajamarca. The effect of this double foci is a particular kind of visibility: the former often reifies the clergymen's intellectual projects; the latter showcases spectacular resistance, which comes from outside the system. This grid of intelligibility does not fit the religious exchanges and relations in Cuzco during the 1540s; it veils their untidy heterogeneity, the limitations and contradictions of the Spaniards' ideas about conversion, and the kind of challenges native peoples posed to them.

The entry into the early religious landscape is the conversion of Paullu Inca, which took place in March 1543. In the usual portrayal of the Inca as a pro-Spanish pawn, his baptism works as a final stroke. In his widely read *The Conquest of the Incas*, for instance, John Hemming casts it as remedying the "only . . . blemish" in the career of the "greedy puppet Inca"; the Inca's conversion "understandably excited" Spanish authorities and frustrated natives, making many of them join Manco Inca in Vilcabamba—or so the story goes (1993:250).[2] This way of casting the baptism sustains and is sustained by a black-and-white portrayal of colonial power relations and a condemnation of the Spanish conquest. Arguably, the effect is the opposite. It trivializes indigenous peoples' acts and subjectivities, and it echoes the Spaniards' field of visibility: what Indians are up to is only what Spaniards can imagine—in this instance, either convert or be pagan. In 1540s Cuzco native actors' politicoreligious projects and ways of conceiving relations with the Viracochas' potencies escaped Spanish designs and at times effectively challenged them. The Spanish authorities, in turn, were not necessarily thrilled by Paullu's initiation, nor saw in it an eagerness to conform.

I begin with a rereading of the event in terms of political timing. Under the auspices of Peru's new governor, Cristóbal Vaca de Castro, the baptism took place in a magnificent ceremony in Cuzco's main church, which faced the core of both the Inca and the Spanish city, the Haucaypata plaza. Behind the conversion one can read a win-win deal. On the one hand, after major political events *encomienda* awards were always revised—a task Vaca undertook in Cuzco after defeating Diego de Almagro "the Lad" in the battle of Chupas, on 16 September 1542. Although Paullu had been on the right side during the conflict (BNE, Ms. 20193, e.g., f. 43v), the threat of reducing the number of Indians given in encomienda was real even to loyalists.[3] On the other hand, responding to Morales's "Relación," Charles V had ordered Vaca to look after Paullu, mentioning in particular his conversion (AGI, L 566,I. 4, f. 271v). In response, and conscious of the adverse political climate at court, the governor diligently informed his king after the battle that at his command, Paullu was being "instructed" (Vaca de Castro [1542] 1921:75). The Inca converted in March 1543; Vaca confirmed his encomienda title as it was on 29 March.

My second rereading of the baptism is in terms of literacy and subversion. In Paullu's encomienda confirmation title, Vaca de Castro, addressing the Inca, after listing his services says, "now with the wish to serve God our lord and enjoy the things of our holy catholic faith and Christian religion you have turned Christian and go dress as such" (BNE, Ms. 20193, f. 12). The joint mention of dressing and conversion is not casual: to Spaniards dressing was a marker that proved—and eventually could improve—an Indian's ranking in the civilization ladder. Paullu's postbaptism dressing style responded to this type of interpellation; it at once acknowledged it and displaced it. Testimonies in Paullu's grandson's *información* stress that the Inca was a magnificent figure in mid-1540s Cuzco, although clearly in different ways to different eyes. Joan de Baldibieso, for instance, remembered Paullu dressed in the finest cloth (*grana*, or velvet, with gold *pasamanos*), mounting a white horse with gold and silver plates in the saddle (ibid., f. 107) and always accompanied by a large retinue (which included a Spanish servant). If in some respects the image bowed to the conquerors' dominance, as the Inca adopted their dressing style, it also unsettled it; Paullu's outfit was both unaffordable to most colonizers and one that showcased him as a cosmopolitan connoisseur—the colors fit well the latest Spanish fashion of the times, Lope Hernández noted (ibid., f. 83v). In addition, Paullu's dressing code addressed also indigenous literates. He wore mostly red, the elder Inca nobleman Don Cristóbal Casiacuc noted, while other Incas baptized the same day wore yellow (ibid., f. 159). This fitted Inca royal distinctions: red was the Inca's color, while yellow was that of initiates in Inca royal ceremonies (Garcilaso [1609]I. 4, c. 2, 1995:208,I. 6, c. 27 and 28, 1995:386, 387).

I suggest that Paullu's conversion has to be understood in the same terms as his dressing style: a double code that enables him to at once co-opt the potencies of the civilizers and escape the latter's designs. I begin with the former. By using the word *potencies*, I want to call attention to the fact that the deity (God) is one element in a continuum of things endowed with energy, which is at times of a more strictly religious nature, while at others of a more strictly fetishistic nature. These potencies were central, I suggest, to Spanish-Inca relations, as both sides recognized them and often used them to define and contest their standing vis-à-vis each other. In what follows, I treat these potencies separately only for clarity's sake, beginning with the god itself.

As is known, among Andean polities, reciprocity ties governed relations between peoples and deities, or *huacas*. In the circle of generosity and indebtedness, in return for offerings and services huacas delivered *cámac*—a powerful generative essence, a potency or energy, much like the Fijian and Hawaiian *mana*. The gift secured a people's well-being and reproduction, as well as their military or political success (Taylor 2000:1–34; Salomon 1991:16, Ziólkowski 1996:219–20). Although forging relations with powerful huacas, including those of adversaries, was common practice (Stern 1982: 39, 57), I suggest that the case in point was unique: the Viracochas' huaca was a totally alien one, who, for instance, spoke through books and in weird tongues, and whose port-paroles asked for exclusivity. This posed the question of how to establish the relation—how to become knowledgeable about the huaca, in what terms to gain the knowledge, and then what to do with it.

Declaring in Seville in 1543 in an official inquiry about Indians' liberty (*libertad de los indios*), Luis de Morales, the Cuzco *provisor* (ecclesiastic judge) briefly mentioned his conversion efforts. He declared that although he had the first sacrament administered to Indians, he exercised some caution; "He had some [Indians] instructed in the faith baptized and those that he felt had good heart to the Christians and were secure; and the others he did not dare *although they demanded it*, because they did a thousand mockeries and went to [Indian] towns and to the hills [*monte*] to live like before" (AGI, P 231, n. 1, r. 4, f. 4v; my emphasis). As the quote makes plain, obtaining the expertise of God's representatives was not simple. The provisor tightly controlled the initiation process that allowed Indians to communicate with the Spaniards' huaca in his own terms, requiring a thorough instruction of those to be baptized and checking for the right attitude and feelings. If religious zeal is to be expected, what the quote reveals of the Cuzco Indians' relation to

Catholicism is not some mocked the conversion process *and yet wanted to convert*. What is striking is that this is the case of Indians neither plainly refusing to convert nor outwardly faking conversion to dodge pressure, both well-known colonial images; in Cuzco, Indians tried to be baptized, even demanded it, although they apparently did not really mean it. How to explain this apparent puzzle? I suggest that their asking and mocking before the refusal expresses a desire to establish a relation with, and gain knowledge of, the Viracochas' huaca, and at once a rejection of the *terms* on which they were offered: yielding to Spaniards and the power relation the Catholic Church was known for.

In this light, Paullu's conversion gains new signification: it was the necessary step to change the terms. After his baptism, in addition to adopting a new dressing style, he founded a chapel adjacent to his palace, hired a priest who held Mass as his chaplain, and paid several hermits who taught Inca nobles about Christianity and to read and write. He even translated regularly across cultures to his followers the knowledge he was acquiring, according to native testimonies in Paullu's grandson's información report (BNE, Ms. 20193, ff. 125, 132v).[4] By doing so, Paullu outdid most Spaniards again; having a private chapel and sponsoring priests publicly stated "Christianness" in ways all Spaniards could understand but few could afford. At the same time, he gained control over the explicit and implicit power relations embedded in the instruction process. In the first case, by sponsoring the clergymen and even taking the translation of knowledge into his own hands, he questioned both the Indians' subordination to Spanish priests and their monopolistic doctrine (ibid., f. 132v); in the second case, he made it possible for Incas to undo the stigmatizing mark of illiteracy, a key Spanish measurement of non-Western peoples' degree of barbarism (Seed 1991; Mignolo 1995).

The move is doubly significant because the elements through which these power relations were set were not ordinary ones. In light of the role both knowledge of Christianity and writing played in Cajamarca and the siege of Cuzco, I suggest that Paullu's postbaptism acts have to be seen as an attempt to co-opt the potencies with which Christians invested both fetishes. That is, the import of the deity—often the only focus of attention—has to be seen as part of a continuum of energies that encompassed and exceeded it. In this regard Paullu's acts are not extraordinary; they express a way of dealing with Western civilizing projects common to other times and places. Hawaiian and Fijian nobles imitated and appropriated Western fashions and power icons—including God and muskets, not only in recognition of the political benefits that followed from doing so, but also in an attempt to have the white peoples' *mana* on their side (Sahlins 1981:29–31; 1985:18, 37–38). Similar intentions guided Mayan lords, who experimented with some Christian liturgical elements when performing their own rites, in recognition of the former's potency (Clendinnen 1987:165–66, 186–87, 192).

In all three cases, control over potencies was constitutive of indigenous political leadership, which was always at once religious. In Paullu's case the conversion was part of a project one can only glimpse but which unsettled Spanish authorities. Several native testimonies tell that the Inca stated publicly his will to be Christian, and that all others should do so as well (BNE, Ms. 20193, ff. 172–172v); he wanted to lead those interacting with the Christian huaca, "to be the first one catechized" (ibid., f. 147v), and "at times playing at others by threats" (ibid., f. 172) asked others to convert after him. The Inca even attempted to take the eremitic habit, which was, however, "forbidden to him by the . . . governor Baca de Castro," the Spaniard Joan de Baldibieso declared (ibid., f. 109).

Why did the Spanish governor find it necessary to stop Paullu from engaging in active predication? After all, the Inca was to all appearances the avant-garde of Christianization and as such deserved encouragement and compliment. A possible answer is that it would have trespassed the limits of what Christians conceived as possible for Indians. As is known, Indians were seen as capable of only some "rational entertainment," and were consequently either rejected straightforwardly or accepted to only some vows. However, in Mexico the Franciscans took Indians into their ranks until the 1570s (Pita Moreda 1992:95–99), and in Peru it was only in 1567 that the Church, in its second Lima council, closed the door to the sacred orders to Indians—and mixed bloods—(Vargas Ugarte 1951–54, 3:43–47). I suggest that the Spanish governor reacted as he did because Paullu's relations with Christianity—as those of many other Indians—escaped Spanish designs.

Already in 1539 the otherwise native-oriented first bishop of Cuzco, Fray Vicente de Valverde, voiced the risk indigenous political leadership entailed. In a long letter to his king, he praised Paullu's help (the "friend Indian") in the fight against Manco Inca but recommended that to strengthen Spanish authority, after their deaths there should be no Inca or lord but the governor (1865:115). Although the bishop's expression of concern would suggest otherwise, his letter silenced more than it said; it did not mention that Paullu Inca troubled Spanish authority not only because of his well-known political and military prowess, but also because of his religious command: since 1537, when he returned from Chile, until his death in 1549, Paullu publicly led Inca religion in colonial Cuzco. In particular, as several eyewitnesses narrate in detail, he fulfilled his role as Inca in massive gatherings during the royal ceremony of initiation, the *huarachicuy* or *cápac raymi* (BNE, Ms. 20193, ff. 37, 60, 65).[5]

The importance of the huarachicuy cannot be overstated. The annual ritual involved a reappropriation of space, time, and subjectivities in the core of the Spanish-conquered city. All male and female Inca of age, as well as their kin, took part in the month long ceremony. During its many stages, initiates went from Cuzco's main plaza, center of both public imperial celebrations and colonial life, to several nearby hills/huacas and back; in each location Inca huacas and ancestors received repeated sacrifices of animals and vegetables as they were ritually recognized (*mochados*) by the initiates.[6] The religious-political statement was clear. The huarachicuy was a key part of the interwoven "fabric of sacred time" (MacCormack 1991:117) through which the Incas reinforced their celestial character, as it linked human time (the maturation of youth) to celestial time (the end of the ceremony coinciding with the summer solstice). This reminder of the order of things also served to socialize future generations into the beliefs and values of the empire (Sharon 1976), actively competing for the production of subjectivities and localities in colonial Cuzco.[7]

Beyond shedding light on Vaca de Castro's reluctance toward Paullu's proselytism, the fact that the Inca led the ceremony until his death tells that his baptism (another ceremony of initiation) did not affect his religious leadership among native peoples; rather, it arguably empowered it, since it enabled him to encompass Christian authorities and to master their potency. Consider the following bizarre images. In 1545, Gonçalo Barbossa recalled (BNE, Ms. 20193, f. 94v), when during the huarachicuy Paullu Inca held a massive ceremony in Cuzco's main plaza, he had the city's recently arrived second bishop, Don Juan Solano, as main guest, sitting by his side under his canopy (*palio*)—likely, both wearing shades of *carmesi*.[8] At once, in the most important colonial city of Peru, the divine privileges and energies that distinguished indigenous authorities were current; the Spaniard Pedro Guerrero, newly arrived in Cuzco in 1544, declared that Paullu Inca caught his attention because Indians in his presence "respected and obeyed him lowering their eyes without looking at his face" (ibid., f. 53v)—the same behavior observed in the presence of Atahualpa twelve years earlier.

The little one can glimpse of early colonial Cuzco's religious landscape does not fit a space in which native peoples either converted or clung to their "traditional" religion, cornered by a zealous Spanish Catholicism. There was no banning of ceremonies, no Inquisition-like trials; nor were there dodging ploys or disguised native ceremonies. Rather than a clear-cut, either/or scenario, some twelve years after Cajamarca, Spaniards and native peoples inhabited a heterogeneous one. Beliefs, potencies, and authorities were plural and untidy. Given that two ways of relating to divine potencies (also plural) coexisted in full sight no doubt undermined the Spaniards' dominance, a question arises: While juggling deities was common to Peru's indigenous peoples (the Inca imperial project was not monotheist), religious pluralism was not a characteristic of sixteenth-century Spain. Why did the Christians tolerate such an unorthodox order of things?

It could be argued that it was a simple matter of resources; the small number of arriving clergymen, who settled only in urban centers (Vargas Ugarte 1953), suggests a slim chance of converting a native population of several million.[9] It is no surprise then that even in Lima, the most Hispanicized city of Peru, toward 1542 conversion was described as almost nonexistent (Martel de Santoyo [1542] 1943) or that two years later Governor Vaca de Castro could claim as an achievement that there were 4,000 converts in the empire (ASM, A. I, e. 5, n. I, f . 290). Yet sheer numbers do not tell the whole story; they cannot explain, for instance, the situation in Cuzco city, where there were several monasteries and churches in place by the 1540s. To understand the untidy religious landscape, the Christians' conversion paths—that is, how they *imagined* conversion to happen—must be taken into consideration. It is the tensions and limitations of these imagined paths—together with the creative views Peru's native peoples held on Christianity—that, I argue, largely account for Cuzco's unorthodox state of culture and society. These tensions and limitations become clear in testimonies and letters narrating quotidian religious scenes, rather than in conversion treatises.

A first imagined path resulted from the Spaniards' (belief in their) immanent superiority. Christianization, encompassing conversion and enculturation, was imagined to happen in a way reminiscent of biological osmosis. The idea transpires in discourses of colonial government. For instance, in 1535, when performing a general granting of encomiendas (*reparto general*), Francisco Pizarro argued that they would in fact benefit Indians, because "with the conversation and good treatment the Christians would do them [they would remain pacific and] be indoctrinated and taught [in the things of the faith] and in all other good customs men must have" (AGI, L 128, f. 154v). That is, contact could only result in conversion. On the one hand, because the Spaniards were superior in deeds and words, and on the other, because the Christians' physical presence kept native peoples away from their rites that were, ultimately, the Devil's work. Pizarro declared when founding the city in March 1534 that Cuzco's (Spanish) neighbors would "take them [Indians] out of the prison and blindness in which the Bad Enemy, our contrary and pursuer, has put them, and of the idolatries and bad customs they have" (RB, II/1960). Leaving aside the question of what would had happened had the Spaniards behaved like good Christians, the Spaniards' presence did not have an inescapable civilizing effect, because their actual deeds failed to match the cannon and were (allegedly) reminiscent of Mahoma's. The discrepancy not only faced those Spaniards actually engaged in conversion by contact and example with the civilizing paradox of how to convince Indians to do what Christians did not, but also opened the door for native peoples to question Spanish claims of ascendancy by at once de-occidentalizing the Christians and outdoing them—as seen in the previous chapter.

A second imagined path to conversion, one that also took Indian inferiority for granted, was transference through similitude: natives had faith, it just needed to be redirected. The idea, traceable to the medieval Church (Alberro 1994), held sway during the Mexican conquest and early evangelization (Cortés [1519] 2000:71–72; Rabasa 1993). In Peru, some Spaniards were quite optimistic about it. In his 1539 letter to Charles V, Valverde, the first Cuzco bishop, repeatedly spoke of Peru's Indians as docile subjects to be easily converted: "the people of the land are very capable and take the doctrine of the holy gospels very well" (1865:102); they are "good Indians" (ibid., 110), rustic "like farmers" in Spain (ibid., 123). Although he gave no details of how conversion would work, some passages suggest the logic of transference. Beyond mentioning that having Indians tithe would not be a problem because they were used to giving to the Sun, Valverde asked all priests to be sent to Peru to "know organ music [canto de órgano] so that the Church was more honored in the divine cult and [the priests] impress the naturals" (ibid., 101). The request fits a known evangelizing technique: teaching through songs built on the natives' taste for music. Dominicans employed it in Central America both to proselytize in unconquered areas (Galmes 1990) and to teach doctrine in rural houses (Pita Moreda 1992:225). In the Andean case, the hope for transference likely worked upon the taki, the mix of dancing and singing that often accompanied ritual acts, from plowing to offering to a huaca to welcoming a high authority.[10] The idea seems to have had some success. The conqueror Juan Camacho reported having seen in San Miguel, north of Peru, groups of Indians singing in the streets the Pater Noster, Ave María, Credo, and the Salva Regina (AGI, P 90a, n. 11, r. 1, f. 214v). In Cuzco, toward 1544, special services for Indians were celebrated with flutes, and after Mass Christian doctrine and organ music were taught in the newly built school; on Fridays, Indians visited all of Cuzco's churches, singing the doctrine on the way, which they also did when plowing, several Peru veterans stated (ASM, A. 1, e. 5, n. 1, ff. 290v, 291, 293v; AHNE, C 240b, f. 65).[11]

I will return to these Christian epiphanies in a moment. For the time being, I am pointing out that not everyone saw Peru's natives as so docile, and, in consequence, transference working so easily. Writing in 1541, the Cuzco provisor, Luis de Morales, told his king that "the major impediment [to Indians becoming acquainted with] the faith . . . are the idolatries they used to use and now use," such as adoring huacas, the Sun, and bultos of past lords. Morales asked Charles V to order that all idolatries and rites and adorations be banned, and all huacas and ancestors' bodies destroyed "because thus it is convenient to the conversion of the naturals and it is time—although some say no for their own ends" (AGI, P 185, r. 24, f. 21).

The quotes suggest that the two obstacles to an all-Christian landscape were that native peoples stubbornly stuck to their huacas and that some

Spaniards' held a tolerant view—perhaps arguing for a "soft beginning," a doctrinal stance acceptable in the flexible pre–Council of Trent atmosphere (MacCormack 1985; Alberro 1994; Estenssoro Fuchs 2003:1–178). However, this image is doubly misleading: first, native peoples did not simply resist but creatively related to Christianity, which in turn forced heterodoxy into being; second, the conquerors held strong beliefs about the nature of their god and about Indians, beliefs which a strong intervention would have questioned. Allow me to elaborate. I suggest that despite their visible differences, at an epistemological level all Spaniards agreed on matters of conversion; it is precisely this certainty that native peoples understood and co-opted to make conversion not an either/or matter. Both elements, certainty and co-optation, become visible in testimonies of conquerors, who were as divided as the experts on questions of the human qualities of those to be converted and how to proceed.

Five months after Paullu Inca was baptized in Cuzco, the royal prosecutor opened in Spain an inquiry against Hernando Pizarro. Question 14 asked the witnesses, all veterans of the conquest, whether Peru's Indians were "meek and pacific and plain people, friends of Christians and prepared [aparejados] and disposed to receive and follow the Christian doctrine and to serve His Majesty" (AGI, P 90a, n. 1, r. 11, f. 77v). The answers can be, broadly, grouped into two categories. The first shattered the bucolic image. Diego de Bazán, for instance, declared that Peru's Indians "are friends of always having war" and "did not want to learn nor know Christian doctrine," were therefore "naturally . . . enemies of Spaniards and of being Christians"; any good treatment to those "dogs" was a waste (ibid., ff. 275v–76). The second category supported the prosecutor's image; Peru's Indians are "people of much reason and understanding, and [he] believes that indoctrinating them . . . they will convert to the faith," declared captain Francisco de Orellana (ibid., f. 120).

The stark opposition is well known to students of Spanish colonialism: the Indian as good savage versus the Indian as evil creature. What I want to stress is that the disagreement is merely apparent; it rests on a shared epistemological certainty: the (belief in the) self-evident truth of the Christian doctrine, which inextricably linked reason and faith. In the case of the positions described in the last paragraph, this translates as follows: according to the first group, "Indians are animals, *that is why* they do not convert";

according to the second, "Indians are rational, *therefore* they will convert."
The shared rationale is that if one thinks, then one becomes Christian. The
explicit divergence could work as an effective mechanism of subalternization. As in the case of *cargar indios* examined in chapter 4, it results in a
civilizing catch-22; faced with either statement, native peoples could only
confirm their inferior condition: if they accepted Christianity, they proved
to be rational and in need of tutelage; if they rejected it, they proved to be
irrational and in need of punishment.

The implicit agreement opened, however, the door to co-optation. Peru's native peoples clearly understood that a catch-22 is effective only if its
conditions of enunciation hold, and then they successfully challenged them.
Some rejected them straightforwardly and chose open resistance—a familiar image of resistance; others, who were "interested" and "curious" about
"things of Christians," crafted a way out of the double bind from within.
The conqueror Gerónimo de Çurvano, for instance, declared that it was
his experience that often "Indians reprehend Christians many things, making them understand that the law we have is good . . . but we are bad and
do not follow it"; some Indians he saw, he acknowledged, even followed
the precepts and Christian doctrine more closely than the Spaniards themselves (AGI, P 90a, n. 1, r. 11, ff. 400–400v). The answer is, in other words,
to decouple the (believed-to-be-irrefutable) knowledge from those carrying
it; it appropriates the fetish (the epistemological certainty), and decenters
it, severing its taken-for-granted Europeanness. In this light, the images of
Indians singing the doctrine in the streets just examined signal something
other than meekness: a means of turning the claim of the self-evident superiority of being Christian to their advantage, a move that—as in Paullu Inca's
case—effectively subverted the Spaniards' claim of dominance.

As we will see in the next chapter, Spanish responses to these challenges
were articulated only in the 1550s by the first ecclesiastic council. For the
moment, I want to point out another reason a strong intervention of the
sort Morales advocated did not take place. I suggest that for Peru's native
peoples, challenges were not seen as requiring an urgent response because
the doctrine of conversion by substitution rested on another epistemological certainty: the anthropomorphic nature of God. The Peru veteran Juan
Camacho declared that when Indians came in peace, the Spaniards told

them that they were conquering the land in the name of the "great emperor of the Christians, and that they were to enlarge the holy catholic faith" and that if the Indians recognized the emperor, he would treat them well "and that these and many other words they told them *because they found them [to be] people that knew nothing more than the sun and wooden figures whom they adored*" (AGI, P 90a, n. 1, r. 11, f. 214v; my emphasis). That is, conversion would happen because Indians adored natural or bestial elements—the sun or wooden figures. To many Spaniards this could not be an obstacle because they had learned to see religion through a Judeo-Christian lens: only those with (false) knowledge of an alternative humanlike god, like Muslims or Jews, could resist conversion; Indians would convert once exposed to true knowledge of the divine—"seeing the light," not only in a metaphoric but in an epistemological sense; it was only a matter of time, and thinking otherwise meant questioning the certainty.[12]

This hypothesis speaks to larger questions. It makes sense that for Spaniards in Peru, even when they continually faced Indians, the Others were never Indians. References to deviations from rightful conduct were expressed as behaving "like Moors" or "like the great Turk"—never "like Indians." In terms of the current emphasis in colonial studies that takes the Self and the Other not as a given but as a historically shifting pair of identities, the situation in Peru was of a displaced, triangular shiftiness: the Spaniards' map of alterities had not changed; they still imagined themselves in comparison to their known Others back in Spain. Also, the hypothesis makes sense that if in colonial India the question of the British was how to keep the natives at fault—Bhabha's (1994:86) "like but not quite," the case under study tells of a window of opportunity in which natives could be both Christian and pagan; that is, could legitimately challenge the need for being "like." In Peru, at that early stage some escaped the "double bind of ocularcentrism" (Levin 1993:4)—either being in the role of dominant observer or of observable object—by being seen as objects of Christianity *and* seeing through its lenses the Christians as non-Christians. They could thus confound the conquerors' gaze, helped by the divergences among Spaniards and the cracks and limits that their epistemological certainties cast on their actions. As a result, conversion was not an either/or matter, nor a neatly defined one, and asserting dominance was demanding. While the Spaniards' responses on the religious terrain were slow to come, on others in which a heterogeneous state of culture and society troubled their claim of ascendancy, they proved more effective.

TO IMITATE AND TO EXOTIZE

After Murra's influential work (1978, 1975), Andean economies have been largely thought to function on nonmarket principles.[13] Instead of the pursuit of profit, reciprocity and redistribution ties mobilized human energy, securing the production and circulation of goods within a given group. Because these ties were at once social and political as well as economic, the movement of goods mapped relations in an inclusive way, blurring Western distinctions. The Inca state, in turn, added a layer to this system, taking surplus from communities and partially returning it in the form of institutionalized generosity. Building on this precontact foundation, studies of the early colonial economy take two different paths. Ethnohistorians focus on native peoples' relations with the new order. While some argue that the Spanish conquest severely disrupted traditional Andean patterns, with the market economy playing a major role (e.g., Wachtel 1971), others suggest that Andean polities successfully engaged Spanish colonialism and in particular used market forces to their advantage (e.g. Stern 1982). On the other hand, the work of social historians scrutinizes the fine grain of the settler society (e.g., Lockhart 1968). From their studies emerges the image of a complex Spanish colonial economy that revolved around the encomenderos, conquerors-entrepreneurs who not only collected tribute but engaged in land accumulation, production, and trade, realizing their Indians' produce and labor force; the latter remain in the margins of the picture.

The problem I would like to address is that regardless of their differences, these postcontact scenarios assume clear-cut differences between colonizers and colonized, implicitly reifying Spaniards as market-minded actors. This obscures the fact that the logic guiding Andeans' and Spaniards' economic practices were different in some regards but similar in others, and also that the latter's acts were often not guided by profit alone. I suggest that not only were there similarities between parties, but that the conquerors actively imitated native practices to develop their colonial enterprises. To restore their distinctiveness, and therefore their claim of dominance, the conquerors resorted to the exotization of native ways of making sense and to forcing Indians into double binds. Once this power dynamics is taken into consideration, the image of the early colonial economy changes, revealing that the tensions animating the religious landscape were not exceptional.

In what follows, I ask the reader to keep in mind that the sources are few and fragmented.[14] The earliest reference to a colonial market (*tiangues*) in Cuzco speaks of a Spanish attempt to assert and objectify an elusive mastery. Although relations during Manco Inca's siege were far from implying subordination, and the exchanges could be read as payment of services, the conquerors labeled "tribute" the gold and silver Incas gave them after trading it in the city's main plaza. As the next piece of information notes, the siege was not an exceptional time in which politics overdetermined markets. In mid-1539 Paullu Inca, and Hernando and Gonzalo Pizarro returned from defeating Colla armies and Manco Inca's armies in the Collasuyo provinces, south of Cuzco. Several Peru veterans informed the royal prosecutor of having seen caravans of llamas entering Cuzco loaded with corn, quinoa, and *chuño*, grains Hernando had looted during the campaign and was then selling in the city's market (AGI, P 90a, n. I, r. II, ff. 159, 363v, 404v). The move at once delivered a political message—a punishment to those ethnic groups that had challenged the Spaniards' authority—and created demand: Indians from the Collasuyo region, several days distant from Cuzco, had to buy back the staple grains in the city's market (ibid., f. 363v).

The fact that the few traceable early market transactions involving Spaniards and native peoples were as much about economy as about politics, besides emphasizing the import of the circulation of goods by Paullu and ethnic lords seen in chapter 5, illustrates that the emergence of colonial markets was not a process in which Andean peoples surrendered their customs to an altogether alien logic—the Incas also blurred distinctions between both fields. In fact, Spaniards copied native customs. During the 1539 campaign, in addition to the aforementioned grains, Hernando Pizarro looted loads of coca and sold them in Cuzco's and other nearby markets (ibid., ff. 363v, 437v, 502v), where it was not simply produce, nor in demand only among Indians. The Spanish carpenter Pedro Román, "the good old man," declared that "sometimes [coca] was given to him in payment of his carpentry works" in the houses of conquerors, such as fixing doors or chairs (ibid.,

f. 161). In other words, seven years after Cajamarca, coca was accepted currency among Spaniards. This reveals both the politics behind later Spanish administrators' labeling of coca as "Indian currency" (Matienzo [1567] 1967: 164), a "magnet stone" (Glave 1989:88) that drew (only) Indians to markets,[15] and an ironic resemblance between the allegedly distinct parties: if, as it was known since the beginning, Spaniards eat their currency, Indians did likewise with theirs.

This crisscrossing similarity is just one expression of the larger process of copying and asserting distinctiveness that characterized early colonial economic relations. The actual heads of the colonial enterprise, the Pizarros, walked in Inca footsteps, and not by accident. Because of the coca leaf's religious and political value among Andean peoples, the Incas paid particular attention to it and even attempted to monopolize its production and circulation.[16] In the Cuzco area in particular, the powerful *panacas* of Inca rulers Pachacuti Inca, Topa Inca Yupangui, and the last pre-Hispanic emperor, Huayna Cápac, developed and controlled most coca production sites as personal property (Villanueva Urteaga 1970; Rowe 1990; Julien 2000b). In turn, thanks to his careful allotment of encomienda awards, Pizarro and his brothers gained control of most of these sites and even copied Inca labor and production structures (Julien 2000b).[17] The same can be said of other major enterprises. Mining, soon the pillar of the Peruvian economy—and since the exploitation of Potosí, of much of the emerging world-system—also involved imitation. The Pizarros were the first in exploiting, toward 1539, the Inca silver mines of Porco; as in the previous case, Pizarro assigned to himself and his brothers large encomienda awards nearby to secure manpower (Varón Gabai 1996:271–359; Presta 1999), a copying that was to be copied. In turn, Vaca de Castro imitated the Pizarros. He sent Indians from several encomiendas that were vacant after the battle of Chupas (16 September 1542) to work Huayna Cápac's gold mines of Carabaya (AGI, J. 467, cpo. 3, cuad. 3, cargo 6); he also sold in Cuzco's market corn, chuño, and coca produced by the vacant groups, and also enforced a selling monopoly (ibid., cpo. 1, f. 26v; cpo. 3, cuad. 2)—which Hernando Pizarro had done in 1539 (AGI, P 90a, r. 1, n. 11, f. 135v).

The fact that to create a "new" economic order the Spaniards engaged in large-scale mimicking, posed the threat of similarity by force. (If equals, there can be no ascendancy claim.) One of the Spaniards' solutions was to exotize native practices, reinstating distinctiveness. The fundament is epistemic. Under the Incas, gold and silver had no exchange value, but a high religious and political one. Gold was considered to grow as a manifestation of the Sun, silver of the Moon. The Sun and the Moon (and other celestial bodies) were huacas venerated because of the reproductive energy they could endow, and they were observed to construct advanced calendars (Berthelot 1986; Silverblatt 1987; Zuidema 1982, 1983). Tellingly, sixteenth-century Spaniards held the same metals in the highest esteem, in fact saw close relations between them and the aforesaid heavenly bodies (gold was to be found in hot lands, closer to the sun; silver in cold areas, closer to the moon), and thought that celestial bodies influenced peoples' lives and observed them to construct advanced calendars. One can see this similarity put to a test in a short story narrated by Pedro Pizarro ([1571] 1965:222). In early 1543, when the conqueror Martínez de Vegazo asked the ethnic lords of his encomienda to show him a rich Sun/sun mine he had heard about, they refused, fearful that they would all die and their crops dry up, as their "sorcerers [hechiceros]" told them.[18] After Vegazo pressured the curacas and told them that their "sorcerers did not speak the truth," they reluctantly agreed to show him the mine. As they prepared to leave, however, the Sun/sun's anger, manifest in an eclipse, stalled the party. A new round of arguments took place, in which Vegazo rehearsed a lesson in astronomy to ease the Indians' "lack of understanding" of the Sun/sun's movements. The trip then resumed, but only to be finally aborted by an earthquake; the lords declared at that point that even if they were killed because of it, they would not show the mine.

In addition to disqualifying native beliefs and deeming their own rational as key, another way in which Christians tried to reinstate their claim of dominance was by forcing Indians into double binds. As part of a political shift at royal court that I will explain later (see the discussion of New Laws in the section "A Revolution of One"), at his return to Spain, the royal prosecutor indicted governor Vaca de Castro. Charge 6 was sending Indians to work in the mines of Carabaya, in which many died, and profiting from it (AGI, J 467, cpo. 3, s/f). While Vaca argued that the Indians worked the mines of their own will and even profited from it themselves (ibid., cpo. 2, s/f)—which was not necessarily a lie[19]—the royal prosecutor's witnesses, posing a double bind, told that the Indians indeed died in the mines due to climate difference (Carabaya was in a hot and humid land, while most miners were from the dry and cold Collao) and yet admitted to "believe that the said Indians would not go willingly to the mines *because they are enemies of work* . . . and if not compulsively pushed they never . . . serve" (loc. cit.; my emphasis).

And yet stating ascendancy was not a one-way street; the same episode could trigger the fear of failing to conform. Prompted by the Indians of the Collao provinces' complaints about the hardships of having to go to the mines, the Dominican provincial fray Tomás de San Martín told all conquerors gathered in Mass in Cuzco that "the governor and the others that had Indians in the mines should reason, because the Turks did not do what they did," imposing on Indians so many obligations that they did not have time to tend their own fields nor to hear doctrine (AGI, J 467, cpo. 4, f. 130). There were, in fact, other things Turks did not do. Rewarding economic activities toward 1543 included some very far from those that sixteenth-century and current accounts tend to privilege. Another source of revenue Vaca de Castro sought to profit from was the Incas' adoration of their former kings. Jealously guarded, their embalmed bodies played a key role in the daily activities of the politicoreligious imperial apparatus, and were huacas to their respective panacas. Fray Tomás de San Martín and Fray Juan de Olías denounced that, appallingly, the governor was in control of Huayna Cápac's body and had one of his servants collect payments from noble Incas wanting to "visit" him (ibid., ff. 133v, 139).[20]

HOW TO CO-OPT A KING'S POTENCY

Striking as it may be, the Christian governor's understanding of the cross-cultural value of Inca bodies was not original. It had been anticipated by Paullu Inca, who toward 1540 allegedly gave Huayna Cápac's embalmed body to Cuzco's provisor, Luis de Morales. The clergyman was as interested in it as the governor, although had a different goal in mind: to bury it, as he allegedly did. There were more twists to the story; all in all, the body was twice buried for good and thrice discovered, always as if for the first time.[21] The comings and goings surrounding this Inca's body—the fact that it is the same body although it could not be so, that it was finally discovered although it had already been so, and that everybody knew of its import although nobody agreed on it—encapsulate well, I suggest, the larger power landscape: an active Spanish-Indian counterpoint of successive acts of imitation and successive declarations of origin. Far from a clear-cut affair, the way in which colonial Peru worked resembled—paraphrasing Foucault (1984:76–77)—"a field of entangled and confused parchments" of meanings "that have been scratched over and copied many times," that knew "invasions, struggles, plundering, disguises, ploys." Although the Spaniards had an advantage that allowed them to introduce to the game authoritative signs Indians could not ignore, the coin could always be flipped. In particular, kings and their cosmologies could make other mimes possible, at times to native peoples' advantage; they could, for instance, secure rights to land.

Although in the long run, the result of Spanish colonialism in Peru was the concentration of the best lands in the hands of rich Spanish families (the famous *estancieros*), the history of the process is complex and meandrous, as many specialized studies show. In part, because if the Spaniards' acts of transformation could secure them land titles (what is usually considered the practice of Castilian law), the acts were not safe from the general dynamic of plundered meanings. Spanish legal acts' efficacy rested on the potency of their Grand Magus, their king, a potency Peruvian indigenous peoples recognized as inevitable and learned to co-opt.

Given the complexity of studying land tenure in Inca and early colonial times, I will examine only a circumscribed—and often overlooked—phenomenon at the core of the transition: the production of reality effects. The best way to define the problem is to situate it in relation to studies of land and the men holding it in terms of Spanish law in practice (*derecho vivo*) (Guevara Gil 1993), and in terms of cross-cultural tenure regimes (Ramírez 1996:42–86). As both approaches show, to establish property rights all parties had to take into consideration Spanish legal procedures and to maneuver successfully across the unknown cultural terrain of actual landholding practices. I suggest, though, that establishing property rights was not reducible to this pair of endeavors, but depended on a previous one: the production of reality effects. On the one hand, for "things" (*cosas*) to turn into "goods" (*bienes*)—that is, into objects of law—a prior definition of their existence has to take place, as "things." On the other hand, cultural differences mattered, but in such an untidy and heterogeneous terrain of political legitimacy and land tenure as Cuzco's, property had less to do with how things *really* were than with the capacity to define reality, making situations mean one thing or another, crystallize in one recognizable form or another. Consequently, the goal of my analysis will not be to establish who owned a given piece of land, but to illuminate how *certainties* of property rights were created—how "effects of truth are produced within discourses that are neither true nor false" (Foucault 1980:118).

In order to discuss the actual cases, I need to present a brief sketch of precontact land tenure. Lands could belong to different entities: to the Inca (representing the empire), particular Incas, and Inca huacas; to ethnic lords (representing an entire group), particular lords, and ethnic huacas. Complicating this taxonomy, the Incas often resettled population pools (*mitimaes*) in foreign ethnic territories and gave them land to support themselves and at times land they had to work for the empire.[22] As a result, the ethnic groups affected often lost access to some of their agricultural lands. In addition to mitimaes, temporary pools (*mitayos*) worked lands for the Incas, at times far away from their original locations. Finally, large ethnic groups had their own mitimaes and mitayos. These variations, together with the political practice of discontinuous territoriality, resulted in a patchwork-like landscape of human and natural resources.

The question is complex also because the very notion of property objectifies a fluid reality; there was no property in a Western sense. At stake was who benefited from what was produced in a given plot. For instance, communal lands worked for the Inca to pay tribute could be labeled as "Inca lands," and they were likely so from the Incas' point of view, since the Inca claimed a conquered group's lands to be his and graciously gave most of it back. But from a community's point of view, its ancestors had made them into productive lands, and the Inca was just receiving their produce. This disagreement was irrelevant in practice because who owned a piece of land was not an issue: insofar as land could not be sold in a market, what mattered was how its produce was appropriated—which was defined politically. Land, labor, and political authority were thus inextricably tied.

What did the Spaniards understand of this complex terrain, and what did they do? Little, it is often argued, and they only messed things up. Pizarro, for instance, split ethnic mitimaes from their curacas when giving encomienda titles, effectively diminishing a group's access to resources in distant ecological niches and weakening its natural lord's authority.[23] I suggest, though, that there was no lack of understanding: Pizarro knew what he was doing. The reasons he did it, and his means of doing it, speak to a first moment of reality making, a moment in which he needed to objectify beings and relations, turning them into apprehensible things.

On 26 March 1534, caught in the predicament of giving encomiendas to fence off Pedro de Alvarado and at once veiling his conquest plan from Manco Inca (see chapter 3), Pizarro dictated in Cuzco his first ordinances. In item 5, in consideration of the fact that Indians spent part of the year away from their lands, and seeking to avoid conflicts among conquerors, Pizarro ordered that "taking the word of the encomienda [depósito] the Indians in that part they shall serve there and shall not return to where they used to live" (PML, MA 155, f. 180v). That is, as if casting a spell, the head conqueror gave the legal word a magical power; beings and relations were being transformed as the news of a given encomienda was reaching those defined as its objects. This moment zero of the colonial order meant to at once strike out the complexities of the indigenous landscape, making encomienda titles effective—the conquistadors/encomenderos would start fighting with each other if Indians did not stay put. Intended to mark people, the word would undoubtedly affect land: if frozen in place, land claims would start overlapping and colliding, since many people would be caught away from their own.

A year later, a new ordinance from Pizarro changed the rules again. He mandated that "mitimaes" should serve the Spaniard who had them in his encomienda title, but if they continued to pay tribute to their curaca of origin, then they should serve the Spaniard who had that curaca (F. Pizarro [1535] 1986:153). This exception made the mitimaes' status depend not on an arbitrary-but-definitive title, but on actual relations. The door to conflicts of all kinds was open. Since no encomendero wanted to lose tribute payers, tenacious legal actions were common.[24] Meanwhile, native actors also took advantage of the opaque panorama. Their actions cloaked by the permanent state of war, native lords, either on their own or allied with their encomenderos, tried to improve their situation; they attempted to regain lands where mitimaes had settled and expel them altogether, or to add mitimaes to their subjects, or to keep control of their mitimaes and the lands they exploited elsewhere.[25]

These and other moves resulted in tense configurations of ethnic borders and statuses, and consequently of land tenure. Although data on the Cuzco area for the period under consideration is scarce, one can still glimpse murky situations whose clarification required mastery to define what things were. The question I examine next is: Since Spaniards deemed only their own words magic, how did native actors sustain land claims in a space where the conquest worked upon a previous layer of radical Inca interventions? I suggest that it was done by mimicry, taking Christian cosmology to its logical ends. In essence, it was an elaboration on the first Cuzco bishop's ideas (see chapter 5), which had involved, in turn, a reappropriation of Inca forms. The move effectively flipped the coin.

In 1556 a complaint was brought before Cuzco's *corregidor* (royal local authority) by Don Felipe Caritopa (LL, Caritopa, n/f). *Yanaconas* (servants) of Francisco Altamirano had ransacked his corn lands named Chuquimaturi, located near Cayaocache, Cuzco valley. After a quick inquiry, the corregidor issued a protective order (*amparo*) in favor of Don Felipe and asked the parties to prove their claim. While Altamirano failed to make a strong case, Caritopa succeeded; his arguments bring different rationales to light. To begin with, the land was collectively owned by several Incas, who managed to get more land confirmed than was originally at stake. In the execution of the amparo Don Joan Paucarguaman, Auca Mycho, Don Joan Vscamayta, and Caritopa took possession, in their names and those of other *orejones*, of the lands, the huts on them, and houses in the town of Cayaocache.

In the *probanza* presented by the orejones, Spanish and Inca notions tangled. In question 2 the Incas stated that they had held the lands and houses for "ten, twenty, thirty, forty years and more." The goal was to establish property rights through continuous possession in accordance with Spanish terms (Guevara Gil 1993:170) and was legally sufficient.[26] Yet in question 3 they asked whether, besides having held the town and the plots in that way, "gave the said town of Cayocache" to the said orejones "Ynga Yupangui, lord that was of this kingdom," and "whether under that title" they have held them. Ynga Yupangui, also called Pachacuti, ninth in the list of Inca sovereigns scholars most commonly use, is known to have done a large reordering of Cuzco valley. What exactly Pachacuti gave, to whom, and to what extent it mattered had to be unclear; it depended on how land tenure in the valley was understood (the Incas were not its native inhabitants), and on how the Incas and the *panacas* were defined—either as actual kings, heads of royal lineages, or, as structuralist scholars suggest, as fictive heads of the social units of a complex, post-rotational system.[27] The orejones, nevertheless, invoked Pachacuti's gift as a title, and to clear away potential uncertainties mimicked Spanish categories. In question 6 they claimed that some twenty-two years ago, Pizarro, "confirming the *merced* that the said Ynga Yupangui made to the said orejones . . . gave the said town to the said orejones Indians so that they lived and had their houses in it."

In other words, two myths, one Inca and the other Spanish, converged to produce land titles. The orejones swiftly merged Spanish and Inca forms, shaping their—likely contestable—pre-Spanish rights into a recognizable, unquestionable form: the merced. By doing so, they (like Valverde in 1539) took the Crown's cosmology to its logical end: the Spanish legal framework determined that because of the papal donation, the natural lords' sovereignty had been transferred to the Spanish king, so he—or his highest representative—should confirm his predecessors' legal acts (another example of the fact that the Crown's claim to semiotic mastery's strength lay in its weakness). The case also reveals both early political trade between Pizarro and Incas and the latter's understanding and appropriation of the potency Spaniards attributed to their acts of government.[28] Recognizing that Pizarro held the magic wand that could (re)define what things and relations among them were, the orejones asked for a wave of it. The Inca noblemen, in turn, cared for the wizard and his relatives. Among those few changing sides during Manco Inca's siege who can be identified was Don Felipe Caritopa; at a time of scarcity, he drove a large flock into Cuzco (*Discurso* . . . [1542–1608?] 1892:37).

The example tells that despite their disadvantageous position in the signifying game, native peoples could be successful at establishing land claims. I am not arguing that Spanish estates did not encroach on native land—they did, or that the legal field was level. At the same time, I do find it important to avoid reinscribing the mystifying tale of impotent Indians facing all-powerful colonizers, which in a last instance confirms all-too-familiar taxonomies. I suggest that it is precisely because the Spanish colonial enterprise was neither as powerful nor as coherent as to escape indigenous flippings of the coin that Spaniards often found it *necessary* to resort to the power asymmetries between parties (i.e., access to legal resources, political connections, economic pressures, institutionalized racism, etc.) in order to prevail.

Nor is it the case that only the indigenous nobility could be successful when fighting over land with Spaniards. Although much less detailed than trials, Cuzco notarial registers are full of ordinary native people, Inca and non-Inca, trading land in Cuzco's valley and nearby areas.[29] And they not only sold land to Spaniards; they also bought it from them—besides buying and selling amongst themselves—in many occasions even trading lucrative coca production sites. Further, land also circulated in an "Inca sphere" (Lamana 1997b) impervious to commodification and below the Spaniards' radar. As Doña Catalina Tocto Vssica declared in 1560, for instance, she had received lands from her husband, Paullu Inca, which were not listed in his will because "as things done between Indians, and not being of the custom of writing down what happens between them, he did not do it" (in Heffernan 1996:206).

A REVOLUTION OF ONE

The heterogeneous state of culture and society of mid-1540s Peru reflected the limitations and contradictions inhabiting the Spaniards' colonial projects and native peoples' creative ways of relating to them; at no point did it express a weak will toward power among conquerors. In fact, the flippings-of-the-coin just examined unfolded in a social context in which the conquerors' hegemonic impulses guarded social hierarchies, actively constraining what Indians could do or say. This tense status quo was tipped off balance by the arrival of Vaca de Castro's successor, the viceroy Blasco Núñez Vela. As is known, Vela's attempt to enforce the absolutist project in Peru triggered four years of strife among Spaniards. Although, as scholars have pointed out, the divergences between the conquerors' and the Crown's political projects were at the center of the dispute, I suggest that it also expressed a major twist in Spanish-Indian colonial relations. Besides threatening to dispossess many key players of their encomiendas, Peru's first viceroy discursively articulated and publicly legitimated some of the native peoples' challenges to his countrymen's claims of dominance, upsetting the unstable status quo.

The colonial experience caught the nascent Spain by surprise. Building central power and a colonial system at once, the Crown faced numerous internal and external challenges, at once political, legal, and moral. In the Indies, as the early colonial experience matured, the question became how to secure the survival and conversion of native (tax-paying) populations given that only conquest *compañías* could put those populations under its control in the first place (Pietschmann 1989). In Peru in the years in question, royal order had few means of direct control. As we have seen many times, the Crown was present mainly through its claim to semiotic mastery—that is, through its claim to provide the only forms that could make the colonial encounter crystallize in handy forms—which proved effective only when locally invited. In addition, the constant state of war helped the Pizarros' political project, which early on had been embraced by the few royal officers.[30] In this milieu, the Crown tried to enroll the clergymen in its colonial project of power building, but with limited success. After Berlanga's 1535–36 inquiry (see chapter 3), the Crown brought in Valverde as his agent, and assigned him a number of tasks upon his return to Peru as first Cuzco bishop (*Instrucción 1536* [1536]1943a). The bishop's first steps announced him as the right man, but the situation soon changed. Denunciations of Valverde's own political project as detrimental to royal authority (e.g., La Gama [1539] 1865:146) led the Crown to support him only as far as his job as defender of Indians was concerned, never a step beyond (e.g., AGI, P 185, r. 20, pza. 1). He also soon sided with Pizarro, who favored Valverde's numerous businesses, saw to the success of his entourage (Hampe 1981), and even awarded him an encomienda (in Julien 1998b:88).

The political status quo did not change with Peru's first nonconqueror governor, Cristóbal Vaca de Castro. To explain why, I need to complicate the image of the Crown I have used as shortcut. During these years, Charles V spent most of his time out of Spain, fighting the Infidels in the Mediterranean and the Heretics in Flanders. The actual control of colonial affairs was in the hands of the Council of the Indies. Pizarro had staunch allies in this collegiate body, among them Francisco de los Cobos, the king's secretary, and the council's president, Fray García de Loaysa. They protected Pizarro's interests, and he reciprocated.[31] Vaca de Castro was another of the active spinners of this web of interests and favors, not an outsider loyal only to his king.[32]

While the political balance in Peru remained stable during Vaca's governorship, the situation at the council did not. Powered by the lobbying of the so-called Indians' Party and the pressure of the Council of Castile, Charles V in person led a review (*visita*) of the council and a major junta that examined the government of the Indies (Shäfer 1935:61–67; Pérez de Tudela 1958). The main outcome was the New Laws of November 1542 (Muro Orejón 1959). They aimed at enforcing the Indians' freedom (chaps. 3, 20–25, 31) and at revolutionizing the way the colonies worked. There would be local royal authorities (corregidores) overseeing city councils (chap. 32), a High Court (Real Audiencia) above them, and a viceroy (chap. 10). The encomienda regime was to end. The titles were not to be passed to a second generation but instead would revert back to the Crown (chap. 30). Additionally, the encomiendas of those who had abused Indians, those guilty in the wars between Pizarro and Almagro (chap. 29), all royal officers, and monasteries and clergyman (chap. 26) also would revert to the Crown. Completing the shift, men of merit, or their descendants, were to be preferred for royal offices (chap. 32). Within the larger strengthening of royal power, 1542 was, or was intended to be, a turning point, foundational to the absolutist project in the colonies.[33]

The one chosen to enforce this revolution-from-above in Peru was Blasco Núñez Vela, who proved to be an absolutist avant la lettre, only lacking absolutist means. He arrived in Lima in May 1544, and after a protracted political conflict was defeated and killed by Gonzalo Pizarro in January 1546, in the battle of Añaquito. Gonzalo governed an unsettled Peru until he too was defeated in April 1548 in the battle of Jaquijahuana by the Crown's new envoy, Pedro de la Gasca, and soon after was executed. Studies of the conflict often focus on the Spaniards alone, specifically on the luck of the encomiendas and the complex military and politicojuridical plot (e.g., Loredo 1941, 1958; Pérez de Tudela 1963; Lohmann Villena 1977). Showing a similar understanding of the conflict's import, work on the conquest of the Incas often jumps ahead to La Gasca's negotiations with the neo-Inca state of Vilcabamba after Gonzalo's defeat, at times arguing that the conflict among

Spaniards had no effect whatsoever on the relations between the latter and Indians (Hemming 1993:259), which is questionable.

Leaving aside the fact that wars among Spaniards took a huge toll on native populations, whose food and manpower were repeatedly ransacked by all passing armies, I suggest that this conflict had an effect on native populations because the battles were not to define what person was in control, but what political project would prevail. At stake were the sources of legitimacy native actors could appeal to, and consequently their own status. And this not because of the encomiendas but because, to put it in terms I have presented before, Vela openly menaced the conquerors' hegemonic pulsations, destabilizing the colonial normal—the series of everyday habits, the configurations of what is usually done, without thinking, that enforced statuses and relations between people, and between people and objects. In particular, the viceroy's words and acts publicly legitimated native peoples' challenges to the conquerors' dominance—they could be carried out in public spaces with no fear of retribution, as they were backed by the royal seal.

Gonzalo Pizarro's campaign and governorship were no thoughtless affair. They were surrounded by a mass of documents—letters, memorials, declarations, powers of attorney, and so on—that testify to its vast reach and juridical underpinnings. To justify actions against Vela in particular, many major players produced probanzas, some of which have survived. Their structure is similar: they portray Vela as an agent of chaos, abusive and perverse, and—therefore—those opposing him as good servants of the king, sensible people who only tried to put out the fires. Although most questions refer to Spaniards alone, some refer directly or indirectly to Indians, and allow a glimpse of quotidian moments of fire.

The earliest probanza was done in September 1544 by Lima's Royal High Court (Real Audiencia). Its magistrates had just imprisoned and shipped Vela back to Spain, and a month later, surrendering to mounting pressure, they would have to name Gonzalo Pizarro as Peru's governor. Of the fifty-nine questions, the few involving Indians make the colonial normal once again visible as well as the way in which the viceroy's actions sabotaged it. Question 7 asked whether it was true that during his arrival, on his way south by land from Trujillo to Lima, Vela emptied all *tambos*, sent the Indians serving them away, and ordered them not to supply travelers "as they were accustomed to and accustomed to doing . . . from immemorial time" (AGI, P 186, r. II, n/f). That is, Vela altered the way things were and had been, the customary order of things. Question 8 followed up; introducing the other two elements central to the colonial normal—need and practical reason—it asked whether, as a result, those traveling had no food nor supplies of any sort and suffered "great work of illness and hunger and necessity" and "because of it were stealing and *rancheando* nearby Indians," causing much damage and many deaths.

The causal order is revealing: traveling Spaniards had no food; *therefore* they had to steal from Indians—and kill some, presumably because the latter resisted the theft. What exactly Vela ordered, and why Spanish travelers could not obtain supplies is not yet clear, but soon becomes so. Question 12 asked, "if the said viceroy ordered the food Indians used to give by grace since immemorial time to be paid in gold," which "scandalized and riled up all Spaniards in the land." Clearly the problem the viceroy caused was not that there were no supplies available, but that Indians had to be paid for feeding and serving Spaniards, an idea conquerors and royal magistrates alike found outrageous. In other words, powering the resultant rancheos there was a need, as the question implied, although not one related to hunger; it was the need to restore deeply embodied understandings of hierarchy and humiliation.

Question 12 closed the argument with an exoticization. It asked if, in addition to the fact that Indians had never been paid, giving them gold was a waste, since "what enters their power never exits it, and they keep it to bury it when they die or for other rites and ceremonies they do, and do not have that on which to spend it, because they go by naked and barefoot" (loc. cit.). That is, not only was it unthinkable to pay an Indian for supplies or services, but in the event of payment, to give gold was absolutely foolish since Indians were irrational beings, had no use for the metal, and would only bury it. The exotizing move involves the estrangement and generalization of native practices. Andean peoples did use gold and silver objects to honor their (wealthy) dead, and buried them with all paraphernalia, but the tomb of no Spanish king, lord, or high-rank clergyman was poor. And like Spaniards, Andean peoples used gold and silver for other ends. I suggest that it is precisely the menace similitude was to dominance, in particular in such a volatile context, that was resented by Spaniards and required exotization. The case was particularly trying because reversing the direction in which metals flowed also reversed the signs, positive and negative, in the argued Indians/Spaniards opposition; it therefore called into question things taken for granted—that Indian practices and beliefs were foolish and particular, while the Spanish were rational and self-evident, thus universal.

The fact that such questions could be asked by High Court magistrates in a legal text shows how deeply embodied Spaniards' hegemonic pulsations were, and explains the nature of Vela's "scandal." The witnesses uniformly agreed, and in cases added nuances that bring back to the fore the most conflictive by-product of the royal cosmology—the Indians' liberty. The royal accountant Agustín de Zárate declared that he saw Vela sending Indians away from the tambos "under the pretense of ensuring their liberty," after which they refused to give anything without payment in gold or silver. The soldiers were angry at the viceroy, and Zárate, when paying, saw that the Indians "had their weight as traders, and were as *ladinos* in the value of weights as a trader in Medina del Campo" (loc. cit.). As in previous examples of the colonial normal, contradictions empower it because they make possible to formulate double binds: proximity—Indians resembled in fact Spanish merchants—works hand in hand with orientalization.[34]

Vela also crushed his countrymen's order of things in more direct ways. He ordered Spaniards to be punished if they stole anything from Indians, which Rodrigo Núñez de Prado confessed, "was a much scandalous and unsettling thing . . . impossible to suffer." The suffering brings us *full-circle*: faced with the enforcement of the Indians as equal beings, Captain Pedro de Vergara declared "Indians to be by nature . . . evil" (they refused to give for free) and added that Spaniards "would rather let themselves die than suffer it" (loc. cit.); that is, beliefs and feelings were not so different—if Indians would rather die than show the Sun's mine to Spaniards, Spaniards would rather die than give gold to Indians.

Resemblances did not end there. The viceroy's attempt to make Indians free vassals was one with the attempt to strengthen royal authority, an attempt that to many eyes had to be powered by the ultimate enemies of Christians: the Devil and the Turks. In September 1546, seven months after Vela's final defeat and death in the battle of Añaquito, the Lima council made a probanza. In it the Dominican principal, Fray Domingo de Santo Tomás, declared that Vela understood Gonzalo Pizarro's claim about the encomiendas and told him that it was "the Devil that has tricked His Majesty, setting him to do in these kingdoms what the Grand Turk does in his, that is not wanting lords of vassals to exist, but rather paying corregidores and justices" (AGI, P 186, r. 13, s.f.). Although not revolutionaries like the men of Castilian communities, who in 1519–21 openly fought the same king in an attempt to define what a modern order should look like (Maravall 1994), Spaniards in early colonial Peru had a clear consciousness of what absolutism was about—the loss of their acquired rights and status—and saw it inspired by the forces of darkness. The Devil's favorite strategy, inducing people to do foolish things (MacCormack 1991), had succeeded even with the very Christian Charles V.

These mid-1540s snapshots of the colonial normal—as those about cargar indios and ranchear from the time of Manco Inca's war—may reinstate the impression of an absolute Spanish control. Yet, at a second glance the passages make clear that Vela created serious problems for the Spaniards in Peru only because native peoples were ready to take advantage of the options he legitimized. Consistent with the fact that, as we just saw, interpretations were plural and dominance disputed, this reveals that the conquerors needed to enforce and police an ascendancy they lacked. As usual, their repertoire of efforts included to reinstate distinctiveness via the exotization of indigenous practices and beliefs, and to force Peru's native peoples into double binds.

The particularity of the conflicts and wars triggered by the absolutist project in the Indies is that it made possible a new kind of challenge to the conquerors' will of dominance: native lords could appropriate two of the former's most ubiquitous fetishes—the king's and God's service—as a means to legitimize their political projects and personas. And, given most conquerors' doubtful allegiances, the outcome was at best a blurring of merits, at worst a reversal of roles. Consider, for instance, these images: After his arrival to Peru's northern coast, Vela pursued his way south by land; on the long trip, the first viceroy to step onto Peru was escorted and celebrated not by the most eminent conquerors, but by a large number of native lords, who traveled with him all the way to Lima; by contrast, the conquerors there resented the viceroy's arrival and allowed him to enter the city only after forcing him to promise political concessions (AGI, P 186, r. 11). Or, while Gonzalo Pizarro formed an army to go from Cuzco to Lima to meet the viceroy, Paullu Inca made the same trip to welcome him. Later on, the Inca offered help to the Crown's new envoy, the bishop Pedro de la Gasca (Calvete de Estrella [1565–67]:1. 4, c. 1, 1964: 393) and joined those who had raised the king's flag in the south of the empire; there, along with other main Incas and many service men, in October 1547 he fought against Gonzalo in the battle of Huarina, and after the defeat joined Gasca's advancing camp in Jauja (BNE, Ms. 20193, e.g., ff. 56, 69). The landscape of heterogeneous political projects and subjectivities is even richer if one considers that those opposing Gonzalo called themselves "the Catholics." In fact, Paullu went to Huarina with Cuzco's bishop, Juan Solano, who energized the Catholics with a Mass before battle (Longo 1996:514), where—if one were to follow the typology's own logic—they must have been fighting infidels.[35]

CHAPTER 7

"The End"

Histories need endpoints, and Pedro de la Gasca's governorship (1548–49) is a convenient one. I do not argue that
a clear watershed took place then—that would contradict my
overall argument—but suggest that some important traits of
the early status quo faded while new ones that would gain center stage began.

Gasca defeated Gonzalo Pizarro in the battle of Jaquijahuana,
on 9 April 1548, and had him executed shortly thereafter. Although
he did not fully enforce the New Laws (Charles V had annulled
some of its most incendiary chapters by then), Gasca advanced
royal order in different ways. I will stress two here. First, he put
in office *corregidores*, the local royal authorities. They oversaw
cabildos' work and limited their power, replacing them as first legal
instance. Once the Real Audiencia (High Court) and the viceroy
replaced, respectively, the conqueror-governor as highest legal
and political instance, the initial institutional frame was all but
gone. Second, Gasca ordered a general survey of the land (*visita
general*) and with the result at hand set the annual tribute each
encomendero should receive (the *tasa*) (Hampe 1989:134–56;
Lohmann Villena 1952). This innovation had a double impact:
it capped the exaction and reduced the encomenderos' direct
power—from then on royal magistrates would set amounts.

The tasa also hastened the commodification of social relations, as it increasingly included gold and silver as part of tribute payments. This was, in fact, part of a larger change: the rearticulation of the entire colonial economic space powered by the exploitation of Potosí's rich silver mines. Best known by its massive production of silver linking Peru to Spain's political hegemony in Europe (and in turn linking Europe to China), Potosí also had a major local impact. Before its realization in the international sphere, the money-commodity was realized in a surging local economy that together with Potosí's rapidly growing population (from 20,000 in 1550 to 100,000 in 1610), effectively displaced Cuzco as the center of economic gravity (Assadourian 1979; Bakewell 1984).

Less spectacular but as important, by 1549 a generational change had taken place among the main characters of the transition. On the Spanish side, Hernando Pizarro was the only main conqueror alive—although imprisoned almost for life in Spain. Among the churchmen, Bishop Vicente de Valverde had died trying to escape Diego de Almagro "the Lad" in 1541, while Luis de Morales was by then back in Spain. On the native side, the Incas who bridged Inca and Spanish times, Manco and Paullu, had died. Manco was murdered in 1544 by a few exiled Almagristas he had hosted in Vilcabamba (Hemming 1993:265–69; Guillén Guillén 1994:127–30; Lamana 1997b:135–37). The relations his son and successor, Sayri Túpac, established with the Spanish Crown tilted toward recognition. Thus, for instance, during Gasca's seclusion to plan the reshuffling of all encomiendas, messengers from Vilcabamba asked him for particular lands and Indians to be reserved (Hemming 1993:270–72). Paullu's death in 1549—the only death due to natural causes—was also followed by changes.[1] His status, the kinds of things he could do because of the historically sedimented senses of order wrapping his persona, constituted an "immaterial inheritance" (Levi 1988) he could not pass to a next generation. After his death, for instance, tolerance toward native peoples' use of public spaces and religious practices in Cuzco city ceased, as *huarachicuy* celebrations were banned. Betanzos ([1551]:I, 14, 1987:70), the Spanish chronicler married to an Inca princess, tells that the Incas continued to carry them out anyway, but they had to do it in hiding in nearby towns.

Since the practices were the same, what had changed was the context of meaning that defined them, now marking them outlaw. This change responded, arguably, to a larger, seemingly contradictory shift in the definition of who was and who was not a sensible being: at the same time that Peruvian native peoples were being progressively able to exercise their status as free vassals, they were being marked as beings at fault in a more institutional manner. As part of a number of minor novelties,[2] toward 1550 *curacas* began appearing in notary registers renting Indian labor and services to Spaniards (Lockhart 1968:207, 217), which no doubt signals a shift in the colonial normal. Yet, by the same time the Peruvian Church had reinscribed the basic hierarchies sustaining the latter. The resolutions of its first ecclesiastic council (1551–52) cast Indians as of limited mental capacity, "people of little understanding" who could only comprehend things if taught slowly (*Concilio* . . . [1552] 1950:17, 20, 34, 46). Native practices were defined as false, in opposition to the Truth (ibid.:16). *Huacas* honored the Devil and had to be destroyed (ibid.:19), and native religious practitioners and leaders jailed and otherwise punished (ibid.:25). Marking a doctrinal watershed, the notion of "inferno" was introduced, and Andean peoples' ancestors were said to inhabit it, being beyond salvation (ibid.:48; Estenssoro Fuchs 2003:66–71, 128). In fact, although salvation was in theory for anyone, because of their lacking condition Indians could only access the basic sacraments (*Concilio* . . . [1552] 1950:28). The council also signaled a political advance: it tightened a 1545 instruction given by the Lima bishop, Jerónimo de Loayza (1943), and was enforceable over the entire archbishopric, which included Loayza's archnemesis, the Cuzco bishop, Juan de Solano (Longo 1996; Mateos 1950), who had a flexible attitude toward native religious practices and authorities.

And yet, at the same time that the Peruvian Church defined order in a stark contrast, adding its two cents to the orientalization of native peoples, during the 1550s the neat opposition "Spaniard versus Indian" began to be undermined by a new social actor's coming-of-age: the progeny of conquerors and native women, the mestizos and mestizas, reached adulthood and claimed a place for themselves, challenging handy racial borders. In Cuzco's case, where the import of mestizos and mestizas was paramount, this challenge resulted in new legal regulations (Ots 1998) and precise institutions of social control (Burns 1999). The emergence of castes in Peru went hand in hand with heated political and religious debates about the shape of the future colonial society (Lohmann 1966; Assadourian 1994; Hemming 1993:360–76; Estenssoro 2003:139–310), debates in which the question of Andean peoples' capacities and distinctive characteristics played a key role. But that is another story.

Basic Political Chronology of the Spanish Conquest

1531 Jan.	Arrival of the small Spanish expedition to the north of the Inca empire. War of succession between Atahualpa Inca and Huascar Inca.
1532 Nov.	The 168 Spaniards capture Atahualpa Inca in Cajamarca. Atahualpa's generals capture Huascar. Soon after, Atahualpa has Huascar killed.
1533 July	Francisco Pizarro and Diego de Almagro, heads of the conquest company, have Atahualpa executed. Allied with another Inca faction, they march southward with some 300 men. Only Atahualpa's generals resist.
1533 Nov.	Spanish entry into Cuzco City, capital of the Inca empire, and coronation of Manco Inca as new Inca sovereign.
1534	Joint Spanish–Inca-ethnic armies continue battling Atahualpa's generals. The Spaniards face the rival conquest company of Alonso de Alvarado.
1535 Jan.	The last of Atahualpa's generals is defeated in the north of the empire. Pizarro and Almagro buy out Alvarado's army.
1535 May	Diego de Almagro and Paullu Inca, brother of Atahualpa and Manco Inca, leave for Chile with 500 and 10,000 men respectively.
1536 May	Manco Inca begins his war. Lima is attacked and Cuzco is besieged for a year. All aid expeditions are exterminated. Pizarro's brother Juan is killed.

1537 April	Diego de Almagro and Paullu Inca return from Chile and take control of Cuzco—Almagro as new governor, Paullu as new Inca king. Ethnic lords recognize both authorities. Manco Inca retreats to an isolated area north of Cuzco and founds a "neo-Inca" state.
1538 April	Hernando Pizarro defeats Diego de Almagro, and executes him in July.
1538 Aug.–1539 Feb.	Paullu Inca and Hernando and Gonzalo Pizarro battle and defeat ethnic lords and Manco's men in the south of the empire.
1540	Spanish priests actively side with Paullu Inca against conquerors.
1541 June	Diego de Almagro's son and some Almagristas kill Francisco Pizarro.
1542 Sept.	Pizarro's successor, Vaca de Castro, defeats and executes Almagro's son.
1544 (mid)	Some Almagrista refugees in Vilcabamba kill Manco Inca, and are in turn killed. Sayri Túpac, Manco's son, is crowned new Inca.
1544 July	Blasco Núñez Vela, Peru's just-arrived first viceroy, imprisons Vaca de Castro and enforces the Crown's "New Laws."
1546 Jan.	Gonzalo Pizarro defeats and kills Vela.
1548 April	Vela's successor, Pedro de la Gasca, defeats and executes Gonzalo Pizarro. Paullu Inca and many ethnic lords join Gasca.
1549 May	Paullu Inca dies of natural causes.

Notes

INTRODUCTION: SITUATED INTERVENTIONS

1. All data on editions are from WorldCat, accessed 20 February 2007. Prescott finished his work in 1847, John Hemming in 1970. The genre continues to be prolific; see, for instance, Kim MacQuarrie's 2007 *The Last Days of the Incas*.

2. Jared Diamond (1997:68–81) also gives historical agency to other tropes of Western imagination, such as epidemics, literacy, and political centralization, factors that eventually provide the context for social agency, not agency itself. Thus, epidemics do not explain Atahualpa's presence in Cajamarca; knowledge-wise Europe was not necessarily more advanced than the Incas—who also had a writing system; and the Spaniards were in America not propelled by Spain's political centralization, but because they wanted to go to China and India—the economic center of their world—and had no other choice but to sail westward (Dussel 1998).

3. Native peoples begin to appear as agents in Peruvian notarial records only toward the 1560s, once the transition is over.

4. Current accounts also use probanzas, but most often to add details to the standard master narrative.

5. All translations of Spanish originals are mine; I have strived to preserve the incongruences of the original texts. Readers interested in the original Spanish text of archival quotes can find most of them in my doctoral dissertation. In the case of indigenous words, I have adopted their most usual Hispanized spelling, adding accents according to modern Spanish use.

I. BEYOND EXOTIZATION AND LIKENESS

1. A panaca was either a lineage composed of all descendants of an Inca, excluding the next Inca and his descendants (Rowe 1985), or a unit of a complex, rotational post

system, each unit assigned to a particular task and associated with a mythical figure (Zuidema 1990). In any case, they were identifiable political fractions.

2. These Indian witnesses testified in Huarochirí, central sierra near Lima, in a trial between the Crown and Pizarro's inheritors. The only Spanish witness adds little to the issues considered here.

3. Cristóbal de Mena ([1534] 1937:80–81) says he saw a spy disguised as a Tallán when exiting Tangarara, who soon returned to Atahualpa. Pedro Pizarro (1965:175) locates the same spy earlier, in Poechos, and adds that after a violent exchange with Hernando Pizarro, brother of Francisco, the spy returned and told Atahualpa that they were bearded thieves who appeared from the sea walking on big sheep. The chronicler Pedro Cieza de León ([c.1553] 40, 1996:124) says that messengers from Túmbez told Atahualpa in Cajamarca—where he was not then—about their aggressive behavior, and he then sent a spy who counted the strangers and returned (ibid. [c.1553]:37, 1996:115).

4. Mena thought that the ducks meant to represent how they themselves would soon look and the "fortresses" that awaited them ahead (1937:81).

5. Kubler's good ideas are hampered by his errors regarding references, particularly those regarding the native political map in the Peruvian northern coastal region.

6. The sacrifice was done by throwing *puna* birds into a fire of *yanlli* wood. Those conducting the ritual carried special painted stones, and asked for their victory and for the enemy's huacas to be weakened.

7. For the role of authorities in the Andes as mediators between secular and supernatural realms, see José L. Martínez Cereceda 1995 and Susan E. Ramírez 1996. For the Inca in particular and his powers, see Franklin Pease G. Y. 1991 and Mariusz Ziólkowski 1996.

8. An interesting parallel in a less exotic context is Roger Chartier's rich analysis of the varied personal feelings toward, and understandings of, the sacred persona of the French king around 1789 (1991:138–66). Being a sacred king was neither a given fact embraced by all men in a given time and culture, nor a "dummy's tale."

9. I use the improper plural to avoid the implication of a single, monolithic native reason.

10. Cieza portrays an arrogant Atahualpa giving a long speech to encourage their captains to capture and enslave the New People, and to sacrifice the horses (44, 1996:135). (For the reverse plan, see Estete [1535?] 1918:25. Besides the fact that Cieza's informants were Huascar's partisans (39, 1996:119), this gives divine providence a chance to punish Atahualpa's arrogance, a topic all Spanish narratives indulge in. In addition to what I have argued above, it makes little sense that powerful generals in command of some 60,000 men needed to be encouraged, at length, to attack a few vandals—there was more at stake.

11. Although the number, arms, and disposition of Atahualpa's squads vary from source to source, those surrounding him carried only hidden stones and slings and an undercover doublet.

12. As this book was ready to go to the press, Xavier Lanata brought to my attention a short essay by Ziólkowski (2002) that uses the category of huaca to explain Atahualpa's behavior in Cajamarca. The present chapter diverges from it in several ways: it offers an encompassing alternative historical narrative, includes actors others than the Inca, studies the unfolding contact process, introduces uncertainty and the production of sense to avoid culturalist readings, and is concerned as much with the events as with their representation.

13. "He saw clearly that his only choice left was to test in person his luck [*fortuna*], that so adverse had been. And to that effect, he fasted and made many sacrifices to idols and oracles" (Sarmiento [1571]:64, 2001:156).

14. Evangelic narratives excepted, of course. Some sources place Atahualpa's request before the book event, some after. But the order changes little—while there was no huaca in sight, he deployed plan B.

15. In short, the text stated that God had created the world, that the pope was his representative, and that as such he had conceded the Spanish king *dominio* over the new lands. Depending on the response of a native lord—whether or not he recognized the Christian king—the door to pacific submission or a just war was juridically opened (see Hanke 1988; Pietschmann 1989).

16. As I have shown elsewhere (1996, 2001), Valverde later had strong clashes with the conquerors, and he sent letters to the king full of criticisms and requests for direct action against them and in favor of the Indians. He was the only Spaniard who took nothing of Atahualpa's ransom (Lockhart 1972:201).

17. Francisco de Xérez ([1534] 1985:111): "What God spoke to us, which is in this book"; Miguel de Estete ([1535?] 1918:24): "That he should see what God ordered, which was in that book"; Juan Ruiz de Arce ([1543] 1953:99): "He left it here, written in this book"; Diego de Trujillo ([1571]1953:139): "Atabalipa said: 'Who says so?' And [Valverde] answered: 'God says so.' And Atabalipa said: 'How does God say it?' And Fray Vicente told him: 'See them here, written.'"; Cataño (AGI, P 90a, n. I, r. II, f. 182): "He showed him the breviary telling him that they were written there." For others the book simply contained the things of God: Hernando Pizarro ([1533]1953:57): "It was about the things of God. And Atabalipa asked for the book and threw it to the ground"; Cristóbal de Mena ([1534] 1937:86): "He started to tell him the things of God . . . but he did not want to take them; and asking for the book, the father gave it to him, thinking that he wanted to kiss it; and he took it, and threw it over his men."

18. From simply reporting (Xérez 1985:111), to saying that things were in no condition for further delay (H. Pizarro 1953:57), to "llorando y llamando a Dios" (Ruiz de Arce [1543] 1953:99), to asking to attack the "perro lleno de arrogancia" (Estete 1918:24).

19. Unlike Diego de Almagro (1535–38) and Cristóbal Vaca de Castro (1541–44), Pizarro and Pedro de la Gasca (1547–49) had narrators, and did far better than the former.

20. Three months after Atahualpa's death, Judge Espinosa ([1533] 1959) wrote to the king from Panama, calling the death a mistake stemming from Pizarro's inability to govern, and offered himself as the best candidate to replace him.

2. CHRISTIAN REALISM AND MAGICALITY

1. I follow here Enrique Anderson Imbert's (1976) distinction between the real, the supernatural, and the preternatural.
2. Atahualpa wanted revenge because the huaca had augured that Atahualpa's father, Huayna Cápac, would heal if exposed to the Sun (he died), that Huáscar would defeat Atahualpa (he lost), and that Atahualpa would defeat the Christians (Estete, in Xérez 1985:127–28; P. Pizarro 1968:183–84).
3. Although soon there were no traces of Pachacamac's ministers, in the 1540s its cult blended with that of the first back slaves, giving birth to the colonial *señor de los temblores* (Rostworowski 1992:132–84).
4. "Several priests" in Mena 1937:91; three priests and Valverde in Lockhart 1972:202.
5. Estete wrote two accounts. One is an independent manuscript; the other is known only through copies included by Xérez ([1534] 1985) and by the chronicler Gonzalo Fernández de Oviedo y Valdés ([1547]: XLVI, 11–14, 1959:5:67–83).
6. Part of a long and multifaceted trial between the Crown and Hernando Pizarro (Schaefer 1931; Varón Gabai 1996). Edmundo Guillén Guillén (1974), who published most of the document, dates it as 1571; yet that is the date of the document ordering the inquiry to take place. The witnesses declared in 1573, when Diego Dávila Briceño was already *corregidor de indios* (highest rural royal authority) of the Yauyo province.
7. He located Atahualpa's death before the events at Pachacamac and divorced the latter from Atahualpa's ransom. As a result, the testimonies contradict each other, are implausible at a chronological level, or both.
8. The same choice is visible in other testimonies. Don Gonzalo Zapayco uses the word *marqués* to open his answer and shifts to *capitán*, which fitted best the alterity he was about to introduce in order to describe the news about Cajamarca—recall that *capitán* (captain, *capito*) is the name Atahualpa knew for Pizarro. Twenty years before these witnesses declared, the royal accountant Zárate ([1555]:I, 12, 1995:55) noted that although Peruvian Indians had indigenous names for *maíz*, *cacique*, and *chicha*—all Mesoamerican terms—they did not use them when talking to Spaniards.
9. Soberly because following Oviedo's version of Estete, I take 1 *carga* = 1 *arroba* = 11.5 kg [25 lb], but the *licenciado* De la Gama ([1533] 1937:43) gives 1 *carga* = 4 *arrobas*.
10. I use Hernando's numbers ([1533] 1952:68) and take 1 gold *peso* = 4.55 grams (.16 oz) and 1 silver *marco* = 227.5 g (8 oz).
11. I am using the Comaroffs' suggestive idea of a "realm of partial recognition," but I do not locate it in the conscious-unconscious action continuum. In a contact-to-

domination time, I find more useful to think of partial recognition as a *necessary temporal realm*, because contact implies a blend that is both beyond and within the actors' recognition and control. It is through unexpected configurations of meaning that provide the necessary lubricant for action that inchoate, opaque forms come into being (acts of recognition through fear, for example). They provide the initial context that makes the two actors being together possible. Whatever comes after works upon this first instance, when parallel realities intersected.

12. For a different view of the events in Jauja, see Waldemar Espinoza Soriano 1973:78–91. His version is based on that of Martín de Murúa ([1590–1611] 62, 1987:215–19), who clearly mixes Calcuchima's interaction with Hernando with that of the three men sent to Cuzco (see the next section), and gives voice and agency against the Incas to an Inca captain—Mayta Inga—who was not there at that time.

13. For Atahualpa's anger at the Sun priests, see Pedro Sarmiento de Gamboa [1571]:66, 2001:161; and Murúa [1590–1611]: 55, 1987:195.

14. While the gift did not have the effect Atahualpa intended, it had other unexpected consequences: three years later the mother of Quispe Sisa, Contarguacho, daughter of Anan Huayllas' lord, would send ethnic troops to help her grandchildren, daughter, and son-in-law against Inca armies besieging them (Rostworowski de Diez Canseco 1989b; Espinoza Soriano 1976).

15. I stress that these testimonies *contradicted* the prosecutor's intent. Also, a witness in Hernando Pizarro's probanza said the same, and his narrative plot makes the answer believable (AGI, Ec. 1007c, pza. 1, f. 153v).

16. See minibiographies of Beltrán, of Pérez de Vivero, and indirectly of Pantiel de Salinas in Lockhart 1972:399–400, 404–6, 393–95. I am by no means suggesting a structural determinism; the distinction simply fits this case.

17. Andean ethnic polities were composed of several subunits (see Pärssinen 1992).

18. Espinoza Soriano's dating of Guacra Páucar's delivery (1973:70–72) is contradicted by Yauyo witnesses, as Guillén Guillén (1974:86) notes. Also, other details do not fit: his use of the objects described by Mena and the *Relación Francesa* (1937 [1534]), or his reading that the three men that went to Cuzco could have killed 100 animals when they were provided with anything they needed by Atahualpa's orders.

19. Some scholars dismiss Felipillo's role entirely, considering it to be a late scapegoat. I accept it because nativelike sources do, and because it makes quotidian sense; the reasons are plausible and the handling of rumors and the production of evidence fit the conquerors' accounts.

20. During a foundry the quality of the metal was assessed and engraved in the piece being registered.

3. CIVILIZING DEEDS AND SNAGS

1. As a sample of an extensive literature, for the Mexican case, see Hernán Cortés [1519–26] 2000:122–23; H. S. Elliot 1989; Tzvetan Todorov 1978; and Inga Clendinnen

1991. For the Maori case, see Hugh Carleton 1948; Thomas Buick 1936; Donald McKenzie 1985; and Marshall Sahlins 1985:67–71.

2. Their holders' actual power was, however, much larger. The institution had a long history. Toward the 1530s, the awardees had to be ready to defend the king and to care for their Indians' conversion (Zavala 1935, 1940; De la Puente Brunke 1992; Seed 1995:78–87).

3. Yet some scholars see in the ordenanzas primarily the expression of a civilizing concern for the goodwill of the Indians (e.g., Porras Barrenechea 1978:284–87, 371; Del Busto Duthurburu 2000:2:237).

4. The exception is the battle of Jauja, where Huanca manpower played a significant role. Along their way, the Spaniards were provided for at times by the imperial apparatus and at others by some ethnic groups, in particular the Hurin Huayllas (AGI, L 204, n. 5) and the Huancas (Espinoza Soriano 1971, 1973).

5. Firearms, too slow and heavy for a fast-advancing cavalry, played a minor role. For a general overview of Spanish and Amerindian weaponry, see Salas 1949; for an analysis of Inca and Spanish weapons, see Hemming 1993:109–15; for a conceptual study of Inca and Spanish warfare strategy and tactics, see John Guilmartin 1991, and Robert Himmerich y Valencia 1998; for a military analysis of some particular Inca-Spanish battles, see Alejandro Seraylan Leiva and José Vega 1981.

6. Manco's son, Diego de Castro Tito Cussi Yupangui ([1570] 1985:6–8), stages a weak Pizarro and a powerful Manco, who welcomes, protects, and cares for the Spaniards, until "years later" he realizes that they were rather devils, whose driving force was greed and sexual appetite—a politically motivated reappropriation of the civilizing discourse. According to Juan de Betanzos ([1551]:II, 28, 1987:289), the realization happened when Pizarro asked Manco for Inca tribute records to give encomiendas. One can date the event at August 1535, since (1) while the 1535 awards come from an itemized register, include lords unknown to the Spaniards, and are very complex (Julien 1998b), the 1534 titles are simple and mention only nearby lords; (2) Pizarro needed to carry out local inquiries in Jauja in mid-1534 in order to give encomiendas there (Berlanga [1535] 1868:297–302); (3) in the 1540 annulment of the 1535 repartimiento general (general awarding of encomienda grants), he said that it had been based on Inca information, which he did not in 1535 when annulling all 1534 titles (AGI, L 128, ff. 154–154v).

7. Raúl Porras Barrenechea (1978:263) gives the exact number of conquerors in Cuzco. The bounty was registered in a foundry that ran from 15 December 1533 to 15 March 1534—that is, parallel to the massive celebrations related to Manco Inca's crowning. Its total exceeded Atahualpa's fabulous ransom (Loredo 1958:97–133).

8. An ethnographic description of the ceques can be found in Bauer 1998, diverging theories about them in John Rowe 1979, 1985; Tom Zuidema 1964, 1990; and Jeanette Sherbondy 1986, 1987.

9. I will return to this instance of mimicry. As is known, Viracocha became native peoples' standard appellation for Spaniard in colonial times. I suggest that this reflected

a number of semantic slippages, in part politically motivated, through which the Spaniards' potency merged with the idea of Viracocha as the source of energy, or *camac* (Szeminski 1985), to end up translating the colonizers' plain exercise of colonial power.

10. See Pizarro's 1529 title in CP 1959:17–24.

11. Of course, foundations have a plainer effect: jurisdiction. Setting the borders implies a claim to the exercise of justice by the cabildo, and to the labor force of the native vassals and other resources encompassed.

12. Although Pizarro had founded Jauja in October 1533, on the way to Cuzco, it was a failed act because no conqueror wanted to be a vecino. The effective foundation took place on 25 April 1534 (Porras Bailenechea 1978:375–78).

13. To strengthen the odds that their civilizing image would be bought, they also sent 2,000 pesos for the hospital and church of Panama.

14. Although in response to his repeated requests to the supreme Consejo de Indias (Council of Indies) asking for an extension, on 23 May 1534 Pizarro received a *real cédula* (royal decree) conceding him twenty-five additional leagues, his governorship was still short of reaching Cuzco (F. Pizarro [1533] 1921; Porras Barrenechea, 1950:126).

15. And one cannot even tell who ordered the service of men and goods to be given in the first place, since Manco Inca, like Atahualpa before, at times ordered the Spanish to be helped.

16. For an overview of the northern campaign, see Hemming 1993:147–63; for detail on the cross-conflict and the conquerors' internal rivalries, see Cieza de León [c. 1553] 1996:chaps. 63, 65–67, 70, 72–76.

17. Although one of the brothers, Atauxo, was Pizarro's personal aid (Molina 1968:80; P. Pizarro 1965:196; Betanzos 1987:289–90; and AGI, Ec 1007c, pza. 1, ff. 265, 361), in all cases, the political project and factions are unclear. Almagro's help was also framed through the logic of payment of services: he received from Manco 19,000 marcos (Berlanga 1868:290; *Fundición . . .* 1868:556).

18. For a moralizing version of the same meeting, see Cieza 1996, chap. 85.

19. The cabildo record is dated 4 July, but it must be August since Pizarro's letter is dated 27 July and Quincoçes's first appearance was on 5 July.

20. For the importance of a colonial-metropolitan circulation of ideas in the British and Dutch cases, see Ann Stoler 1995; Richard Helgerson 1992; and Frederick Cooper and Stoler 1997.

21. Not driven by a civilizing impulse "to see the land," as the conqueror Pedro Pizarro tells ([1571] 1965:199) and current narratives at times repeat. Pizarro was as unlucky in finding the huaca's treasure as his brother Hernando was in 1533. He brought from the coast only 872 pesos melted on 2 July as "oro de compañía" (Cook 1968:87).

22. To control the council, he also named Soto new governor-lieutenant and his brother Juan general captain.

23. Although the legal file is lost, there are indices of the strategy chosen to bury the problem: in July 1535 Pero Sancho, the notary of Cuzco's foundation, and Diego de Naruáez, Cuzco cabildo's notary after him, swore that Pizarro's ordenanzas had never been cried (both lied, and it is not by chance that Cuzco cabildo's first book, where the ordinances were registered, disappeared until 1572). Had Pizarro managed to redirect the ransom/servicio toward himself, this would have debased part of the problem.

24. The first time was toward the end of October 1535, at night, and with Manco surrounded by a large number of servants; the second attempt was less conspicuous, but failed too (Cieza 90, 1996:311–13; Molina 1968:87).

25. See Tito Cussi 1985: 8–20, and ARC, Bet. 5, ff. 724, 738v, 919, 977; Cristóbal de Molina (1968:87); *Causa . . . 1540* 1889; Oviedo 1959: bk. 47, chaps. 7 and 8; Juan Gómez Malaver and Pedro de Oñate 1889:278; AGI, Ec 1007c, pza. 1; and P 90a, n. 1, r. 11, ff. 1–567. For the rape, see Catherine Julien 2000c. The constant uncertainty, a researched technique that results in the suspension of any context for action and self, is today part of the Western torture expertise; it was extensively used by the French during the Algerian liberation war (Branche 2001:133) and is being used by the United States in the Guantánamo Detention Center (Ratner and Ray 2004).

26. A classificatory sister of Manco told her partner, Captain Hernán Ponçe de León, that Manco should not be allowed to leave and that Villac-Umu had come to Cuzco to take him away. She corroborated her version before Hernando (AGI, P 90a, n. 1, r. 11, ff. 166v, 473v). Doña Beatriz Yupangui, daughter of Huayna Cápac, told the same to her partner, the conqueror Mancio Sierra (AGI, L 205, n. 1, ff. 11, 13); Hernando, to cover up his plan, threatened Mancio with killing Doña Yupangui (ARC, Bet. 5, f. 1053).

27. The ransom metal was never assessed. Berlanga estimated it in 100,000 pesos, but 35,000 marcos and 30,000 pesos could be worth up to 200,000 pesos, as Sierra valued it (AGI, P 107, r. 2, f. 7).

28. Berlanga's report was part of a larger attempt to strengthen the king's control over the Spanish colonial expansion, an attempt reflected in the language of the *capitulaciones* (the legal agreements between the Crown and the head of a compañía), which progressively shifted away from that of contract toward that of *merced* (Pietschmann 1987).

29. According to medieval Castilian law, when a captain of his majesty captured a lord all belonging to the lord belonged to the king, since the captain was his subordinate (Partida 2, título 25, ley 5). This advance of royal order was likely powered by the magnitude of the ransom, ten times that of the first Mexican foundry (Loredo 1958:122).

30. Aware of the situation in Cuzco and of Manco's key role, the bishop had asked Pizarro that should the Inca rebel, he not be executed but imprisoned and sent to Spain (Berlanga [1535] 1868:311).

31. Only the claim over the servicio would resurface, to end up being in the 1560s one more piece in a tax trial against the Pizarros (AGI, L 566,1. 4, ff. 322, 324–25).

4. ILLUSIONS OF MASTERY

1. I am indebted to Clendinnen's (1991) analysis of the Mexican conquest for pointing out the importance of narrating how victory is achieved.

2. For Spanish casualties, see Himmerich y Valencia 1998:402. Inca casualties range from 20,000 according to a man of Cuzco, Diego de Baçán (AGI, P 90a, n.1, r.11, f. 275v), to 50,000 according to Inca sources reported by the chronicler Cieza de León ([c.1553]:21, 1991:98).

3. To give a sense of how important this was, even well-trained European infantry could suffer losses of more than 60 percent if caught off guard (Haythornthwaite 1979:52).

4. For all lunar dates, see the moon calendar at http://paulcarlisle.net/mooncalendar/ visited August 2007.

5. The fall also involved a change of sides: Tito Cussi (1985:22), Manco's son, mentions two classificatory brothers of his father fighting against him, one of them Inquil, whom other sources list as Manco's main captain (Murúa:66, 1987:234).

6. On each new moon, when retreating, Manco's men carried out offerings (RS [c. 1539]: 1879:36) directed to the Sun, and sacrificed birds, likely intended to disempower his enemies' huacas, as Atahualpa had done years before.

7. There is no doubt that these reported dialogues are structurally particular; Tito Cussi's is a royal account, therefore the kinds of reasonings and elements used are those responding to Inca governing ideology. Hence, if one need not believe that this is what the defeat was all about to all Inca and ethnic eyes, it certainly tells what mattered for those supporting Manco.

8. Although the church's official charts date 1536 Corpus Christi on 15 June (Cappelli 1906:165), it is a mobile feast that depends on the date of Easter, which in 1536 Cuzco was out of phase. Witnesses in AGI, P 90a, n. 1, r. 11, and the author of the RS date Easter Sunday on 23 April 1536, not on 16 April, as the official charts had it (Cappelli 1906:164)—and not on the ninth either, as it would have been according to the lunar phases. Therefore Corpus Christi's actual celebration must have taken place on Thursday, 22 June.

9. Another step in undoing the conquerors' portrayal of the war is to consider that the entire siege was fought over a huaca. Cuzco was a deity, access to it was strictly regulated, and its landscape full of religious and political significance embodied in innumerable shrines its inhabitants recognized and revered. As Juan Rodríguez declared in a probanza, losing Cuzco would have meant losing it all "because the said city . . . was and is dwelling and guaca and shrine of the Incas and other naturals of the city" (AGI, P 114, r. 2, f. 48v).

10. Indeed, Indians captured to gain information said that Manco had more than 200 human heads and 150 horse skins, which was true, and that Pizarro had abandoned Lima by sea, which was not (RS, [c. 1539] 1879:52–53).

11. Not all scholars agree, though; see Carol Mackey et al. 1990; Martti Pärssinen 1992:26–50; Jeffrey Quilter and Gary Urton 2002; Frank Salomon 2001, 2004; and Urton 1998.

12. Recall that the Viracocha label was a result of Atahualpa's initial co-optation of the Spaniards' potency. See papers as animated objects, evidence of the Spaniards' power, in Garcilaso de la Vega [1609]:IX, 29, 1995:625; and the Spaniards' sly use of it in Oviedo [1547]:XXIX, 28, 1959, 5:323—yet recall that most conquerors could not read.

13. The Incas were of no particular royal lineage. While chroniclers never indicate their social affiliation (Murúa:66, 1987:223; Tito Cussi 1985:23; *Discurso* 1892:36–37), in a probanza made in 1579–80 to defend their tax and labor exemption privileges, members of each of the eleven panacas claimed to have been in the city "serving His Majesty" (AGI, L 472). A varied, multiethnic origin characterized the Peruvian yanaconas (AGI, L 123).

14. Within those limits, numbers vary from source to source. The only exception is the anonymous *so* [c. 1543?] 1884:387, which says 30,000 "friend Indians" helped Hernando in his attack against Ollantaytambo in the siege's tenth month. I dismiss that figure because—among other reasons—Hernando in his probanza mentions as proof of his friendliness toward and good treatment of Indians the fact that 7,000 "friend Indians" were in Cuzco with him (AGI 1007c, pza. 1, f. 346v); 30,000 would have strengthened his case.

15. The witnesses in Hernando's probanza coincided in this regard with those in the *fiscal's* (prosecutor's), and only made the rationale explicit: such was the right treatment of *any* Indian failing to come in peace, regardless of the circumstance (AGI, Ec 1007c, pza. 1, ff. 405, 459v).

16. A case reminiscent of other neo/colonial Western contexts, and a theme thoroughly fleshed out by Taussig (1987). Recognizing a culture of terror prevents reading the Christians' violence as a result of the collapse of all rules of sociability (e.g., Guilmartin 1991:43, after Clausewitz 1943).

17. Both questions build on a previous inquiry done by Diego de Almagro in 1537 (AGI, P 90a, n. 1, r. 11, f. 8).

18. The metal registered was obtained during the siege alone. Some melted only silver, others only gold, others both (AGI, C 1824). I take 1 peso as equal to 4.55 grams (.16 oz), and 1 marco as equal to 28.8 grams (1 oz).

19. These victories are the source of the human heads and horse skins examined in the previous section (see note 10, above).

20. For a detailed study of the attack on Lima, see Hemming 1993:203–6; Espinoza Soriano 1973:157–65, 1976; María Rostworowski de Diez Canseco 1988:70–76, 1989b:22–29; Guillén Guillén 1994:96–100; and José Antonio Del Busto Duthurburu 2000:2:236–43.

21. The same internal split characterized the Chachapoya mitimaes in Cuzco. Although often seen as allies and even guardians of the Spaniards, some joined Manco Inca's war people (Murúa:66, 1987:233) and played an important role in stopping a counterattack against Manco's stronghold in Ollantaytambo (*so* 1884:387–88). In fact, even cases thought of as of "loyal behavior" can be deceiving. For example, the fact that after his failure to take Cuzco, Manco killed a Chachapoya curaca in

Amaibamba and took many of his men, as the curaca's brother claimed in 1579 (in Rostworowski 1963), tells that until that point these mitimaes had remained in their land, their curacas had remained in office, and their superior curaca had indeed been Inca; all which was possible only if during the entire siege they had—at least—not countered Manco.

22. Because hegemony operates through consensus, reciprocity in this regard is assumed in each interaction.

23. Available studies examine in detail later years. Lockhart (1968:207) mentions only work agreements between curacas and Spaniards, which began slowly and unevenly in the mid-1540s; Luis Glave's (1989) study of trade focuses on the years after the 1550s.

24. I am following Mieke Bal's (1994) and Jean Baudrillard's (1994) insightful pieces on collecting; in particular, their observations of the relations between collecting, narrative, and function.

25. I will examine in detail the Indians' legal status in the next chapter.

26. Molina's text is an example of the internal Spanish critique, whose elements were in turn developed by the second, North-European modernity to craft the "Black Legend." The latter sustained claims of distinctiveness and superiority that belied the sameness of imperial projects (see Lamana 2008).

5. EMERGENCE OF A NEW MESTIZO CONSCIOUSNESS

1. I am following Michel-Rolph Trouillot's (1995) ideas of the unthinkable and of discourses and practices being out of pace.

2. As we saw in chapter 3, to whom Cuzco belonged was far from clear. For a description of the different titles, see Hemming 1993:216, n. 216.

3. For a detailed analysis of Paullu's coronation and the end of Manco's siege, see Gonzalo Lamana 1997a.

4. Alvarado had left Lima in November 1536 with 500 heavily armed men, and slowly opened his way up the sierra in an all-out war against Manco's men (Guillén Guillén 1994:100–102).

5. Alvarado, in turn, promised Pizarro's powerful secretary, Antonio Picado, that he would definitively "pacify" the Huancas, which were a large part of Picado's encomienda (P. Pizarro [1571] 1965:212).

6. The exchanges' complexity far exceeds the range of the present study; I analyze it in Lamana n.d.

7. The bodies, as heads of the *panacas*, organized most of the politicoreligious celebrations of the Inca elite. There is contradictory information regarding which Inca bodies exactly Manco and Paullu had in their power (see Hampe 1982; Guillén Guillén 1983; Lamana 1996).

8. Almagro had freed Hernando during the negotiations. For the most complete account of the conflict, see Cieza [c.1553] 1991. For present-day studies, see Del Busto 2000: 2:295–330; Rubén Vargas Ugarte 1966:118–32; and Juan Pérez de Tudela 1963.

9. After Vitcos, Manco had tried to regain control of the central sierra by waging an all-out war against the Huancas, only to retreat then to Vilcabamba (Guillén Guillén 1994:112–13). In late 1538 Manco had crushed a Spanish force of thirty footmen sent after him. Although the 1539 joint attack was successful, the Inca escaped again.

10. Rómulo Cúneo Vidal (1925:169–73) published a slightly different and shorter document than the one I have used, dated 20 January 1539. He does not indicate the source.

11. See the will in *Revista Peruana* (1879) 2(4):250–58; and RAHC (1953) 4:91–102.

12. The Spanish king gave Paullu his coat of arms on 9 May 1545 (AGI, L 566,I. 5, f 163).

13. It declared Indians to be human beings, rational, and therefore capable of receiving the faith (Hanke 1937).

14. The text also lessened the effect of radical critical voices inside the church upon conquerors, strengthened Spain's position before the other Catholic European powers that had been left out of the conquest, and satisfied the king's conscience (Pietschmann 1989:80–82, 96–99, 105, 122).

15. Faced with the double standard Paullu crafted a mimetic way out, paradigmatic of his relation with the Viracochas: he converted with his main wife, Catalina Tocto Ussica, with whom he had two sons, and he also had at least forty-two children with other women. (Dunbar Temple [1949–50:638] mentions 32 children, but lists 42 in n. 20.)

16. Inca governors also received their dúhos directly from the Inca (Murúa:c. 13, 1987:378). There was a detailed imperial taxonomy of dúhos that publicly denoted hierarchy—see Guaman Poma's classification synthesized in José Martínez Cereceda 1995:75.

17. The main towns of Hernández's encomienda were some 7 and 84 km (4 and 52 mi) west of Cuzco (Loredo 1941:312).

18. Manco also had his priests cast weakening spells on Paullu (AGI, L 204, n. 11, f. 13v). Both acts can be seen as antecedents of Vilcabamba's propaganda campaign, identified by Jean-Philippe Husson (2001).

19. Not long before, in mid-1539, Pizarro in retaliation for a trick from Manco Inca killed several main Incas who had come in peace and were thus the king's vassals (Hemming 1993:245–46).

20. Of the 109 requests Morales's "Relación" contained, the Consejo de Indias approved 43 immediately. See the reales cédulas issued between 7 October and 29 November 1541, in AGI, L 566. Although no letter written by Paullu has survived, his requests can be inferred from some of the reales cédulas concerning him.

21. It is likely that what made relations between Spaniards and ethnic lords legitimate were social forms other than titles; for instance, as in the case of Pizarro and Contarguacho (see chapters 2 and 3 in this volume), marital alliances included the Viracochas in native webs of kinship, which regulated social relations at large.

6. POWER AS MOVES

1. After having had Almagro executed, Hernando Pizarro left for Spain in 1539 to defend his case. There, he would spent most of his life in prison (Schaefer 1931; Varón Gabai 1996:157–62).

2. I mention Hemming's book in particular because it is, even today, the most complete account of the "facts" of the conquest, and often referred to by both specialized and general literature. In what concerns Paullu, Hemming builds on Ella Dunbar Temple's pioneer work (1937, 1939, 1940) and in this case perfects it— although she steadily condemned Paullu, the paramount example of the "claudicante y entreguista" antipatriot (1949–50:638), she passed no judgment on his conversion (1940:57–60).

3. An encomienda grant was supposed to last two lives, but it could be revoked or the number of Indians reduced if the encomendero lost political favor. As a result, an encomendero routinely asked each new governor to confirm his encomienda titles (see Loredo 1958; Lockhart 1968; De la Puente 1992; and Julien 1998a, 2000b).

4. Paullu familiarized himself with the Christians' cosmology, initially through Morales (AGI, P 185, r. 24, f. 18v) and later through a Franciscan friar (BNE, Ms. 20193, f. 122v).

5. While the testimonies of the native witnesses in Paullu's grandson's 1599 información are silent about it—they consistently portray a zealous Christian Inca—the Spanish and Mestizo witnesses, more invested in confirming Paullu's authority as Inca, narrate the colonial huarachicuy in detail.

6. For the most detailed descriptions of the ceremony, see Betanzos I, 14, 1987:65–70; Cristóbal de Molina "el Cuzqueño" 1989:97–110; Cieza 7, 1985:46–49; Garcilaso VI, 24–27, 1995:378–86; and Bernabé Cobo XIII, 25, 30, 1956:2:207b–12b, 219b–20a.

7. I am building on Arjun Appadurai's (1996:178–79) use of "locality." While in his analysis, initiation ceremonies inscribe localities onto bodies, I suggest that in contexts of competition over space, as in sixteenth-century Cuzco, the relation should be thought as mutually constitutive.

8. Red was the color of cardinals, purple that of bishops.

9. Although each encomendero had to hire a priest who would take care of his Indians' conversion, by the 1540s Spaniards did not reside in the countryside.

10. For precontact instances of taki, see John Murra 1978:46–47; Steve Stern 1982:8–20; for colonial ones, see Juan Carlos Estenssoro Fuchs 1992.

11. Schools for native lords' children opened under Vaca de Castro's administration, and soon the Dominicans had several in the Collao area, south of Cuzco (AGI, J 467, ff. 130–130v).

12. This certainty makes explicit the rationale behind Valverde's argument why Indians would tithe—they would because they gave to the Sun. See the same kind of certainty expressed some forty years later in intellectual terms by José de Acosta [1590]:V, 2, 1995:301–2.

13. In particular in the highlands; there are dissident works (e.g. Hartmann 1971a, 1971b), but they remain marginal. In Peru's northern coast, according to Rostworowski (1989a), the economy was based on specialized work and trade.

14. There are also notarial records, but they most often convey neat categories of interaction reifying Spanish legal forms.

15. Coca appears in Cristóbal de Vaca de Castro's 1543 *tambos'* regulations as an accepted means of payment by Spaniards to Indians (1908:469).

16. In the long scholarly debate over Inca monopoly on coca production, even staunch deniers of monopoly (e.g., Parkerson 1984) concede that it likely took place in the Cuzco area.

17. Pizarro assigned himself in encomienda the rich Yucay valley, a state of the last emperor, Huayna Cápac, asking for as much tribute as the Inca did (ARC, Bet. 5, 1587, f. 861v).

18. Mariusz Ziólkowski (1985:159) has dated the event.

19. Mining in colonial Peru could be both profitable and dangerous for native peoples, depending on the local conditions and period (see Bakewell 1984:3–60; and Stern 1982:81–89).

20. A misleading phrasing; to *mochar* the body was rather an obligation to those close to the emperor.

21. The last time in 1559; see different takes on the story and information about Huayna-Cápac's body in Lamana 1996; Guillén Guillén 1983; and Hampe 1982.

22. The latter is the case when the mitimaes' task was agricultural production. They could have other duties, such as policing imperial borders, taking care of royal estates, dissolving local allegiances, and so on (see Murra 1978; Rowe 1982; M. La Lone and D. La Lone 1987; and Salomon 1987).

23. Land tenure and ethnic power became topics of heated debate among Spaniards in the 1550s, 1560s, and 1570s, debate Carlos Assadourian studied extensively (1994: 92–279).

24. See, for example, the case of the Carumbas, Lupaca mitimaes in Arequipa whose possession was fought over for years by Martínez de Vegazo, Gómez de Tordoya, and Hernando de Silva (Trelles Aréstegui 1991).

25. See the example of the Chaclla and the Canta near Lima (Rostworowski 1988); in Cajamarca and Chimbo more complex conflicts took place (Espinoza Soriano 1969–70, 1976–77, 1983–85).

26. Although according to Spanish law who worked a piece of land and for how long did not determine ownership (tenants were not owners), there was an exception that in the colonies became a rule: continuous use of land could result in property rights if after thirty years no one claimed to receive damage from it (it became *sin perjuicio*).

27. See the diverging views on Inca royal organization and the subsequent organization of Cuzco's valley in Pierre Duviols 1980; Julien 1998b, 2000; Pärssinen 1992;

Rostworowski 2001; Rowe 1945, 1979, 1985, 1995, 1997; Sherbondy 1986, 1987, 1993, 1996; and Zuidema 1964, 1990, 1997.

28. This also disrupts, once again, the Spanish chroniclers' accounts of the conquerors' self-sustainability.

29. I do not analyze these records here because only registers written after 1560 have survived.

30. For a study of the Pizarros, see Varón Gabai 1996.

31. For example, Pizarro took good care to collect the royal grant of 1 percent of all gold and silver melted in Peru given to Cobos (Hampe 1983), and gave good encomiendas to Loaysa's brother, the bishop of Lima (A. Acosta 1996).

32. Commissioned among other things to do justice after the Almagristas' complaints (see the "Instructions" in Lewis Hanke 1978:1:20–36), Vaca was in fact Loaysa's man, as their private correspondence shows (Loaysa [1540] 1884a, [1540] 1884b).

33. A process at no point free of political contradictions and complex legal tensions (see Ramos 1970; and Pietschmann 1987).

34. The exchange involved an explicit although unmentioned irony: the scales and weights were, likely, the ones encomenderos in the north coast gave their Indians to pay *them* tribute, since they were not used in native markets. (See the use of weights in tribute payments in the north of the empire in *Visita hecha* . . . [1540] 1975, and indigenous mechanisms of exchange in local markets in Hartmann 1971.)

35. A comprehensive analysis of the agentive participation in the wars on the part of Peru's native people exceeds the scope of the present study; it is clear, though, that many Andean lords found it convenient supporting the royal and Catholic cause.

7. "THE END"

1. Even his passing challenged categories: buried as Christian, he was mourned according to traditional Inca ways (Hemming 1993:273).

2. Among others, agricultural production ceased to be in the encomenderos' hands as some other Spaniards began supplying urban markets (Lockhart 1968:25), merchants consolidated and began settling down (ibid., 91), and tight makers of status, such as the use of *don* loosened with the generation of the conquerors' sons (ibid.:39).

Glossary

Andas: litters, of many different kinds and ranks

Atao: warlike luck, expression of someone's huacas' support

Borla: Spanish for fringe, in particular that of the Inca

Bulto: body double of an Inca or of other high-ranking characters. Original body parts, such as fingernails or hair, were used to make it

Cabildo: municipal council

Cacique: Caribbean word imported by the Spaniards, equivalent to *curaca*

Cámac: energy, power, generative essence, animating force

Cargar indios: to use Indians as loaders; in this period, most often forcibly

Chicha: Andean drink made of fermented corn. It was indispensable in many political, religious and social ceremonies

Compañía: a conquest company; a private enterprise that had obtained the Crown's legal authorization to pursue the conquest of a given territory

Curaca: native lord

Encomendero: holder of an encomienda grant

Encomienda Grants: cessions from the Crown to conquerors of its right to collect tribute from its vassals; in exchange, the awardees had to be ready to defend the king and care for their Indians' spiritual well-being

Hanan: the half of highest rank of a dual sociopolitical entity

Huaca: sacred, powerful being/shrine, with many possible embodiments

Hurin: the half of lowest rank of a dual sociopolitical entity

Información: *see* Probanza

Merced: grant

Mita: rotational labor service

Mitimae: members of an ethnic group residing away from the groups' main settlement

Mocha: the act of mochar

Mochar: to pray, to adore, to venerate; also, to recognize the authority and power of some high-ranking individual or deity. It often involved pulling out eyebrow hairs and blowing them toward the one being recognized

Orejón: man of Inca royal blood

Panaca: either a lineage composed of all descendants of an Inca, excluding the next Inca and his descendants, or a unit of a complex, rotational post system, each unit assigned to a particular task and associated with a mythical figure; in any case, identifiable political fraction

Peso: Spanish monetary unit, equivalent to 0.16 ounce or 4.55 grams

Probanza: legally recorded deposition by witnesses brought forward and questioned by an interested party, which could be a person or an institution, private or public (if carried out by a royal officer commissioned to certify a private person's request, it is called *información*). A probanza certified a certain state of affairs; it could be presented as a proof element in a trial, sent to the king in support of a claim, or kept on file for other uses

Provisor: ecclesiastic judge

Ranchear: to loot, to rob, to plunder, when the act is committed by a Spaniard or someone under Spanish authority, and the victim is Amerindian

Rancheo: the act of ranchear

Real Audiencia: highest legal local colonial authority

Real Cédula: royal decree

Requerimiento: the act of requerir

The Requerimiento: the crown-mandated text requesting political submission that all compañías had to read to native lords when first encountering them

Requerir: to request in legal terms. The act involved reading a statement explaining the status quo to the one to whom the request was being made. That person had to accept or refute it, and the exchange was often registered before a notary.

Señor natural: natural lord

Tambo: lodging site for travelers

Visita: inspection to establish tribute amounts

Yanacona: a native retainer, someone who has lost any rights to ethnic resources

References

The references are divided into three sections: archival documents, published documents, and other references. A list of the abbreviations and acronyms appears at the beginning of appropriate sections.

PRIMARY SOURCES

Archival Documents

References in quotation marks indicate the use of the archive's own description of the document.

Abbreviations
    Bet.: Colección Betancour
    c: Contaduría
    Ec: Escribanía de Cámara
    J: Justicia
    L: Lima
    P: Patronato
    n.: número (number)
    n.d.: no date
    pza.: pieza
    r.: ramo
    s.f: sin foliación (no pagination)

AGI: Archivo General de Indias (Seville) (Formerly part of the Archivo General de Simancas, Valladolid.)
c 1824. Caja del Cuzco, 1535–58. Fundición de oro y plata hecha del 12/II al 26/IV de 1537.
Ec 496b. "[Roto] y escrituras de obligaçión e cartas de ventas . . . que tenía doña Françisca Pizarro en Trujillo sobre la execuçión de los 60000 pessos."

Ec 1007b. Proceso contra Françisco Piçarro por la muerte de Diego de Almagro, hecho por Diego de Almagro el Mozo, por Diego de Alvarado y otros.

Ec 1007c. Pza. 1 (ff. 1–995). "Probanza de Hernando Piçarro en la causa criminal que contra él seguía el señor Fiscal y don Diego de Almagro y consortes sobre la muerte que dio a don Diego de Almagro." 1544–45.

J 413. "Litigio del cacique e indios de Chaclla . . . contra el cacique e indios de Canta . . . sobre demarcación de límites." 1558–70. [Published entirely in Rostworowski 1988.]

J 467. Cuerpo (cpo.) 1 (165 ff.). "Residencia tomada al Licenciado Cristóbal Vaca de Castro governador que fue en las Provincias del Perú, a sus tenientes . . . por el Licenciado Alonso Alvarez oidor de la Audiencia de Lima sobre la buena administración e Justicia." 1543–44.

J 467. Cuerpo 2 (10 ff.). Respuesta de Vaca de Castro a las acusaciones del fiscal Villalobos.

J 467. Cuerpo 3 (152 ff.). "Consejo. Memorial del pleito del liçençiado Villalouos fiscal de Su Magestad con el Liçençiado Vaca de Castro del Consejo Real." n.d., s.f.

J 467. Cuerpo 4 (163 ff.) Traslado del proceso original iniciado por Blasco Núñez Vela y los oidores de la residencia a Vaca de Castro, dado en Panamá el 24/ XII/1544.

L 118. Probanza de méritos y servicios de Lope Sánchez. Cuzco, 25/II/1539.

L 118. Probanza de méritos y servicios de Martín de Salas. Cuzco, 7/III/1539.

L 123. Cédula de depósito de indios de Francisco Pizarro en Juan de Manueco. Cuzco 27/III/1534.

L 123. Petición de los yanaconas de Juan Arias Maldonado. s.f.

L 128. Pleito de Francisco de Baluerde sobre el derecho a los indios de su mujer, Paula de Sylba. Lima.

L 136. Probanza de méritos y servicios de don Christóbal Pomarica, cacique y segunda persona del repartimiento de Atunxauxa. Santa Fe de Hatun Xauxa, 1598.

L 149. Cédula de depósito de indios de Francisco Pizarro en Tomás Vázquez. Cuzco 26/III/1534.

L 153. Probanza de méritos y servicios de Pedro Alonso Carrasco. La Plata, mayo de 1566.

L 204, n. 5. Probanza de méritos y servicios de Martín de Ampuero en nombre de su mujer Inés Huayllas Yupangui. Los Reyes, 1/VII/1538.

L 204, n. 11. "Probança fecha ad perpetuam rei memorian . . . a pedimento de Pavlo Ynga sobre los seruiçios que a su magestad ha fecho e de cómo es bueno e amygo de los xpianos e otras cosas segun que en ella se contiene." Cuzco, 6/IV–15/V/1540.

L 204, n. 12. Probanza de méritos y servicios de Pedro del Barco. Cuzco, 12/IV/1540.

L 205, n. 1. "Información de los seruiçios echos a su magestad en las prouinçias del Perú por Juan Serra de Leguiçamo vezino de la çiudad del Cuzco." Los Reyes, 12/I/1559.

L 472. "Prouança de los yngas desçendientes de Mango Capac." Cuzco, 1579–80.

L 565, libro 1. ff. 117v–119. Real cédula con instrucciones para Francisco Pizarro sobre el reparto de las encomiendas y otros asuntos. Zaragoza, 8/III/1533.

L 565, libro 2. ff. 117–117v: Real Cédula a Francisco Pizarro concediéndole 25 leguas más a su gobernación. Zaragoza, 8/III/1533.

L 565, libro 2. ff. 117v–20v: Real Cédula a Francisco Pizarro con instrucciones sobre el repartimiento general. Zaragoza, 8/III/1533.

L 565, libro 3. ff. 229–30: Real Cédula al gobernador del Perú mandando devolver indios a Juan Hortiz, a quien se los había sacado Hernando Pizarro. Madrid, 11/VI/1540.

L 566, libro 4. ff. 27–29: Real Cédula a don Cristóbal Vaca de Castro sobre derechos del rey a lo que se obtiene en las conquistas. Madrid, 19/V/1540

L 566, libro 4. f. 271v: Real Cédula a don Cristóbal Vaca de Castro sobre que tenga especial cuidado de Paullu Inca. Fuenzálida, 29/X/1541.

L 566, libro 4. f. 288: Real Cédula a Paullu Inca confirmándole la propiedad del palacio de Colcampata. Sevilla, 29/XI/1541.

L 566, libro 4. f. 289v: Real Cédula a don Cristóbal Vaca de Castro sobre agravios a Paullu Inca. Sevilla, 29/XI/1541.

L 566, libro 4. ff. 324v–25: Real Cédula a don Cristóbal Vaca de Castro sobre el servicio del Cuzco. Valladolid, 14/V/1542 (includes letter from Pizarro of 17/V/1535).

P 28, r. 55. Información de Francisco Pizarro contra el tesorero Alonso Riquelme por alteraciones que producía. Túmbez, 13/IV/1532.

P 28, r. 56. "Memoria de las cosas primeras que acontecieron en los chachapoyas." 1555[?].

P 90a, n. 1, r. 5. Instrucción de Francisco Pizarro a Hernando de Soto nombrándolo teniente de gobernador del Cuzco. Jauja, 27/VII/1534.

P 90a, n. 1, r. 6. Fes de Diego de Naruáez y Pero Sancho de que las ordenanzas de Francisco Pizarro no fueron pregonadas. Cuzco, 16–17/VII/1535.

P 90a, n. 1, r. 11. ff. 1–73. Información del gobernador Diego de Almagro contra Hernando Pizarro. Cuzco de la Nueva Toledo, IV/1537.

P 90a, n. 1, r. 11. ff. 74–567. "Probanza del licenciado Villalobos . . . en el pleito entre el Fiscal, Yñigo López de Mondragón, y otros en nombre don Diego de Almagro, contra Hernando Pizarro, por la muerte de don Diego de Almagro y otros delitos." Valladolid, 1543.

P 90a, n. 1, r. 13. Documento 1. Querella del fiscal Villalobos contra los gobernadores Francisco Pizarro y Diego de Almagro y otros por fraude a la real hacienda. s.f.

P 93, n. 9, r. 6. Probanza de méritos y servicios de Antón Domingo. Cuzco, 3/III/1539.

P 107, r. 2. Objeto 1 (ff. 2–89v). Probanza de méritos y servicios de Mancio Serra de Leguizamo. Los Reyes, 28/I/1562.

P 107, r. 2. Objeto 4 (s.f.). Testamento de Mancio Sierra. Cuzco, 18/IX/1589.

P 114, r. 2. Probanza de méritos y servicios de Diego Peralta. La Plata, 13/XI/1566.

P 185, r. 16. Probanza del procurador de Lima contra el gobernador don Diego de Almagro. Lima, 24–29/IX/1537.

P 185, r. 20, pza. 1. Real Cédula al Obispo Valverde en respuesta a su carta de 1539. 1540[?].

P 185, r. 24. "Relación que dio el provisor Luis de Morales sobre cosas que debían proveherse para las provincias del Perú." Sevilla, 1541.

P 186, r. 1. Pleito homenaje hecho por Blasco Núñez Vela por requerimiento de los vecinos de Los Reyes sobre guardar los privilegios de la ciudad. Los Reyes, 17/V/1544.

P 186, r. 11. Traslado dado a pedido del procurador de la ciudad y reino, Francisco de Benavides el 20/XI/1546, de la probanza hecha el 19/IX/1544 por los señores licenciado Çepeda, el doctor Tejada, el licenciado Alvarez, oidores de la Audiencia y Chancillería de Su Magestad.

P 186, r. 13. Probanza del cabildo y regimiento de Lima contra excesos cometidos por Blasco Núñez Vela. Los Reyes, 9/XI/1546.

P 192, n. 1, r. 10. Carta de Francisco Pizarro al secretario Juan Vázquez de Molina. Cuzco, 29/VI/1535.

P 231, n. 1, r. 4. "Información sobre la libertad de los indios hecha por petición de Gregorio López, del Consejo de Indias y visitador de la Casa de Contratación." Sevilla, VI/1543.

AGNA: Archivo General de la Nación, Argentina (Buenos Aires)
Sala 9, 31–5-8 (Colonia, Sección Gobierno, Justicia, Legajo 27, expediente 784). "Expediente obrado a instancias de don José Palavicino como apoderado del Lic. don Nicolás Tadeo de Miranda, clérigo presbítero domiciliado del obispado de La Paz, sobre los privilegios y excenciones que a éste corresponden como descendiente de don Alonso Tito Atauchi Inca."

AHNE: Archivo Histórico Nacional, España (Madrid)
Códices, 240 B. "Autos hechos por el licenciado Vaca de Castro en el processo del leuantamiento de don Diego de Almagro en las prouincias del Pyrú." 76 ff. n.d.

AHNP: Archivo Histórico Nacional, Perú (Lima) (Formerly called Archivo General de la Nación.)
Derecho Indígena y Títulos de Encomienda (DI), legajo 31, cuaderno 622. Información a pedido de don Gonzalo Nango Misari contra Carva Alaya, por el curacazgo del pueblo de Guaripampa, en Huringuaylas. 1597.
Protocolo Notarial, Protocolo Ambulante (PA), 717. Testimonio de la toma de posesión del galeón de Pedro de Alvarado por Diego de Almagro ante Domingo de la Presa y Hernando de Valderrama. Puerto de Los Reyes, 5/I/1535.

ARC: Archivo Regional del Cuzco (Cuzco) (Formerly called Archivo Histórico del Cuzco and Archivo Departamental del Cuzco.)
Bet. 4, 1574 (ff. 95v–168v). Probanza hecha en el Cuzco por parte de don Martín García de Loyola y doña Beatriz Coya en el pleito con el fiscal de SM. 11/II–1/IV de 1574.

Bet. 5, 1587 (ff. 648–871v). Probanza hecha en el valle de Yucay y en Xaquixaguana por parte de don Martín García de Loyola y doña Beatriz Coya en el pleito con el fiscal de SM. 14–24/XII/1587.

Bet. 5, 1589 (ff. 872–1067). Probanza hecha en la ciudad del Cuzco por parte de don Martín García de Loyola y doña Beatriz Coya en el pleito con el fiscal de SM. 10/III/1589.

ASM: Abadía del Sacromonte (Granada)

Armario (A.) 1, estante (e.) 5, número 1. "Relación sacada de las probanças y scripturas por parte del illustrísimo señor liçençiado Christóbal Vaca de Castro."

BNE: Biblioteca Nacional de España (Madrid)

Manuscrito (Ms.) 20193. "Memorial de D. Melchor Carlos Inga a S.M. en que . . . pide merced y recompensa por los señoríos de su abuelo que S.M. gozaba."

BNP: Biblioteca Nacional del Perú (Lima)

BNP, A-397. Registro de escrituras públicas otorgadas ante Diego Gutiérrez. Ff. 360–67: Testamento incompleto de Alonso de Mesa. Lima, n.d.

HL: The Huntington Library (San Marino, Calif.)

PL218–1. Carta del Cabildo del Cuzco a Carlos V. Cuzco, 27/VII/1537.

LL: Lilly Library (Indiana University, Bloomington) (Files have no call number; they are identified by name of the parties and date.)

Cayo Topa . . ."Pleito con don Juan Tambo Uscamaita y los demás indios sobre las tierras Quinchapaba y Amanguanaya." 16/VII/1560–7/V/1561.

Caritopa . . ."Pleito entre don Felipe Caritopa, cacique, y Francisco Altamirano, menor, sobre las tierras de Cayocache." 6/X/1556–23/II/1557.

Guacra Paucar . . ."Causa con Francisco Guacra Paucar y Francisco Ticsi Cancaguacra sobre el cacicazgo de segunda persona del repartimiento de Luringuanca." 18/XI/1600–22/I/1602.

Puric Huanca . . ."Pleito sobre el cacicazgo principal en Huánuco." 22/V/1576–17/VIII/1612.

PML: The Piermont Morgan Library (New York, N.Y.)

MA 155. "Hordenanças fechas por el Sr. Don Francisco de Toledo y otras cosas de rrepublica." (It includes Cuzco's first *cabildo* book.)

RB: Real Biblioteca (Palacio Real, Madrid) (Formerly called Biblioteca de Palacio.)

II/1960. Testimonio de la fundación cristiana del Cuzco, 24/III/1534. 6 ff.

Published Documents

Italicized original dates indicate that the text was published right after or close to its finishing date.

BAE (cont.): *Biblioteca de autores españoles desde la formación del lenguaje hasta nuestros días (continuación)*. M. Menéndez y Pelayo (ed.), 1905–. Madrid: Ediciones Atlas.

CBC: Centro de Estudios Regionales Andinos "Bartolomé de Las Casas." Cuzco.

CDIA: *Colección de documentos inéditos relativos al descubrimiento, conquista y colonización de las posesiones españolas en América y Oceanía, sacados, en su mayor parte, del Real Archivo de Indias.* Don Joaquín F. Pacheco, don Francisco de Cárdenas and don Luis Torres de Mendoza (eds.), 42 vols., 1864–84. Madrid: Several Presses.

CDIHCH: *Colección de documentos inéditos para la historia de Chile desde el viaje de Magallanes hasta la batalla de Maipo, 1518–1818.* José Toribio Medina (ed.), 30 vols., 1888–1902. Santiago de Chile: Imprenta Ercilla.

CP: *Cartas del Perú: Colección de documentos inéditos para la historia del Perú.* Vol. 3, 1959. Raúl Porras Barrenechea (ed.). Lima: Edición de la Sociedad de Bibliófilos Peruanos.

CSIC: Consejo Superior de Investigaciones Científicas. Spain.

FCE: Fondo de Cultura Económica. Mexico City–Lima–Buenos Aires.

GPCP: *Gobernantes del Perú, Cartas y Papeles: Siglo XVI, Documentos del Archivo de Indias.* Roberto Levillier (ed.), 14 vols., 1921–26. Madrid: Colección de publicaciones históricas de la Biblioteca del Congreso Argentino.

HYC: *Historia y Cultura.* Lima.

IEP: *La Iglesia de España en el Perú: Colección de documentos para la historia de la Iglesia en el Perú que se encuentran en varios archivos.* Emilio Lissón Chávez (ed.), 5 vols., 1943–47. Seville: Editorial Católica Española.

IFEA: Institut Français d'Etudes Andines. Lima.

PUCP: Pontificia Universidad Católica del Perú. Lima.

RAHC: *Revista del Archivo Histórico del Cuzco.* Cuzco: Universidad Nacional San Antonio Abad.

RH: *Revista Histórica.* Organo del Instituto Histórico del Perú. Lima.

Acosta, José de. 1995 [1590]. *Historia natural y moral de las Indias.* Madrid: Dastin.

Almagro, Diego de. 1884 [1534]. "Carta a SM de Diego de Almagro, dyziendo que el gobernador Francisco Piçarro . . . ofreció volver con gente armada para quitar la gobernacion a Pizarro." CDIA, vol. 42, 104–13. Madrid: Imprenta Manuel Hernández.

Berlanga, Fray Tomás de. 1868 [1535]. "Pesquisa hecha en Lima por el obispo de Tierra Firme . . . gobernador, tesorero y contador de la Real Hacienda de aquel reino." CDIA, vol. 10, 237–332. Madrid: Imprenta J. M. Pérez.

———. 1921 [1536]. "Carta del obispo de Tierra-firme, D. Tomás de Berlanga, dando cuenta de las diferencias entre Almagro y Pizarro." GPCP, vol. 2, 37–50.

Betanzos, Juan de. 1987 [1551]. *Suma y Narración de los Incas.* March Manuscript. Edited by María del Carmen Martín Rubio. Madrid: Atlas.

Calvete de Estrella, Juan Cristóbal. 1964–65 [1565–67]. "Rebelión de Pizarro en el Perú y vida de don Pedro Gasca." In Juan Pérez de Tudela Bueso (ed.), *Crónicas del Perú,* 4:227–409, 5:1–157. BAE (cont.), vols. 167–68.

Causa . . . 1889 [1540]. "Causa criminal seguida y sustanciada en el Consejo . . . entre Diego de Almagro, Diego de Alvarado y otros conquistadores del Perú contra

Francisco, Hernando y Gonzalo Pizarro y otros, sobre la muerte de Diego de Almagro." CDIHCH, vol. 5, 361–488.

Cieza de León, Pedro. 1984 [1553]. *La crónica del Perú*. Edited by Manuel Ballesteros Gaibrois. Madrid: Historia 16.

———. 1985 [c. 1553]. *El señorío de los Incas*. El Escorial Manuscript. Edited by Manuel Ballesteros Gaibrois. Madrid: Historia 16.

———. 1991 [c. 1553] *Crónica del Perú: Cuarta parte*. Vol. 1: *Guerra de las Salinas*. Hispanic Society of America manuscript. Carlos Guibovich Pérez (ed.). Lima: PUCP.

———. 1994 [c. 1553]. *Crónica del Perú: Cuarta parte*. Vol. 2: *Guerra de Chupas*. Hispanic Society of America manuscript. Gabriela Benavides de Rivero (ed.). Lima: PUCP.

———. 1996 [c. 1553]. *Crónica del Perú: Tercera parte*. Vatican Manuscript. Edited by Francesca Cantù. Lima: PUCP.

Cobo, Bernabé. 1956 [1653]. "Historia del Nuevo Mundo." In Francisco Mateos (ed.), *Obras del padre Bernabé Cobo de la compañía de Jesús*. BAE (cont.), vols. 91–92.

Comisión. 1943 [1536]. "Comisión al Obispo Valverde, sobre los tesoros del Perú." IEP, 1 (2), 60–61.

Concilio . . . 1950 [1552]. "Constituciones para indios del primer Concilio limense (1552)." Edited by Francisco Mateos. *Missionalia Hispánica* 7(19): 5–54.

Cortés, Hernán. 2000 [1519–26]. *Cartas de relación*. Edited by Mario Hernández Sánchez-Barba. Madrid: Dastin.

Dávila Briceño, Diego. 1881 [1586]. "Descripsion y relacion de la provincia de los Yauyos toda . . . hecha por Diego Davila Brizeño, corregidor de Guarocheri." In Marcos Jiménez de la Espada (ed.), *Relaciones geográficas de Indias*. 4 vols. Vol. 1, 61–78. Madrid: Ministerio de Fomento.

De la Gama, Antonio. 1937 [1533] "Carta del licenciado de la Gama la S.C.C.R.M. del XVIII de julio de 1533." In Raúl Porras Barrenechea (ed.) *Las relaciones primitivas de la conquista del Perú*, 42–43. Paris: Imprimeries Les Presses Modernes.

Discurso . . . 1892 [1542–1608]. "Discurso sobre la descendencia y gobierno de los ingas." In Marcos Jiménez de la Espada (ed.), *Una antigualla peruana*, 5–47. Madrid: Imprenta de M. Ginés Hernández.

Enríquez de Guzmán, don Alonso. 1960 [c. 1543]. *Libro de la vida y costumbres de don Alonso Enríquez de Guzmán, el caballero noble desbaratado*. Edited by Hayward Keniston. BAE (cont.), vol. 126.

Espinosa, licenciado. 1959 [1533]. "El licenciado Espinosa al gobernador." CP, 66–75.

Estete, Miguel de. 1918 [1535?]. "El descubrimiento y la conquista del Perú." Edited by Carlos Larrea. *Boletín de la Sociedad Ecuatoriana de Estudios Históricos Americanos* 1(3): 1–51.

Fundición . . . 1868 [1535]. "Relación del oro, plata y piedras preciosas que se fundieron . . . en la fundición del Cuzco . . . hasta último de Julio del mismo año." CDIA, vol. 9, 503–82. Madrid: Imprenta de Frías y Compañía.

Garcilaso de la Vega. 1960 [1617]. "Historia general del Perú." In Carmelo Sáenz de Santa María (ed.), *Obras completas del Inca Garcilaso de la Vega*. BAE (cont.), vols. 134–35.

———. 1995 [1609]. *Comentarios reales de los incas*. 2 vols. Carlos Araníbar (ed.). Mexico City: FCE.

Gómez Malaver, Juan, and Pedro Oñate. 1889 [1539]. "Carta al rey de Pedro de Oñate y Juan Gómez Malaver acreditando el valor, celo y actividad de don Alonso Enríquez de Guzmán . . . y en el servicio de la corona." CDIHCH, vol. 5, 277–79.

Gonçález Holguín, Diego. 1952 [1608]. *Vocabvlario de la lengva general de todo el Perv llamada lengua Qquichua*. Edited by the Instituto de Historia. Lima: Imprenta Santa María.

Guaman Poma de Ayala, Felipe. 1987 [c. 1615]. *Nueva crónica y buen gobierno*. 3 vols. Edited by John V. Murra, Rolena Adorno, and Jorge L. Urioste. Mexico City: Siglo XXI.

Hilaquita, Diego, and Francisco Hilaquita. 1976a [1555]. "Dos provanzas hechas, la vna en Lima . . . que dicen ser del emperador Atabalipa." In Udo Oberem (ed.) *Notas y documentos sobre miembros de la familia del Inca Atahualpa en el siglo XVI*, 1–25. Guayaquil: Talleres gráficos del núcleo de Guayas.

———. 1976b [1556]. "Probanza de que don Francisco y don Diego fueron hijos de Atagualpa . . . piden al rey con que vivir." In Udo Oberem (ed.), *Notas y documentos sobre miembros de la familia del Inca Atahualpa en el siglo XVI*, 27–56. Guayaquil: Talleres gráficos del núcleo de Guayas.

Huarochirí . . . 1987 [1608?]. *Ritos y tradiciones de Huarochirí*. Edited by Gerald Taylor. Lima: IEP-IFEA.

Información 1567 . . . 1970 [1567]. "Información ad perpetuam dada en 13 de enero de 1567 ante la real justicia de la ciudad del Cuzco . . . a pedimento de la muy ilustre señora doña María Manrrique Coya." Edited by Horacio Villanueva Urteaga. RAHC 13:149–84.

Instrucción 1536 . . . 1943a [1536]. "Instrucción general para el obispo don Fray Vicente de Valverde." IEP, vol. 1 (2), 54–59.

———. 1943b [1536]. "Instrucción sobre los tesoros del Perú al Obispo Fr. Valverde." IEP, 1(2), 61–63.

Instrucción . . . 1978 [1543]. "Instrucción al Lic. Vaca de Castro." In Lewis Hanke (ed.), *Los virreyes españoles en América durante el gobierno de la Casa de Austria: Perú*, vol. 1, 20–36. BAE (cont.), vol. 280.

Jauja, cabildo de. 1884 [1534]. "Carta a Su Magestad del ayuntamiento de Xauxa, con varias notycias de gobierno y fazienda e dando las gracias por las mercedes que le a concedido." CDIA, vol. 42, 114–34. Madrid: Imprenta de Manuel G. Hernández.

La Gama 1865 [1539]. "Carta del licenciado la Gama al Emperador sobre las disidencias de Pizarro y Almagro y otros asuntos de la gobernacion del Perú." CDIA vol. 3, 142–48. Madrid: Imprenta de Manuel B. de Quirós.

Loaysa, García de. 1884a [1540]. "Carta del cardenal de Sevilla Garcia de Loaysa dyrigida al Lycenciado Vaca de Castro . . . que pueden servirle para su gobierno." CDIA, vol. 42, 178–79. Madrid: Imprenta Manuel Hernández.

———. 1884b [1540]. "Carta del cardenal de Sevilla Garcia de Loaysa dyrigida al Lycenciado Vaca de Castro . . . que pueden servirle para su gobierno." CDIA, vol. 42, 180–83. Madrid: Imprenta Manuel Hernández.

Loayza, Jerónimo de. 1943 [1545]. "Instrucción sobre la doctrina dada por el arzobispo de Los Reyes . . . que se a de tener en la doctrina de los naturales." IEP, 1(4):135–45.

Matienzo, Juan de. 1967 [1567]. *Gobierno del Perú*. Edited by Guillermo Lohmann Villena. Paris: Institut Français d'Etudes Andines.

Mena, Cristóbal de. 1937 [1534]. "La conquista del Perú llamada la Nueva Castilla . . ." In Raúl Porras Barrenechea (ed.), *Las relaciones primitivas de la conquista del Perú*, 79–101. Paris: Imprimeries Les Presses Modernes.

Mesa, Alonso de. 1927 [1542]. "Cartulario de los conquistadores del Perú: El capitán Alonso de Mesa." Edited by B. T. Lee. *Revista del Archivo Nacional del Perú* 5(1): 1–12.

Molina, Cristóbal de ("el Almagrista") [Bartolomé de Segovia]. 1968 [c. 1553]. "Relación de muchas cosas acaescidas en el Perú." In Francisco Esteve Barba (ed.), *Crónicas peruanas de interés indígena*, 59–95. BAE (cont.), vol. 209.

Molina, Cristóbal de ("el Cuzqueño"). 1989 [1573]. "Relación de las fábulas i ritos . . . del consejo de su magestad." In Henrique Urbano and Pierre Duviols (eds.), *Fábulas y mitos de los incas*, 47–134. Madrid: Historia 16.

Murúa, Martín de. 1987 [1590–1611]. *Historia general del Perú*. Wellington manuscript. Edited by Manuel Ballesteros Gaibrois. Madrid: Historia 16.

Oviedo y Valdés, Gonzalo Fernández de. 1959 [1547]. *Historia general y natural de las Indias*. Edited by Juan Pérez de Tudela Bueso. BAE (cont.), vols. 117–21.

Partidas . . . 1758 [1252–84]. *Siete partidas del sabio rey D. Alfonso el Nono, copiadas de la edicion de Salamanca del año de 1555 . . . corregida, de orden del Real consejo, por los Señores D. Diego de Morales, y Villamayor . . . y D. Jacinto Miguel*. Valencia: J. T. Lucas.

Pizarro, Francisco. 1865 [1537]. "Carta de Francisco Pizarro al Obispo de Tierra-Firme, sobre sus diferencias con Almagro." CDIA, vol. 3, 58–63. Madrid: Imprenta de Manuel B. de Quirós.

———. 1921 [1533]. "Carta de Francisco Pizarro al secretario Samano . . . y en especial para que se amplíen los límites de su gobernación." GPCP, vol. 1, 1–2.

———. 1986 [1535]. "Ordenanzas generales sobre la conversión y trato de los naturales y obligaciones de los beneficiarios de depósitos de indios." In Guillermo Lohmann Villena (ed.), *Francisco Pizarro, testimonio,*152–55. Madrid: CSIC.

Pizarro, Francisco, et al. 1868 [1534]. "Este es un traslado bien e fielmente sacado de una carta misiva dada a los señores justicia e regimiento de la ciudad de panamá . . . cuyo tenor es el siguiente." CDIA, vol. 10, 134–332. Madrid: Imprenta J. M. Pérez.

Pizarro, Hernando. 1953 [1533]. "Carta de Hernando Pizarro a los oidores de la audiencia de Santo Domingo." In El Conde de Canillejos (ed.), *Tres testigos de la conquista del Perú*, 51–69. Buenos Aires: Espasa-Calpe.

———. 1959 [1535]. "Hernando Pizarro al emperador: Los Reyes, 15/XI/35." CP, 175–77.

Pizarro, Pedro. 1965 [1571]. "Relación del descubrimiento y conquista de los reinos del Perú." In Juan Pérez de Tudela Bueso (ed.), *Crónicas del Perú*, vol. 5, 167–242. BAE (cont.), vol. 168. Madrid: Atlas.

Polo Ondegardo, Juan. 1940 [1561]. "Informe del Licenciado Juan Polo de Ondegardo al Licenciado Briviesca de Muñatones sobre la perpetuidad de las encomiendas en el Perú." Edited by Carlos Romero. RH 13:125–96.

———. 1990 [1567]. "Los errores y supersticiones de los indios, sacados del tratado y aueriguación que hizo el licenciado Polo." In Juan Guillermo Durán (ed.), *Monumenta catechetica hispanoamericana (siglos XVI–XVIII)*, vol. 2, 562–83. Buenos Aires: Pontificia Universidad Católica Argentina.

Probanza 1573 . . . 1974 [1573]. "Lima año de 1561: Probanza hecha por parte del señor fiscal en el pleito que seguían contra la Real hazienda doña Françisca Pizarro y don Hernando Pizarro su marido . . . y en razón de los 20000 vasallos que se le conzedieron con el título de marqués de las Charcas." In Edmundo Guillén Guillén, *Versión Inca de la conquista*, 9–129. Lima: Milla Batres.

Ramos Gavilán, Alonso. 1988 [1621]. *Historia del Santuario de Nuestra Señora de Copacabana*. Edited by Ignacio Prado Pastor. Lima: Talleres Gráficos P. L. Villanueva S.A.

Relación del sitio . . . *(RS)*. 1879 [c. 1539]. "Relación del sitio del Cuzco y principio de las guerras civiles del Perú hasta la muerte de Diego de Almagro, 1535 a 1539." In Marqués de Fuensanta del Valle and Sancho Rayón (eds.), *Colección de libros españoles raros y curiosos*, vol. 13, 1–195. Madrid: Librería de Murillo.

Relación de varios sucesos . . . 1889 [c. 1540?]. *Relación de varios sucesos de la conquista del Perú*. CDIHCH, vol. 4, 197–212.

Relación Francesa . . . 1937 [1534]. "Relación francesa de la conquista del Perú." In Raúl Porras Barrenechea (ed.), *Las relaciones primitivas de la conquista del Perú*, 69–78. Paris: Imprimeries Les Presses Modernes.

Ruiz de Arce, Juan. 1952 [1543]. "Advertencias de Juan Ruiz de Arce a sus sucesores." In El Conde de Canillejos (ed.), *Tres testigos de la conquista del Perú*, 71–119. Buenos Aires: Espasa-Calpe.

Sancho, Pero. 1986 [1534]. "Relación destinada a SM de cuanto ha sucedido en la conquista y pacificación . . . y la prisión del cacique Atabalipa." In Luis A. Arocena (ed.), *La relación de Pero Sancho*, 60–215. Buenos Aires: Plus Ultra.

Santa Cruz Pachacuti Yamqui Salcamaygua, Juan de. 1993 [1615–40?]. *Relación de antigüedades deste reyno del Pirú*. Edited by Pierre Duviols and César Itier. Cuzco: IFEA-CBC.

Santoyo, Martel de. 1943 [1542]. "Relación que hace a Su Magestad el licenciado Martel de Santoyo sobre lo que debe proveer y remediar en los reynos del Perú y en otras partes." IEP, I(3): 99–120.

Sarmiento de Gamboa, Pedro. 2001 [1571]. *Historia de los Incas*. Edited by Ramón Alba. Madrid: Miraguano Ediciones–Ediciones Polifemo.

Sucesos ocurridos . . . *(SO)*. 1884 [1543?]. "Sucesos ocurridos en la conquista del Perú antes de la llegada del lycenciado La Gasca." CDIA, vol. 42, 376–403. Madrid: Imprenta de Manuel G. Hernández. (Anonymous, written by Juan Sánchez de Badajoz.)

Tasa . . . 1975 [c.1570–90]. *Tasa de la visita general de Francisco de Toledo.* Edited by Noble David Cook. Lima: Universidad Nacional Mayor de San Marcos.

Tito Cussi Yupangui, Diego de Castro. 1985 [1570]. *Ynstruçión del Ynga don Diego de Castro Titu Cussi Yupangui . . . tocante a los negoçios que con Su Magestad en su nonbre, por su poder a de tratar.* Edited by Luis Millones. Lima: Ediciones El Virrey.

Trujillo, Diego de. 1953 [1571]. "Relación del descubrimiento del reino del Perú . . . hasta 15 de abril de 1571." In El Conde de Canillejos (ed.), *Tres testigos de la conquista del Perú,* 123–46. Buenos Aires: Espasa-Calpe.

Vaca de Castro, Cristóbal de. 1908 [1543]. "Ordenanzas de tambos." Edited by Antonio Rodríguez Bonilla. RH 3:427–92.

———. 1921 [1542]. "Carta del licenciado Cristóbal Vaca de Castro al Emperador . . . y de otros importantes asuntos." GPCP, vol. 1, 53–75.

Valverde, Fray Vicente de. 1865 [1539]. "Carta de Obispo del Cuzco al emperador sobre asuntos de su iglesia y otros de la gobernación general de aquel país." CDIA, vol. 3, 92–137. Madrid: Imprenta de Manuel B. Quirós.

———. 1943 [1539]. "Fee de cierta sentencia que dio el Obispo del Perú." IEP, 1(3): 11–15.

Visita hecha . . . 1975 [1540]. "Visita hecha en el valle de Jayanca [Trujillo] por Sebastián de la Gama." HYC 8:215–28.

Xérez, Francisco de. 1985 [1534]. *Verdadera relación de la conquista del Perú.* Edited by Concepción Bravo Guerreira. Madrid: Historia 16.

Zárate, Agustín de. 1995 [1555]. *Historia del descubrimiento y conquista del Perú.* Edited by Franklin Pease G. Y. and Teodoro Hampe Martínez. Lima: PUCP.

SCHOLARLY ARTICLES AND BOOKS

Abbreviations

AEA: *Anuario de Estudios Americanos.* Escuela de Estudios Americanos. Sevilla.

BAE (cont.): *Biblioteca de autores españoles desde la formación del lenguaje hasta nuestros días (continuación).* M. Menéndez y Pelayo (ed.), 1905–. Madrid: Ediciones Atlas.

CBC: Centro de Estudios Regionales Andinos "Bartolomé de Las Casas." Cuzco.

FCE: Fondo de Cultura Económica. Mexico City–Lima–Buenos Aires.

HYC: *Historia y Cultura.* Lima.

IEP: Instituto de Estudios Peruanos. Lima.

IFEA: Institut Français d'Etudes Andines. Lima.

PUCP: Pontificia Universidad Católica del Perú. Lima.

RAHC: *Revista del Archivo Histórico del Cuzco.* Cuzco: Universidad Nacional San Antonio Abad.

RH: *Revista Histórica.* Organo del Instituto Histórico del Perú. Lima.

RMN: *Revista del Museo Nacional,* Lima.

Acosta, Antonio. 1996. "La Iglesia en el Perú colonial temprano: Fray Jerónimo de Loaysa, primer obispo de Lima." *Revista Andina* 14(2): 53–71.

Adorno, Rolena. 2000. "The Negotiation of Fear in Cabeza de Vaca's *Naufragios*." In Stephen Greenblat (ed.), *New World Encounters*, 48–84. Berkeley: University of California Press.

———. 1993. *Guamán Poma: Writing and Resistance in Colonial Peru*. Austin: University of Texas Press.

Alberro, Solange. 1994. "Acerca de la primera evangelización en México." In Gabriela Ramos (ed.), *La venida del reino*, 11–30. Cuzco: CBC.

Althusser, Louis. 1971. "Ideology and Ideological State Apparatuses." In *Lenin and Philosophy, and other Essays*, 136–70. London: New Left Books.

Amin, Shahid. 1989. "Gandhi as Mahatma: Gorakhpur District, Easter UP, 1921–2." In Ranajit Guha, and Gayatri Chakravorty Spivak (eds.), *Selected Subaltern Studies*, 281–342. New York: Oxford University Press.

Anderson Imbert, Enrique. 1976. *El realismo mágico y otros ensayos*. Buenos Aires: Monte Avila Editores, C.A.

Anzaldúa, Gloria. 1987. *Borderlands / La Frontera*. San Francisco: Aunt Lute Book Company.

Appadurai, Arjun. 1996. *Modernity at Large*. Minneapolis: University of Minnesota Press.

Arocena, Luis A. (ed.). 1986. *La relación de Pero Sancho*. Buenos Aires: Plus Ultra.

Assadourian, Carlos S. 1979. "La producción de la mercancía dinero en la formación del mercado interno colonial: El caso del espacio peruano, siglo XVI." In Enrique Florescano (ed.), *Ensayos sobre el desarrollo económico de México y América Latina, 1500–1975*, 223–92. Mexico City: FCE.

———. 1994. *Transiciones hacia el sistema colonial Andino*. Lima: IEP–El Colegio de México.

Bakewell, Peter. 1984. *Miners of the Red Mountain*. Albuquerque: University of New Mexico Press.

Bakhtin, Mikhail M. 1973. *Problems of Dostoevsky's Poetics*. Ann Arbor, Mich.: Ardis.

Bal, Mieke. 1994. "Telling Objects: A Narrative Perspective on Collecting." In John Elsner and Roger Cardinal (eds.), *The Cultures of Collecting*, 97–114. Cambridge, Mass.: Harvard University Press.

Barros, Carlos. 1990. *Mentalidad justiciera de los Irmandiños, siglo XV*. Madrid: Siglo XXI.

Bataille, Georges. 1955. *Lascaux; Or the Birth of Art: Pre-Historical Painting*. Paris: Skira.

———. 1986. *Erotism: Death and Sensuality*. San Francisco: City Lights.

Baudrillard, Jean. 1994. "The System of Collecting." In John Elsner and Roger Cardinal (eds.), *The Cultures of Collecting*, 7–24. Cambridge, Mass.: Harvard University Press.

Bauer, Brian S. 1998. *The Sacred Landscape of the Inca*. Austin: University of Texas Press.

Belaunde Guinassi, Manuel. 1945. *La encomienda en el Perú*. Lima: Ediciones Mercvrio Peruano.

Berthelot, Jean. 1986. "The extraction of precious metals at the time of the Inka." In John Murra et al. (eds.), *Anthropological History of Andean Polities*, 69–88.

Cambridge: Cambridge University Press, Editions de la Maison des Sciences de l'Homme.

Bhabha, Homi K. 1994. *The Location of Culture*. London: Routledge.

Bloch, Marc. 1993. *Los reyes taumaturgos*. Mexico City: FCE.

Bourdieu, Pierre. 1978. *Outline of a Theory of Practice*. Cambridge: Cambridge University Press.

———. 1985. "The Social Space in the Genesis of Groups." *Theory and Society* 14(6): 723–44.

———. 1996. *The State Nobility: Elite Schools in the Field of Power*. Stanford, Calif.: Stanford University Press.

———. 1998. *Practical Reason: On the Theory of Action*. Stanford, Calif.: Stanford University Press.

Brading, David. 1991. *Orbe indiano*. Mexico City: Fondo de Cultura Económica.

Branche, Raphaëlle. 2001. *La torture et l'armée pendant la guerre d'Algérie*. Paris: Gallimard.

Buick, Thomas L. 1936. *The Treaty of Waitangi*. New Plymouth, New Zealand: Thomas Avery.

Burns, Kathryn. 1999. *Colonial Habits*. Durham, N.C.: Duke University Press.

Cappelli, A. 1906. *Cronologia e calendario perpetuo*. Milan: Ulrico Hoepli.

Carleton, Hugh F. 1948. *The Life of Henry Williams, Archdeacon of Waimate*. James Elliot (ed.). Wellington: A. H. and A. W. Reed.

Carpentier, Alejo. 1974. *Tientos y diferencias*. Havana: Unión de Escritores y Artistas de Cuba.

Chartier, Roger. 1991. *Les origines culturelles de la révolution française*. Paris: Editions du Seuil.

Clausewitz, Karl von. 1943. *On War*. New York: Modern Library.

Clendinnen, Inga. 1987. *Ambivalent Conquests*. Cambridge: Cambridge University Press.

———. 1991. "'Fierce and Unnatural Cruelty': Cortés and the Conquest of Mexico." *Representations* 33:65–100.

Comaroff, Jean and John. 1991. *Of Revelation and Revolution*. Vol. 1. Chicago: University of Chicago Press.

———. 1992. *Ethnography and the Historical Imagination*. Chicago: University of Chicago Press.

———. 1997. *Of Revelation and Revolution*. Vol. 2. Chicago: University of Chicago Press.

Connerton, Paul. 1989. *How Societies Remember*. Cambridge: Cambridge University Press.

Connolly, Robert, and Robin Anderson. 1987. *First Contact*. New York: Viking Penguin.

Cook, Noble D. 1968. "Los libros de cargo del tesorero Alonso Riquelme con el rescate de Atahualpa." *Humanidades* 2:41–88.

Cooper, Frederick, and Ann L. Stoler (eds.). 1997. *Tensions of Empire: Colonial Cultures in a Bourgeois World*. Berkeley: University of California Press.

Coronil, Fernando. 1996. "Beyond Occidentalism: Towards Nonimperial Geohistorical Categories." *Cultural Anthropology* 11(1): 51–87.

———. 1997. *The Magical State*. Chicago: University of Chicago Press.

Cummins, Tom, and Joanne Rappaport, 1998. "Between Images and Writing: The Ritual of the King's *Quillca*." *Colonial Latin American Review* 7(1): 7–32.

Cúneo Vidal, Rómulo. 1925. *Historia de las guerras de los últimos Incas peruanos contra el poder español*. Barcelona: Editorial Maucci.

Daniel, Valentine E. 1987. *Fluid Signs*. Berkeley: University of California Press.

Das, Veena. 1998. "Wittgenstein and Anthropology." *Annual Review of Anthropology* 27:171–95.

Dean, Carolyn. 1999. *Inka Bodies and the Body of Christ*. Durham, N.C.: Duke University Press.

De Certeau, Michel. 1990. *L'invention du quotidien: 1 Arts de faire*. Paris: Gallimard.

———. 1991. "Travel Narratives of the French to Brazil: Sixteenth to Eighteenth Centuries." *Representations* 33:221–26.

De la Cadena, Marisol. 2000. *Indigenous Mestizos*. Durham, N.C.: Duke University Press.

De la Puente Brunke, José. 1992. *Encomienda y encomenderos en el Perú*. Seville: Excelentísima Diputación Provincial del Sevilla.

Del Busto Duthurburu, José Antonio. 1994. *Historia general del Perú: Tomo IV*. Lima: Editorial Brasa S.A.

———. 2000. *Pizarro*. 2 vols. Lima: Ediciones COPÉ.

Derrida, Jaques. 1992. "Before the Law." In D. Attridge (ed.), *Jacques Derrida: Acts of Literature*, 181–220. New York: Routledge.

Diamond, Jared. 1997. *Guns, Germs, and Steel*. New York: W. W. Norton and Company.

Dirks, Nicholas B. (ed.). 1992. *Colonialism and Culture*. Ann Arbor: University of Michigan Press.

Domínguez Ortiz, Antonio. 1974. *El antiguo régimen: Los Reyes Católicos y los Austrias*. Madrid: Alfaguara III, Alianza editorial.

Douglas, Mary. 1966. *Purity and Danger*. London: Routledge.

———. 1970. *Natural Symbols*. New York: Pantheon Books.

Du Bois, W. E. B. 1995. *The Souls of Black Folk*. New York: Signet Classic.

Dunbar Temple, Ella. 1937. "La descendencia de Huayna Cápac (continuación). Paullu Inca." RH 11(3):284–323.

———. 1939. "La descendencia de Huayna Cápac (continuación)." RH 12:204–45.

———. 1940. "La descendencia de Huayna Cápac: Conclusión del capítulo 'Paullu Inca.'" RH 13:31–77.

———. 1949–50. "Los testamentos inéditos de Paullu Inca, Don Carlos Inca y Don Melchor Carlos Inca." *Documenta* 2(1): 630–51.

Durkheim, Emile. 1982. *The Rules of Sociological Method and Selected Texts on Sociology and Its Method*. Edited by Steven Lukes. New York: Free Press.

Dussel, Enrique. 1998. "Beyond Eurocentrism: The World-System and the Limits of Modernity." In Frederic Jameson and Masao Miyoshi (eds.), *The Cultures of Globalization*, 3–31. Durham, N.C.: Duke University Press.

Duviols, Pierre. 1980. "Algunas reflexiones acerca de la tesis de la estructura dual del poder incaico." *Histórica* 4(2): 183–87.

———. 1986. *Cultura andina y represión.* Cuzco: CBC.

———. 1993. "Estudio y comentario etnohistórico." In Joan de Santa Cruz Pachacuti Yamqui Salcamaygua, *Relación de antigüedades deste reyno del Pirú*, 13–126. Cuzco: IFEA-CBC.

Elliott, H. S. 1989. "The Mental World of Hernán Cortés." In *Spain and Its World, 1500–1700*, 27–41. New Haven, Conn.: Yale University Press

Espinoza Soriano, Waldemar. 1967. "Los señoríos étnicos de Chachapoyas y la alianza Hispano-Chacha." RH 30:224–332.

———. 1969–70. "Los mitmas yungas de collique en Cajamarca, siglos XV, XVI y XVII." RMN 36:9–57.

———. 1971. "Los Huancas aliados de la conquista: Tres informaciones inéditas sobre la participación indígena en la conquista del Perú. 1558–1560–1561." *Anales Científicos de la Universidad Nacional del Centro del Perú* 1:3–407.

———. 1973. *La destrucción del imperio de los incas.* Lima: Retablo de papel.

———. 1976. "Las mujeres secundarias de Huayna Cápac: Dos casos de señoralismo feudal en el imperio Inca." HYC 42:247–98.

———. 1976–77. "La pachaca de Pariamarca en el reino de Caxamarca, siglos XV–XVIII." HYC 10:135–80.

———. 1983–85. "La etnia Chimbo, al oeste de Riobamba: el testimonio de la etnohistoria." RMN 47:165–257.

Estenssoro Fuchs, Juan Carlos. 1992. "Los bailes de los indios y el proyecto colonial." *Revista Andina* 10(2): 353–402.

———. 2003. *Del paganismo a la santidad.* Lima: IFEA-PUCP.

Evans-Pritchard, E. E. 1969. *The Nuer.* New York: Oxford University Press.

Feldman, Allen. 1991. *Formations of Violence.* Chicago: University of Chicago Press.

Fish, Stanley. 1980. *Is There a Text in This Class?* Cambridge, Mass.: Harvard University Press.

Florescano, Enrique. 1997. *Memory, Myth and Time in Mexico.* Austin: University of Texas Press.

Foucault, Michel. 1969. *L'archéologie du savoir.* Paris: Gallimard.

———. 1971. *L'ordre du discours.* Paris: Gallimard.

———. 1975. *Surveiller et punir.* Paris: Gallimard.

———. 1980. "Truth and Power." In Colin Gordon (ed.), *Power/Knowledge: Selected Interviews and Other Writings, 1972–1977*, 109–33. New York: Pantheon Books.

———. 1984. "Nietzsche, Genealogy, History." In Paul Rabinow (ed.), *The Foucault Reader*, 76–100. New York: Pantheon Books.

———. 1991. "Governmentality." In Graham Burchell et al. (eds.), *The Foucault Effect*, 87–104. Chicago: University of Chicago Press.

Frazer, James G. 1911. *The Golden Bough*. 3rd ed., pt. 1, vol. 1. London: Macmillan.

Furet, François. 1984. *In the Workshop of History*. Chicago: University of Chicago Press.

Galmes, Lorenzo. 1990. "Fray Luis Cáncer, O.P. y su doble experiencia misionera y pacificadora." In José Barrado (ed.), *Los Dominicos y el Nuevo Mundo*, 258–85. Salamanca: Editorial San Esteban.

Ginzburg, Carlo. 1980. *The Cheese and the Worms*. New York: Penguin Books.

———. 1983. *The Night Battles*. Baltimore: Johns Hopkins University Press.

———. 1989. *Clues, Myths and the Historical Method*. Baltimore: Johns Hopkins University Press.

Gisbert, Teresa. 1990. "Pachacamac y los dioses del Collao." *Historia y Cultura* (La Paz) 17:105–21.

Glave, Luis M. 1989. *Trajinantes*. Lima: Instituto de Apoyo Agrario.

Gramsci, Antonio. 1992. *Prison Notebooks*. New York: Columbia University Press.

Guevara Gil, Jorge A. 1993. *Propiedad agraria y derecho colonial*. Lima: PUCP.

Guha, Ranajit. 1988. "The Prose of Counter-insurgency." In Ranajit Guha and Gayatri Chakravorty Spivak (eds.), *Selected Subaltern Studies*, 45–88. New York: Oxford University Press.

———. 1997. *Dominance without Hegemony*. Cambridge, Mass.: Harvard University Press.

Guillén Guillén, Edmundo. 1974. *Versión Inca de la conquista*. Lima: Milla Batres.

———. 1979. *Visión peruana de la conquista*. Lima: Milla Batres.

———. 1983. "El enigma de las momias incas." *Boletín de Lima* 28(5): 29–42.

———. 1984. "Tres documentos inéditos para la historia de la guerra de reconquista Inca." *Bulletin de l'Institut Français d'Études Andines* 13(1–2): 17–46.

———. 1994. *La guerra de reconquista Inka*. Lima: R A ediciones.

Guilmartin, John F., Jr. 1991. "The Cutting Edge: An Analysis of the Spanish Invasion and Overthrow of the Inca Empire, 1532–1539." In Rolena Adorno and Kenneth Andrien (eds.), *Transatlantic Encounters*, 40–69. Berkeley: University of California Press.

Haliczer, Stephen. 1996. *Sexuality in the Confessional*. New York: Oxford University Press.

Hampe Martínez, Teodoro. 1981. "La actuación del obispo Vicente de Valverde en el Perú." *HYC* 13–14:109–53.

———. 1982 "Las momias de los Incas en Lima." *RMN* 46:405–18.

———. 1983. "Incidencia de los 'Derechos de Cobos' en la hacienda peruana (1527–1552)." *AEA* 40:253–95.

———. 1989. *Don Pedro de la Gasca (1493–1567)*. Lima: PUCP.

Hanke, Lewis. 1937. "Pope Paul III and the American Indians." *Harvard Theological Review* 30:65–102.

———. 1978. *Los virreyes españoles en América durante el gobierno de la Casa de Austria*. BAE (cont.), vols. 280–84.

———. 1985. *La humanidad es una*. Mexico City: Fondo de Cultura Económica.

———. 1988. *La lucha por la justicia en la conquista de América*. Madrid: Colegio Universitario de Ediciones Itsmo.

Hartmann, Roswith. 1971a. "Mercados y ferias prehispánicos en el área andina." *Boletín de la Academia Nacional de Historia* (Quito) 54(118): 214–35.

———. 1971b. "Algunas observaciones respecto al trueque y otras prácticas en las ferias de la sierra ecuatoriana." *Archiv für Völkerkunde: Museum für Völkerkunde in Wien und von Verein Freunde der Völkerkunde* 25:43–55.

Havel, Václav. 1987. "The Power of the Powerless." In *Vaclav Havel: Or Living in Truth*, 36–122. London: Faber and Faber.

Haythornthwaite, Philip. 1979. *Weapons and Equipment of the Napoleonic Wars*. Poole: Blandford Press.

Heffernan, Ken. 1996. *Limatambo: Archeology, History and the Regional Societies of Inca Cusco*. Oxford: Basingstoke Press.

Helgerson, Richard. 1992. "Camões Hakluyt, and the Voyages of Two Nations." In Nicholas B. Dirks (ed.), *Colonialism and Culture*, 27–63. Ann Arbor: University of Michigan Press.

Hemming, John. 1993. *The Conquest of the Incas*. London: Macmillan.

Himmerich y Valencia, Robert. 1998. "The 1536 Siege of Cuzco: An Analysis of Inca and Spanish Warfare." *Colonial Latin American Historical Review* 7(4): 387–418.

Husson, Jean-Philippe. 2001. *La mort d'Ataw Wallpa*. Geneva: Patiño.

Hyslop, John. 1990. *Inka Settlement Planning*. Austin: University of Texas Press.

Itier, César. 1993. "Estudio y comentario lingüístico." In Joan de Santa Cruz Pachacuti Yamqui Salcamaygua, *Relación de antigüedades deste reyno del Pirú*, 129–78. Cuzco: IFEA-CBC.

Julien, Catherine. 1982. "Inca Decimal Administration in the Lake Titicaca Region." In, George A. Collier et al. (eds.) *The Inca and Aztec States, 1400–1800*, 119–51. New York: Academic Press.

———. 1998a. "La encomienda del Inca." In *Actas del IV Congreso Internacional de Etnohistoria*. Vol. 2, 489–516. Lima: PUCP.

———. 1998b. "La organización parroquial del Cusco y la ciudad incaica." *Tawantinsuyu* 5:82–96.

———. 2000a. *Reading Inca History*. Iowa: University of Iowa Press.

———. 2000b. "Inca State and the Encomienda: Hernando Pizarro's Holdings in Cuzco." *Andean Past* 6:229–76.

———. 2000c. "Francisca Pizarro, la cuzqueña, y su madre, la coya Ynguill." *Revista del Archivo Regional del Cuzco* 15:53–71.

Kubler, George. 1945. "The Behavior of Atahualpa, 1531–1533." *Hispanic American Historical Review* 25(4): 413–27.

La Lone, Mary B. and Darrell E. 1987. "The Inka State in the Southern Highlands: State Administrative and Production Enclaves." *Ethnohistory* 34(1): 47–62.

Lamana, Gonzalo. 1996. "Identidad y pertenencia de la nobleza cusqueña en el mundo colonial temprano." *Revista Andina* 14(1): 73–106.

————. 1997a. "Estructura y acontecimiento, identidad y dominación: Los Incas en el Cusco del siglo XVI." *Histórica* 21(2):235–60.

————. 1997b. "Dominación y distancia cultural: Incas y españoles en el Cusco del siglo XVI." *Memoria Americana* 6:19–41.

————. 2001. "Definir y dominar: Los lugares grises en el Cuzco hacia 1540." *Colonial Latin American Review* 10(1): 25–48.

————. 2005. "Beyond Exotization and Likeness: Alterity and the Production of Sense in a Colonial Encounter." *Comparative Studies in Society and History* 47(1): 4–39.

————. 2008. "Of Books, Popes, and Huacas; or, the Dilemmas of Being Christian." In Margaret R. Greer et al. (eds.), *Rereading the Black Legend: The Discourses of Racial Difference in the Renaissance Empires*, 117–49. Chicago: University of Chicago Press.

————. n.d. "Words in Reality: Colonial Acts of Transformation in 16th-Century Peru." MS in author's possession.

Lee, B. T. 1926. "Gobierno colonial: Encomenderos y encomiendas." *Revista del Archivo Nacional del Perú* 4(1): 1–21.

Levi, Giovanni. 1988. *Inheriting Power.* Chicago: University of Chicago Press.

Levin, Michael David (ed.). 1993. *Modernity and the Hegemony of Vision.* Berkeley: University of California Press.

Lévi-Strauss, Claude. 1956. *Tristes tropiques.* Paris: Librairie Plon.

Lockhart, James. 1968. *Hispanic Peru.* Madison: University of Wisconsin Press.

————. 1972. *The Men of Cajamarca.* Austin: University of Texas Press.

————. 1985. "Some Nahua Concepts in Postconquest Guise." *History of European Ideas* 6:465–82.

Lohmann Villena, Guillermo. 1952. "El corregidor de Lima." AEA 9:131–71.

————. 1966. *Juan de Matienzo, autor del Gobierno del Perú: Su personalidad y su obra.* Seville: Escuela de Estudios Hispano-Americanos.

————. 1977. *Las ideas jurídico-políticas en la rebelión de Gonzalo Pizarro.* Valladolid: Casa-Museo de Colón y Seminario Americanista, Universidad de Valladolid.

Longo, Carlo. 1996. "Juan Solano, O.P. (1505 ca.1580), segundo obispo del Cuzco, y la fundación del 'Colegium S. Thomae de Urbe.'" *Revista Andina* 14(2): 509–24.

Loredo, Rafael. 1941. "Alardes y Derramas." RH, 16(3): 199–324.

————. 1958. *Los repartos.* Lima: Librería e Imprenta D. Miranda.

Lynch, John. 1998. "Habsburg Monarchy and Its Agents." In *Spain 1516–1598*, 66–81. Oxford: Blackwell.

Lyotard, Jean François. 1973. *Des dispositifs pulsionnels.* Paris: Union Générale d'Editions. [1994 revised edition. Paris: Editions Galilée.]

MacCormack, Sabine. 1985. "'The Heart Has Its Reasons': Predicaments of Missionary Christianity in Early Colonial Peru." *Hispanic American Historical Review* 65(3): 443–66.

————. 1989. "Atahualpa and the Book." *Dispositio* 14(36–38): 141–68.

————. 1991. *Religion in the Andes.* Princeton: Princeton University Press.

Mackey, Carol, et al. (eds.). 1990. *Quipu y yupana*. Lima: Consejo Nacional de Ciencia y Tecnología.

MacQuarrie, Kim. 2007. *The Last Days of the Incas*. New York: Simon and Schuster.

Maravall, José A. 1994. *Las comunidades de Castilla*. Madrid: Alianza editorial.

Martínez Cereceda, José L. 1995. *Autoridades en los Andes: Los atributos del señor*. Lima: PUCP.

Marx, Karl. 1977. *Capital*. Vol. 1. Ben Fowkes (trans.). New York: Vintage books.

Marx, Karl, and Friedrich Engels. 1998. *The Communist Manifesto*. Martin Malia (ed.). New York: Penguin.

Mateos, Francisco. 1950. "Constituciones para indios del primer Concilio limense (1552)." *Missionalia Hispánica* 7(19): 5–54.

Mauss, Marcel. 1990. *The Gift*. London: Routledge.

McKenzie, Donald F. 1985. *Oral Culture, Literacy and Print in early New Zealand: The Treaty of Waitangi*. Wellington, New Zealand: Victoria University Press.

Mignolo, Walter. 1995. *The Darker Side of the Renaissance*. Ann Arbor: University of Michigan Press.

———. 1999. "Philosophy and the Colonial Difference." *Philosophy Today* 43:36–41.

———. 2000. *Local Histories / Global Designs: Coloniality, Subaltern Knowledges, and Border Thinking*. Princeton: Princeton University Press.

Muro Orejón, Antonio. 1959. "Las leyes nuevas de 1542–1543." *Anuario de Estudios Americanos* 16:561–619.

Murra, John V. 1975. *Formaciones económicas y políticas del mundo andino*. Lima: IEP.

———. 1978. *La organización económica del estado Inca*. Mexico City: Siglo XXI.

Nora, Pierre. 1989. "Between Memory and History: Les Lieux de Mémoire." *Representations* 26:7–25.

Oberem, Udo. 1995. "La "reconquista" de Manco Inca: Su eco en el territorio de la actual república del Ecuador." In Udo Oberem and Segundo Moreno Y. (eds.), *Contribución a la etnohistoria ecuatoriana*, 56–68. Quito: Banco Central del Ecuador–Abya-Yala.

Obeyesekere, Gananath. 1992/1997. *The Apotheosis of Captain Cook*. Princeton: Princeton University Press.

Ots, Mauricio V. 1998. "Los grupos raciales en las ordenanzas municipales del Cuzco indiano." *Revista Andina* 16(2):363–92.

Pagden, Anthony. 1982. *The Fall of the Natural Man*. Cambridge: Cambridge University Press.

Parkerson, Phillip T. 1984. "El monopolio incaico de la coca: ¿Realidad o ficción legal?" *Historia y Cultura* (La Paz) 5:1–28.

Pärssinen, Martti. 1992. *Tawantinsuyu*. Helsinki: Societas Historica Finlandiae.

Pease G. Y., Franklin. 1991. *Los últimos incas del Cuzco*. Madrid: Alianza Editorial.

———. 1995. *Las crónicas y los Andes*. Lima: PUCP-FCE.

Pemberton, John. 1994. *On the Subject of "Java."* Ithaca, N.Y.: Cornell University Press.

Pérez de Tudela Bueso, Juan. 1958. "La gran reforma carolina de las indias en 1542." *Revista de Indias* 18(73–74): 463–509.

———. 1963. "Observaciones generales sobre las guerras civiles del Perú." In *Crónicas del Perú*, ix–cxxi. BAE (cont.), vol. 164.

Pietschmann, Horst. 1987. "Estado y conquistadores: Las capitulaciones." *Historia* 22:249–62.

———. 1989. *El estado y su evolución al principio de la colonización española de América.* Mexico City: FCE.

Pita Moreda, María T. 1992. *Los predicadores novohispanos del siglo XVI.* Salamanca: Editorial San Esteban.

Porras Barrenechea, Raúl. (ed.). 1937. *Las relaciones primitivas de la conquista del Perú.* Paris: Imprimeries Les Presses Modernes.

———. 1950. "Jauja, capital mítica." RH 18:117–48.

———. 1978. *Pizarro.* Lima: Editorial Pizarro S.A.

———. 1986. *Los cronistas del Perú (1528–1650) y otros ensayos.* Lima: Banco de Crédito del Perú and Ministerio de Educación.

Pratt, Mary L. 1992. *Imperial Eyes.* New York: Routledge.

Prescott, William H. 1998. *History of the Conquest of Peru.* New York: Modern Library.

Presta, Ana M. 1999. "Gonzalo Pizarro y el desarrollo de Porco: Patronazgo y clientelismo en un yacimiento charqueño inicial, 1538–1576." Paper presented to the "VI Reunión de Historiadores de la Minería Latinoamericana." Lima.

Quilter, Jeffrey and Gary Urton. 2002. *Narrative Threads.* Austin: University of Texas Press.

Rabasa, José. 1993. "Writing and Evangelization in Sixteenth-Century Mexico." In Jerry M. Williams and Robert E. Lewis (eds.), *Early images of the Americas*, 65–92. Tucson: University of Arizona Press.

Rafael, Vicente L. 1993. *Contracting Colonialism.* Durham, N.C.: Duke University Press.

Ramírez, Susan E. 1996. *The World Upside Down.* Stanford, Calif.: Stanford University Press.

Ramos, Demetrio. 1970. "El problema de la fundación del Real Consejo de las Indias y la fecha de su creación." In Demetrio Ramos et al. (eds.), *El Consejo de las Indias en el siglo XVI*, 11–48. Valladolid: Universidad de Valladolid e Instituto Gonzalo Fernández de Oviedo.

Rappaport, Joanne. 1994a. *Cumbe Reborn.* Chicago: University of Chicago press.

———. 1994b. "Object and Alphabet: Andean Indians and Documents in the Colonial Period." In Elizabeth Hill Boone and Walter Mignolo (eds.), *Writing without Words*, 271–92. Durham, N.C.: Duke University Press.

Ratner, Michael and Ellen Ray. 2004. *Guantánamo.* White River Junction, Vt.: Chelsea Group Publishing.

Rawlings, Helen. 2002. *Church, Religion and Society in Early Modern Spain.* New York: Palgrave.

Rojas Gabriel, Manuel. 1995. *La frontera entre los reinos de Sevilla y Granada en el siglo XVI (1390–1481)*. Cadiz: Universidad de Cádiz.

Rony, Fatimah T. 1996. *The Third Eye: Race, Cinema and the Ethnographic Spectacle*. Durham, N.C.: Duke University Press.

Rosaldo, Renato. 1980. *Ilongot Headhunting*. Stanford, Calif.: Stanford University Press.

Rostworowski de Diez Canseco, María. 1963. "Dos manuscritos inéditos con datos sobre Manco II, tierras personales de los Incas y mitimaes." *Nueva Corónica* 1(1): 223–39.

———. 1983. *Estructuras andinas de poder*. Lima: IEP.

———. 1988. *Conflicts over Coca Fields in XVIth Century Peru*. Ann Arbor: University of Michigan.

———. 1989a. *Costa peruana prehispánica*. Lima: IEP.

———. 1989b. *Doña Francisca Pizarro*. Lima: IEP.

———. 1992. *Pachacamac y El señor de los milagros*. Lima: IEP.

———. 2001. *Historia del Tawantinsuyu*. Lima: IEP.

Rowe, John H. 1945. "Absolute Chronology in the Andean Area." *Antiquity* 3:265–83.

———. 1946. "Inca Culture at the Time of the Spanish Conquest." In Julian H. Steward (ed.), *Handbook of South American Indians*, Vol. 2, 183–330. Washington, D.C.: Government Printing Office.

———. 1979. "Account of the Shrines of Ancient Cuzco." *Naupa Pacha* 17:2–80.

———. 1982. "Inca Policies and Institutions Relating to the Unification of the Empire." In George a Collier et al. (eds.), *The Inca and Aztec States, 1400–1800*, 93–118. New York: Academic Press.

———. 1985. "La constitución inca del Cuzco." *Histórica* 9(1): 35–73.

———. 1990. "Machu Picchu a la luz de documentos del siglo XVI." *Histórica* 14(1): 139–54.

———. 1995. "Los Incas no reales." *Revista del Museo Inka* 25:121–26.

———. 1997. "Las tierras reales de los Incas." In Rafael Varón Gabai and Juan Flores Espinoza (eds.), *Arqueología, antropología e historia en los Andes*, 277–87. Lima: IEP–Banco Central de Reserva del Perú.

Sahlins, Marshall. 1976. *Culture and Practical Reason*. Chicago: University of Chicago Press.

———. 1981. *Historical Metaphors and Mythical Realities*. Ann Arbor: University of Michigan Press.

———. 1985. *Islands of History*. Chicago: University of Chicago Press.

———. 1995. *How "Natives" Think*. Chicago: University of Chicago Press.

Said, Edward W. 1978. *Orientalism*. New York: Vintage Books.

Salas, Mario A. 1950. *Las armas de la conquista*. Buenos Aires: EMECÉ.

Salomon, Frank. 1982. "Chronicles of the Impossible: Notes on Three Peruvian Indigenous Historians." In Rolena Adorno (ed.), *From Oral to Written Expression: Native Andean Chronicles of the Early Colonial Period*, 11–39. Syracuse, N.Y.: Syracuse University.

———. 1987. "A North Andean Status Trader Complex under Inka Rule." *Ethnohistory* 34(1): 63–77.

———. 1991. *The Huarochirí Manuscript: A Testament of Ancient and Colonial Andean Religion*. Austin: University of Texas Press.

———. 2001. "How an Andean 'Writing without Words' Works." *Current Anthropology* 42(1): 1–27.

———. 2004. *The Cord Keepers: Khipus and Cultural Life in a Peruvian Village*. Durham, N.C.: Duke University Press.

Saussure, Ferdinand de. 1995. *Course de linguistique générale*. Paris: Payot.

Sayer, Derek. 1994. "Everyday Forms of State Formation: Some Dissident Remarks on 'Hegemony.'" In Gilbert M. Joseph and Daniel Nuget (eds.), *Everyday Forms of State Formation*, 367–77. Durham, N.C.: Duke University Press.

Schaefer, Ernst. 1931. "El proceso de Hernando Pizarro por la muerte del Adelantado Almagro." *Investigación y Progreso* 5(3): 43–46.

Schäfer, Ernesto. 1935. *El Consejo Real y Supremo de las Indias*. Vol. 1. Seville: Imprenta M. Carmona.

Seed, Patricia. 1991. "'Failing to Marvel.' Atahualpa's encounter with the Word." *Latin American Research Review* 26(1): 7–32.

———. 1995. *Ceremonies of Possession in Europe's Conquest of the New World, 1492–1640*. Cambridge: Cambridge University Press.

Semiński, Jan. 1987. "Why Kill the Spaniard? New Perspectives on Andean Insurrectional Ideology in the 18th Century." In Steve Stern (ed.), *Resistance, Rebellion and Consciousness in the Andean World, 18th to 20th Centuries*, 166–92. Madison: University of Wisconsin Press.

Seraylan Leiva, Alejandro, and José Vega. 1981. *Historia general del Ejército Peruano*. tomo. 3, vol. 2. Lima: Ministerio de Guerra, Comisión Permanente de Historia del Ejército del Perú.

Serulnikov, Sergio. 2003. *Subverting Colonial Authority*. Durham, N.C.: Duke University Press.

Sharon, Douglas. 1976. "The Inca *Warachicuy* Initiations." In Johannes Wilbert (ed.), *Enculturation in Latin America*, 213–36. Los Angeles: University of California Press.

Sherbondy, Jeanette E. 1986. "Los Ceques: Código de canales en el Cusco incaico." *Allpanchis* 18(27): 39–75.

———. 1987. "The Incaic Organization of Terraced Irrigation in Cuzco, Peru." In William M. Denevan et al. (eds.), *Pre-Hispanic Agricultural Fields in the Andean Region*, Proceedings of the 45th International Congress of Americanists, 365–71. Oxford: B.A.R.

———. 1993. "Water and Power: The Role of Irrigation Districts in the Transition from Inca to Spanish Cuzco." In William P. Mitchell and David Guillet (eds.), *Irrigation at High Altitudes*, 67–97. Arlington, Va.: American Anthropological Association.

———. 1996. "Panaca Lands: Re-invented Communities." *Journal of the Steward Anthropological Society* 24(1–2): 173–210.

Silverblatt, Irene. 1987. *Moon, Sun, and Witches: Gender Ideologies and Class in Inca and Colonial Peru*. Princeton: Princeton University Press.

———. 1988. "Imperial Dilemmas, the Politics of Kinship, and Inca Reconstructions of History." *Comparative Studies in Society and History* 30(1): 83–102.

———. 2004. *Modern Inquisitions: Peru and the Colonial Origins of the Civiized World*. Durham, N.C.: Duke University Press.

Spalding, Karen. 1974. *De indio a campesino*. Lima: Instituto de Estudios Peruanos.

———. 1984. *Huarochirí*. Stanford, Calif.: Stanford University Press.

Stern, Steve. 1982. *Peru's Indigenous Peoples and the Challenge of Spanish Conquest*. Madison: University of Wisconsin Press.

———. 1992. "Paradigms of Conquest: History, Historiography and Politics." *Journal of Latin American Studies* 24 (Quincentennial supplement): 1–34.

Stoler, Ann L. 1995. *Race and the Education of Desire*. Durham, N.C.: Duke University Press.

Szeminski, Jan. 1985. "De la imagen de Wiraqučan según las oraciones recogidas por Joan de Santa Cruz Pachacuti Yamqui Salcamaygua." *Histórica* 9(2): 247–64.

Tandeter, Enrique, et al. 1995. "Indians in Late Colonial Markets: Sources and Numbers." In Brooke Larson et al. (eds.), *Ethnicity, Markets, and Migration in the Andes*, 196–223. Durham, N.C.: Duke University Press.

Taussig, Michael. 1987. *Shamanism, Colonialism and the Wild Man*. Chicago: University of Chicago Press.

———. 1993. *Mimesis and Alterity*. New York: Routledge.

———. 1997. *The Magic of the State*. New York: Routledge.

———. 1999. *Defacement*. Stanford, Calif.: Stanford University Press.

Taylor, Gérald. 1987. *Ritos y tradiciones de Huarochirí: Manuscrito quechua de comienzos del s. 17*. Lima: IEP.

———. 2000. *Camac, camay y camasca y otros ensayos sobre Huarochirí y Yauyos*. Cuzco: IFEA-CBC.

Thomas, Nicholas. 1991. *Entangled Objects*. Cambridge, Mass.: Harvard University Press.

———. 1994. *Colonialism's Culture*. Princeton: Princeton University Press.

Thompson, Edward P. 1966. *The Making of the English Working Class*. New York: Vintage Books.

Todorov, Tzvetan. 1978. *La conquista de América*. Mexico City: Siglo XXI.

Tomás y Valiente, Francisco. 1973. *La tortura en España*. Barcelona: Ariel.

———. 1979. *El derecho penal de la monarquía absoluta (siglos XVI–XVII–XVII)*. Madrid: Tecnos.

Trelles Aréstegui, Efraín. 1991. *Lucas Martínez de Vegazo*. 2nd expanded ed. Lima: PUCP.

Trouillot, Michel-Rolph. 1995. *Silencing the Past*. Boston: Beacon Press.

Turner, Víctor. 1967. *The Forest of Symbols*. Mexico City: Siglo XXI.

Urbano, Henrique. 1981. *Viracocha y Ayar*. Cuzco: CERA "Bartolomé de Las Casas."

Urton, Gary. 1998. "From Knots to Narratives: Reconstructing the Art of Historical Record Keeping in the Andes from Spanish Transcriptions of Inka Khipus." *Ethnohistory* 45(1): 409–38.

Vansina, Jan. 1985. *Oral Tradition as History*. Madison: University of Wisconsin Press.

Vargas Ugarte, Rubén. 1951–54. *Concilios limenses*. 3 vols. Lima: Tipografía Peruana S. A. Rávago e Hijos.

———. 1966. *Historia general del Perú*. Vol. 1. Lima: Milla Batres.

———. 1953. *Historia de la Iglesia en el Perú*. Vol. 1. Lima: Imprenta Santa María.

Varner, John Grier, and Jeannette Johnson Varner. 1983. *Dogs of the Conquest*. Norman: University of Oklahoma Press.

Varón Gabai, Rafael. 1996. *La ilusión del poder*. Lima: IEP-IFEA.

Vázquez Núñez, Guillermo. 1931. *Manual de historia de la orden de Nuestra Señora de la Merced*. Toledo, Spain: Editorial Católica Toledana.

Villanueva Urteaga, Horacio. 1970. "Documento sobre Yucay en el siglo XVI." RAHC 13:1–148.

Wachtel, Nathan. 1971. *La vision des vaincus: Les Indiens du Pérou devant la conquête espagnole, 1530–1570*. Paris: Gallimard.

Williams, Raymond. 1977. *Marxism and Literature*. Oxford: Oxford University Press.

Zavala, Silvio. 1935. *La encomienda indiana*. Madrid: Centro de Estudios Históricos.

———. 1940. *De la encomienda y propiedad territorial en algunas regiones de la América española*. Mexico City: Porrúa.

Ziólkowski, Mariusz. 1985. "Hanan pachacp unanchan: Las "señales del cielo" y su papel en la etnohistoria andina." *Revista Española de Antropología Americana* 15:147–82.

———. 1996. *La Guerra de los Wawqi*. Quito: Abya-Yala.

———. 2002. "El Inca y el breviario, o del arte de conversar con las huacas." In Javier Flores Espinoza and Rafael Varón Gabai (eds.), *El hombre y los Andes*, 597–609. Lima: IFEA-PUCP.

Žižek, Slavoj. 1989. *The Sublime Object of Ideology*. London: Verso.

Zuidema, Tom. 1964. *The Ceque System of Cuzco*. International Archives of Ethnography. Leiden: E. J. Brill.

———. 1982. "The Sidereal Lunar calendar of the Incas." In Anthony F. Aveni (ed.), *Achaeoastronomy in the New World*, 59–107. Cambridge: Cambridge University Press.

———. 1983. "Towards a General Andean Star Calendar in Ancient Peru." In Anthony F. Aveni and Gordon Brotherston (eds.), *Calendars in Mesoamerica and Peru*, 235–62. Oxford: B.A.R.

———. 1990. *Inca Civilization in Cuzco*. Austin: University of Texas Press.

———. 1997. "La política matrimonial incaica según Juan de Betanzos: Un ejemplo implicando a los reyes Inca Roca y Yahuar Huácac." In Rafael Varón Gabai and Juan Flores Espinoza (eds.), *Arqueología, antropología e historia en los Andes*, 289–300. Lima: IEP–Banco Central de Reserva del Perú.

Index

Abancay, Spanish-Inca relations in, 166–72

absolutism: colonial reorganization and, 24–25; emergence of, 193; state building in colonial Peru and, 218–20, 224

achronicity, in accounts of Atahualpa's capture, 63–64

agency: in Cajamarca contact, 28; coronation of Paullu Inca and role of, 162–66; historical narrative and role of, 2–25, 233n2; Manco Inca's war and role of, 130–32; of native peoples, 2

Aguirre, Juan de, 141

Aldana, 56

Aliaga, Jerónimo de, 117–20

Allaulli, Francisco Caro, 38

Almagro, Diego de, 93–94, 106–8, 125; Alvarado and, 110–11; compañía and, 31; coronation of Paullu Inca and, 162–73; execution of, 171–72; expeditions of, 146; Manco Inca's war and, 111–12, 125, 143–44, 159, 239n17; Pizarro and, 117, 220; Villac-Umu ransom episode and, 118, 122

Almagro, Diego de ("the Lad"), 193, 196–97, 228

Altamirano, Francisco, 216

alterity: colonial narratives and, 78–81; conquerors' reconfiguration of, 175–76; containment of, and partial recognition, 76–81; encounter with Atahualpa and, 20, 29–30, 53–64; narratives of Atahualpa's capture and, 72–76

Althusser, Louis, 13–14, 110

Alvarado, Alonso de, 162–63, 168, 243n4

Alvarado, Pedro de, 106–8, 215; payments to, 110–11, 117

Amin, Shahid, 79

Añas Collque, 170

Andean politics, in nativelike sources, 34–35

anti-inferiority politics and capture of Atahualpa, 53

Anzaldúa, Gloria, 17, 79, 161

Apaiche, Don Hernando, 109

Appadurai, Arjun, 245n7

asymmetry: of colonial normal, 147–57; of historical sources, 7–25; in Manco Inca's war, 127–32

Atahualpa: alleged arrogance of, 54, 184–85, 234n10; alleged spies of, 39,

Atahualpa (*cont.*)

234n3; Betanzos's account of, 35; capture of, at Cajamarca, 53–64; Cuzco treasure collection and, 81–84; execution of, 92–95; failed contact with, 46–53; imprisonment of, 65–95; nativelike sources and accounts of, 36–39; order in Cajamarca established by, 84–85; politics of, 41–46; ransom negotiations for, 66–68, 89–92; resistance of, to Spaniards, 32–33; sacred status of, 85–89; size of squads for, 55, 234n11; Spanish encounter with, 4–5, 16, 20–25, 27, 29

atao (warlike luck), 57, 131, 170

Atauxo, 239n17

Atrico, Martín, 73

Baçán, Diego de, 142

Bakhtin, Mikhail, 11

Baldibieso, Joan de, 197, 200

battlefields: colonial and indigenous scholarship concerning, 3; in Manco Inca's war, 22–23

Bazán, Diego de, 140, 205

beard tugging, native accounts of, 39–41

Beltrán, Hernán, 88–89

Benalcázar, 55, 107

Berlanga, Fray Tomás de, 120, 122–23, 219, 240nn27–28

Betanzos, Juan de, 34–35, 39, 43–44, 47, 57–58; Cuzco treasure collection and, 82; on Inca religious practices, 228–29; on Pizarro-Manco encounter, 238n6

Bhabha, Homi, 33, 106

bird sacrifice, 39–41, 234n6

body: cross-cultural valuation of, 212–18; first contact and, 19–25; worldview and, 10–11

Borderlands / La Frontera, 17

border thinking: Atahualpa's encounter and, 29–30; mestizo identity and,

191; nativelike narratives and, 10–11; Viracocha label and, 43–46

borla (royal insignia), 162–64, 170

Bourdieu, Pierre, 84

bricolage and Viracocha label, 43–46

British-Maori treaty of Waitangi, 10, 98, 101

Bueno, Martín, 84, 88

bulto (body double), 57, 83–84

Cajamarca: alterity and sense in contact scene, 27–30; Atahualpa's meeting at, 49–53; capture of Atahualpa at, 53–64; cohabitation in, 84–89; failed coherence at, 46–49; historiography concerning, 28; Spanish encounter at, 20–21

Calcuchima, 75, 82, 103, 237n12

Camacho, Juan, 204

cámac (personal potency), 57, 102, 170, 198

Cañares, 139

cannibalism, in nativelike sources, 36–37

Cantas, 145, 246n25

capitulaciones (Spanish legal agreements), 240n28

cargar indios: colonial references to, 206; colonial normal and reappropriation of, 14, 86–89; cross-cultural interaction and, 23; rationalization of, 152–57, 176, 182–83

Caritopa, Don Felipe, 216–18

Casiacuc, Don Cristóbal, 197

Castro, Antonio de, 166

Cataño, Pedro, 61, 94

Catch-22. *See* double bind

Catequil, 36–37

Cayotopa, 146

ceque system, 105

Çermeño, Pedro, 169

Chachapoyas, Inca rivalry with, 139, 146, 242n21

chaco, 109–10

Challco Yupangui, 146

Chartier, Roger, 234n8

Chicana identity, gray space of, 190–91

Christianity: Atahualpa and contact with, 20–25; capture of Atahualpa and perspective of, 59–64, 235n14; in colonial narratives, 79–81; conversion efforts among Incas and, 195–208; early conquest attempts and, 31; Paullu Inca and, 23–24; policy of fear and, 48–49; in Spanish colonial narrative, 16–19; Spanish-Indian interaction and exposure of, 173–83; Viracocha and, 45–46

Christian realism: civilizing discourse and, 97; imprisonment of Atahualpa and, 65–95; magicality and, 15–16

Christians, Spanish self-presentation as, 5

Cieza de León, Pedro, 46, 234nn3, 10; conquest narrative of, 82–84, 159

Ciquinchara, 41–46, 48, 52, 54

civilizing discourse: of Manco Inca's war, 112–24; narratives and visibility and, 97–124; quotidian interaction and, 149–57; ransom fraud incident and, 123–24; rationality and state building, 116–17

civil war in Peru, colonial perspectives on, 193–95

Clendinnen, Inga, 43, 241n1

clergy: advocacy of Inca rights by, 173–88; conversion of Incas by, 195–208; generational change in, 228–29

Coaque, Spanish arrival at, 31

Cobos, Francisco de los, 120, 219–20

coca: as colonial currency, 24, 186–88; trading and looting of, 209–10, 246nn15–16

cohabitation, in Cajamarca, 84–89

colonial difference: colonial normal and, 155–56; indigenous blurring of, 16–17

colonial imprint: concepts and dialogues concerning, 12–19; eyewitness narratives with, 77–81; historical legacy of, 1–25

colonialism: Andean economic practices and, 208–12; capture of Atahualpa and, 62–64; magicality of, 14–15

colonial normal: asymmetry in, 147–57; clash of, with equality, 175–83; colonial difference and, 155–56; colonial-native cohabitation in Cajamarca and, 86–89; definition of, 14; habit memory and, 155–57; hegemony and, 127, 147–57, 164, 171, 173, 177, 181, 183, 189, 218, 221–25; justification of dominance and, 155–57; Manco Inca's war and, 125, 147–57; New Laws and, 224; Paullu Inca's challenge to, 180–83

colonial semiosis, capture of Atahualpa in context of, 59

Comaroff, J. and J., 13, 80, 147, 236n11

compañía: alliance with Inca elite, 99–105; at Cajamarca, 46–49, 54–64; census of, 238n7; conquest of Inca and, 30–33; rational image of, 54–55

conquest narratives, 77–84; Christianization theme in, 16–19; civilizing discourse in, 98–124; civil war in Peru and, 193–95; on colonial cohabitation in Cajamarca, 86–89, 237n15; colonial normal in, 147–57; conversion of Indians in, 197–208; coronation of Paullu Inca in, 162–73; European superiority affirmed in, 6; as historical background, 10, 100–105, 233n4; horse imagery in, 68–76, 81, 104–5; indigenous economic practices and, 209–12; interpretation of ordinances (ordenanzas) in, 103, 238n3; Jauja expedition in, 107–10; land tenure in, 214–18; lapses in, 11–12; Manco Inca's war in, 112–13, 121–32, 134–38, 141–47, 241nn8–10; mestizo politics in, 159–61; narcotic effect in, 33; native actors in,

conquest narratives (*cont.*)
139–47; native alternative histories vs.,
4–25; partial recognition in, 80, 236n11;
Paullu Inca's status in, 174–83; privileging in, 7–25; ransom negotiation
accounts in, 90–92, 114; rationality and
state building in, 116–17; Vela regime
and, 221–25; Vilcaconga incident and,
103; Villac-Umu ransom episode in,
117–24, 239n21
Conquest of the Incas, The, 2, 77, 162, 196
containment, in nativelike sources, 37
Contarguacho, 237n14, 244n21
conversion: in colonial narratives, 16–19,
79–81; early conquerors' attempts at,
31, 48–49; native contact with, 20–25;
of Paullu Inca, 23–24, 183, 196–200;
quotidian interaction and, 24, 173–83;
transformation of indigenous culture
and, 195–208; Viracocha and, 45–46.
See also clergy.
Cortés, Hernán, Moctezuma's encounter
with, 10, 98, 101
Council of Castile, 220
Council of the Indies: absolutism and,
218–20; Cuzco cabildo's appeal to, 115
Council of Trent, 176–77, 205
cross-cultural interaction: during Manco
Inca war, 23; valuation of Inca bodies,
212–18
cross-gender relations and conquest-
native cohabitation in Cajamarca, 88–89
cultural difference: colonialism and,
28–29; Cuzco social order and, 193–95;
Manco Inca's war and, 127–32; military superiority and, 3; mimicry and
mimesis and, 135–38; re-introduction
of, 5; Spanish belief in superiority of,
16–17; universality and transparency
of, 63–64
curacas: conquest-native cohabitation
and, 86–89; dúho as legitimation

of, 184–88; political status of, 109,
180–83; ransom negotiations and,
89–92
Curi Huaranga, Don Hernando, 91
Çurvano, Gerónimo de, 142, 206
Cussi Yupangui, Diego de Castro Tito,
33, 42, 46, 131–32, 137–38, 170–71, 238n6,
241nn5, 7
Cuxi Yupangue, 38–39
Cuzco: alternative Indian political
structure in, 183–88; colonial imprint
on, 1–25; conquerors' entry into (1533),
10, 21; foundry in, 113, 117–24, 144,
242n18; Hernando Pizarro's founding
of, 106–10, 112–17, 239n11; land tenure
and, 215–18; Manco Inca's attack on,
98, 125–57; native actors in, 138–47; religious interaction in, 173–83; treasure
collection in, 81–84

Dávila Briceño, Diego, 236n6
De Certeau, Michel, 11, 78–81, 189–91
De la Cadena, Marisol, 79
de la Gasca, Pedro, 25
del Barco, Pedro, 113
Despinoza, Juan, 150
dialogic indices, 11, 29–30
Diamond, Jared, 3, 233n2
difference: Inca politics and role of,
42–46; mimicry and mimesis and,
135–38
Dirks, Nicholas, 13
documents as objects, in colonial power
relations, 136–38
dogs, terrorization of Indians with,
175–78
domination and dominance: colonial
normal as justification for, 155–57;
conflation of, 3; contact and, 19–25;
cultural difference and, 28–29; gray
spaces and, 188–91; indigenous challenges to, 218–25; Manco Inca's war

in context of, 126–27, 132–57, military
superiority and, 3, 127–32; politics of
fear and, 48–49; Western hegemony
and, 13–19

double bind: absolutism and, 24, 223–24;
cargar indios and, 23; certainty of
Christian superiority, 208; imperial-
ism and subalternization, 6–7; indigenous narratives and, 35–37; market
forces and, 209, 211–12; nature of
Indians and subalternization, 6–7, 161

double consciousness, 17, 46, 185–86;
mestizo identity and, 190–91; ransom
negotiations and, 89–92

"double mistaken identity," in Manco
Inca war narratives, 143

Du Bois, W. E. B., 17, 46, 161, 185–86,
191

dúho political ceremony, 183–84, 244n16

Dunbar Temple, Ella, 245n2

Durkheim, Emile, 152

economic entrepreneurship: Andean
practices of, 208–12, 246n13; quotidian
interaction and, 24, 186–88

encomienda grants: demise of, 220–25;
duration and revocation of, 197,
245n2; government structures and,
227–28; land tenure and, 215–18;
Pizarro's distribution of, 103, 112, 118,
149–50, 173, 238n2; political order and,
184–88

Engels, Friedrich, 112

Enlightenment vision: Cajamarca
contact accounts and, 28; colonial
ideology and, 150–51

Enríquez de Guzmán, Don Alonso, 138,
141

epistemology: border thinking, 10–11;
43–46; colonial superiority and. 3, 6,
53–64, 155–56; situated interventions,
10–11; subalternization and, 16–19

equality, colonial normal clash with,
175–83

Espinoza-Soriano, Waldemar, 91, 146,
237n18

estancieros, 213

Estete, Miguel de, 41, 55, 70, 75, 80–81;
crowning of Manco Inca and, 102

European superiority: capture of Atahualpa in context of, 53–64; conquest
narratives as affirmation of, 6

evangelic narratives: capture of Atahualpa and, 235n14; conversion of
Indians and, 203–8

Evans-Pritchard, E. E., 141

exotization: economic practices and,
208–12; as mechanism of subalternization, 5–25; sameness and, 29, 222–24

Feldman, Allen, 62

Felipillo, 93, 237n19

field of visibility: Christian realism and,
69, 76, 104; civilizing discourse and,
97–98; conversion and, 195; competing regimes of, 189; and intelligibility,
112; monotopic visibility and; 162–64;
nativelike texts and, 163–64; in past
and current accounts, 111, 160; in
Spanish narratives, 9, 21, 33, 97

first contact: British-Maori encounter, 10,
98, 101; historiographical interpretation of, 19–25; newness as element of,
33–35, 42–46; objectification in, 37–39

Foucault, Michel, 17, 188, 190, 213

Garcilaso de la Vega, 33, 46, 57–59, 109,
138

Gasca, Pedro de la, 220–21, 227–30

Ginzburg, Carlo, 11, 70, 79

gold, in colonial Peru, 141–47, 211–12,
222–25, 247n34

Gonçalo Barbossa, 201–2

González, Franciso, 177

Gonzalo Zapayco, Don, 71–72, 236n8
goods, De Certeau's analysis of consumption of, 189–91
government structures in Peru, installation of, 227–30
Gramsci, Antonio, 13, 147
gray space: alternative genealogy of, 188–91; double consciousness and, 17, 46, 185–86; new mestizo consciousness and, 160–61, 190–91
Guachapuro, 47–48
Guacra Páucar, Don Jerónimo, 91–92, 109–10, 237n18
Guaman Poma de Ayala, Felipe, 33, 35, 46, 58–59, 88, 161, 191
Guaman Ramach, Don Francisco, 102–3
Guerrero, Pedro, 202
Guha, Ranajit, 10, 13, 77–78, 139
Guillén Guillén, Edmundo, 236n6
Guns, Germs, and Steel, 3, 233n2
Gutiérrez, Gonzalo, 154

habit memory: colonial normal and, 155–57; definition of, 14
habitus and colonial cohabitation, 84–89
Haitian revolution, 168
hanan pacha (upper world), 131
Hatun Jauja cuarcas, 145–46, 149–50
hegemony: clergy and, 173–83; colonial dynamics and, 13–19; colonial normal and, 147–157; either/or thinking and categories of, 17, 161, 191; eyes of, 59; frames for, 7, 46; hegemonic projects and, 123, 173; Manco Inca's war in context of, 126–27; mental deficiency image and, 127–32
Hemming, John, 2, 28, 77; capture of Atahualpa discussed by, 55; on conversion of Paullu Inca, 196, 256n2; on coronation of Paullu Inca, 162; on Manco Inca's war, 131
Hernández, Francisco, 177

Hernández de Espinossa, Sebastián, 183–84, 244n17
historical realism and Atahualpa's encounter, 29
historical sources, alternative and asymmetrical, 9–25
historiography: colonial narratives and, 76–81; of first contact, 19–25; gray space and, 190–91; privileging of conquerors' sources and, 9–25
History of the Conquest of Peru, 2
Hojeda, Juan de, 141
horse imagery: in colonial narratives, 68–76, 81, 104, 165; execution of Atahualpa and, 94–95; magicality and, 21–25
huacas: capture of Atahualpa and, 58–64, 235n12; in conquest narratives, 138, 241n9; cultural differences in views of, 40–41, 69–76; economic activities and, 210–11; Inca politics and, 44–46, 111–12; native attachment to, 204–5; in native narratives, 36–37; reciprocity and, 198; religious practices of, 229–30; as tricksters, 42–46
Huanacacure, Spanish attack on, 133–38
Huancas, 90–93, 106–7; conquerors' interactions with, 148–49; in Jauja, 109–10; manpower strength of, 102, 238n4; political autonomy of, 145–46
Huarachicuy: Paullu Inca's ceremony of, 160; political importance of, 200–208, 245n5; Inca leading ceremony of, 160–73
Huáscar Inca: Atahualpa and, 32–33, 36–39, 46–50, 54, 57; imprisonment of, 65; murder of, 86–89; Quizquiz and, 82–84; rivalry of, with Atahualpa, 68, 105, 236n2
Huayna Cápac, 39, 85, 100, 122, 141, 210, 212, 236n2, 246n17
Hurin Huancas, 109, 145, 149
Hurin Huayllas, 145, 238n4

Illa Topa, 145

Imbert, Enrique Anderson, 14

improvisation, at Atahualpa-Pizarro meeting, 50–53

Inca elite: compañía's alliance with, 99–105; Manco Inca's elimination of, 111–12; Manco Inca's war and, 130–32; Manco-Paullu rivalry and, 170–71, 233n1, 243n7; Paullu Inca and, 172–73

Inca Empire: colonial imprint on, 1–25; compañía's arrival in, 30–33; diversified allegiances in, 141–47; genealogy in, 242n13; hegemony in, 13; historical sources on conquest of, 2; land tenure in, 214–18, 246n22; politics of, 41–46, 146–47; secondary actors in, 138–47; similarities with Spanish Empire, 2–3; tribes and provinces of, 3–5

Indians' liberty (*libertad de los indios*) concept, 175–83; clergy conversion efforts and, 198–99

Indians' Party, 220

indigenous culture: Christianity appropriated by, 16–17; economic practices and, 208–12, 215–19; political practices in, 109–10; religious resistance and, 195–208

informaciones, as historical source, 10

Inquil, 241n5

inquiry, in nativelike sources, 35–37

interpellation: Althusser's concept of, 13–14; colonial normal and Inca authority, 110; crown civilizing discourse, 116, 163; double binds and 154; dressing codes and, 197; Pizarro in Cuzco cabildo, 115

Inti-Raymi (Sun festival), 111, 134; Corpus Christi and, 134, 241n8

intra-Inca conflict and Cuzco treasure collection, 81–84

Jauja, Pizarro expedition to, 74–76, 80–81, 105–15, 237n12, 238n6, 239n12

Kubler, George, 40, 234n5

Lanata, Xavier, 235n12

land tenure: cross-cultural valuations of, 213–18; power asymmetry and, 17–18; quotidian interaction and, 24; truth effects and, 17–18

langue, theory of, 12

La Puná Island, 32

Las Casas, Bartolomé de, 178–79

Las Casas–Sepúlveda debate, 155–57

Laws of Burgos, 175

legitimacy of native actors and domination, 220–25

Lerma, Pedro de, 168

Leyes Nuevas: absolutism and, 24–25; libertad de los indios and, 175–83, 198–99

Lima: conversions in, 202–3; Jauja city moved to, 110, 120–21; Manco Inca's war and siege of, 144–45

literacy: conversion of Paullu Inca and, 197–98; potencies and, 212–18; in Spanish colonial narratives, 16–19

liturgy, Indian converts' knowledge of, 204–8

Loaysa, Fray García de, 219–20, 247nn31–32

local documents, as historical sources, 10

locality, huarachicuy ritual of, 201, 245n7

Lockhart, James, 95, 119, 143

logistics: colonial-native interaction and role of, 148–57; colonial normal and, 175–83; Spanish reappropriation of privileges, 147–57

looting (*rancheo*), 147, 151, 176, 187–88; in Cajamarca, 87–89; colonial justification of, 221–25

Loredo, Rafael, 95

Lyotard, Jean François, 173

lunar cycle, in Manco Inca's war narratives, 128–32, 136, 241nn4, 6

MacCormack, Sabine, 29, 56–59, 69
magicality: Atahualpa contact in context of, 21–25; Christian realism and, 15–16; definition of, 14–15; imprisonment of Atahualpa and, 65–95
Manco Inca, 21–22; aftermath of war by, 23; coronation of Paullu Inca and, 161–64; crowning of, 100–102; death of, 228; degradation of authority of, by Spanish conquerors, 121–22, 169–70, 240nn25–26; elimination of Inca elite by, 111–12; encomienda system and, 187–88; founding of Jauja and, 107–10, 239n15; land tenure and, 217–18; leadership of, 200–201; Paullu Inca's rivalry with, 170–73, 183–84, 244n9; Pizarro's encounter with, 100–105, 179–80; at Vilcabamba, 159, 188–91, 196, 244n18; war of, 112–14, 125–57
Manicheanism and colonial normal, 155–57
Marca Chimbo, 141, 150
Marcalloclla, Don Pedro, 90
market relations: Andean practices of, 208–12, 246n13; exotization and, 208–12; gold and, 81–84; quotidian interaction, 24, 186–88
Martín, Cristóbal, 153
Marx, Karl, 15, 112
Mayta Inga, 236n12
Mayta Yupanqui, 100, 102
Melchor Inca, 163, 165
memory, role of, and Manco Inca's war, 133–38
Mena, Cristóbal de, 39, 48, 234nn3–4
Mencia (Inca woman), 177
mental deficiency, implication of, and Manco Inca's war narratives, 127–32
Mercado, Diego de, 120

Mesa, Alonso de, 110, 177
mestizo consciousness: civil war in Peru and, 194–95; emergence of, 159–91; and Foucault's genealogy, 17, 188, 190, 213; Paullu Inca and, 23, 188–91; postcolonial phase of, 227–30
Mexico: conquest of, 6; conversion of Indians in, 200–201
Mignolo, Walter, 16, 155–56
military superiority: cultural superiority equated with, 3; logic of, in colonial narratives, 125–27; in Manco Inca's war narratives, 127–32, 241n3; Spanish horsepower and weaponry and, 102–3, 238nn4–5
mimesis: Manco Inca's war and role of, 126–27, 132–38; mimicry and, 135–38; potencies and, 200–208, 212–18
mimicry: civil war in Peru and role of, 194–95; colonial and native economic practices and, 210–12; mimesis and, 135–38; production of order through, 177; Viracocha and role of, 105, 238n9
mining: in colonial Peru, 211–12, 246n19; government structures, 227–28
mitimaes (population pools), 214–18, 246n22, 24
Mocha, Don Diego, 38, 61
Moctezuma: Cortés's encounter with, 10, 98; speech of 1519 by, 101–5
Molina, Cristóbal de, 149, 163
Montesinos, Fray Antonio de, 179
Morales, Luis de, 174–77, 180–85, 197–98, 204–6, 212–13, 228, 245n4
Murra, John, 208
Murúa, Martín de, 174
mythification: of capture of Atahualpa, 53–64; in colonial narratives, 79–81; in nativelike sources, 35–37

Naruáez, Diego de, 240n23
nativelike narratives: capture of Ata-

hualpa and, 54–64; colonial imprint on, 2–25; containment in, 37; coronation of Paullu Inca and, 165–66; as historical source, 10–11; inquiry in, 35–37; land tenure in, 216–18; Manco Inca's war and, 128–32, 138–47, 241n7; newness in, 33–35; objectification in, 37–39; Paullu Inca's probanza, 185–88; Paullu Inca's status in, 174–83; on Pizarro-Manco encounter, 103–5, 238n6; privileging of conquerors' sources vs., 9–25; Spanish sources compared with, 33, 39, 234n2; Viracocha references in, 43–46

natural lord (*señor natural*) concept, 175–83; alternative Indian political structures and, 184–88

necessity, logic of, and colonial-native interaction, 153–57

negotiation of fear and Atahualpa, 48–49

New Laws of November, 220, 227

newness: in nativelike sources, 33–35; political conversion of, 42–46

notarial records: bias and coding in, 9; native agents' appearance in, 233n3

Nueva crónica y buen gobierno, 191

Nuñez de Prado, Rodrigo, 223

Obeyesekere, Gananath, 43, 79

objectification: of document, 136–38; in nativelike sources, 37–39

occidentalism: capture of Atahualpa in context of, 53–64; definition of, 15; myth of mastery in, 177–78

Ocllo, Cuxirimay, 34–35

Olías, Fray Juan de, 212

ontology and subalternization, 16–19

order, contested production of, in colonial Peru, 19–25

ordinances (*ordenanzas*), of Pizarro in Cuzco, 103, 238n3

Ordoñez, Juan Bautista, 124

orejones (Inca noblemen), 141–42; land tenure and, 216–18

Orgóñez, Rodrigo, 170

Orientalism, definition of, 15

Other: Christian realism concerning, 15–16; in conquest narratives, 78–81, 134–38; conversion of Incas and concept of, 206–8; De Certeau's discussion of, 189–91; exoticization and erasure of, 5–25; performative vs. presciptive action and role of, 167–73; unpredictability of, 34–35

Oviedo y Valdés, Gonzalo Fernández de, 163

Pachacámac, expedition to, 54, 68–76, 105, 165, 236n3

Pachacuti Inca, 210, 216–18

Palla, Doña Isabel Yaruc, 146

panaca (lineage of descendants), 38–39, 170–71, 210, 217, 233n1, 243n7

Pancorbo, Juan de, 103

Pantiel de Salinas, Juan, 89, 144

partial recognition, colonial narratives and, 80, 236n11

passive deterrence strategy, 46–49

Paullu Inca: alternative political structure established by, 183–88; Christian conversion of, 183, 196–208, 244n15; coronation of, 160–73; death of, 228, 247n1; economic practices and, 209; expedition of, with Spaniards, 106, 112; Manco Inca's war and, 125; mestizo consciousness and legacy of, 23, 160, 188–91; religious authority of, 162–66; rivalry with Manco Inca, 146; Spanish interaction with, 173–83

Pazca: killing of, 170; Manco Inca's confrontation with, 111–12, 130–32

Pérez, Cristóbal, 150

performative vs. presciptive action, characteristics of, 166–73

sources, research methodology concerning, 7–25. *See also* conquest narratives; nativelike narratives

sheep imagery and narratives of Atahualpa, 72–73

similarity and exoticization, 5–25

similitude and economic practices, 201–8

situated interventions and nativelike narratives, 10–11

snapshots and colonial narratives, 78–81

social forms and coronation of Paullu Inca, 166–73

social historiography: Andean economic practices and, 208–12; Cajamarca contact and, 28

Solano, Don Juan de, 202, 229–30

Soto, Hernando de, 39–40; Atahualpa's failed meeting with, 49–53; capture of Atahualpa and, 55, 61; expedition against Quizquiz, 100; Jauja expedition of, 107; Villac-Umu ransom episode and, 118, 239n22

Spanish colonialism: conflict among conquerors and, 159; difference, similarity, and mastery in, 5–25. *See also* conquest narratives

Spanish conquerors: clergy and, 173–83; conflict among, 159; de-occidentalization of, 5; horse power of, 102–3, 238nn4–5; land tenure concepts of, 214–18; lapses in accounts by, 11–12; lies in accounts by, 21–22; narcotic effect of narratives by, 33; narratives by, 77–81; privileging of narrative sources of, 9–25; similarities with Incas, 2–3

structuralism and langue theory, 12–13

subalternization: imperial mechanism of, 5–7; mestizo consciousness and, 161; in narratives of Paullu Inca coronation, 163–66; reality and, 16–19

Sublimus Deus papal bull, 175, 244n13

supernatural imagery: capture of Ata-

hualpa and role of, 55–56; imprisonment of Atahualpa and, 68–76; in Manco Inca's war narratives, 134–38; Spaniards' characterization of Incas with, 14–15

tacit-explicit dynamic: colonialism and, 13–14; colonial normal and, 147–57; hegemony and, 13–19

taki ritual, 204

Tallanes and Inca politics, 41–46

tasa, installation of, 227–28

Taussig, Michael, 76

tax trial of Hernando Pizarro, 71, 232n6; Spanish conquest narratives of, 102–3

terror, colonial culture of, 48–49, 140–41, 177–78, 242n16

"third eye" and double bind of ocularcentrism, 17, 190–92

Tiçoc (Sun priest), 102

tithe payments in Cuzco, 179–83, 207, 245n12

Tizo Yupanqui, 170

Tocari, Don Garcia, 91–92

Tocto Ussica, Doña Catalina, 170, 218, 244n15

Todorov, Tzvetan, 41

Topa Inca Yupanqui, 38, 210

torture, Spanish conquerors' use of, 69–70, 74–75, 105, 140–41, 165, 175–76, 242n15

transference and conversion of Incas, 203–8

transparency and accounts of Atahualpa's capture, 62–64

Trouillot, Michel-Rolph, 241n1

Trujillo, Diego de, 39

truth effects and Cuzco land disputes, 17–18

Túmbez, 32

Túpac Huallpa, 99–100

Turuégano, Juan de, 154

Unan Chullo, 50–52
uncertainty: domination and maneuvering of, 73–74; encounter with Atahualpa and, 20; as research technique, 240n23
universality: transparency and, 62–64; Western claim of, 5–6, 161, 233

Vaca de Castro, Cristóbal, 193, 196–97, 201–2, 210–12, 220, 247n43
Valverde, Fray Vicente de, 29, 56–64, 123–24, 219, 235n16; advocacy of Indian rights by, 174–75, 177, 181–83; conversion of Indians and, 203–8; death of, 228; on risks of Indian political leaders, 200–201
Vázquez de Molina, Juan de, 120
Vegazo, Martínez de, 211–12
Vela, Blasco Núñez, 218–25
Vergara, Antonio de, 87
Vilcabamba: attack on, 172–74, 244n9; founding of, 159; Manco Inca in, 183–84
Vilcaconga, 103
Villac-Umu (Sun priest), 102, 112, 122, 240nn25–26; capture of, 118; Manco Inca's war and, 129; ransom of treasure of, 117–24
Villalobos, Juan de, 140, 152–53
violence, Spanish conquerors' use of, 69–70, 74–75, 105, 140–41, 154–55, 186–88, 242n15, 244n19
Viracocha, 28, 33; Christianity and, 45–46; in conquest narratives, 137–38, 242n12; Con's disappearance from, 43–46; Inca politics and, 86–89; Manco-Pizarro encounter and, 104–5; in nativelike sources, 35, 37–38; Spaniards as, 53; spies' accounts of, 41–42; Western mythmaking concerning, 43–46

visibility, sustenance of, and civilizing discourse, 97–124
Vispa Ocllo, 109–10
Vitoria, Francisco de, 178–79
Vivero, Alonso Pérez de, 87–89

weaponry: in Manco Inca's war, 132; of Spanish conquerors, 102–3, 238nn4–5
Williams, Raymond, 13, 147, 150
women: conquerors' sexual exploitation of, 176–77; conquest-native cohabitation in Cajamarca and, 88–89; as political operators, 150; as porters for Spanish conquerors, 149; as warriors, 140–42
writing: civilization linked to, 136–38, 206–8; fetishization of, 16–19; huacas as books, 58; power relations and role of, 199–208; superiority conveyed with, 62–63; and "writing lesson," 136–38

Xérez, Francisco de, 29, 55, 61–62, 85; civilizing discourse in narrative of, 98, 100

Yacobilco, Sebastián, 38, 54, 71, 74
yanaconas: colonial transactions with, 148–57; land tenure and, 216; Manco Inca's war and, 138–47, 242n13
Yauyos: as Inca trading partners, 145; Pizarro tax trial and testimonies, 71–76, 236n6
Yupangui, Doña Beatriz, 240n26
Yupari, Juan, 90–91

Zárate, Agustín de, 223
Zope-Zopahua, 111

Gonzalo Lamana is an assistant professor in the Department of Hispanic Languages and Literatures at the University of Pittsburgh.

Library of Congress Cataloging-in-Publication Data
Lamana, Gonzalo, 1966–
Domination without dominance : Inca-Spanish encounters in early colonial Peru / Gonzalo Lamana.
p. cm. — (Latin America otherwise)
Includes bibliographical references (p.   ) and index.
ISBN 978-0-8223-4293-9 (cloth : alk. paper)
ISBN 978-0-8223-4311-0 (pbk. : alk. paper)
1. Incas—History. 2. Incas—First contact with Europeans. 3. Peru—History—Conquest, 1522–1548. 4. America—Discovery and exploration—Spanish. I. Title.
F3429.L17 2008
985'.02—dc22   2008028436